Neuronal Man

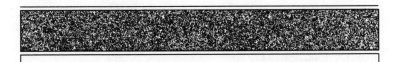

NEURONAL MAN

The Biology of Mind

by Jean-Pierre Changeux

TRANSLATED BY DR. LAURENCE GAREY

OXFORD UNIVERSITY PRESS
New York   Oxford

Oxford University Press

Oxford   New York   Toronto
Delhi   Bombay   Calcutta   Madras   Karachi
Petaling Jaya   Singapore   Hong Kong   Tokyo
Nairobi   Dar es Salaam   Cape Town
Melbourne   Auckland

and associated companies in
Beirut   Berlin   Ibadan   Nicosia

Originally published in France as *L'Homme Neuronal* by Fayard. Copyright © 1983
  by Librairie Arthème Fayard
First published in English in the United States in 1985 by Pantheon Books,
  a division of Random House, Inc., New York
First published in English in Great Britain in 1986 simultaneously in paperback and hardcover
  by Oxford University Press, Walton Street, Oxford OX2 6DP
First issued in paperback in the United States in 1986 by Oxford University Press, Inc., 200 Madison Avenue,
  New York, New York 10016, by arrangement with Pantheon Books

Oxford is a registered trademark of Oxford University Press

Library of Congress Cataloging-in-Publication Data
Changeux, Jean-Pierre.
  Neuronal man.
  Translation of: L'homme neuronal.
  Bibliography: p.
  Includes index.
  1. Neuropsychology.   2. Brain.   I. Title.
QP360.C45513   1986   612'.82   86-18122
ISBN 0-19-504226-3 (pbk.)
ISBN 0-19-217750-8 (UK hardcover)

Printing (last digit): 9 8 7 6 5 4 3 2 1

Printed in the United States of America

Contents

List of Illustrations

Preface to the Oxford Edition

Neuronal Man was written in 1982 and has been regularly revised in subsequent printings and also for its English translation. Although the most up-to-date neurobiological data were, of course, taken into account during the initial editing of the work, it was not intended simply to be fashionable and, as such, doomed to becoming rapidly outdated. It represents, rather, an attempt to reflect in depth upon the neurosciences and their implications for mankind, based as much on the history of ideas and the evolution of knowledge as on the most recent discoveries. The examples used to illustrate the arguments put forward in the book were necessarily limited in number and presentation at the outset, but they were chosen with sufficient care to ensure that they still remain valid.

New facts have, of course, emerged to enrich our knowledge. There is room here for no more than a brief résumé of these data, so I will mention just those which are especially remarkable either for their originality or for the results they bring about.

Among the latter, I will refer first, in the chapter on "Animal Spirits," to the fact that, contrary to a frequently held belief, one neurone synthesizes not just one neurotransmitter but in reality several at the same time.[1] This coexistence of several chemical messengers dramatically increases the range of signals available to the nerve cell with which to communicate with its neighbors. Similarly, neurone chemistry has been constantly developing, in particular as a result of the identification of the structure of receptors for various neuronal "messengers" and, more especially, of the ionic channel specific to the sodium ions responsible for the propagation of the nerve impulse.[2]

For the chapter on "Mental Objects" a huge body of theoretical work, currently growing at an explosive rate, has had to be taken into account. This research draws its inspiration as much from the physics of disordered states of matter, such as the "spin glass"[3] as from work on artificial intelligence and, of course, on the neurobiology of the higher functions of the brain. [4] The traditionally hierarchical and computational (or digital) views about the functioning of computers have been improved upon or, quite simply, replaced by models where the massive parallelism of the input and the analogical character of the representations predominate. In psychology also functionalist theories—whose purpose is to explain the psyche in terms of (if not to reduce it to) formal operations which are independent of their neuronal substrata—are tending to break the spell of their platonic seduction, and attempts at synthesis between psychology and the neurosciences are appearing more and more fruitful. But it has to be admitted that the code for mental representations, in space and in time, still has to be worked out, and it is there that one of the most important discoveries in the future development of the neurosciences has yet to be made.

The biology of the development of the nervous system presented in the chapters on "The Power of the Genes" and "Epigenesis" has developed spectacularly over recent years, in particular through the identification of genes that we have called "communication genes." They have been regrouped into two distinct categories: one family encodes for surface proteins, such as CAM (cell adhesion molecules), which intervene in the adhesion between embryonic cells from the very first stages of development (but also in later stages) and during the formation of the nervous system;[5] a second family code for regulatory proteins, which act at the level of chromosone genes in the same way as the "repressor" defined in the regulation of the synthesis of β-galactosidase in the *E. coli* bacillus. Initially identified in the *Drosophila* (fruit fly),[6] certain of these genes determine the segmentation of the body (for example, their mutation causes the loss of one segment in two); others, known as homeotic, define the identity of each segment (for example, their change transforms a cephalic segment with an antenna into a thoracic segment with a leg). These genes have been found in vertebrates and, in particular, in mammals.[7] They can manifest themselves several times in the course of development, and the product of some of them appears, selectively, in the embryonic nervous system. The central nervous system of mammals, the spinal cord and, of course, the encephalon display a repeated segment structure. It is tempting to see in this the result of the action of segmentation genes and/or of homeotic genes which might have manifested themselves very early, at the neural disc stage, even before the formation of the groove and its closing into the neural tube. From there we might go on to speculate that the extremely rapid expansion of the frontal lobe—which, in the course of the evolution of primates, leads to man (see the chapter on "Anthropogenesis")—may not simply be the result of the prolonged actions of some of these genes. In the near future molecular biology will doubtless provide the answer to a question which has concerned humanity for thousands of years.

The deliberately physicalist philosophy of *Neuronal Man* and the extension of the Darwinian model to the development of the neurone network, as well as to the genesis of mental objects, has sometimes provoked strong reactions which are not all of a scientific nature. The reader should bear in mind that the author of this book has neither claimed to describe exhaustively the functioning of the human brain nor wished to impose a totalitarian view of the human sciences; he desires merely to offer subjects for consideration to a wider public than that of the specialists and, especially, to establish an interface, which is still far from adequate, between the life sciences and the human sciences.

Notes

1. Hökfelt, T., Johansson, O. & Goldstein, M. (1984). Chemical anatomy of the brain. *Science, 225,* 1326–1334.
2. Noda, M. et al. (1984). Primary structure of *Electrophorus electricus* sodium channel deduced from cDNA sequence. *Nature, 312,* 121–127.
3. Toulouse, G., Dehaene, S. & Changeux, J.-P. (1986). A spin glass model of learning by selection. *Proc. Natl. Acad. Sci.* (USA), *83,* 1695–1698.
4. Edelman, G. & Finkel, L. (1984). Neuronal group selection in the cerebral cortex. In *Dynamic apsects of neocortical function* (G. Edelman, E. Gall & W. M. Cowan, eds.). New York: John Wiley, pp. 653–695.
5. Edelman, G. (1985). Molecular regulations of Neural Morphogenesis. In *Molecular bases of development* (G. Edelman, E. Gall & W. M. Cowan, eds.). New York: John Wiley, pp. 35–60.
6. Gehring, W. (1985). The molecular basis of development. *Scientific American, 253,* pp. 153ff.
7. Awgulewitsch, A., Utset, M., Hart, C. P., McGinnis, W. & Ruddle, F. (1986). Spatial restriction in expression of a mouse homeo box locus within the central nervous system. *Nature, 320,* 328–335.

Preface

Neuronal Man was born in 1979 as a result of a discussion with Jacques-Alain Miller and his colleagues on the review *Ornicar?* (which has since become *L'Âne*). This lively dialogue between psychoanalysts and neurobiologists demonstrated, against all expectations, that the protagonists could talk to each other and even come to an agreement. It is often forgotten that Sigmund Freud was a neurologist, for since his *Project for a Scientific Psychology* of 1895, the multiple avatars of psychoanalysis have cut off its real biological basis.[1] Could this renewed dialogue with the "hard" sciences be the sign of an evolution, a return to basic sources—perhaps even a new departure?

There was another positive aspect to this meeting: it allowed us to judge the distance we must travel before such exchanges can become constructive and a synthesis finally emerge. Perhaps the time has come to rewrite Freud's *Project* and to lay the foundation for a modern biology of the mind.[2] That is certainly not the pretension of this book; its scope is more limited—to inform and if possible interest readers in the neurosciences. In the last twenty years, our knowledge in this field has undergone an expansion matched only by the growth of physics at the beginning of the century and molecular biology in the 1950s. The impact of the discovery of the synapse and its functions is comparable to that of the atom or DNA. A new world is emerging, and the time seems ripe to open this field of knowledge to a wider public than the specialists and, if possible, to share the researchers' enthusiasm. Since the *Ornicar?* discussion, I have felt the need to bring together recent data relating to developments in the neurosciences. There was no question of presenting an exhaustive picture of contemporary research on the nervous system. A choice had to be made, and I will certainly be accused of partiality in this choice. I admit it. Several years of teaching at the Collège de France have convinced me that a fruitful exchange with one's audience can be established only on the basis of a few simple but solid ideas. I hope that my partiality will be interpreted as a concern for educating.

The human sciences are in vogue. Much has been said and written about psychology, linguistics, and sociology, but the brain itself has been to a large extent excluded.[3] This is not purely by chance. No, the stakes are too high for that. Yet this deliberate neglect is relatively recent. Might it be a question of prudence? Perhaps it is feared that attempts to give a biological explanation of the psyche or mental activity will fall into the trap of simplistic reductionism. Perhaps it would be better to uproot the human sciences from their biological subsoil. Surprisingly, disciplines that began with a physicalist viewpoint, like psychoanalysis, have begun to defend an almost complete autonomy of psychic phenomena, accentuating the traditional split between mind and body.

Throughout history, research on the nervous system has run into bitter ideological obstacles and visceral fears, on the right as well as the left. Any research that directly or indirectly challenges the immaterial nature of the soul threatens faith and risks being burned at the stake. There is also an understandable fear of the social impact of biological discoveries that, if abused, could become weapons of oppression. It might be wiser to cut the deep bonds that link the social to the cerebral. Rather than meet the problem head on, why not hide away this dangerous organ and "decerebrate" the social order?

Finally, the best writings in the human sciences generally deal with problems that touch one personally, like political involvement, sex life, or the education of children. The quest for the "internal" mechanisms underlying these concerns appears much less interesting. In the short term, this search will not lead to a code of good conduct, nor disclose the secret of happiness, nor permit us to predict the future (unless the knowledge so acquired stimulates a deeper reflection on human nature and the world around us).

Seen from another planet, human behavior would seem rather surprising. We are one of the rare species that kills our kind deliberately. Even worse, sometimes we condemn an individual murder while rewarding those responsible for collective homicide and the inventors of terrible war machines. This absurd madness has pursued man throughout history, from the invention of the Stone Age ax to the perfecting of thermonuclear bombs. It has resisted all religions and all philosophies, even the most magnanimous. As emphasized by Arthur Koestler, it is hard-wired into the organization of the human brain. But man also decorated the Sistine Chapel, composed the *Rite of Spring*, discovered the atom. "What is this chimera called man? What novelty, what monstrosity, what chaos, what contradiction, what prodigy!"[4] What can be in the head of this *Homo* who shamelessly attributes to himself the epithet *sapiens?*

This book would never have seen the light of day without the initiative and the diligence of Odile Jacob, who followed its publication so competently and attentively. The work benefited from scientific contacts, conferences, and discussions made possible by the Neuroscience Research Program, directed initially by Francis O. Schmitt in Boston and more recently by Gerald Edelman and Vernon Mountcastle in New York. Seven years of teaching in the Collège de France in front of an ever-critical audience eager for knowledge have helped my research and documentation as well as influenced my choice of examples and, of course, my synthesizing reflections.

Finally, my thanks are due to P. Benoît, C. Bertheleu, S. Carcassonne, H. Condamine, J. Costentin, H. Hecaen, and A. Klarsfeld for their critical reading of the manuscript and constructive comments and also to J. Cartaud, M. Donskoff, M. Fardeau, J. Gaillard, C. Sotelo, A. Trautmann, and S. Tsuji for providing valuable information. The illustrations owe much to the careful and painstaking photography of P. Lemoine.

Neuronal Man

The "Organ of the Soul"—from Ancient Egypt to the Belle Époque

> The nervous system has been discovered with a slow-
> ness only explicable by the numerous difficulties that
> have always opposed this sort of research.
> —Franz Joseph Gall, *On the Functions of the*
> *Brain and Each of Its Parts*

MAN THINKS WITH HIS BRAIN.

In 1862 Edwin Smith, an American collector, bought a papyrus scroll in a junk shop in Luxor. Over fifty years later, James Breasted, at the time director of the Oriental Institute at the University of Chicago, deciphered it.[1] This medical manuscript contains seventeen columns, fragments of a surgical treatise in which, for the first known time in history, the brain is actually named as such. The hieroglyphs of the papyrus date it to the seventeenth century B.C., but it is probably a copy of an earlier text of the Ancient Empire written in about 3000 B.C. In it, one finds a list of forty-eight cases of head and neck injuries, described very concisely and systematically; each case includes a title, details of the examination, the diagnosis, and the treatment. In case number 6, we read how, with an open wound of the skull, one sees "corrugations" similar to those that "form on molten copper"—the first highly evocative description of cerebral fissures and convolutions. Case 8 is important: the scribe notes that a "smash" in the skull was accompanied by a deviation of the eyes and that the patient "shuffled" when walking. This observation must have surprised him, for he re-peated four times in a few lines that the wound was "in the skull," as if wishing to emphasize the paradox of a motor handicap in the limbs so far from the lesion. Further on, in case 22, we read: "If thou examinest a man having a smash in his temple. . . . If thou callest to him he is speechless and cannot speak." In case 31, the Egyptian surgeon tells us that after dislocating the vertebrae in his neck, a patient was not conscious of his arms and legs, that his phallus was erect, and that he urinated and ejaculated unconsciously.

Each of these cases provides a precise description of symptoms now known to accompany fractures of the skull or the cervical vertebrae. The objectivity of the Egyptian surgeon marks even his style of writing: "If thou examined" such and such a lesion "thou shouldst find" such and such a symptom. He resists magical formulas and does not hesitate to repeat on several occasions: "an ailment not to be treated." With our twentieth-century knowledge and perspective, we must avoid over-interpreting such a fragmentary text. Nonetheless, despite several errors, this papyrus comprises the first known document in which the brain's role in controlling limbs or organs at a considerable distance from it is established.

Did the ancient Egyptians understand the profound implications of their observations? It does not seem so, because for them, as for the Mesopotamians, the Hebrews, and even Homer, it was not the brain, or "encephalon," but the heart, the source of life, that harbored intelligence and feeling. "It is indeed there," writes Lucretius, "that fear and terror leap. It is there that joy gently throbs." The history of cerebral function begins with a separation, which persists to our time, between the objective interpretation of facts and the subjective sensations we experience.

The forerunners of Socrates, from the seventh to the fifth century B.C., established and developed a philosophy of a different nature.[2] It was rather ambitious in trying to "model" both the universe and man. Ideas concerning spirit and matter were not yet unambiguously defined, but perhaps there was some merit in this. Earth, air, fire, and water and later, with Lucretius and Democritus, the "atoms," constituted the substance of the world, man, and even, it seems, his thoughts for, according to Parmenides, thought and being were one and the same thing.

Of the ancients, Democritus came closest to many of our modern concerns. For him, sensation and thought had a material basis and depended on concrete, "fine, polished and round" atoms; all sensations and images resulted from a change in the position of these particles in space. In his view these "psychic atoms" were spread throughout the body. But he wrote: "The brain watches over the upper limbs like a guard, as citadel of the body, consecrated to its protection." And he added that "the brain, guardian of thoughts or intelligence," contains the principal "bonds of the soul." He thus differed from the poet of the *Iliad* by abandoning the heart in favor of the brain. Nevertheless, he called the heart "the queen, the nurse of anger," and believed that "the center of desire is in the liver." Despite such statements, which tend to make us smile, Democritus produced two major concepts in the history of ideas concerning the brain. He distinguished several intellectual and affective faculties and assigned them to precise locations in the body. One of them—thought—was situated in the brain. His psychic atoms constituted the material basis for exchanges between the brain, the other organs of the body, and the world outside, thus anticipating the notion of nervous activity.

Around the time of Pericles, Hippocrates and his colleagues consolidated and enriched Democritus' thesis with clinical observations. Like the surgeon of Edwin Smith's papyrus, they studied head injuries and showed that they could cause motor deficits. But they made the further discovery that these impairments were on the left when the right side of the brain was involved—that is, on the side of the body opposite that of the head injury. Hippocrates also discovered that "if the brain is irritated, intelligence is impaired, the brain enters into spasms, and the whole body convulses. Sometimes the patient does not speak, he suffocates. This affection is called apoplexy or epilepsy. At other times, intelligence is disturbed and the patient comes and goes, thinking and believing things remote from reality and carrying the features of the disease in his mocking smile and strange visions." Hippocratic medicine already distinguished neurological and mental diseases and rightly attributed them to the brain. But we are surprised to read: "The brain is like a gland . . . white and friable."

In the *Timaeus* Plato developed these pre-Socratic theses with his theory of the three parts of the soul. He distinguished the intellectual part from the irascible and concupiscible parts, placing the first in the head and attributing to it the virtue of immortality. He united it to the other two—mortal—parts by the spinal cord. With Plato and Hippocrates, the "cephalocentric" thesis was formulated quite explicitly. According to it, the seat of thought was the brain.

This point of view, so obvious to us today, was the subject of a long and lively polemic. Aristotle led minds astray for centuries on this point. He who, it is said, had never seen a human brain, revived the ideas of Homer and the Hebrews by insisting that the heart was the seat of sensations, passions, and the intellect. The brain, for him, was composed of earth and water and served simply to cool the organism! It lowered the temperature of blood loaded with food and brought on sleep. How can we explain such a strange idea? Aristotle, like Plato, did not know of the existence of nerves, but had observed blood vessels and the way they converged toward the heart. Was this a means of putting the periphery of the body in contact with the central command organ? Aristotle also noticed, quite correctly, that the exposed brain was not sensitive to mechanical stimulation while the heart was. Furthermore, there was nothing resembling the vertebrate brain in such animals as worms, insects, and shellfish. Aristotle judged these observations sufficient to abandon Plato's doctrine.

Aristotle's error, however, did not prevent him from developing thoughts on the "soul," a concept that he introduced unequivocally into the natural sciences. Anticipating the theories of Epicurus, he wrote: "The soul never thinks without images." These images, whose origin was in the sense organs, constituted "representations" or "copies" of the objects that produced them. Thanks to these images, the intellect could also anticipate and prepare for the future in the present, "as if it could see things." These preoccupations resemble certain problems in modern cognitive psychology (see Chapter 5).

Greek medicine was in general faithful to Hippocratic theories and avoided the "cardiocentric" idea. Alexandria took the place of Athens. The notions of the pre-Socratic atomists were known there through Epicurus. With Herophilus and Erasistratus in the third century B.C., knowledge of the brain progressed rapidly. Abandoning analogies with animals, so dear to Aristotle, they were the first to dissect the human body. At that time, even touching a corpse was considered "abject." Yet they dissected criminals whom, as Celsus wrote, "the kings removed from the prisons to give to them, and they examined them while they were still breathing." Herophilus is said to have dissected thousands of bodies. This—fortunately exceptional—enterprise led to the distinction of the cerebellum from the brain and the spinal cord. They showed that the brain contained cavities, or ventricles; that its surface, or cortex, was folded into convolutions; and that nerves were different from blood vessels, that they originated not in the heart, as Aristotle thought, but in the brain or the spinal cord. They also distinguished nerves concerned with "movement" and those with "feeling" —that is, motor and sensory nerves. In addition, they noticed that in man, whose intelligence was superior to that of other animals, the convolutions of the brain were much more complex than in other animals. In Europe it was not until the seventeenth century that this level of anatomical knowledge of the human brain was surpassed.

Anatomical data alone, however, were not enough to undermine Aristotle's thesis. It was almost five hundred years after the school of Alexandria before Galen succeeded in this by introducing a new method. He was not satisfied with a mere description of the nervous system; he experimented and established brain physiology as a science. He was particularly concerned with the cavities, or ventricles, and differentiated these from the "substance" of the brain, which "resembled that of the nerves." Following up the work of Herophilus and Erasistratus, he distinguished three ventricles: one at the front of the brain, divided in two; one in the center; and one at the rear. He noted that if the substance of the brain was cut at a given point, the animal did not lose consciousness or movement. For this to happen, the section had to penetrate as far as the ventricles. A lesion of the posterior ventricle had the most disturbing effect on the animal. Galen demonstrated that the brain played the central role in controlling bodily and mental activity and that this activity originated in the cerebral substance itself. His experiments dealt a fatal blow to cardiocentric theses. Nevertheless, backed up by numerous philosophical and naturalistic works, and perpetuated by medieval scholars, Aristotle's erroneous opinions survived until the eighteenth century. A feeling of uncertainty can be found in William Shakespeare's *Merchant of Venice:* "Tell me, where is fancy bred, or in the heart, or in the head?" And elsewhere Honoré de Balzac's "Heartaches of an English Cat" have naturally nothing to do with cardiac disease.

BODY AND SOUL

For Plato and Galen, the rational soul had its seat in the brain. But this teaches us nothing about the nature of the soul or its relations with the body. What is more, the diverse meanings of the word "soul" are matched only by its ambiguity. Its significance varies from one culture to another, and from one author to another. Some look upon it as a principle of life, others believe that the soul can be reduced to abstract thought, that is, to a higher cerebral function. Advances in biology, first at the cellular and then at the molecular level, have disposed of the first of these meanings. From the time of Galen to the eighteenth century, discussions bearing on the second meaning of the word centered on establishing the relationship between the organization of the brain and its functions.

Galen, the physiologist, developed the idea of a "psychic pneuma" produced and stored in the ventricles. According to him, the pneuma, "the organ of the soul," circulated in the nerves and allowed the brain to communicate with the organs of sensation and movement. This pneuma became the "animal spirits" of the classical age and then, in the eighteenth century, "nervous fluid." Galen, much more an observer than a philosopher, nevertheless hesitated to go further than Democritus had. Could the pneuma, the *organ* of the soul, also be the *substance* of the soul or even the soul itself? He seemed unable to decide. Nevertheless, aware of the dictum of Moses, he refused to confuse madness with possession by the devil and suggested a lesson to meditate upon: "Do not consult the gods to discover the directing soul, but consult an anatomist."

Pursuing the analytical approach of Herophilus and Erasistratus, Galen broke the soul down into several functions. He divided it into faculties: motor, sensory (including the five senses), and rational. The rational soul was itself composed of functions, which he named imagination, reason, and memory. Nevertheless, having little real data, Galen did not give these functions precise locations in the brain. Without drawing on any new observations, the Church Fathers, particularly Nemesius, bishop of Emesa, and St. Augustine in the fourth and fifth centuries, set forth their opinions on this point. They placed imagination in the anterior ventricles, intellect in the middle ventricle, and memory in the posterior ventricle. However simplistic, this conception had the major advantage of giving specific functions to discrete brain regions. It formed the first model of cerebral localization, and numerous drawings and engravings illustrated it for more than a thousand years until the seventeenth century (Figure 1).

Medieval scholars forgot the work of Herophilus and Erasistratus; moreover, their original texts disappeared. With the Renaissance, the dissection of animals, and above all of the human body, began again. Leonardo da Vinci, at the Santa Maria Nuova Hospital in Florence, made a wax cast of the cerebral ventricles of an ox for the first time between 1504 and 1507; he also made precise drawings of the cerebral convolutions. Andreas Vesalius in Italy (Figure 2) and Constanzo Varolio and Fresnel in France produced more and more precise descriptions of cerebral morphology, demonstrating its complexity. Gradually, the oversimplified ventricles were abandoned as sites of psychic functions in favor of the real "substance" of the brain. Nemesius'

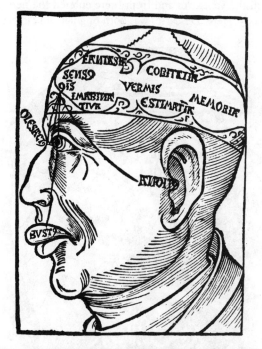

Figure 1. This engraving, dating from the beginning of the sixteenth century, represents one of the first attempts to subdivide the soul into basic faculties and to localize these faculties in discrete regions of the brain. These first "phrenologists," who were also Fathers of the Church, erroneously attributed the functions of the soul to the hollow ventricles of the brain. In the first ventricle one finds fantasy, common sense, and imagination. In the second, separated from the first by the Vermis, thought and judgment; in the third, memory. (From G. de Rusconibus, 1520.)

sketches were replaced by sumptuous anatomical plates, but the functional significance of the structures described remained unclear.

Researchers and philosophers found themselves in a tricky situation. The political climate was such that they hesitated to openly oppose the official doctrine on the immaterial nature of the soul for fear of being condemned. In the writings of that time it is difficult to differentiate between the author's real thoughts and what he had to write in order to survive, even his flattery of the authorities. In this light, it is easier to understand the curious synchretism of René Descartes. For him, as for Aristotle, the flow of blood from the heart to the brain produced animal spirits. Reminiscent of Nemesius' ideas, these animal spirits "flowed" in the ventricles and from there entered the nerves to influence the body. Here, Descartes was both original and radical. For him,

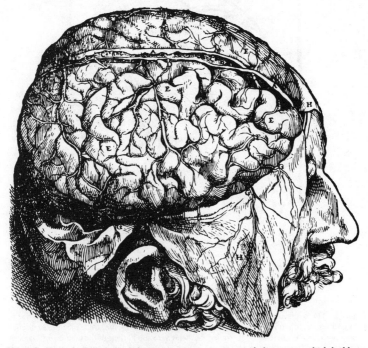

Figure 2. With the Renaissance, there was a return to anatomical observation, which had been abandoned since the school of Alexandria. In *De humani corporis fabrica* (1543), Vesalius supplied faithful illustrations of the form of the brain, with the cerebral convolutions and their blood vessels.

the body was a machine. He compared it to an organ in which animal spirits acted like the air in pipes. But man was different from animals because of his soul, which Descartes in no way confused with animal spirits. He was a dualist and rejected Plato's tripartite theory, believing the soul to be unique, immaterial, and immortal.

How could such radically opposed and even contradictory ideas be reconciled? Descartes, better at reasoning than anatomy, made use of the pineal gland, which had the virtue of being single, for "the other parts of our brain are double, and we can only think about one thing at any one time." It is there, according to Descartes, that the soul joins the body. There, the circulation of animal spirits is controlled, although these spirits in turn act upon the pineal gland "when certain parts of the body move or are stimulated." This incongruous role of the pineal rightly astonished both theologians and anatomists. It could not get past the criticism of an alert philosopher like Benedict de Spinoza.

Posterity has retained one essential aspect of Descartes' view: his concept of the human body as a *machine* consisting of bones, nerves, muscles, veins, blood, and skin. When he applied this concept to an analysis of the stimulation of movement by visual or auditory signals, he arrived at diagrams remarkably similar to those used today to describe the reflex arc.

Thomas Willis (Figure 3) never achieved the same philosophical level as Descartes. He was an observer. With the artistic help of the architect of St. Paul's, Christopher Wren, he produced the best pictures of the brain so far. He showed that the folds of the cerebral cortex covered a certain number of "subcortical" centers, such as the striatum, the thalamus, and the corpus callosum that unites the two hemispheres. He distinguished a cortical *gray matter*, responsible, in his mind, for animal spirits, from a deeper *white matter*, distributing the spirits to the rest of the organism, to which they gave sensation and movement. He even spoke of the "explosive" virtues of animal spirits. We are very close to modern concepts of the respective functions of gray and white matter in the production and conduction of nervous activity. Nevertheless, like Descartes, and perhaps in order to attract the blessing of the powerful archbishop of Canterbury, Willis still accepted the idea of an immaterial, reasoning soul unique to man, somewhere beyond the blade of his scalpel. Descartes united body and soul with the pineal gland; Willis gave this function to the striatum. Indeed, contemporary authors differed considerably on this point. Every newly discovered

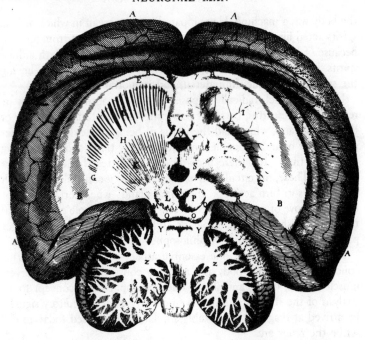

Figure 3. In the seventeenth century, Willis in England finally abandoned the doctrine of ventricles and correctly gave primacy to the cerebral cortex. In this figure we see the cortex folded back to each side after sectioning the brain between the two hemispheres. The surgical cut has split the corpus callosum (B, in white), which connects the two hemispheres, and reveals subcortical nervous centers, such as the thalamus (K). Willis also distinguished the surface gray matter from the deeper white matter. This distinction is particularly clear in the section of the cerebellum (Z) at the bottom of the figure. (From T. Willis, 1672.)

structure became a potential junction between body and soul. The efforts of Descartes or Willis to situate the soul in a precise area of the brain were, without doubt, in line with the tenet of localization. But, always, they stumbled against a belief in the unique and indivisible nature of the soul; their efforts thus seem retrogressive compared with those of Galen or Nemesius.

Another line of thought was introduced by Pierre Gassendi, who, at the beginning of the seventeenth century, revived the ideas of the Greek atomists and Lucretius. Although still trying to reconcile the official doctrine of the Church, to which he belonged, he announced to the Collège de France that animals also have a memory. They can reason and possess other psychological characteristics similar to those of man; therefore, they must also have a soul. What is more, for Gassendi, the soul was not situated in any particular part of the body.

Thus, a lively polemic developed concerning the soul of animals. The outcome was certainly not a humanization of animals but rather an animalization of man. Whether we like it or not, this was the time of the historical devaluation of the soul. Gassendi's disciple, Guillaume Lamy, wrote: "I use the words soul and [animal] spirits without differentiation. There should be no confusion because they are the same thing." A century later, the dualism of Descartes was rejected by those it had inspired. Vaucanson, a master in the art of building automatons, with the help of a surgeon, Claude Le Cat, made a duck that could flap its wings and eat and digest seeds. He even conceived an "artificial man." Finally, Julien Offray de la Mettrie wrote, at the risk of severe punishment, that it was quite possible to remove the soul from Cartesian theories without losing much and that man himself could be put in the category of these mechanical animals. For Pierre Cabanis, the "brain secretes thought as the liver secretes bile." The theory of the immaterial nature of the soul disappeared progressively from works devoted to the brain sciences. We have had to wait three thousand years to rediscover the concepts of the Greek atomists in their original simplicity and for these thoughts to be expressed with complete freedom.

PHRENOLOGY

The explosion of ideas brought about by the Encyclopedists engendered two theories, published at the beginning of the nineteenth century, that revolutionized biological thinking: Jean-Baptiste de Lamarck's transformism and Franz Joseph Gall's phrenology. In both cases the theory is fundamentally correct; it is the application that can be criticized.

Gall, a professional physician and anatomist, had considerable experience with dissection.[3] He was familiar with the organization of the brain, but described little that was new. Nevertheless, his experience allowed him to speculate that the cerebral cortex represented the highest level of the brain and that the development of this area characterized mammals and man. He also pointed out the anatomical uniformity of the cortex (an observation that will be developed later). Spread out, either naturally as in cases of hydrocephalus or experimentally, using a weak spurt of water, the cortex seemed to form a continuous mantle in spite of its folds. It was made of the same material as the ganglia in direct contact with the organs. He identified the same gray and white matters in both the central and the peripheral nervous systems. In the tradition of La Mettrie and Cabanis, he secularized the brain.

Gall stood out from his contemporaries in his theories and his methods. His aim was to analyze cerebral functions and localize them without the help of introspection. He advocated abandoning speculative philosophy in favor of trying to understand mental faculties from the naturalistic, physiological point of view. Gall therefore rejected Plato's and Galen's concepts of the rational soul and, of course, Descartes' dualism. He stood far apart from the "sensualist" theories of John Locke and Etienne Bonnot de Condillac, according to which mental faculties and instincts derived from sensations. In Gall's view, man possessed a great number of "moral and intellectual faculties," which he accepted as innate, essential, and irreducible. He established an empirical list of these, drawing on everyday language, the biographies of famous men, and descriptions of mental disturbances or manias that, he claimed, represented the exaggeration of one or other of these faculties. This list, which he judged provisional, contained twenty-seven entries, of which seven were specific to man. Among these twenty-seven faculties, one finds the reproductive instinct (or sexual drive), the love of progeny (or maternal behavior), the taste for combat (or aggressiveness), verbal memory, understanding of words, and the sense of location and spatial relations. More recent research has confirmed the independence of many of these. On the other hand, pride, authority, glory, metaphysical thought, poetic talent, and devotion leave us perplexed. Gall assigned to each of these faculties a specific cerebral localization. Every aspect of behavior had its own "organ," confined to a precise area of the highest functional division of the brain—the cerebral cortex.

How was this map established? Access to the brain is difficult. Gall postulated that the skull was a faithful representation of the surface of the cortex. So it was enough to palpate the skull and correlate certain bumps with faculties that were particularly developed in certain individuals. This was *cranioscopy*. Gall collected skulls of criminals or mentally ill patients and busts of famous men. After careful examination, he established maps of the bony features corresponding

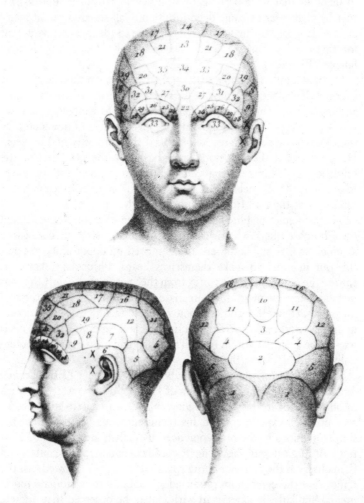

Figure 4. A fanciful representation of Gall's model. Gall's phrenology gave precise cortical localizations for twenty-seven mental faculties. The doctrine of phrenology engendered a lively polemic, in which it is often difficult to distinguish between truly scientific controversy and ideological quarrels. Gall was considered a left-wing materialist! Although fundamentally as important to the history of ideas as the theory of evolution, the initial concepts of phrenology and particularly its detailed application left much to be desired. With little solid data, Gall was obliged to study the shape of the skull rather than the structure of the cerebral convolutions. Often his twenty-seven faculties surprise us in their naiveté; note that there are even thirty-five represented in this figure! (From F. Broussais, 1836.)

15

to faculties that were particularly well developed in his subjects. Either by chance or by some deep intuition, Gall situated verbal memory and language in the frontal region, close to the location we accept for them today. But for other faculties, Gall's topography is pure fantasy (Figure 4).

It is quite understandable that, on the basis of such superficial observations, Gall's "model" came in for severe criticism, which grew more and more vehement as phrenology rapidly came to symbolize materialism. Gall was prohibited from teaching in Vienna and persecuted by the Church; exiled to Paris, he provoked the animosity of Napoleon. He wrote about the emperor that if he had wished to "destroy the tendency toward materialism as he wanted to . . . he would have had to use 300,000 bayonets and as many cannons in order to separate the functions of the soul from those of the body."

The principles of phrenology extended the ideas of Nemesius and the Church Fathers, whose ventricular model had stressed localization as much as Gall's. The phrenologists missed no opportunity to point this out in order to make themselves heard. Phrenology, however, shifted the emphasis to the cortex from the ventricles—a shift that was inevitable in view of advances in anatomy and the division of the soul into many concrete faculties. Some of these faculties could be found in animals and could therefore be approached experimentally. This is one of the essential virtues of Gall's model, and a feature of all potentially useful biological theories.

Pierre Flourens, who eventually became a member of the French Academy and officer of the Legion of Honor, and who was very much in official favor for his dualistic view, put Gall rudely to the test. An accomplished experimentalist, his techniques went further than the simple incisions in the brain practiced by Galen. He performed ablations, or surgical removals, of anatomically defined areas or centers and then observed the behavior of the operated animal. He showed that the removal of the cerebellum produced an inability to coordinate movements. Similarly, in agreement with Galen, he observed that discrete lesions in the medulla, near the posterior ventricle, disturbed certain vital functions, such as respiration. His results supported the idea of localization and his use of ablation became a favored method for establishing maps of cortical localization. Yet his experiments, and above all his interpretation of the role of the cortex, led him to the opposite conclusion. According to Flourens, "a large section of the cerebral lobes can be removed without loss of function. As more is removed all functions weaken and gradually disappear. Thus, the cerebral lobes operate in unison for the full exercise of their functions." In his opinion, the cerebral cortex functioned as an indivisible whole. It was the seat of the "essentially single" faculty of perception, judgment, and will. For Flourens, the cortex was the last refuge of the soul or, if one prefers, of the spirit. Without hesitation, he mixed metaphysics with politics in interpreting his experiments. But he went too far and many of his findings on the cortex are now contested.

For example, his surgical technique was often blind. Although supposedly removing only the cortex, he often also simultaneously destroyed subcortical structures. It was Gall's turn to criticize him. What is more, Flourens experimented mainly on birds or lower vertebrates, in which we now know the cortex is far less differentiated and functionally less important than in mammals and particularly humans. Also, his behavioral analysis of the operated animals was too rudimentary for a serious investigation of the faculties catalogued by Gall. As is often the case, an ideological debate grew into a controversy based on deficient experimental technique.

Anatomical research on the cerebral cortex became more and more precise. We possess accurate, almost photographic, descriptions of the gyri and sulci—the folds and fissures—of the cerebral cortex from this period by François Leuret and Pierre Gratiolet. They rapidly became indispensable guides in all cortical mapmaking. Demarcated by the fissures of Sylvius and Rolando, the frontal, temporal, parietal, and occipital lobes, as well as the insula, were named (Figure 5).

The first irrefutable proof in favor of Gall's model was derived neither by cranioscopy nor by animal experimentation. Jean Baptiste Bouillaud, Gall's student, worked on humans and was particularly interested in one of the faculties that Gall had emphasized: language. He made use of the "natural experiments" provided by accidental cranial trauma or spontaneous cerebral lesions and related them to disturbances of language. Bouillaud initiated the anatomical study of language disturbances that was to become neuropsychology. He established that there could be selective paralysis of the tongue and organs of phonation without paralysis of the limbs, as well as limb paralysis without loss of articulate speech. He localized the function of language, in accord with Gall's phrenology, in the anterior cortical lobe. Bouillaud wrote: "The loss of language depends sometimes on the loss of memory for words,

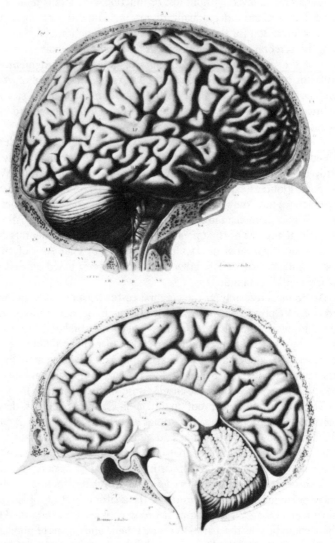

Figure 5. During the romantic period, anatomists, inspired by Gall's theories, examined and reproduced the cortical convolutions in abundant detail and with rarely equaled precision. In this beautiful nineteenth-century plate, we can distinguish in the *lower* figure the sectioned corpus callosum (cc), the ventricles, and the brainstem, giving way to the spinal cord. (From F. Leuret, 1839; L. Gratiolet, 1857.)

sometimes on the loss of muscular movements that make up memory." These essentially clinical observations, published in 1825, in the midst of the ideological controversy created by Flourens, made little impression on contemporary scientists despite their rigorous nature.

Paul Broca obtained recognition much later. On April 18, 1861, he presented to the Anthropological Society of Paris the case of a certain Leborgne, whose autopsy he had performed the previous day. The patient had been admitted twenty-one years earlier to the asylum of Bicêtre, soon after losing his speech. He expressed himself with signs and seemed to possess all his intellectual faculties, but he could pronounce only a single syllable, which was responsible for his nickname —"Tan." A postmortem examination of his brain revealed a lesion situated principally in the middle part of the frontal lobe of the left hemisphere. If Broca was convincing, it was because the anatomical facts he (and his followers) presented could no longer be denied. A lesion of the left frontal lobe causes the loss of speech, or *aphasia.* The quarrels between the phrenologists and their critics were soon left behind. Broca emphasized that the phrenologists, with their cranioscopy, had too often neglected an anatomical examination of the patient. For this, he wrote, it was "necessary to indicate exactly the name and place of the lesioned convolution." By establishing rigorous correlations between anatomical and behavioral features, Broca gave the first demonstration of the discrete cortical localization of well-defined faculties, the fundamental basis of Gall's "organology." Although the lesion he observed was unilateral, it was sufficient to cause aphasia. Thus, he revealed an asymmetry between the two hemispheres that Gall had not suspected. In some ways he was close to Descartes' attempt to unite body and soul in a single midline point of the brain, thus preserving the integrity of the "ego."

The years around 1900 became the "belle époque" of cerebral localization. The progress in clinical anatomy set in motion by Bouillaud and then Broca matched that of the experimentalists. Korbinian Brodmann, in 1909, gathered data from both monkeys and humans. He divided the cortex into fifty-two areas, each with a number but, more important, a function. Area 4, in the frontal lobe, was responsible for motor activity; area 17 in the occipital lobe, for vision; areas 41 and 42 in the temporal lobe, for hearing; areas 44 and 45 corresponded to Broca's area. Extensive and poorly identified *association* areas united these primary motor and sensory *projection* areas and were probably

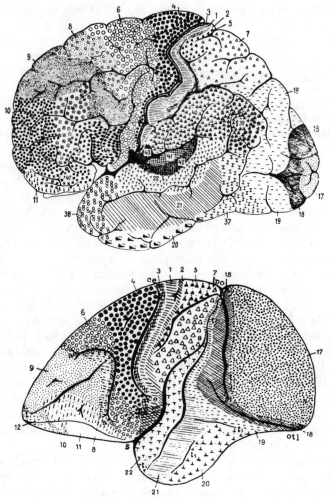

Figure 6. In this map of the cortical areas published in 1909 by Brodmann, the *upper* figure shows the brain of a man and the *lower,* the brain of a monkey. The names and numbers of these areas are still used today. The different areas were established by studying minor anatomical differences in thin cortical sections with the microscope; further experimental study of lesions and electrical stimulation has permitted the attribution of specific functions to each area. In comparing the maps of the monkey and the man, we see a large number of areas in common, such as the primary projection areas of the sense organs. Vision is in the occipital area 17, relatively larger in the monkey than in man. Hearing is in temporal areas 41, 42, and 22, while bodily sensation is in parietal areas 1, 2, and 3. Area 4 is the motor area. In man the so-called association areas, particularly the frontal areas 8 to 11 and 44 to 47, are remarkably well developed.

concerned with more integrative functions. Brodmann's map, still used today, brought Gall's work up to date. This "new phrenology," in which precise functional localization replaced the naive naming of faculties, was based not on an approximate cranioscopy but on undeniable anatomical and functional criteria (Figure 6).

Those with a holistic view of the mind were not to be defeated. On the contrary, Henri Bergson proclaimed from the heights of his chair that "the hypothesis of an equivalence between the psychological state and the cerebral state implies a pure absurdity." A more fertile and subtle point of view was expressed by neurologists such as Henry Head, who took up the theories put forward fifty years earlier by John Hughlings Jackson but left in oblivion. He based his views on the observation that a localized lesion of a particular cerebral area never led to a complete loss of function. The localization of the lesion could therefore not correspond strictly to that of a function. For Hughlings Jackson and Head, the more a process was complex and voluntary, the more it mobilized multiple cerebral areas. A cortical lesion disorganized an ordered sequence of physiological processes rather than destroying a cortical "center"; indeed, they thought the concept of a center should be replaced by a "preferential integration focus." They did not reject the principle of localization but emphasized the difficulties of applying it in too narrow a way in the cerebral cortex. In order to analyze brain function objectively, as we shall see, we must account for important relays—indeed, "integration foci"—that are not cortical. Criticisms from the holistic viewpoint led to a better definition of localization and highlighted a complexity of organization that was easy to underestimate.

THE NEURON

From antiquity until Broca's time, little was needed in the way of specialized instruments in order to demonstrate cortical localization. It was enough to open the skull, expose the brain, and observe with the naked eye. But there was a gradual evolution in the care taken with observation and, above all, interpretation. In contrast, deciphering the fundamental structure of the "nervous substance" depended directly on the development of an optical instrument: the microscope—first using natural light and more recently, since the 1950s, an electron beam.[4]

In the seventeenth century it was already known, particularly from the work of Willis, that the brain contained gray and white matter. But what was the composition of this matter? Were there cells, such as those discovered in plants and in blood by Robert Hooke in 1665? Would the fine structure of the brain be analogous to that of the liver or the heart? If this were the case, the brain would be, as Cabanis suggested, an organ like any other.

To answer these questions, the microscopists had to overcome another difficulty particular to nerve tissue. On account of its softness, it is difficult to cut thin sections of brain for microscopic observation. For many years one had to be satisfied with tearing it and teasing it between two needles. Then, at the beginning of the nineteenth century, it was discovered that it could be hardened, while preserving its structure, by "fixing" it with "wood vinegar," alcohol, formalin, chromic acid, or osmic acid. It could then be stained, embedded in an even harder supporting material (such as paraffin or, later, plastic), and then sectioned. The first sections made were several tens of microns thick (a micron is one thousandth of a meter). More recently it has become possible to section at a few nanometers (billionths of a meter), thus making the tissue transparent not only to light but to electrons. Since the nineteenth century, the chemical industry has supplied microscopists with dyes permitting the staining of the internal architecture of the cell, thus revealing the diversity of its structure.

In 1685 Marcello Malpighi observed the surface of the brain for the first time with a magnifying lens. First he had boiled it and then, after removing the meninges, flooded it with ink to increase the contrast. He saw little, transparent, whitish bodies, which he described as "minute glands." Did this observation really correspond with their form, or was it a resurgence of Hippocratic ideas? These "glands" continued to be observed for several years, but disappeared with the use of new methods. They were reproducible but artificial—aberrations due to a very primitive optical system or the result of preparing the nerve tissue too crudely. The history of microscopic study of the nervous system began with an artifact. It was not to be the last.

We owe to the Dutch scientist Anton van Leeuwenhoek the first faithful descriptions of a microscopic organization peculiar to the nervous system. "I have often, with great pleasure," he wrote in 1718,

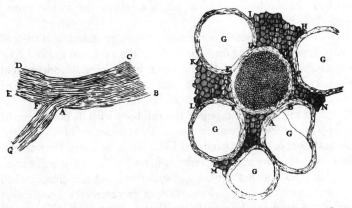

Figure 7. One of the first drawings to show nerve fibers is this section of a nerve seen through a light microscope by van Leeuwenhoek in 1718. On the *left* is a longitudinal section showing the organization of the fibers into bundles. The cross-section on the *right* shows the sheaths around the nerve bundles, with the fibers themselves illustrated in the center of the figure. Van Leeuwenhoek mistakenly believed that these fibers were hollow.

"observed the texture of the Nerves, which are composed of very minute vessels of an incredible thinness, and which, running along by the sides of each other, constitute a Nerve."[5] The word "vessel" is surprising. He believed they were really hollow. Was this an optical illusion? Indeed, van Leeuwenhoek used a rather crude microscope with a single lens. Could he have been influenced by Aristotle's confusion of nerves and blood vessels, or by the idea that animal spirits were necessarily gaseous or liquid? Nerve fibers are not strictly hollow, but many are surrounded by an enveloping membrane, or *myelin sheath.* These "nerve cylinders" (later called "axis cylinders," and then, "axons") make up the white matter of the brain and the peripheral nerves (Figure 7).

Microscopic anatomy made little significant progress for nearly a century until René Dutrochet in 1824 described and drew "globular corpuscles" in the ganglia of snails and slugs. For him, these were "the elements that produce nervous energy, which the nerve fibers are destined to conduct." He correctly named them "small cells." Thus, the nerve cell made its first appearance in scientific literature and was characterized by its cell body, or *soma.* A few years later, Gabriel Valentin noted that some of these "spheres" in the cerebellum possessed protoplasmic "tails," later recognized as multiple and widely ramified like the branches of a tree, thus giving rise to the name *dendrites*.

The relationship between the nerve fibers, or *axons*, and the cell bodies provoked a lively discussion. Were the axon and the cell body part of the same unit or did the nerve fibers form an independent network? In spite of achromatic microscope lenses and the routine staining of sections, many years elapsed before the microscopists gradually solved the puzzle and united the cell body with its dendrites and axons (which were incidentally frequently confused). O.F.C. Deiters, in a posthumous publication dated 1865, finally proposed the image of the nerve cell as we accept it today (Figure 8). The nerve cell, like all cells, has a body with a nucleus and cytoplasm, but it is characterized by two types of distinct prolongations, or processes: the axon, always single, and the dendrites, usually multiple and branched. Nerve tissue is, indeed, composed of cells like other tissues, but their cell bodies, situated in the gray matter, have long, branched prolongations quite unique to nerve cells. In addition, they are packed in a "nerve glue," or *glia*, composed of more ordinary cells.

How do the nerve cells described by Deiters unite to form nerve tissue? An objective reply to this question raises a major technical difficulty. Nerve cells do not interact through their cell bodies, easily seen with the microscope, but through their axons and dendrites, and the size of their terminal branches is at the limit of the resolving power of the light microscope. A debate, or rather a polemic, developed around 1870 and was not definitively ended until after 1950, with the introduction of electron microscopy.

The stakes were the following: for adherents of the reticular or *nerve-net* hypothesis, the nerve cells formed a *continuous* network like the canals of Camargue seen from the air. For believers in the *neuron* hypothesis, nerve cells, like trees in a forest or the fragments of a mosaic, were independent but *contiguous* units. Just when, with Broca, the principle of localization was gaining on the holistic view, a similar debate reappeared, but at a different level.

Joseph von Gerlach, leader of the nerve-net group, was working on the human cerebral cortex. In 1872, with his technique of staining with gold chloride, he revealed two distinct fiber networks. One fine network, formed of dendrites, seemed to connect the cell bodies. The other, coarser, seemed to be axonal in origin. The dendritic network was the first of these artifacts to be questioned by Camillo Golgi, who

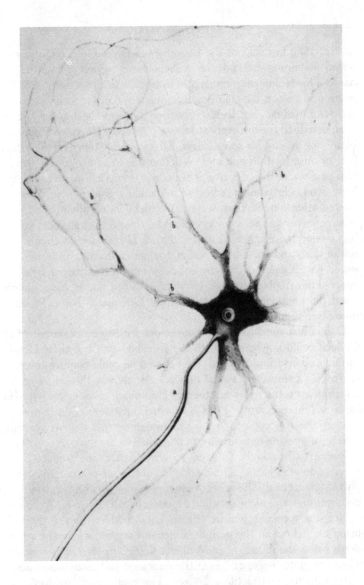

Figure 8. After the discovery of fibers in the nerves and in the white matter and of cell bodies in the gray matter, it still took several decades for microscopists to connect the fibers to the cell bodies. Here we see one of the first complete and correct drawings of a neuron (taken from the anterior horn of the spinal cord), published in 1865, in a posthumous work by Deiters. In the center one can distinguish the cell body, or soma, with its nucleus; the multiple, branching dendrites (b), converging toward the cell body; and the single axon (a) leaving it.

was teaching histology at the University of Pavia. Golgi had just perfected a staining method, the *reazione nera*, which still carries his name. This technique impregnates in black a small proportion of the neurons in a block, but stains each completely, down to its finest axonal and dendritic branches. In 1909 Santiago Ramón y Cajal, Golgi's direct rival, described the discovery as follows: "A piece of nervous tissue had been lying around for several days, hardening in Müller's fluid, either pure or mixed with osmic acid. Whether due to a histologist's distraction or a scientist's curiosity, it was then immersed in silver nitrate. Very soon, glistening needles with sparkling golden reflections attracted attention. Sections were made, dehydrated, illuminated, and observed. An unexpected spectacle! On a perfectly translucid yellow background there appeared scattered black filaments, smooth and narrow or spiny and thick; black bodies, triangular, stellate, fusiform! One would have thought they were ink drawings on transparent Japanese paper. They troubled the eye. Everything looked simple, clear, unconfused. Nothing remained but to interpret. One merely had to look and note" (see Figure 15).

Golgi's first conclusion was that the dendritic network described by Gerlach could not be seen with the *reazione nera;* but there Golgi's inspired observations stopped. He believed he could confirm the existence of a continuous axonal network. What was the origin of his attachment to the nerve-net theory? He himself gives us the reply in his Nobel Prize lecture of 1906: "I have never had reason, up to now, to give up the concept which I have always stressed, that nerve cells, instead of working individually, act together. . . . However opposed it may seem to the popular tendency to individualize the elements, I cannot abandon the idea of a unitary action of the nervous system." It was only to be expected. The belief in a nerve net took over from the holistic, even spiritualistic, ideologies that Flourens had defended so vigorously.

Golgi, a specialist on the cortex, knew nothing of the research being carried out in the peripheral nervous system, where the motor nerve meets the muscle fiber. Wilhelm Kühne, in 1869, affirmed that when the motor nerve arrives at the muscle, it ends and "never penetrates into the contractile cylinder." The motor endplate forms an intermediate layer separating the "axon cylinder" from the muscle. At this level, Kühne contended, there could be no continuity between the axon and its target. His argument was not irrefutable; moreover, there was still a certain hesitation about accepting that

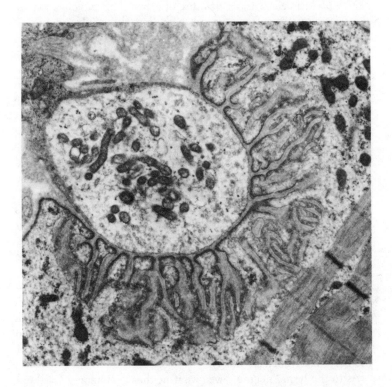

Figure 9. A synapse between a motor nerve and a human skeletal muscle observed by electron microscopy at a final magnification of 20,000. In the center is the nerve terminal (the circular shape), containing vesicles and mitochrondria (the dark "sausages"). On the right is the muscle fiber, containing bundles of contractile fibrils and crossed from time to time by dark stripes. A space—the synaptic cleft—separates the very fine membrane of the nerve terminal from the thicker, folded membrane of the muscle fiber. As Ramón y Cajal proposed, the nerve net is discontinuous. (Original micrograph by Michel Fardeau.)

what was true for the peripheral nervous system was also true for the brain (Figure 9).

In 1887 two Swiss scientists, Wilhelm His and Auguste Forel, within a few months of each other, launched the first serious attacks on the nerve-net theory. For both, the argument was not based simply on observations of the adult brain. His, an embryologist, had done post-doctoral work with Claude Bernard. He discovered that in the early stages of development the nervous system is made up of independent, closely packed cells without neurites, or axons. This prolongation appears later, growing from the cell body, but the whole remains an independent unit. There is never any formation of a "net" apart from that consisting of axonal branches.

Forel was a psychiatrist. At this time, psychiatrists were interested in anatomical research and made important contributions to it. Even Sigmund Freud published anatomical works in the 1880s, which he believed supported the nerve-net theory. Forel performed experiments on the degeneration of axonal and dendritic trees following sectioning of the axon. He showed that in certain well-defined cases, degenerative effects spread as far as the cell body and the dendrites but remained limited to the damaged unit, not extending through the entire tissue as implied by the nerve-net hypothesis.

Finally, Ramón y Cajal in Madrid launched a series of violent attacks on Golgi, whose technique he used to accumulate a remarkable number of observations on the morphology of the nerve cell and its processes, as well as on their degeneration and regeneration. The first attack came in 1888. He was working on the cerebellum, in which some cells possess an axon forming a basket around the cell bodies of other giant cells— the Purkinje cells. He showed that this basket was anatomically independent of the target cell and certainly not continuous with it. The death blow came in 1933, with an impressive review "Neuronismo o reticularismo?" which had been made necessary by the persistence of the nerve-net (reticular) theory.

As to the term "neuron," we owe it neither to Ramón y Cajal nor to His, but to Wilhelm Waldeyer (1891), about whom Ramón y Cajal wrote that all he had done was to "publish in a daily paper a résumé of his research and invent the term neuron." Whether true or false, Waldeyer had a feeling for words, for we also owe the term "chromosome" to him.

The electron microscope confirmed the neuron theory in a spectacular manner. It permits magnifications a thousand times greater than the light microscope. Its resolving power reaches a billionth of a meter— a nanometer. In the region where a nerve terminal contacts its target, the cell membranes do not fuse but are separated by a gap about 20 nanometers wide; neurons are therefore juxtaposed and not continuous with each other.[6] This junction was named a *synapse*, not by an anatomist but by the English physiologist Sir Charles Sherrington in 1897.

ELECTRIC CURRENT
AND "MEDICINAL SUBSTANCES"

The idea that the brain controls body movements or that it interprets information received from the outside world through the sense organs implies that it communicates with the periphery. What system of signals is used? With Democritus' psychic atoms, and then Galen's pneuma, came the concept of a "subtle agent" traveling along the nerves. In classical times animal spirits were usually considered to be liquids or even gases. Descartes compared them to air circulating in the "organ" of the body. For Sir Isaac Newton, on the other hand, it was a question of an "intangible ether." At the beginning of the eighteenth century, electricity was already mentioned in this context, for it had just been discovered.

The "substantiation" of animal spirits could take place only after the introduction of the concept of the excitability of nerve or muscle tissue —that is, once the possibility had been established of artificially obtaining a reaction from these tissues through experimental intervention. It is remarkable that this notion was suggested in the 1650s by Francis Glisson, professor of physics at Cambridge, who was reacting to the materialist, mechanistic view of Descartes. Glisson believed he could demonstrate "vital forces" by analyzing the variety of different movements—the "irritability"—of fibers that, according to him, made up all tissues and organs. He emphasized that when nerves were present a special property emerged: "sensitivity." Experimental analysis of this property was only undertaken a century later by the Swiss scientist Albrecht von Haller. He employed various forms of stimulation, both mechanical (a scalpel, a jet of air) and chemical ("spirit of wine, lapis infinalis, oil of vinegar, bitter antimony"), which he applied to a wide variety of tissues such as skin, blood vessels, meninges, and glands. He demonstrated that, contrary to Glisson's opinion, only muscles contract, but that, as Glisson indicated, the property of sensitivity is directly related to the presence of nerves.

The nature of the agent or "energy" used by excited nerves to provoke muscular contraction still was not known. For many, it remained a matter of "vital forces," incomprehensible at that time and probably forever. It is therefore easy to understand that the publication in 1791 of Luigi Galvani's *Commentary on the Effect of Electricity on Muscular Motion* caused a revolution in ideas matched only by that developing at the time on the political front. In 1780 Galvani had observed that discharges of static electricity from Leyden jars could cause muscles to contract. Since antiquity, it had been known that a strange creature—the torpedo fish—could give electric shocks when touched. Nevertheless, Galvani and his wife, Lucia, were greatly surprised when, on September 20, 1786, while trying to show the effect of atmospheric electricity on the contraction of a frog's leg, they saw that the limbs of the frog contracted *spontaneously* when the preparation was suspended on an iron bar with a copper hook implanted in the spinal cord. All this took place on a clear day, with no sign of a storm. Galvani concluded that the frog itself produced "animal electricity," circulating through the nerves, stimulating the excitable muscle fibers, and forcing them to contract, and that the most important organ "secreting" this electricity was the brain. In other words, Galvani suggested that animal spirits were identical to electricity (Figure 10).[7]

His conclusion was immediately the target of lively criticism by his compatriot Conte Alessandro Volta, a professor at the University of

Figure 10. Illustration of the laboratory used by Galvani and his collaborators for their experiments on animal electricity at the end of the eighteenth century. The equipment is very simple. One can see, suspended from the ceiling and stretched across the room from left to right, the metal wire on which Galvani and his wife one day hooked the specimen of frog's limbs, which contracted due to the rudimentary electrical battery thus set up. (From L. Galvani, 1791.)

Pavia. Volta claimed that Galvani had not proved the existence of animal electricity; he had simply shown an effect of "metallic electricity." It was the contact between the copper hook and the iron bar that caused the contraction of the frog's muscles. Volta was right. Moreover, a few years later he developed a battery, which today bears his name, based on this principle. Galvani, with the help of his nephew Aldini, quickly replied to Volta's objection with an experiment using no metal. He dissected the frog's spinal cord and, bending one of the hind limbs in which he had exposed the muscles, he put it in contact with the cord. This circuit caused a contraction of the limb, only possible if the frog itself had produced electricity.

The controversy over "metallic" versus "animal" electricity came to an end only with the development of an adequate measuring instrument. With the galvanometer, named after Galvani, Carlo Matteucci in 1838 recorded for the first time the production of an electric current by a muscle. He called this *courant propre*. The muscle not only responded to an electrical stimulus, but, in accord with Galvani's ideas, produced electricity, which could be measured in the same way as a voltaic current. Electrophysiology was born.

At this stage of the development of knowledge, the use of instruments—and particularly the introduction of methods borrowed from physics—had a considerable impact. An attempt was made to "reduce" the biological phenomena of excitability and sensitivity to physical mechanisms. Emil Du Bois-Reymond, a German descended from a family of French Huguenots, founded a school of materialist thought in Berlin. This "mechanical physiology" anticipated modern biophysics and in a few decades expurgated once and for all any "vital" content from animal spirits. In 1848 Du Bois-Reymond demonstrated that the signal propagated along a nerve and in the contracting muscle was a wave of electrical "negativity," an "action potential." Then Hermann von Helmholtz applied to nerves ballistic methods like those he had used to measure the speed of a bullet leaving the barrel of a gun. The action potential traveled less rapidly than an electrical current in a copper wire, at a speed less than that of sound (between 25 and 40 meters per second in the nerve he used). It was, nevertheless, sufficiently fast to account for the rapidity of human movements and thought.

The pioneers of animal electricity worked with dissected frogs. The typical arrangement consisted of the rear limbs attached to the lumbar spinal cord. Were the results obtained from such a simple arrangement valid when applied to nervous centers, and in particular the cerebral cortex? François Magendie, Pierre Flourens, and Matteucci himself tried to stimulate the cortex with electricity or various chemical "irritants." They did not obtain any response. Could Aristotle have been right? The results supported the spiritualistic theory of Flourens, well established in this first half of the nineteenth century; they seemed incontestable. In 1870, however, Gustav Fritsch and Edward Hitzig, thirty-two-year-old physicians in Berlin, had the audacity to contest them. Aware of the clinical observations on aphasia published by Bouillaud some thirty-five years earlier, one of them accidentally noted that passing a galvanic current through the posterior part of a man's skull, and even through the temporal region, caused eye movements. They were both so confident about this observation that they undertook to repeat the experiment systematically in animals. They chose a dog, closer to man on the zoological scale than Flourens' pigeons. Lacking financial support, they installed their operating room in Hitzig's apartment. The stimulus was provided by the opening and closing of a galvanic battery at an intensity sufficient to cause a perceptible sensation on the tip of the tongue. It was enough to cause muscular contraction in the opposite half of the body when applied by electrodes to precise points on the surface of the cortex. A strong stimulus made the entire half of the body contract, while with weak stimulation contractions were limited to a few muscles. Motor activity was found to be restricted to a particular part of the cortex, localized on the "convexity of the brain, in its anterior part." The importance of Fritsch and Hitzig's experiments was much more than this elementary demonstration of the motor areas. They had formed an inseparable link between Galvani and Broca, between electricity and cerebral function.

Volta's objection to Galvani's work is obviously also applicable to an overinterpretation of Fritsch and Hitzig's findings. The demonstration that certain areas of the cerebral cortex are sensitive to electrical stimulation does not mean that the cortex itself produces electricity. In 1875, however, Richard Caton, a young physiology assistant at the Liverpool Royal Infirmary, showed that such is the case. He placed an electrode on the surface of the gray matter of a rabbit and, with his galvanometer, *recorded* weak currents, varying spontaneously in direction. When he exposed the retina to a bright light, he found a large negative current in the occipital region of the cortex. At one and the same time, Caton discovered electroencephalography and evoked potentials. The cells that made up the cerebral cortex produced action potentials similar to those found in peripheral nerves by Du Bois-Reymond. Gall had "secularized" the brain by showing that it was composed of the same gray and white matter as the peripheral nervous system; Caton and his successors completed the demonstration by associating cerebral activity with electrical phenomena.

But are the "action currents" of Du Bois-Reymond sufficient to account for all the signaling in the nervous system, central as well as peripheral? If the neuron theory is right, what happens at the ends of the nerves—for example, at the junction between a motor axon and a muscle? Already Du Bois-Reymond envisaged "that there must be *either* a stimulating secretion, perhaps in the form of a thin layer of ammonia or lactic acid or some other substance on the surface of the contractile tissue, in such a way that a vigorous excitation of the muscle follows, *or* an electrical influence." Thus, the hypothesis of a chemical mechanism responsible for crossing the neuromuscular junction was already suggested. It was to take shape only with the arrival on the scene of a very old discipline concerned with poisons, drugs, and medicines: pharmacology.

Experimental analysis of the action of "toxic and medicinal substances" only really began with Claude Bernard in 1857, when, through an ingenious series of experiments, he attempted to understand the effect of curare, the active principle of the arrow poison of South American Indians. This substance paralyzes prey when it penetrates the circulatory system. But where does it act? On the nerves, the muscles, or the site of their connection? Bernard first showed that curare did not block a galvanic muscle contraction. Nor did it act on sensory nerves, but only on the activity of motor nerves at their extreme periphery. Nevertheless, Bernard was wrong when he concluded that curare caused "the natural death of the motor nerve." Edmond Vulpian, an assiduous follower of his lectures at the Collège de France, noticed this and in 1866 gave the correct answer: curare interrupts the communication between nerve fibers and muscle fibers. Could this communication rely on a chemical substance similar to curare?

In 1904 T. R. Elliott provided the solution, using not the junction between motor nerves and voluntary muscle but the "sympathetic" innervation of the cat's bladder. A few years earlier, a very active substance, adrenaline, had been purified and crystallized from the adrenal medulla. When injected into the circulation, adrenaline does not block the effect of the stimulation of the nerves as curare does in voluntary muscle. On the contrary, it acts *in the same way* as the nerve and causes the relaxation of the bladder. On the other hand, both the action of the nerves and that of adrenaline are blocked by toxins extracted from rye ergot. Elliott concluded that adrenaline could be the chemical stimulant released each time a nerve impulse arrives at the periphery. Several years later, acetylcholine was identified as the natural substance released by voluntary motor nerves and whose action is blocked by curare. Acetylcholine and adrenaline were the first in a long list of *neurotransmitters*— natural chemical substances produced by nerve cells, which are responsible for transferring the nervous signal from one side to the other of the synaptic cleft. At the anatomical discontinuity between the nerve cell and its targets, chemistry relays electricity.

Nevertheless, the extension to the brain of mechanisms first recognized at the periphery encountered a long delay, perhaps not unrelated to the spiritualistic notions, conscious or not, of the scientists themselves. The role of chemical agents, the neurotransmitters, in helping the nerve signal cross the synapse, was proposed by Elliott in 1904. Yet in 1949 many physiologists still contested that such a mechanism existed in the central nervous system. Chemistry in the periphery perhaps, but the more fluid and intangible electricity for the seat of the soul! During the 1940s, however, came the discovery by pharmacologists and chemists that acetylcholine was present in various regions of the brain, particularly the cerebral cortex.[8] Brain neurons also responded to acetylcholine. Then, in 1954, Marthe Vogt showed that noradrenaline, just isolated by Ulf von Euler and closely related to the adrenaline with which Elliott had worked, was also present in the hypothalamus. Bengt Falck, Nils-Ake Hillarp, and their colleagues at the Karolinska Institute in Stockholm, using yellow or green fluorescent marking, showed that in histological sections of the brain, aminergic neurons—containing noradrenaline or closely related transmitters— appear in discrete and well-localized groups.[9] The participation of these neurons in important cerebral functions could no longer be doubted. Galen's pneuma had been reduced to sodium, potassium, or calcium ions (see Chapter 3) or acetylcholine, noradrenaline, or some other neurotransmitter, produced in specific, localized parts of the brain and moving along well-defined pathways. Animal spirits could now be iden-

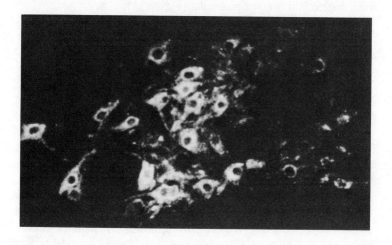

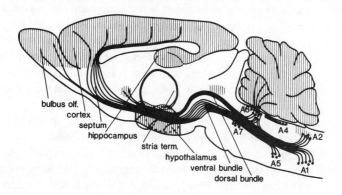

Figure 11. A new chapter in the history of the brain opened with the discovery of neurotransmitters. Neurons could be distinguished not only by their shape and their electrical activity, but also by the chemical substances they synthesized and secreted at their synapses. The *upper* figure here shows neurons of the locus coeruleus in a section of a rat's brainstem after exposure to formalin vapor, which gives them a green fluorescence characteristic for the presence of noradrenaline. (From A. Dahlström and K. Fuxe, 1964.)

The *lower* figure presents a "chemical map" of noradrenaline neurons. Groups of cell bodies are indicated by the letter A, while axon bundles are in black and the areas in which they end are hatched. The locus coeruleus is A6. (From U. Ungerstedt, 1971.)

tified as movements of atoms and molecules. The science of the nervous system had become molecular (Figure 11).

THE "GOOD SENSE" OF HISTORY

This rapid look into the past, admittedly colored by the prejudices of contemporary neurosciences, is sufficient to put into perspective the lines of research and theoretical attitudes that have repeatedly and systematically had a positive impact on the growth of our knowledge. It is of prime importance to adopt an analytical approach, to break down the anatomical or functional framework into simple elements. Throughout history, localizationist and divisionist doctrines have led, and are still leading, to the most radical discoveries, and there is no doubt that they are of immense value for progress. In essence, the aim of the analytical method is to simplify, although it sometimes leads to the simplistic. Glisson, the spiritualist, put forward excitability and sensitivity in the face of the mechanistic Cartesian view. At the beginning of this century, and even today, holistic arguments put us on our guard against overly simplistic interpretations such as might, for instance, be based solely on the cortical cartography of Brodmann, and against the danger of masking the complexity of the interrelationships of the multiple cerebral centers, cortical or noncortical. Holistic theories, in spite of their spiritualistic flavor, should not be rejected without careful study. Even if they cannot be considered "explanatory," they are sometimes useful in limiting the conclusions of analytical experimentation, and in that way stimulating new problems.

Another progressive line of inquiry is to relate anatomical and behavioral features, to search out the material basis of a function, first of all independently of nervous activity, and then taking it into consideration. From the Egyptian surgeon to Herophilus and Eristratus, from Galen to Nemesius, from Gall to Broca, this method has always led to discoveries and continues to bear fruit in the most advanced domains of contemporary neurobiology.

Finally, physicalistic endeavors to find physico-chemical bases of cerebral functions are in general fertile. For instance, the pneuma—first animal spirits then nervous fluid—became animal electricity, then action potentials, and finally the flow of electrically charged ions. The demonstration of the activity of neurotransmitters at the synapse provides yet another example.

If we take up the cogitations and reveries of the spiritualists, these steps are neither seductive nor comforting. But that is not our task—it is to understand how our brain works.

2

The Component Parts of the Brain

Immense numbers of individual units, the neurons,
completely independent, simply in contact with each
other, make up the nervous system.
—Santiago Ramón y Cajal, *Histology of the
Nervous System*

In the depths of antiquity, Greek and Egyptian priests secretly constructed "articulated gods," which they used to impress the crowds. In a different context, Vaucanson in 1738 demonstrated his "digesting duck"; activated by levers and cogs, it beat its wings, swallowed grain, and evacuated it after it had passed through its body. Today, robots paint car bodies carefully and precisely and sophisticated computers control the journeys of spaceships to the limits of the solar system. We invent machines to replace ourselves; they therefore mimic our gestures and even our acts. Naturally, we compare ourselves to the machines we have constructed. For Descartes, only the body was a machine, but for La Mettrie "the soul is merely a vain term of which we have no idea. Let us conclude boldly that man is a machine."

With Norbert Wiener, cybernetics took up this thesis. The human brain was no longer comparable to the mechanism of an automaton or a clock; rather it resembled, and functioned as, a computer. Was this merely an image, a metaphor? If La Mettrie wrote that the machine of the body "winds up its own springs," can one imagine pushing the analogy as far as identifying our organs or cells with steel sheets, rubber tubes, or even transistors and integrated circuits? The reader may rest assured. It is not my intention to identify the brain with a clock, to treat the nerve cells as cogwheels, or even to make the organization of neuronal networks resemble at all costs the circuits of a computer or any other artificial mechanism. On the contrary, my aim is to explore the nervous system through all available means: to identify its anatomical components, to define their mutual relationships, and, finally, to describe its organization. This dissection of the cerebral machine will stop, in a first analysis, at the level of the cell, beyond which the truly original property of the nervous system to organize itself into a communication network using axons and dendrites as wires is lost. The neuron today is situated at the convergence of two lines of research: that of the chemist and molecular biologist, who consider it a system of interacting macromolecules, and that of the neurobiologist and embryologist, who, on the contrary, look upon it as a basic unit from which the brain is constructed. The level of organization chosen here to split the nervous machine into its component parts, then, is that of the neuron and its synapses.

THE MACROSCOPIC VIEW OF THE BRAIN

In his *Anatomy Lesson*, Rembrandt painted the cerebral hemispheres of a cadaver dissected by Dr. Joan Deyman. On the left of the painting, the assistant surgeon is holding the skullcap in his hand, revealing grayish convolutions richly irrigated with blood vessels. Once out of the skull, this mass of tissue—the encephalon—can be subdivided into three major parts. At the front are the cerebral hemispheres, at the back the cerebellum, while the brainstem joins these two parts to the spinal cord.

Since the Renaissance, to observe the brain has meant, first of all, to reproduce its form in drawings or photographs and to label its parts. Another method is to measure the brain, for which an easy parameter is its weight. Anthropologists usually deal only with the skull, which is more easily preserved than the soft tissues. As the brain is firmly attached to the skull by the meninges, the internal volume of the skull can be used as a measure of the brain's weight, for its capacity is only a few percent more than that of the brain itself. The human brain tips the scales at an average of 1,330 grams, with wide variation from one individual to another. The cases of Anatole France and Gall himself are often cited as the smallest values known (between 1,000 and 1,100 grams), while Oliver Cromwell and Lord Byron are among the highest (at more than 2,000 grams). Broca paid considerable attention to brain weight. He even wrote that the mean brain weight of fifty-one unskilled workers was 1,365 grams while that of twenty-four skilled workers reached 1,420 grams. A century later, when Eugène Schreider repeated these observations, he found them impossible to confirm.[1] In fact, the *absolute* weight of the brain has no significance in itself. There can be little doubt that the proportions of the body remain relatively constant while the size of individuals varies. It is only to be expected that the dimensions of the brain will vary with those of the body. Indeed, it seems that Broca did not take this aspect into account in interpreting his results. The least skilled workers, doubtless of humble background and undernourished during their childhood, were on the average smaller than the others.

With what bodily parameter, then, can one compare the weight of the brain? In wild animals, the weight of the body changes little with ecological conditions and is often used as a reference. In humans, body weight varies enormously. Our height varies less with social environment and is often used in statistical studies. Under this criterion, "normal" brain weight varies constantly and much more widely in human populations than among wild animals. A significant difference also seems to exist between the sexes. According to a study by W. Spann and H. O. Dustmann in 1965, adult males have on average 8.3 grams of brain per centimeter of height while females have only 8 grams, so that men have a slight advantage of about 50 grams for a height of 1.65 meters. This sexual dimorphism, which also appears in cranial capacity, can be found among the anthropoid apes as well.[2] It is most marked in gorillas, with humans situated between chimpanzees and orangutans.

Several living animal species have a much greater absolute brain weight than man. For instance, elephants and whales have brain weights, respectively, of up to about 6,000 and 9,000 grams. However, compared with their body weight, their brain weight represents only one ten-thousandth in the first case and one six-hundredth in the second. The weight of the human brain, on the other hand, is about one-fortieth that of the body. But in this game, man is beaten by such small mammals as the marmoset or the ferret, whose brain weight is one-twelfth of the body weight!

So what parameter can we choose to compare the weight of the brain in order to establish a reasonable correlation with evolutionary trends in comparative anatomy, to permit humans to stand out from elephants on the one hand and marmosets on the other, and for our "superiority" to manifest itself, insofar as it exists? Many attempts have been made since the end of the nineteenth century. The most satisfying one is based on an analogy.[3]

Let us take, at random, a few adult subjects from species of different sizes and classify them by weight in increasing order: shrew, marmoset, chimpanzee, man, gorilla. This series is comparable to that of growth of the young to the adult in any one species, as if a gorilla were born a shrew and in growing became a marmoset and then a chimpanzee. One can then analyze the distribution of the weights of adults using methods adapted to the quantitative description of growth. One cell divides into two, then each divides again, giving four, then eight, then

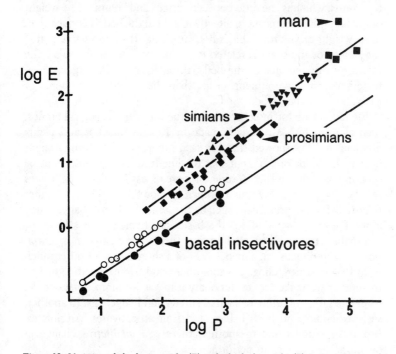

Figure 12. Variation of the brain weight (E) with the body weight (P) in insectivores and primates. Each point represents a different species. The data, expressed on double logarithmic coordinates, form a series of parallel straight lines, each corresponding to a homogeneous zoological group in terms of cerebral performance. The data are normalized to values derived from a series of primitive, "basal" insectivores (black dots). Just above these are the higher insectivores (open circles); then the primitive monkeys, or prosimians (black diamonds), such as the lemurs, tarsiers, and bush babies. The higher monkeys are represented by black triangles. At the top of the scale come the hominoids (black squares)—the orangutan, the chimpanzee, the gorilla, and finally, at the top right, modern man. (From R. Bauchot and H. Stephan, 1969; H. Stephan, 1972.)

sixteen: this is an exponential progression. An exponential function can be transformed into a linear function by using logarithmic coordinates. So let us use logarithmic coordinates to express values of brain weight (E) on the y axis as a function of body weight (P) on the x axis (Figure 12). To begin with, this study can be made with species from the same zoological group. Let us take, for example, the insectivores, ranging from the shrew to the hedgehog. We obtain a straight line, but its slope is not equal to 1. The weight of the brain does not increase linearly with that of the body, but tends to decrease in its relative proportion with higher body weights. The value of the slope is 0.63. This is close to two-thirds, which is the ratio between surface and volume. The weight of the brain then seems more directly related to the body's *surface* than to its weight or volume. This is not surprising. It is reasonable that if the weight of the brain is related to its function, it should follow the increase in the surface of the body, through which the organism interacts with its environment, rather than the weight of the bones or the volume of the blood.

Is what is true for insectivores also true for other zoological groups, such as primates? An analysis made by Roland Bauchot and Heinz Stephan in 1969 showed that for each group the data form straight lines with a slope of 0.63, but that the line from one group cannot be superimposed on another. A series of more or less parallel straight lines results. The line for the simians, which include the hominids, is higher than that for the prosimians such as the lemur and bush baby, which is itself higher than that for the basic insectivores. This still seems reasonable. Along a given straight line, there is no change in organization, only in dimension. The behavior of a shrew does not differ much from that of a hedgehog. On the other hand, from one straight line to another we make an "evolutionary leap" as we jump, for example, from one group of animals, such as shrews and hedgehogs, to another, such as lemurs and bush babies, and from insectivores to primates. From one parallel line to another, there is a *qualitative* change in organization and also in performance.

The distance between the parallel straight lines gives us information on the evolutionary changes in the relationship between body and brain, or "encephalization," which can be found from fish to reptiles, from reptiles to mammals, from insectivores to monkeys, and to humans. Using these data, Bauchot and Stephan defined an "index of encephalization," which eliminated the factor of absolute weight and permitted the qualitative changes to be described. Each parallel line can be defined by a characteristic point, corresponding to an animal within the group, corrected to unit weight. In other words, one can consider a "theoretical chimpanzee" having the same body weight as the shrew and equal to 1. The insectivores are a very homogeneous group and serve as a reference. To simplify matters, let us arbitrarily designate the relationship of brain weight to body weight as 1. Our "theoretical chimpanzee" at unit weight will then have a brain weighing 11.3 times that of an insectivore of the same weight. *Homo sapiens* would have a mean index of 28.7. This means that, for the same body weight, man has a brain weight 28.7 times that of the basic insectivore. Or, if there were a giant shrew as big and as heavy as a man, its brain would weigh only about 46 grams.

On this scale man overtakes all other vertebrates. The chimpanzee comes close behind, with an index only 2.5 lower. The seals attain coefficients above 15, and dolphins and other dentate cetaceans have coefficients above 20! But the quite exceptional intelligence of these marine mammals is well known. It must be recognized, however, that these measurements of brain weight are quite rough. They do not take into account important differences in organization.

THE EXPANSION OF THE NEOCORTEX

Herophilus and Eristratus, and later Gall, emphasized that the cerebral hemispheres make for the most essential difference between man and various animal species. The brain of the fish has many points in common with Nemesius' model (see Figure 1). Less compact than the brain of higher vertebrates, it extends the spinal cord and develops around cavities: the two anterior ventricles and the middle and posterior ventricles (Figure 13). The hemispheres appear as a swelling of the dorsal wall of the anterior ventricles, but at this stage of evolution they still represent only a small portion of the brain. In their floor are masses of gray matter—the *basal ganglia*, which are important for the control of movement. In the walls around the middle ventricle, one finds the *thalamus*, which is an essential relay in pathways going to the hemispheres, as well as the *hypothalamus*, which is important in controlling the basic behavior of the organism as well as in regulating the secretion of hormones, especially from the pituitary gland. Finally the *cerebellum,* the organ of balance, is attached to the dorsal wall of the posterior ventricle. It is in the anterior part of this wall that we find the aminergic neurons, discovered by the Swedish scientists already mentioned (see Figure 11).

This general plan of the brain, though highly schematic, is preserved throughout the course of evolution, from fish to man. Only the relative development, complexity, and mutual relationships of the different parts change. A careful comparison of the brains of present-day fish, amphibians, reptiles, and mammals illustrates these changes and permits us to trace their evolutionary history. In fish, a highly developed sense of smell plays a primary role in the search for food. The cerebral hemispheres are very thin and specialized for olfaction. A similar olfactory center is found in amphibians and reptiles, but it occupies only the ventral half of each hemisphere. It survives in a still smaller form in mammals and humans, where it takes the form of a pear-shaped lobe hidden on the lower surface of the brain. In the partially terrestrial amphibians and the reptiles, the senses, particularly vision, develop and another type of cortex appears in the dorsal part of the hemispheres. It "associates" sensory and motor functions, but it, too, is not destined for development in man. It retreats to the inside of the brain, becoming the hippocampus. A third "experiment," this time successful, takes place in the more highly developed reptiles. In front of the two cortical structures already mentioned, a thickening appears—a "new cortex," or *neocortex.* It takes over the projection functions of the sense organs

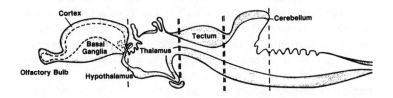

Figure 13. Schematic diagram of the brain common to all vertebrates, including humans. It is made up of a series of vesicles and constrictions. (1) The *forebrain* consists of three vesicles. Two of these form the cerebral hemispheres (although we only see one in this side view), with the olfactory bulb in front and the basal ganglia below. Further back is the third vesicle, with the hypothalamus and thalamus in its walls. (2) The *midbrain* thickens in the dorsal portion into a "roof," called the tectum. (3) The *hindbrain* has the cerebellum on its dorsal surface, and on its ventral and lateral surfaces, further back, the medulla. (Modified from A. S. Romer, 1955.)

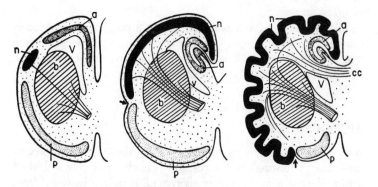

Figure 14. This diagram illustrates the expansion of the neocortex from reptiles (on the *left*) through a primitive marsupial (in the *center*) to man (on the *right*). The most primitive part of the cortex (p) is specialized for olfaction and moves back, as does another slightly less primitive area (a), which goes "inside" to form the hippocampus in mammals. On the other hand the neocortex (n, in black), which is small or absent in reptiles, invades the cerebral hemispheres of mammals, particularly primates and man. Also shown are the basal ganglia (b), ventricle (v), and corpus callosum (cc). (From A. S. Romer, 1955.)

and the association functions in a most striking manner. In man, one can see almost nothing else (Figure 14).

Bauchot and Stephan found a quantitative expression for this differential evolution of the neocortex. To each brain region, they assigned a "progression index," defined in the same terms as their index of encephalization. In the case of the neocortex, if one takes this index as equal to 1 in insectivores, that of the higher monkeys ranges from 8 to 25, that of a chimpanzee is 58, while that of man reaches 156. The index for the basal ganglia in man, however, increases only from 1 to 16.5. As for the olfactory bulb, its index diminishes from 1 in the insectivores to 0.07 in the chimpanzee and 0.023 in man.

The spectacular differential development of the neocortex is mainly due to an increase in its surface area, which poses a serious geometry problem. If the human brain were shaped like a cube, the neocortex would have a surface of 700 square centimeters. But the fully mature cerebral cortex has a mean surface area of 2,200 square centimeters. To permit its packing in the restricted volume of the skull, its surface becomes folded and two-thirds of the cortex is hidden in the depths of sulci, or fissures. The number of convolutions, or gyri, increases from almost none in primitive animals through the primates to reach a maximum in man.

From fish to man, the brain represents a proportionately greater fraction of the body weight. In mammals the neocortex does the same thing in relation to the brain. The brain of modern man represents the most advanced stage of this cerebral "corticalization."

MICROCIRCUITS

Since Willis and Gall, it has been known that the mammalian neocortex—referred to simply as the cortex—is made up of gray and white matter, like the rest of the nervous system. It differs, however, from other nervous centers in the relative disposition of this matter. From the end of the eighteenth century, observations by the naked eye of slices of cortex revealed a linear white line following all the contours of the convolutions and giving this part the appearance of a striped ribbon. In 1840 J. G. F. Baillarger, an alienist in the asylum of Charenton, studied this internal organization with the legitimate aim of discovering an anatomical basis of mental illness. He placed thin slices of cortex, taken from thirty patients who had died in various circumstances, between two glass plates and examined them with the naked eye. Although he noticed no significant differences between mentally ill and normal individuals, he made several important observations. First of all, in the cerebral cortex, as opposed to other nervous centers such as the spinal cord or the "ganglia," the gray matter was outside the white matter. Furthermore, throughout its extent, the cortex presented a stratified structure, with six parallel layers.

Baillarger did not employ the technical means necessary to observe the details of the organization of this cortical layering. To do this, one must use a microscope to observe the cells. One also needs an understanding of the basic structure of the nerve cell and of the relations of the cell body to the axon and dendrites (see Chapter 1). The discovery of the details of the cellular organization of the cortex came relatively late compared with that of the peripheral nervous system. Once again, we owe it to psychiatrists.[4]

Microscopic examination of a section of cortex, using, for example, the Golgi staining technique, reveals a predominant type of neuron, which outnumbers all others (Figure 15). These are the *pyramidal cells,*

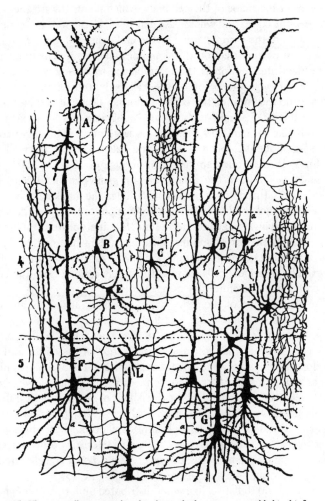

Figure 15. The main cell categories found in the cerebral cortex are assembled in this figure. The neurons are stained in black by the Golgi method. The entire cell body, dendrites, and axons can be marked in this way. The *pyramidal* cells (A to G) can be recognized by a conical cell body, an apical dendrite climbing vertically toward the cortical surface, and rootlike basal dendrites. The axon (a) descends to the deep part of the cortex and finally leaves it. The other, *stellate* cells remain within the cortex (H to M). They are often given names reflecting the diversity of their treelike forms, such as the "double bouquet" cell (H), whose axon blossoms into a bushy configuration, or the "short axon" cell (L), with its long horizontal branches. This section is taken from the temporal cortex of a twenty-four-day-old kitten, but similar categories of cells are found in man. (From S. Ramón y Cajal, 1909.)

named after the shape of the cell body, which points toward the outer surface of the cortex and whose base may reach 80 microns in diameter. In a section of the cortex stained by the Golgi method, these cells look like a forest of pine trees on the slopes of a mountain. The branching of the dendrites reinforces the resemblance to a conifer. An *apical dendrite* prolongs the point of the cell body and climbs vertically through the thickness of the cortex to form a terminal bouquet in its superficial layer. Several *basal dendrites* radiate around the base of the cell body like so many low branches. A large number of microscopic appendages, about 2 microns long, and called *spines*, cover all the dendrites. In man one can count an average of at least 20,000 per pyramidal cell. But in the case of certain giant pyramidal cells, like Meynert cells, this number can reach 36,000 in the monkey.[5] The axon of the pyramidal cell leaves the cell body opposite the apical dendrite and runs downward, giving from time to time collateral branches, before leaving the cortex and disappearing in the white matter. These axons constitute the major output, or *efferent*, pathways of the cerebral cortex. The pyramidal cells channel the orders coming from the cerebral cortex and therefore play a major role.

The classification of the other types of neuron, artificially grouped under the label *stellate cells*, is still the subject of controversy. One thing, however, is clear: their principal axon does not leave the cortex. They participate in the "intrinsic" organization of the cortex and are therefore *interneurons*. They allow communication between pyramidal cells as well as forming targets for some of the incoming nerve fibers. These stellate neurons usually have a cell body of oval or spherical shape and are generally smaller than pyramidal cells. They never have such abundant spines as pyramidal cells and many do not bear any spines. Their axonal and dendritic trees have characteristic forms carrying evocative names such as basket cells, double bouquet cells, neurogliform, fusiform, and short axon cells (see Figure 15).[6]

Pyramidal and stellate cells are not distributed uniformly throughout the cortical thickness. In 1867 Theodor Meynert showed that the laminated form of the cortex observed with the naked eye by Baillarger was due to the distribution of different categories of neurons in parallel layers (Figure 16). They are usually numbered I to VI from the surface downward. Layer I has no pyramidal cell bodies, but they abound in layers II, III, V, and VI, and are generally larger in the deep layers than in the surface layers. Stellate cells are sandwiched in layer IV.

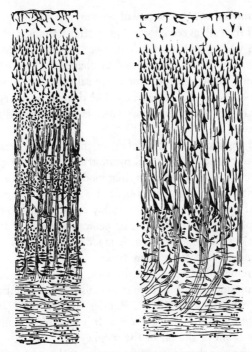

Figure 16. In *Psychiatry*, published in 1884, Meynert showed that the cellular architecture of the cortex varied from one area to another. On the *left* is a section through a sensory-cortex area (the visual cortex). Here stellate cells accumulate in three dense layers, giving rise to the name "granular cortex." On the *right* is the motor cortex with large pyramidal cells.

The most striking feature of the cellular architecture of the mammalian, and particularly the human, cortex is its great morphological uniformity. Samples taken from frontal, parietal, temporal, or occipital areas show pyramidal and stellate cells of very similar form and distribution. Throughout its extent, the cerebral cortex seems to be composed of the same cellular elements and the same categories of cells.

The term "category," because of its importance in interpreting the organization of the cortex, just as that of the nervous system in general, deserves some attention.[7] Under this term we shall group neurons for which, within a given center, the shape of the cell body and axonal and dendritic trees is the same. Recently, certain biochemical criteria have been added to these morphological distinctions—for instance, the type of neurotransmitter synthesized or the reaction of cellular components to specific antibodies.[8] A category of neurons can, then, be defined by the shape of the cell (as seen, for instance, after staining with the Golgi method), as well as by the set of molecules that it synthesizes, essentially proteins but also lipids and polysaccharides. Thus neurons that have the same shape and the same chemical composition will belong to the same category. This category will be defined by its repertoire or "card" of active genes, that is, those which can be expressed as proteins in adult tissue (see Chapter 6).

Although their size and the details of their treelike arrangements vary, one can consider all cortical pyramidal cells as belonging to the same category. It may be, however, that modern biochemical study will lead to their subdivision. Yet even if this happens, the number of categories of pyramidal cells will probably remain small: tens or hundreds, compared with the billions of neurons present in the human cortex. The cerebral cortex, then, is made up of a small number of cellular elements repeated a many times.

Another remarkable fact is that the same categories are found at all stages of evolution from primitive mammals to man. Contrary to the hopes of the first cytologists, like Ramón y Cajal, there are no cell categories specific to the *human* cortex. It is built of the same components as the brain of the rat or the monkey.

At this point one should note that in spite of the relative uniformity in the organization of the cerebral cortex, there *are* differences between areas—differences that the trained eyes of Meynert and the first brain histologists had already noticed (see Figure 16).[9] For instance, the cortex is not equally thick everywhere, and the density of cells and the distribution of different neuron categories through the six layers vary from one area to another. The thin primary visual projection area (Brodmann's area 17), for example, contains abundant stellate, or granule, cells, suggesting the name "granular cortex." On the other hand, the remarkably thick motor cortex (area 4) has many large pyramidal cells, almost to the exclusion of stellate cells—whence the name "agranular cortex." Could this variability, in part the basis of Brodmann's maps, be the result of major differences in the number and distribution of cortical neurons?

Recent quantitative studies by A. J. Rockel, R. W. Hiorns, and T. P. S. Powell in 1980 have shown that this is not the case. They did not concern themselves with local variations in thickness or cell density, but chose to count the total number of neurons in a "core" perpendicular to the surface of the cortex and of a constant cross-section of 25 by 30 microns. The rather surprising result, observed first in the macaque monkey, was that they found the same number of neurons in such a sample in all cortical areas, granular or not, with the exception of the visual area, which contained two and a half times the 110 cells found in other areas. The total number of neurons in the cortical thickness thus seems very uniform throughout.

When these researchers undertook similar measurements in the cortex of other animals — mice, rats, cats, and even humans — the number of cells in a sample was the same — except, again, in the visual area, where primates and humans had two and a half times more neurons. Not only are the categories of pyramidal and stellate cells the same from mouse to man, but the total number of cells under a given surface area does not vary in the course of mammalian evolution. These quantitative microscopic results agree with those obtained by the comparative anatomical approach. The evolution of the cortex in the mammal has concerned mainly its surface area.

Obviously, this increase in area is accompanied by an increase in total number of neurons, which can easily be estimated. Powell's results show that there are about 146,000 neurons per square millimeter of cortical surface in all mammalian species. The cortex of the two hemispheres of the human has an area of about 2,200 square centimeters. It thus contains at least 30 billion neurons (which is more than the 10 or 20 billion suggested until recently). The area of the cortex of the chimpanzee and gorilla is about 500 square centimeters. Thus, they would have between 7 and 8 billion cortical neurons. As for the rat, with 4 to 5 square centimeters of cortex, it would have only 65 million cortical neurons. As the same categories of cells are found in the cortex from primitive mammals to humans, there must be a considerable increase in the number of neurons in any given category.

This particular evolutionary tendency is not the only one found in the history of species. On the contrary, in the invertebrates, such as the sea slug *(Aplysia),* the nervous system consists of a small number of cells but a wide variety of cell types (see Figure 26). There are fewer cells but more categories. Notable exceptions among the invertebrates are the cephalopods, the octopus and the squid, in which we find the same evolutionary tendencies as in the mammals but in parts of the nervous system that are not analogous to the cortex. In these animals the number of cells per category increases more rapidly than the number of categories. As we shall see later, this is a simple, economic way of increasing complexity.

WIRING

Electron microscopy permits the study of structural details from a few thousandths of a micron (the size of large molecules), to a few tens of microns (the size of a cell body). It permits a final confirmation of Ramón y Cajal's theory of the discontinuity of the nerve net (see Chapter 1). We see that neurons are juxtaposed at characteristic synapses. In the cortex, these synapses are usually quite small (a few microns); they consist of an axon terminal, containing many vesicles, and a postsynaptic membrane, clearly separated by a cleft a few nanometers (thousandths of a micron) wide.[10] The postsynaptic profile frequently corresponds to the spines—elements that, as we have already seen, almost cover the surface of pyramidal cell dendrites and show up clearly with Golgi staining (Figure 17).

One might have thought that the increased magnification and resolution provided by the electron microscope would reveal a new world in the cerebral cortex. Certainly the synaptic organization of the cortical network has been confirmed, yet the images obtained are somewhat disappointing. The synapses look even more uniform in structure than the neuron categories. With some difficulty, we can distinguish two types of synapses. When the thickness of the postsynaptic membrane is greater than that of the presynaptic membrane, we call it an *asymmetrical* synapse (see Figure 17, bottom). When the two membranes are of similar thickness, we speak of a *symmetrical* synapse. In other words, the cerebral machine is assembled with a very small number of "screws,"— in fact, only two main sorts.

Anatomists face another difficulty. A random section of the cortex contains an enormous number of synapses, something like 600 million per cubic millimeter. There must be about 10^{14} or 10^{15} synapses in the human cortex. Even counting a thousand per second, one would need between 3,000 and 30,000 years to count them—a superhuman task made still more difficult by the fact that the synapses are found in the midst of axons, dendrites, and cell bodies, seemingly inextricably mixed

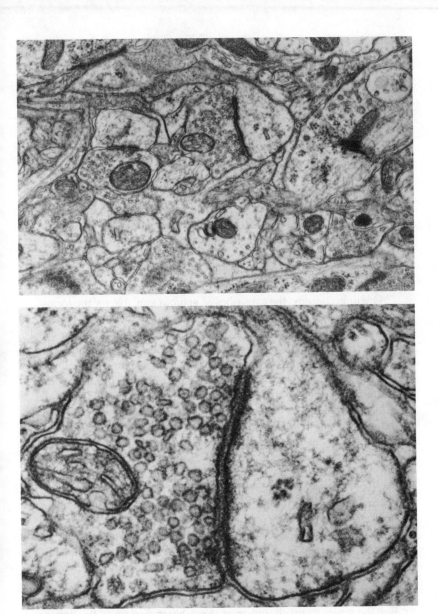

Figure 17. Ultra-thin section of the cerebral cortex of a mouse seen under an electron microscope. At the *top*, at medium magnification of about 36,000, is a view of the extremely dense network of nerve terminals, easily identifiable by the presence of synaptic vesicles, and dendrites interspersed by glial cells. At the *bottom* is a detail of an asymmetrical synapse magnified about 100,000 times. On the left is the nerve terminal, with one mitochondrion and many vesicles. On the right is a dendritic spine. Between the two, one can see the synaptic cleft outlined by pre- and postsynaptic thickenings. (Original micrograph by Constantino Sotelo.)

up in a "jungle" where the branches of hundreds, even thousands, of different trees are entangled (see Figure 17, top). Thanks to the magnification and resolution of the electron microscope, the leaves and the smallest branches are easily recognizable, but they are so similar that it is very difficult to identify the trunks to which they belong.

How can we unravel such complexity? First, we must try to determine simple organizational rules, even if they do not allow us to describe more than the overall principles. Then, tracing techniques must be worked out to find one's way in this labyrinth. Anatomists have tried, for example, to follow a single nerve process in successive serial sections from the same block of tissue. More recently, they have combined electron microscopy, which allows clear identification of a synapse, with cell-staining techniques that permit the unambiguous identification of the neuron category. The data are still fragmentary but a few rules are beginning to emerge.

One rule concerns the categories of neurons available for the formation of cortical networks. Whereas the Golgi technique stains only a small percentage of all neurons, electron microscopy reveals all the cell structures present in a section of cortex. Furthering their quantitative analysis of the cellular organization of the primate cortex, Powell and his colleagues used electron microscopy to distinguish pyramidal cells and various forms of stellate cells and to count all the cells of each category in the same vertical "core" of cortex.[11] Although data were available only for two cortical samples, one in the motor area and the other in the somatosensory cortex, Powell concluded that the percentage of pyramidal and stellate cells is the same in these two functionally distinct areas, although the distribution of cell types clearly varies from one cortical layer to another. The cortical network may be constructed not only from the same building blocks, but also from the same number of blocks, whatever the cortical area.

The other rules deal with the connections of the input and output lines of the cortex. Since Richard Caton and his successors, we know that the sense organs project to specialized cortical areas (see Chapter 1) which, as Ivan Pavlov stated, participate in the "analysis" of sensory signals. So the sensory pathways form an important input to the cortex. But the sense organs do not send nerve fibers directly to the cortex. Whatever the sensory modality, axons stop on their way in subcortical centers, principally in the nuclei of the thalamus. Other neurons relay there, and it is their axons that continue to the cortex. But this input to the cortex by the thalamus is not limited to the sensory pathways. All cortical areas, including motor and association areas, receive fibers from a specific thalamic nucleus. Thus a remarkable uniformity of organization exists at the level of cortical input (Figure 18).

Axons from the thalamus, however, are not the only incoming lines, or *afferents,* to the cortex; fibers coming from the cortex itself constitute another important input. Each cortical area receives a considerable number of axons coming from other areas of the same or opposite hemisphere. Because they associate several areas, they are called *association* fibers. Thalamic and association fibers penetrate the cortex from

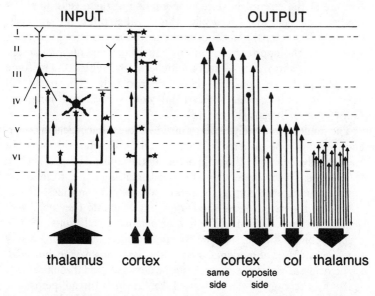

Figure 18. Highly simplified diagram of the principal input and output pathways of the cerebral cortex. In reality the pathways are much more complex and still incompletely understood. It is known that there are detailed variations between one cortical area and another. In the visual cortex (one of the best-understood examples), nerve fibers coming from the sense organ (the eye) relay in the thalamus with neurons, whose axons enter the cortex and branch in a ball-like arrangement mainly in layer IV (shown here schematically by the pitchfork beginning at the thalamus). In layer IV the axons establish synaptic contacts (represented by stars) with dendrites of pyramidal cells (oriented vertically) and also with stellate cells (often oriented horizontally). Another important input pathway is made up of the axons of pyramidal cells coming from other cortical areas in the same or the other hemisphere. Pyramidal cells in different layers send their axons to different parts of the brain. For instance, those whose cell body is in layer VI send their axons to the thalamus; those in layer V send them to other subcortical nuclei—in the case of the visual cortex, to the superior colliculus (col). Cells in layers II, III, and IV send axons to other cortical areas on the same or the opposite side. (Adapted from L. J. Garey, 1976; O. D. Creutzfeldt, 1978; E. L. White, 1981.)

below, climbing vertically toward its surface. Axons originating in other parts of the cortex are generally distributed in several levels of the cortex. On the other hand, thalamic fibers stop in well-defined layers, particularly layer IV and part of layer III. Layer IV can then be considered the main gateway to the cortex (Figure 18).

Let us now follow a thalamic fiber when it reaches layer IV and attempt to define the "intrinsic" circuits with which it comes in contact. It spreads out in a ball-like tree, whose fine branches establish synapses with the dendrites and cell bodies in the layer. An important series of contacts is made with the dendritic spines of pyramidal cells. Because of the essentially vertical orientation of these cells, impulses tend to be propagated "vertically" through the cortex. Stellate cells, some of whose axonal and dendritic trees are also organized vertically, also receive an important proportion of thalamic afferents and participate in this traffic of impulses. In addition, thalamic fibers contact some stellate cells whose axons are oriented "horizontally." These cells will exert a *lateral* influence. There is thus both vertical and horizontal propagation of signals (Figure 18).

The results of the analyses performed by these intracortical microcircuits will finally be gathered by the pyramidal cells, whose axons, as we have already seen, form the main output of the cortex. However, before leaving the cortex, these axons send collateral branches, forming re-entry loops into the cortex; the process of analysis continues.

Finally, the signals leave the cortex, but where do they go? More generally speaking, what is the fate of pyramidal cell axons? [12] The precise reply to this question was obtained only recently, using a very ingenious method of marking based on the use of an enzyme, horseradish peroxidase, whose effects can easily be demonstrated through a color reaction in sections of nerve tissue. Like Ariadne's thread, peroxidase permits the anatomist to begin at the end of the axon and follow it back to the cell body. If one injects the enzyme at the target of a neuron, where the axon branches, it will be taken up by the nerve terminals and transported backward along the axon to the cell body, which becomes easily identifiable by its color reaction. We can therefore relate the cell body to the target of its axon over distances of several centimeters. The main "exit" channels of the cortex, most of which are outlets of the pyramidal cells, can thus be identified.

The first output of the cortex is to the cortex itself. (see Figure 18). A large proportion of the axons that leave it return to it, either on the same or the opposite side. They form the association inputs that we have already discussed. Other outgoing, or *efferent,* axons end outside the cortex at lower, or subcortical, levels. So, in fact, it seems as if the purpose of many cortical signals is to feed back information to the cortex itself.

The second target of cortical fibers is the thalamus. As already noted, the main entries to the cortex are the axons coming from the neurons of the thalamus. Some fibers leaving the cortex thus return toward the neurons that sent their axons to the cortex. Feedback circuits with reentries to the cortex are thus formed at this level, too.

A third efferent pathway takes the axons well away from the cortex and the thalamic nuclei. These axons contribute to systems involved in analysis or motor commands, which are experienced as behavior. These centers, which are not in the thalamus, differ according to the area of cortex considered. Without drawing up a list here, one might mention, as an example, the route from the visual cortex to the superior colliculus in the midbrain (see Figure 18). But some axons go even further. Those of certain pyramidal cells in the motor cortex leave the brain to enter the spinal cord and terminate directly on the motor neurons that control muscular contraction.

Thus, cortical efferent axons follow three principal routes: to the cortex, to the thalamus, and to centers that are neither cortical nor thalamic. This subdivision holds for all cortical areas. One might ask, then, whether a relationship exists between the layer in which the cell body is located and the destination of its axons. Using peroxidase as a tracer, we can answer this question with great precision (see Figure 18). The pyramidal cells that send their axons to the thalamus are located in the deepest layer of the cortex (layer VI) or in the lower part of layer V. This is true for all thalamic nuclei. The cell bodies of pyramidal cells sending axons to nonthalamic subcortical centers, such as the superior colliculus for the visual area or the spinal cord for the motor area, are situated in layer V. Axons that project back to the cortex come from neurons in the more superficial layers II and III, although a few are situated in layer V. The organization of cortical efferents thus follows general rules, independent of the functional significance of the specific cortical area.

In sum, cortical connections obey a number of important organizational rules common to the entire cortex. The general principles of wiring are the same throughout the cortex, regardless of its functional specialization. The networks consist of the same cell categories and of similar numbers of cells in each category. Input and output have similar organizations, and the internal microcircuits are similar. In view of this, the function of a cortical area would seem more determined by the point of departure of its inputs and the final destination of its outputs than by the intrinsic organization of its local circuits. To take up the metaphor of the brain as a computer, one thinks immediately of the chips or microprocessors whose external wiring determines their role in the machine. Stretching the analogy further, one might consider the cerebral cortex as an assembly of modules. But can one go as far as that?

MODULES OR CRYSTALS

To repeat: the exact details of cortical connections are still poorly defined. For this, we await quantitative investigations with new methods. We are therefore forced to use models that offer only a partial and simplified representation of the real organization. To my mind, their use is justified only insofar as they assist anatomical investigation and comprehension.

The first simple model of the cortex that comes to mind is the one just mentioned: a "modular" organization, in which the cortex is made up of geometrically defined, repetitive units. The first physiological investigations of the cortex suggested such an organization. Let us look at them in detail.

The experimental protocol used by Vernon Mountcastle recalls the first experiments of Caton.[13] The electrical activity of the cortex was recorded during the stimulation of peripheral sense organs. However, instead of using a large electrode, a microelectrode of 2 to 4 microns in diameter was used, thus allowing the activity of a *single* neuron to be recorded (see Chapter 3). As the microelectrode penetrated the cortex, it recorded the activity of the cells it encountered. Mountcastle observed that as different sensory receptors were stimulated, such as those in the skin or the joints, particular neurons responded. He then noticed that in the cat and the monkey, if the microelectrode penetrated vertically—perpendicular to the cortical surface—all the neurons encountered responded to the *same* cutaneous or articular sensory modality. On the other hand, an oblique penetration yielded an abrupt jump from one sensory modality to another. Thus was born the idea that cortical neurons are distributed in vertical columns, each representing one modality, specific to, for example, skin or joint sensitivity. In other words, the columns differed not only in their geometry in the cortex, but in their peripheral connections. They could be considered to be "modules" of cortex (Figure 19).

David Hubel and Torsten Wiesel repeated these experiments on the visual cortex, still using the cat or the monkey, but with different stimulation parameters.[14] Bars of light were projected in the animal's

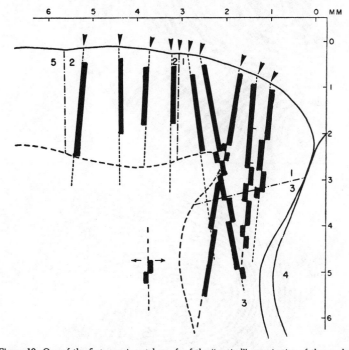

Figure 19. One of the first experimental proofs of the "vertical" organization of the cerebral cortex by Powell and Mountcastle. The somatosensory cortex (areas 1–3) is here seen in a transverse section. Each arrowhead indicates the point of entry of a microelectrode that was progressively lowered through the cortex. The skin or deep tissues were stimulated and the evoked responses recorded by the microelectrode as it encountered cortical cells. When the electrode descended perpendicular to the cortical surface, all the cells encountered responded to the same sensory modality: either the skin (represented by the thick line on the left of the penetration) or by deep tissues (the line on the right). When the electrode penetrated obliquely (as on the right of the figure), there was an abrupt jump from cells responding to one type of stimulation to those responding to the other type (see the jags in the lines). Each transition corresponds to a crossing from one vertical column of "modality-pure" neurons to another. (Modified from T. P. S. Powell and V. B. Mountcastle, 1959.)

visual field and the cortical response to the right or left eye recorded. Hubel and Wiesel confirmed Mountcastle's observations. Neurons in the same vertical columns reacted to the same sensory modality—in

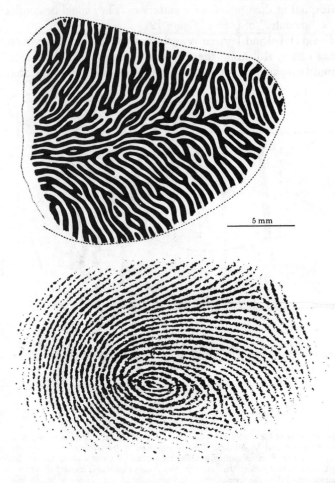

Figure 20. Bird's-eye view of the surface of the visual cortex of a macaque monkey reconstructed from tangential sections. When a microelectrode penetrates vertically in regions represented here by a black band, only neurons responding to a single eye are encountered. When the electrode passes from a black to a white band, the neurons respond to one eye, then the other. The bands represent vertical "slabs" (seen here edge-on), forming a pattern like the coat of a zebra or a fingerprint (the latter is shown in the *bottom* figure at the same scale). (From D. H. Hubel and T. N. Wiesel, 1977.)

this case, the eye that best stimulated the cells in that column. The diameter of each of these "ocular-dominance" columns was constant, about 400 microns. These observations, then, support a model of the cortex composed of modules arranged side by side like cans in a grocery store.

It was not long, however, before problems arose. The first concerned the way in which the left- and right-eye dominance columns were distributed in the cortex. When the cortex is looked at tangentially, the columns are not at all like a collection of vertical barrels as in the temple of the thousand columns at Chichén Itzá. Recent anatomical observations by Hubel, Wiesel, and their collaborators show that there are not really columns in the visual cortex but a system of vertical *slabs,* placed side by side like books on a library shelf (Figure 20).[15] In the tangential plane, they reveal a network rather like the black and white stripes of a zebra. The first electrophysiological penetrations had been too widely dispersed for the real organization of the slabs to be noticeable, for in a vertical section of the cortex they do in fact look like columns or, to keep the analogy of a library, like the backs of the books on the bookshelf. These slabs, of a constant width of about 400 microns, are up to several millimeters long. Can one reasonably consider such a slab to be the cortical module? By definition, the hypothesis of modular organization implies fixed dimensions for the module, at least for any given modality. But Hubel and Wiesel, in a series of experiments that will be considered later (Chapter 7), were able to change the dimensions of the left- and right-eye dominance columns. The most radical way of doing this was to remove an eye at birth: the slabs corresponding to the other eye then occupied the entire cortical area in the adult brain, that is, they were double the size of normal ones. Thus, the left- and right-eye dominance columns do not have fixed dimensions (see Figure 68).

Detailed physiological and anatomical analysis of these slabs showed that their thickness corresponds to the size of the ball-like tree of axons entering the cortex from the thalamus. As already stated, they mainly end at layer IV. Now, layer IV is crossed by a forest of vertical branches —the apical dendrites of pyramidal cells situated in the deeper layers and especially the ascending and "bouquet" dendrites of some stellate cells. Rafael Lorente de Nó proposed that the contacts established between thalamic axons and these dendritic branches served as points of departure for "vertical chains" of neurons. Perhaps modules are not composed of a fixed number of cortical neurons but rather resemble a cortical "fabric" woven in three dimensions. The ball-like tree of the thalamic afferents in layer IV would give the neurons there characteristics derived from the thalamus such as, for instance, left-eye or right-eye dominance. In this case it would be the *extrinsic* innervation of the cortex from the thalamus that determined the organization in regular slabs, rather than an *intrinsic* arrangement of the neurons themselves.

This is made even clearer by the observation that, when one explores properties other than the simple response to the left or right eye, new slabs appear. For instance, if bars of light of different orientation are presented in the cat's or monkey's visual field, once again one encounters neurons responding to a given orientation grouped in vertical columns. But the orientation columns thus defined are only 25 or 30 microns wide. There are then "minimodules" within bigger "hypermodules." Furthermore, the network of orientation columns crisscrosses the ocular-dominance columns. The two networks appear to be independent.[16] So which of the two categories constitutes the reference module?

The concept of modular organization thus seems too simple. With what can we replace it? One way of tackling this is to look at systems simpler than cortex, still with a layered organization but containing fewer cells and, above all, fewer synapses. For instance, we might consider the retina or the cerebellar cortex. Could they serve as models of the cerebral cortex?

The cerebellar cortex has been widely studied both anatomically and functionally.[17] In all the higher vertebrates, including man, it contains five types of cell, repeated many times. Only the *Purkinje cells* send their axons out of the cortex; one might consider them to be homologous to pyramidal cells. The granule cells may be homologous to small stellate cells, with the three other cell types perhaps homologous to the large stellate cells of the cerebral cortex. But everything looks much simpler, for the Purkinje cells form only one layer (Figure 21), as do also the granule cells, situated below the Purkinje layer. This organization makes it easier for us to detect any sign of regularity in the topology of the neurons and their synapses. Such regularity exists, but not in the form of hypothetical modules. It appears in the organization of the cell bodies as a horizontal "woof" in the plane of the cortex. The cell bodies show up as knots in the network. The dimensions of this mesh are constant for a given neuron category but differ when one considers different neuron categories. The retina has an analogous organization (Figure 22).[18] So why not imagine that the cerebral cortex is also organized in cellular "crystals," piled up to form the various cortical layers? Such a model would clearly conform with the uniform number of neurons per unit of surface area seen throughout the cortex by Powell and his colleagues. It also supports the existence of a vertical chain if, as is indeed known, the neurons of each crystal have their axons and dendrites oriented mainly along the vertical axis, thus allowing the interconnection of neurons of different, superimposed crystals. Each two-dimensional crystal would constitute the horizontal woof of a three-dimensional fabric.

Is this piled-up cellular crystal model better than the modular one? Does it better take into account the architectonic differences already mentioned between a granular sensory cortex and a motor or associa-

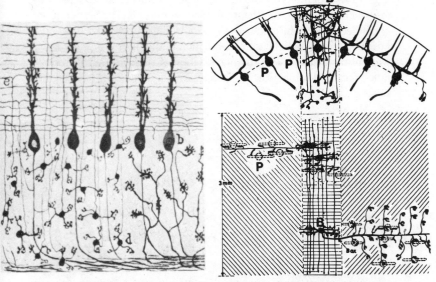

Figure 21. Crystal-like organization of Purkinje cells in the cerebellar cortex. On the *left* a drawing by Ramón y Cajal from 1911 shows a section of the cortex in a plane parallel to the animal's axis of symmetry. The Purkinje cells (b) are seen with their dendritic tree in profile. On the *right*, at the *top*, a drawing by Eccles et al. from 1967 follows a plane perpendicular to the animal's axis of symmetry; here the schematized bushy dendritic trees of Purkinje cells (P) are spread out and seen head on. At the *bottom* is a bird's-eye view of the tangential organization of the cerebellar cortex. The Purkinje cells (P) are dotted. Also shown are basket cells (B), which are homologous to certain stellate cells in the cerebral cortex; they show a regular organization ("Bax" designates the axon of a basket cell).

tion cortex? As we know, these differences are due not to the number of neurons but rather to the detailed distribution of axonal and dendritic trees and to the density of connections. Are the differences related to the input and output of the cortex? Various recent tracing techniques have shown that indeed the density of input varies greatly and in a discontinuous fashion from one area to another. A granular sensory cortex would logically receive a large number of axons from the thalamus. As they terminate mainly in layer IV, this layer should be particularly thick. The number of inputs from other cortical areas will be low in the sensory cortex but will predominate in association areas. One also finds variability in the outputs of different areas. In general, the farther the termination of an axon is from the cell body, the greater is the size of the cell body. The pyramidal cells of layer V of the motor cortex, whose axons go as far as the spinal cord, have giant cell bodies. The diverse architecture of cortical areas can thus be at least partially explained by considering the inputs and outputs and the permutations of connections established with the various, superimposed cellular crystals. The crystal model ensures a variation in the thickness of the layers without disturbing the entire organization of the cortex. It provides a much greater flexibility than a juxtaposition of modules of fixed dimension.

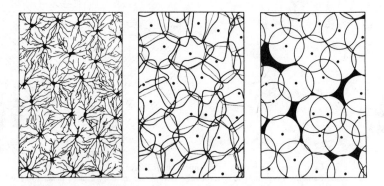

Figure 22. Regular distribution of "alpha-ON" ganglion cells in the retina. The dendritic trees are superimposed along the edges, and the cell bodies are not randomly distributed. In the *center* diagram, the edges of the dendritic trees are represented by continuous lines. In the figure on the *right*, circles of constant radius have been drawn from the cell body. The regularity is less striking than in the center figure. Cells of the same category are organized in a crystal-like manner. (From H. Wässle et al., 1981.)

According to this necessarily very simplified model, the functional specificities of each cortical area will be determined by the connections established by the inputs and outputs (this is also the case for modular organization). But a functional remodeling may take place through reciprocal interactions between cellular crystals and input-output systems. Let us consider the supposedly homogeneous category of pyramidal cells (the same reasoning will hold if they are eventually divided into subcategories). One would expect that even if the general shape appears to be similar, the precise connections, and therefore the detailed shape, of dendritic and axonal trees will differ from one layer to another of the same cortical area and, within the same layer, from one area to another. The set of macromolecules synthesized, or active genes (see Chapter 6), that define the category must therefore be complemented by the set of connections that define the *singularity* of each cell taken individually within the same category.[19] The set of singularities is therefore considerable. In a given area, within a given layer and in the same cellular crystal, each neuron will differ from its neighbors by its singularities. For example, in the motor cortex each pyramidal cell could be labeled according to the muscle whose contraction it controls (see Chapter 4). Contrary to certain current ideas, there is very little redundancy in the functional organization of the cortex. A complete description of the cortical machinery would therefore include several tens of billions of neuronal singularities, where each singularity included the effects of several tens of thousands of synaptic contacts. Although theoretically possible, can such an enumeration be carried out in practice? The task is colossal.

FROM MOUSE TO MAN

No category of cell, no particular type of circuit is specific to the human cerebral cortex. The components of our cerebral machinery derive from a stock very similar, if not identical, to that of the mouse. The major event in the evolution of the mammalian brain, as we have seen, is the expansion of the neocortex. This growth is accompanied by an increase in the total number of neurons, and thus in the number and complexity of the operations which the cortex can perform. The number of cellular elements per unit of surface area has not changed. The cortical thickness varies, but much less than its surface area. On average, the cortex of man is only three times thicker than that of the mouse, although the increase is not uniform in all layers. It affects particularly layers III and V, the main sources of cortical-to-cortical connections. The more the surface area of the cortex expands, the more the number of neurons capable of establishing association connections increases; the area of the association cortex thus becomes relatively greater than that of primary sensory and motor areas (see Chapter 4). This translates, finally, into an increase in the mean number of connections per neuron, with a consequent burgeoning of the dendritic and axonal trees, reaching a maximum in man. Nevertheless, the increase in the mean number of synapses per neuron is not directly proportional to the increase in cortical area. Far from it. The density of synapses per cubic millimeter of cortex is of the same order in the rat as in man. Because the thickness of the cortex increases only a maximum of three times, the mean number of synapses per neuron in man can hardly exceed three times that of the rat, whereas the area of the cortex is four hundred times greater. The increase in the mean number of synaptic contacts is thus not enough to explain entirely the increase in complexity of the cerebral cortex in the course of mammalian evolution. Other parameters intervene, such as the diversification of cortical areas (see Chapter 4).

At the levels of both the macroscopic anatomy of the cortex and its microscopic architecture, no sudden qualitative reorganization marks the passage from the "animal" brain to the human brain. There is, on the contrary, a continuous *quantitative* evolution in the total number of neurons, the diversity of areas, the number of possible connections between neurons, and, therefore, the complexity of the neuronal networks that make up the cerebral machine.

3

Animal Spirits

> We must remember that all our provisional ideas in
> psychology will one day be explained on the basis of
> organic substrates. It seems then probable that there
> are particular chemical substances and processes that
> produce the effects of sexuality and permit the per-
> petuation of individual life.
> —Sigmund Freud, "On Narcissism"

It is not enough to diagram the wiring of the cerebral machine in order
to understand how it functions. Dismantling it in this way merely
provides us with a static description. To understand its functioning
requires knowledge of a different, dynamic order. How do the parts
work together? Under what conditions do the valves and switches that
make up the machine open and close?

All forms of communication use transmitters and receivers linked by
channels carrying "signals." At the turn of the century, the great
anatomist, Santiago Ramón y Cajal put arrows on his drawings of
neurons to indicate the most plausible direction of current flow. In
effect his drawings represented circuits. Understanding the functions
of the brain implies a comprehension of the communication between
neurons. The wires of our "internal telephone" are nerve fibers: axons
and dendrites. They link transmitters and receivers, sometimes over
great distances when compared with the size of a cell body. Signals then
travel along the wires of the nervous machine. In theory, a signal can
be defined as a variation of a physical parameter with time. Transmitters produce this variation. After traveling along a specific channel, the
signal finally arrives at a receptor, which distinguishes it from background noise.

Since antiquity, and in the tradition of Galen, man has wondered
about the nature of the physical "devices" used by nerves. Hypotheses
have evolved through the centuries with the growth of physical and

technical knowledge, and in particular with advances in the transmission techniques used in man-made machines. Pneumatic or hydraulic theories prevailed in the seventeenth and eighteenth centuries, electrical ones in the nineteenth century, and electrochemical and chemical ones today. Let us look at the means used by the cerebral machine, sense organs, and motor centers to create, propagate, and transmit the communication signals that make up nervous activity.

CEREBRAL ELECTRICITY

In 1929 Hans Berger published an article on the electroencephalogram (EEG) of man which had tremendous impact. In terms of basic knowledge, nothing new was revealed. In 1875 Richard Caton had written: "In every brain hitherto examined, the galvanometer has indicated the existence of electric currents"; moreover, "the electric currents of the gray matter appear to have a relation to its functions." But Berger developed a recording system adapted to man, which did not necessitate the opening of the skull. It was enough to apply electrodes to the surface skin of the head and record variations in electrical potentials.

The brain waves that Berger recorded on the surface of the skull cannot be compared to the 300 volts and 0.5 amperes of the discharge of the electric eel. To measure them, one must use a very high-gain amplifier to display variations of electrical potential on a screen (Figure 23). They are very weak, a few tens of microvolts (millionths of a volt), and they oscillate at low frequency. In an adult, at rest with the eyes closed, the recorded waves look very regular, with a mean frequency of ten cycles per second. These are the *alpha* or *resting waves*.

When the subject opens his eyes, the waves change instantly. Their amplitude drops dramatically by at least a half and their regular form disappears. The mean frequency of these *beta waves* is a little more than double that of the alpha waves. In addition, their shape is extremely variable, in contrast to the repetitive nature of the alpha waves. For this reason, beta waves are also called *activity waves*.

Could the transition from alpha to beta waves on opening the eyes be simply the effect of light on the retina? If we continue the recording, with the subject's eyes closed, but we now ask the subject to listen to the ticking of a watch, once again the alpha rhythm disappears and beta waves replace it. Further, if the subject opens his eyes in the dark, again

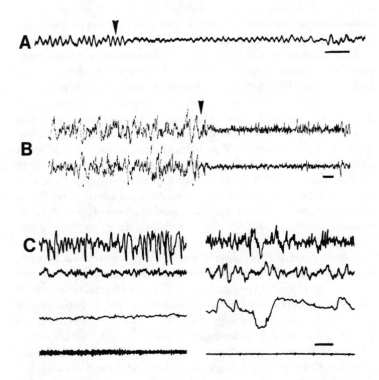

Figure 23. Electroencephalographic (EEG) recordings. When Hans Berger applied electrodes to the skin over the skull in 1929, he recorded weak fluctuations in electrical current resulting from the overall brain activity.

A: One of Berger's first recordings. The subject was awake but resting and the activity is rhythmic and regular, at a frequency of about ten cycles per second (alpha waves). When the back of the subject's right hand is touched with a glass rod (arrow), the recording becomes irregular, the amplitude lower, and the rhythm more rapid. When the subject fixes his attention, beta activity appears. Progressively, as attention is diminished, the alpha waves reappear. Bar length: 0.5 seconds. (From H. Berger, 1969.)

B: The waking state. At the beginning, we see the slow, high-amplitude waves, or delta waves, characteristic of so-called slow-wave sleep (bar length: 1 second). At the arrow, a tactile stimulus wakes the subject and the alpha rhythm reappears. (From S. Sharpless and H. Jasper, 1956.)

C: Slow-wave sleep (on the *left*) and paradoxical sleep (on the *right*). The *upper* trace is from an electrode in the region of the visual cortex; it shows the transition from slow, high-amplitude delta waves to a faster "paradoxical" rhythm. The bursts of paradoxical sleep are clearly visible in the *second* recording in the external occipital region. During paradoxical sleep the eyes move (as seen in the *third* recording from the top), and the muscular tone (*bottom* recording) decreases. Bar length: 1 second. (From P. Salzarulo, 1975.)

beta waves replace the alpha waves. Thus activity waves are not due to a particular sensory stimulus, whether visual, auditory, or tactile. Rather, they are the result of a more generalized process related to the subject's *attention* (see Chapter 5).[1]

Even with the eyes open, if attention wanders resting waves reappear. If the subject then calculates, say, all the taxes he will have to pay that year, the alpha rhythm is temporarily depressed. There are unequivocally different EEG wave forms corresponding to different states of "mental" activity. This becomes even clearer when the subject falls asleep. The passage from the waking to the sleeping state is accompanied by a progressive transformation of alpha waves to much slower *delta waves* at three to five cycles per second, but they reach an amplitude of several hundred microvolts. From time to time these slow waves are replaced by episodes of intense electrical activity, brief bursts of high frequency. These waves correspond to phases of *paradoxical* or *rapid-eye-movement (REM) sleep*, perhaps related to dreams (see Chapter 5).[2]

In general terms these observations establish a correlation between brain activity and electrical phenomena. Do they permit us to conclude that the two represent the same thing? There are several objections to this. Alpha or beta waves can be recorded, if not over the entire surface of the skull, at least over large parts of it. Thus they are much too generalized to really represent detailed brain activity, which should logically show much more diversity. In addition, alpha waves, like the slow waves of sleep, have a repetitive form, making them look like "carrier" waves. They seem unsuited to conveying raw information. On the other hand, beta waves have no obvious regularity. Finally, all these phenomena are slow compared with the speed of many brain processes. Are the electrical phenomena recorded by electroencephalography simply epiphenomena of a much more complicated set of processes?

To answer such a crucial question requires a more detailed analysis. A significant step forward is made when one submits the waking subject to controlled experimental stimulation. One can, for example, apply a slight electric shock to the fingertips and record the response in a particular cortical area, such as the somatosensory cortex. With a single shock, no significant activity is recorded. Only if one eliminates random fluctuations by adding together tens or hundreds of traces with the help of a computer is the *evoked potential* revealed. The first characteristic signs of this response occur very rapidly, only twenty to forty milliseconds after stimulation, and continue for nearly half a second.[3] Such recordings remind one, in man, of Caton's original findings. They suggest that the beta waves recorded in the alert subject contain, or envelop, other more elementary electrical activity provoked by peripheral sensory stimulation.

Further progress in analyzing cerebral electrical activity could take place only with the use of higher-resolution recording techniques than those employing electrodes placed on the surface of the head. Animals were used so that the electrodes could be placed on the cortex itself or even penetrate it. With an electrode about a millimeter wide inserted in the cortex, it is possible to record an evoked response to a single stimulation very similar to that obtained by summing the evoked potentials.

One can attain a different level of analysis by using a very fine electrode—a microelectrode—the tip of which may be less than 5 microns, (smaller than a nerve cell body).[4] The electrical picture changes dramatically. Now, one no longer records only very low-amplitude field effects, gathered from several centimeters of brain surface, but a "crackle" of very brief impulses, each lasting about a millisecond, seemingly coming from distinct sources. Their intensity increases and then decreases as the microelectrode advances micron by micron. These discrete sources are found throughout the cortex and produce spontaneous activity at a mean frequency that varies from one source to another, ranging from less than one impulse per second to a hundred or more per second (Figure 24).

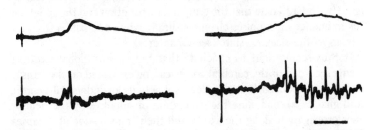

Figure 24. Electrical response in the rat to stimulation of the skin of the paw. There are two levels of recordings. The *upper* trace represents a "global" recording of the response obtained with an electrode in the somatosensory cortex (areas 1–3). The *bottom* trace reveals something of the underlying microstructure as recorded from single cells: either one (on the *left*) or several (on the *right*). Short, discrete impulses appear, coinciding with the evoked potential. Bar length: 4 milliseconds. (Modified from L. J. Bindman and O. C. J. Lippold, 1981.)

One can now repeat the experiment involving electrical stimulation of the fingertips, while a microelectrode penetrates the somatosensory cortex. Instead of a continuous wave, one records bursts of impulses that may reach frequencies of a hundred per second (Figure 24). The sources of this cortical activity respond to peripheral stimulation in a variety of ways, manifesting a diversity that was not even suspected before. There can be little doubt that each generating source of electrical impulses is in reality a single nerve cell. The use of microelectrodes allows us to break a continuous cortical electrical activity down into discontinuous entities with respect to both their source (the neurons) and the impulses they generate—in other words, in both space and time.

The reverse of this breakdown into more elementary activity would be to reconstitute EEG waves from single-unit recordings. This task is difficult for practical reasons. In a cubic millimeter of human cortex, there are tens of thousands of neurons, all capable of producing impulses. One would have to record them all at the same time in a volume of cortex of several cubic millimeters. At present such a technique does not exist, although it is probable that something approaching it will be developed in the near future (see Chapter 5). Attempts to reconstitute regional electrical activity are thus limited to mathematical models, which are still far too simple and based on fragmentary data. Nevertheless, the data we possess do allow a partial interpretation of evoked responses and even of alpha rhythm, which may result from an autorhythmic activity in closed loops between cortical and thalamic neurons (see Chapter 2). What is more, single-unit recording of cortical neurons agrees with EEG data that the temporal distribution and the spontaneous frequency of impulses change radically when one passes from the waking to the sleeping state (see Chapter 5).

It thus seems right to conclude that the various global electrical events recorded in the cerebral cortex can be explained on the basis of —and thus reduced to—the electrical activity of individual neurons (and glial cells), including the generation of impulses by the neuron, their propagation along the axons, and their transmission at synapses. The transition from global measurement to single-cell recording represents a revolution in the interpretation of data in brain electrophysiology.

THE NERVE SIGNAL

When Glisson discovered the "sensitivity" of nerves, he thought that he had put his finger on a "vital" property. With Galvani's findings in the peripheral nervous system, and those of Fritsch and Hitzig in the cerebral cortex, sensitivity became a form of "physical" response to an electrical discharge. Matteucci and, later, Du Bois-Reymond showed that his response was itself an electrical discharge. So nerves and nerve cells have the double property of *producing* and *reacting* to electricity, thus serving as both transmitters and receptors in an electrical communication system.

Although the nerve signal can be recorded as an electrical phenomenon, it does not flow in the same way as a current in copper wire. It is in fact a "wave of negativity," to use Du Bois-Reymond's term, generated in the cell body and propagated along the axon at a constant amplitude and a speed always below that of sound (Figure 25). The duration of this impulse is no more than a few milliseconds. Its velocity is between one-tenth of a meter per second in certain primitive animals such as the jellyfish, and rather more than a hundred meters per second in some mammals. The speed increases with the diameter of the nerve fiber and explains the delay of between ten and a hundred milliseconds observed between the stimulation of sense organs and the response recorded in the cortex.

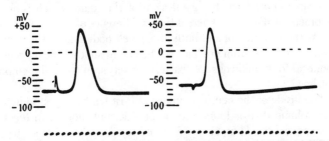

Figure 25. The nerve signal. The propagated electrical wave was recorded from a microelectrode inside the giant axon of a squid. Very similar recordings are obtained from an intact axon in the animal (on the *left*) or after dissection and isolation of the axon (on the *right*). One can even remove the cytoplasm from the axon (keeping the membrane intact), refill this "tube" with saline solutions, and still record very similar nerve impulses. Time scale: 2,500 dots per second. (From A. L. Hodgkin, 1964.)

The duration of a given nerve impulse is invariable. A resting, or refractory, period separates two successive impulses by a "blank" of a few milliseconds. The amplitude of a given impulse (of the order of a tenth of a volt) is also invariable. Wherever they are recorded or however they are produced, nerve impulses always have a similar shape. A very uniform, even universal, system of electrical impulses ensures communication in the nervous system. The signals propagated can almost be reduced to the characters and spaces of a very simplified Morse code.

Thus the nervous machine functions by using a system of electrical impulses conducted over distances as much as a meter or more, without loss of amplitude. But nerve fibers are not made of copper wire. What is the origin of this "nervous electricity" and from where does the energy come to propagate it? The cell membrane plays a fundamental role in generating this electricity.

Like all living cells, the neuron is surrounded by a membrane. Composed of lipids and proteins, it is like a very thin film, 5 to 10 nanometers thick, or about one-thousandth of the cell's diameter. Nevertheless, this film is sufficiently solid to form the boundary of the cell and ensure its integrity.

Let us again consider recordings made in the cortex with a microelectrode. If instead of simply remaining in the vicinity of a nerve cell, we perforate its membrane and penetrate its interior, the electrical potential jumps abruptly to a stable value called the *resting potential*. We obtain the same result if we carry out this experiment on a more easily accessible nerve fiber, the giant axon of the squid, which is about a millimeter in diameter. There is then a difference of electrical potential across the cell membrane, both at the cell body and in the axon. Its value varies little from one part of the cell to another, being generally about 50 to 90 millivolts. A "battery" is set up in the cell membrane, but how?

The inside of the neuron contains at least ten times less sodium per unit volume than is found on the outside, but more than ten times more potassium. Thus, energy is stored across the membrane "barrier" in the form of chemical concentrations. It is this chemical energy that will be converted to electrical energy.

The conversion from chemical to electrical energy makes use of a basic property of sodium and potassium atoms: their loss of a negatively charged electron when they are placed in an aqueous solution. In this way the sodium and potassium atoms acquire a positive charge. They become positive *ions* and, if displaced, will create an electrical current. On one side of the membrane, then, there is an excess of sodium ions and on the other an excess of potassium ions. If the membrane let them pass freely, the electrical currents created by their movements in opposite directions would cancel each other out. But the membrane acts as a selective filter. At rest, only potassium ions can pass, not sodium ones. An electromotive force develops, directly related in value and sign (negative inside) to the ratio of the potassium concentrations on each side of the membrane. Thus, the conversion of a difference in chemical concentration into an electrical potential can be explained in simple physico-chemical terms.

But are we not going backward to get ahead? For if differences in chemical concentrations give rise to these electrical phenomena, what causes these differences and, above all, how are they maintained across the cell membrane? A special molecule intervenes, one that has been isolated and purified in a homogeneous form. This protein, referred to as an *enzyme pump,* crosses the membrane, captures the ions on one side, and transports them back to the other. As this transport is accomplished against a gradient, energy is harnessed from ATP, (adenosine triphosphate), a substance produced by cell metabolism and well known to biochemists. The enzyme pump, or ATPase, breaks down the ATP molecule and uses the energy so released to transport sodium and potassium ions across the membrane. There is thus no mystery surrounding the energy used by the neuron to produce electricity. Its origin is in fact quite simple. It is based on ATP, the "small change" of practically all energy supplies of the cell. ATP provides the energy needed to form a difference in ion concentrations across the membrane and the membrane spontaneously converts this gradient into an electrical potential.

The membrane at rest is therefore "under tension." The enzyme pump and cell metabolism maintain a permanent electrochemical potential across the membrane, and this potential can be used freely to produce nerve impulses. One property of the membrane, however, has not yet been mentioned. In the resting state, sodium ions cannot cross, although there is a difference of concentration, with very few sodium ions inside the cell. At the beginning of this century, Julius Bernstein, the author of the theory of resting potential, suggested that a nerve impulse was due to the temporary collapse of this membrane barrier.

In 1902 E. Overton took up the idea and gave supporting evidence that sodium ions from the outside were important in the genesis of the nerve impulse. Finally, in 1952, Alan Hodgkin and Andrew Huxley gave a complete demonstration of the ionic workings of the nerve impulse using an exceptional specimen, which has already been mentioned: the squid's giant axon. It is so large that one can empty its cellular contents, preserving its membrane in the form of a tube, and then fill it with solutions of varying compositions.

The outcome of their remarkable series of experiments was conclusive. The initiation of a nerve impulse is primarily due to an increased permeability of the membrane to sodium ions. The electrical potential controls this opening of the membrane. When it reaches a threshold value, it unlocks channels through which sodium ions rush in an almost "explosive" manner to the inside of the cell, with no other energy requirements than the "vacuum" created by the enzyme pump. The passage of sodium ions creates an electrical current and therefore a change of potential. In less than a tenth of a millisecond, the nerve signal is released. The electrical potential reverses its sign and reaches a value of about + 20 millivolts, a value imposed by the ratio of the sodium concentrations on the two sides of the membrane. The response thus immediately reaches a maximum amplitude of about 100 millivolts. Then the sodium channels close and other channels selective for potassium ions temporarily open. The membrane potential returns to its resting value and the impulse is over, having lasted a millisecond. It takes the form of a self-propagating solitary wave.

Hodgkin and Huxley concluded their remarkable experimental analysis with a theory that used only a few molecular channels to account in a complete and quantitative manner for the electrical characteristics of the nerve impulse and its propagation. Two were enough. The principal one was clearly the sodium channel, the opening of which was governed by the electrical potential.

The tremendous impact of the findings and theoretical interpretations of Hodgkin and Huxley was due not only to their rigor and logic but also to their universal nature. Whether in a squid's giant axon, a rat's sciatic nerve, or a neuron of the cerebral cortex, the propagation of the nerve impulse can be explained by similar, if not identical, basic mechanisms. Later, following more and more experimental data, came the crowning achievement, which proved the soundness of this theory:

the isolation of the sodium channel in the form of a specific chemical substance.

What Glisson called intangible "sensitivity" can now be explained in physical terms, in particular in terms of electrical fields and their effects on the opening of molecular channels. The generation of electricity shown by Matteucci is explicable by the transport of sodium and potassium ions through the channels. As to the energy used, it is a natural product of cell metabolism.

OSCILLATORS

Communication within a neuronal network is established by solitary waves traveling along the nerves. But where do these signals come from? The electroencephalogram clearly shows that even in the absence of obvious sensory stimulation, even during sleep, the cerebral cortex produces intense electrical activity. A microelectrode in any cortical nerve cell shows that there is spontaneous generation of electrical impulses. This phenomenon is generalized. Even neurons in tissue culture, such as those derived from a tumor like a neuroblastoma, produce spontaneous action potentials. The analysis of these impulse generators has been facilitated by the remarkable temporal regularity of the impulses. They act as oscillators. This is the case, for example, of the "bursting" neuron R15 of the sea slug *(Aplysia)*.

The sea slug possesses a highly dispersed nervous system, ideally adapted to experimentation (Figure 26, see also Chapters 2 and 8). There is no brain or spinal cord, but approximately 100,000 neurons are gathered in compact ganglia in different parts of the body. Each ganglion consists of a small number of neurons; there are, for instance, about 2,000 in the abdominal ganglion. The organization and function of the ganglia are virtually identical from one sea slug to another.[5] Because of the small number of neurons, it is possible to identify many of them, particularly the so-called giant ones. Their cell bodies, almost visible to the naked eye, sometimes reach more than a tenth of a millimeter in diameter. In the posterior part of the abdominal ganglion is neuron R15. When a glass microelectrode penetrates its membrane, an astonishing monologue is recorded (Figure 27B). Bursts of ten to twenty impulses occur every five to ten seconds with the regularity of

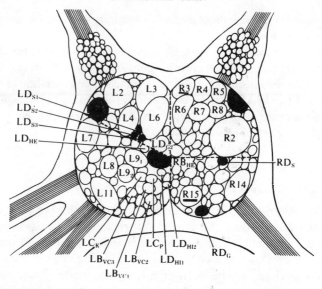

Figure 26. Abdominal ganglion of the sea slug *Aplysia californica*. It is made up of about 2,000 neurons, of which more than 50 have a giant cell body, which is easily identifiable. (From E. R. Kandel, 1976.)

a pendulum. If one isolates the ganglion, the oscillations persists, as they do even when the neuron R15 itself is isolated. The oscillatory activity of the neuron does not depend on the connections it establishes within the nervous system of the sea slug. It is a spontaneous "intrinsic" activity of the nerve cell.

When a neuron alone uses such a language, it inevitably engenders a certain mystery. What dictatorial spirit gives its orders so regularly? First, is this oscillatory behavior compatible with the laws of thermodynamics? Ilya Prigogine and his collaborators examined this question in the more general context of a theory of oscillations in chemical systems.[6] Their first conclusion was that oscillation cannot appear in a thermodynamic system if it is closed but only if it is open and continuously exchanges energy with the outside world. Their second conclusion was that oscillations never develop near equilibrium. The system must be out of equilibrium but in a stable state. It must in fact constitute a "dissipative" structure. The cell, and particularly the neuron, satisfies these two conditions. It continuously exchanges energy with the outside world by consuming nutritive substances such as glucose and by cell metabolism, which produces ATP. It is in a stable state but out of equilibrium, for it maintains a permanent unequal distribution of ions across its cytoplasmic membrane, thanks to the constant effort of the enzyme pump.

The third and last conclusion of Prigogine's work concerned the characteristics of chemical reactions within a given system as well as the flux of matter and energy between this system and the outside world. Nonlinear relationships must exist between forces and flux. This is manifested concretely when reactions take place in an "explosive" manner in time and when reactions become coupled—for example, following the so-called cybernetic feedback between the final result of a chain reaction and the initial reaction. The explosive release of a nerve impulse clearly satisfies this condition of nonlinearity.

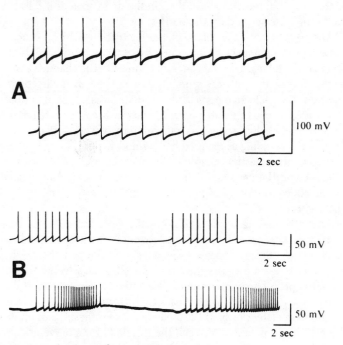

Figure 27. Spontaneous activity of identified neurons in the sea slug. In *A,* we see regular oscillatory activity, such as that recorded in neuron R3; in *B,* in regular bursts of impulses, such as those recorded in neuron R15. In both cases the *upper* line represents a recording from the intact neuron in the animal and the *lower* line, one after isolation of the ganglion. Spontaneous activity persists after isolation. (From B. O. Alving, 1968.)

Thus the oscillitory behavior of a neuron fits the laws of thermodynamics. This was predictable, but needed proof. Now let us look at how, concretely, these oscillations are produced.

Oscillations are composed of quite ordinary volleys of nerve impulses, produced by the mechanism proposed by Hodgkin and Huxley for impulses in the squid's giant axon. The new element is the regular repetition of these impulses in the form of bursts, as well as the regular repetition of these bursts. In fact each burst is superimposed on an oscillation-generating system, a basic oscillator or "pacemaker" that causes a slow fluctuation in the membrane potential of the neuron.[7] The potential oscillates between two extreme values, on each side of the threshold for the nerve impulse. Whenever the potential reaches the threshold, an impulse is released, then another, and so on, as long as the potential remains above the threshold. As soon as it falls below it, the impulses cease and the burst stops.

The pacemaker—the source of the fluctuation (which occurs over some tens of seconds)—is made up of two molecular channels. They open slowly, taking several seconds, in contrast to the channels involved in the propagation of nerves impulses, which act in milliseconds. In addition, their selective permeability to ions differs. One is permeable to potassium, the other to calcium. The electrical potential and the calcium (which like sodium is pumped out of the cell) maintain a "feedback" coupling as required by thermodynamics, for the potential created by the potassium channel influences the opening of the calcium channel, and the opening of the potassium channel is itself regulated by the concentration of calcium entering by its own channel (Figure 28).

At the beginning of an oscillation, the electrical potential diminishes; as a consequence, the calcium channel, which is slow and reacts to potential changes, opens. Calcium enters the cell. Before being pumped out again it causes the other slow channel, selective for potassium, to open. Then potassium can leave the cell. In leaving, it causes an increase in potential. We are back to the beginning. The membrane potential oscillates slowly. If the oscillation is of sufficient amplitude for the membrane potential to reach the threshold for a nerve impulse, a burst will form on the crest of each slow oscillation. The length of the burst will depend on the amplitude and the duration of the oscillation. If this amplitude is at the threshold level only for a very short time, the burst will consist of only one or two impulses (see Figure 27A). The

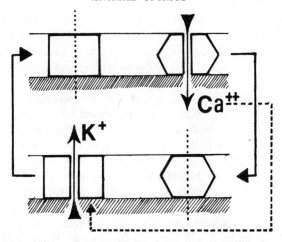

Figure 28. Highly simplified diagram of the workings of a basic oscillator. It is made up of two slow ion channels: one selective for potassium ($K+$) on the left, the other for calcium ($Ca++$) on the right. The "regenerative" entry of calcium diminishes the electrical potential. Once in the cytoplasm, the calcium opens the potassium channel (broken arrow) and the potassium leaves the cell, thus causing an increase in electrical potential. Then the internal calcium is eliminated by an enzyme pump, the potassium is recovered, and the cycle begins again. A regular oscillation of the electrical potential of the cell membrane results.

burst may not even appear at each oscillation, only when it is particularly large. Rather than a "bursting" clock, we now have a stochastic, or random, impulse generator. Thus neuronal oscillators are regulated as much by the membrane potential as by the internal calcium concentration.

Thus, only four molecular channels, three ions, two pumps, and ATP are needed to create an adjustable biological clock, functioning constantly and spontaneously. Oscillators using similar principles have been found wherever they have been looked for in most types of nerve cells, and even in non-nerve tissue, from the sea slug to mammals. They are very widely distributed devices that alone account for a large part of the spontaneous activity recorded at various levels of the nervous system.

What is the function of this spontaneous activity? On the one hand, psychologists hesitate to consider mental work as spontaneous activity; on the other hand, physiologists, in the tradition of Sir Charles Sherrington and the cyberneticists, study responses that are clearly related to peripheral stimulation. Indeed, in essence, the propagated impulses seem the same, whether they are spontaneous or "evoked." Even the distinction between spontaneous impulses and those evoked by an interaction with the environment, is in doubt. In several well-established cases, the evoked activity *begins* with spontaneous impulse generation.

The most striking example is that of sensory receptors, whose function is to "transduce" physical signals received from the outside world into nerve impulses. In the last resort they are at the origin of all evoked activity. Let us look at the vestibular receptors in the inner ear, which are responsible for our perception of gravity and movement in three-dimensional space. In the awake monkey, an electrode on the vestibular nerve will record a sustained spontaneous activity of about twenty impulses per second. If one turns the monkey's chair in a given direction, the activity will increase to, say, thirty impulses per second. In the opposite direction it will diminish to, perhaps, fewer than ten per second. The spontaneous activity present before the physical stimulation permits a double registration, allowing the two directions to be distinguished and offering greater possibilities for coding. The response of the receptor organ, and consequently the evoked response in the central nervous system, may appear either in an increase in frequency of impulses or in a decrease.

The vestibular apparatus in the inner ear is composed of two sorts of cellular elements: impulse-generating neurons, whose axons are directed toward the central nervous system, and the sensory cells themselves. The latter bear a tuft of sensory cilia, which are bathed in a liquid that fills the interior of the vestibule and can contact minute "pebbles"at their extremities. Under the principle of inertia, movements of the head provoke a displacement of the liquid and the cilia are deflected. This affects the membrane potential much as moving a control column affects the flight path of an airplane. Moved in one direction, the cilia bring about a decrease in membrane potential; moved in the other, they engender an increase. One may imagine forward movement opening calcium channels and backward movement closing them. A mechanical signal is transformed into an electrical signal. This electromechanical effect is transmitted to the next nerve cell, whose membrane potential is modified and, consequently, the impulses it produces change in rhythm.[8]

Thus, variations in a physical parameter in the environment are translated into variations in nerve impulses. This is true whatever the variable to which the sense organ is responding, be it gravity, light, or chemical activity. A chain of successive reactions, explicable in strictly physico-chemical terms, regulates the spontaneous activity of the oscillator, which preexists all interaction with the outside world. The impulses produced are therefore independent from the physical stimulus to which the organ is sensitive. The sense organs behave like regulators of molecular clocks. The stimulation that they receive from the outside world sets them forward or backward and corrects their timing. There is no direct analogy, however, between the physical stimulus received from the environment and the nervous signal produced.

The impulses emitted by peripheral oscillators are transmitted to central nuclei, including the cerebral cortex. This evoked activity in fact constitutes only a fraction of the total activity that can be observed, even in the absence of obvious sensory stimulation. The ability to generate impulses, as we have seen, is not reserved to sensory receptors. It is a general characteristic of nerve cells, and even of some non-nerve cells such as certain glandular cells. The nervous machine contains multiple impulse generators, at many levels of both the central and the peripheral nervous systems.

FROM ONE NEURON TO ANOTHER

Impulse generators produce electrical signals that spread throughout the complex network of cables and connections that join together sensory cells, neurons, and effector organs. The direction of propagation is always the same, from the dendrites to the cell body and from the cell body to the axon terminals. The neuronal network is therefore organized in series of "one-way" circuits.

This situation is in some ways paradoxical. We know from Chapter 1 that axons and dendrites are not in continuity. Nerve circuits consist of neurons juxtaposed at the synapses; there is a "break" between one neuron and another. How can such discontinuity allow the passage of electrical signals from one neuron to another? Does it explain the "polarity" of the propagation of nervous signals?

When one stimulates the middle of an axon electrically, an impulse is set off, which travels as easily toward the cell body as toward the axon terminal. In other words, there is no intrinsic polarity to the direction of impulse propagation in the axon. So how can one explain that nerve impulses always travel in the same direction?

The answer to our questions was suggested by Sir Charles Sherrington in 1906 in his book *The Integrative Action of the Nervous System.* He compared the bidirectional propagation in a nerve trunk with the unidirectional propagation in a reflex arc. His proposal was that the "characters distinguishing reflex-arc conduction from nerve-trunk conduction may . . . be largely due to intercellular barriers," to a "nexus" between neuron and neuron, thus to the properties of the synapse. Two opposing theses emerged and remained in conflict for fifty years. Electrophysiologists contended that the nerve impulse crossed the synapse electrically. Pharmacologists, aware of the experiments of Claude Bernard, preferred to think of chemical transmission. In the 1950s the debate came to an end. Physiologists and pharmacologists agreed that both forms of transmission existed. There were electrical synapses *and* chemical synapses.

Electrical synapses are characterized by a very tight apposition of the cytoplasmic membranes, less than 2 nanometers apart in electron micrographs. There can be virtually no delay in the propagation of the nerve impulse, as if there were electrical continuity between the cells. In such conditions one would not expect a polarity in the direction of signal transfer. In some cases one can observe more efficient transmission in one direction than in the other, but most often these synapses have a nondirectional coupling which "synchronizes the clock" for large populations of neurons.

The idea of chemical transmission intervening in nerve signal processing in addition to electrical transmission came not from a chemist but an electrophysiologist of genius, Emil Du Bois-Reymond (see Chapter 1). The development of this concept, however, owed much to the work of pharmacologists, such as T. R. Elliott in 1904, John Langley in 1905, and above all Sir Henry Dale. They were interested in the mode of action of natural or synthetic chemical substances on target organs. For simplicity's sake, they began by studying peripheral organs such as the sartorius muscle of the frog and the dorsal muscle of the leech. When they compared the effect of certain chemical substances to that of the motor nerves innervating the organs, they observed striking similarities. Such was the case for a natural compound extracted from nerve tissue and already synthesized in the late 1860s by the chemists A. Crum-Brown and T. R. Frazer. This ester of choline —*acetylcholine*— is synthesized by some motor nerves. It is released by electrical stimulation of motor terminals. One can legitimately consider acetylcholine as a "chemical mediator" or *neurotransmitter,* transmitting the signals across the gap separating the motor nerve from striated muscle.

The scheme of chemical synaptic transmission thus looks like this:

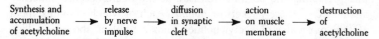

| Synthesis and accumulation of acetylcholine | → | release by nerve impulse | → | diffusion in synaptic cleft | → | action on muscle membrane | → | destruction of acetylcholine |

The validity of this scheme is supported by several convergent observations.

Electron microscopy reveals major differences between electrical synapses and those supposedly using a neurotransmitter, such as the neuromuscular junction. Chemical synapses possess a morphological polarity that imposes a functional polarity. First of all, the synaptic cleft is more than ten times wider, (20 to 50 nanometers) than the electrical junction. In addition, the two sides of the cleft have a very different morphology. On one side there is a nerve terminal, full of vesicles 30 to 60 nanometers in diameter. The other side has no vesicles but rather a membrane thickening or "postsynaptic density." Synapses of this type are not only found in the peripheral nervous system (see Figure 9) but, as we have seen, are also common in the cerebral cortex (see Figure 17). One can even isolate them in a test tube and demonstrate that the vesicles in nerve terminals contain the neurotransmitter.[9]

Recordings with intracellular microelectrodes reveal electrical signals typical of this type of synapse.[10] If the motor nerve is stimulated, a response can be recorded in the muscle fiber. If the electrodes are reversed and the muscle stimulated electrically, there is no response in the nerve. The signal passes in only one direction, from the motor nerve to the muscle: the synapse functions as a "valve," in a strictly unidirectional fashion. Another difference from electrical synapses is that the first changes recorded at the muscle membrane appear after a delay of 0.3 to 0.8 milliseconds, which is quite significant when compared with the duration of the nerve impulse—a millisecond or more.

All these features can be explained simply on the basis of chemical transmission. Acetylcholine is present only in the nerve terminal and not in the muscle. The chemical signal can travel only from the nerve to the muscle and transmission is therefore polarized. In addition, the release of acetylcholine, its diffusion in the synaptic cleft, and its action on the muscle membrane all take time. The resulting delay will obviously be longer than that found in electrical transmission.

How the nerve impulse induces the secretion of acetylcholine when it invades the nerve terminal is still not completely clear. We do know, however, that acetylcholine forms small "packets" and that each impulse reaching the terminal releases, at the neuromuscular junction, about 300 of these packets or *quanta*, each of which contains about 10,000 molecules of acetylcholine. Thus a total of about 3 million acetylcholine molecules accumulates in the synaptic cleft in a very short time, less than a millisecond. If one recognizes that this is an *absolute* number of molecules, it is not so very high, for in the unity of quanitity of matter, or *mole*, there are 6.02×10^{23} molecules. Yet the volume of the synaptic cleft is so small that the *local* concentration caused by the release of a few million molecules reaches a very high value. At rest, the "leakage" of acetylcholine into the synaptic cleft is less than 10^{-9} moles per liter. When an impulse arrives, this concentration rises abruptly almost a million times. It reaches 10^{-4} or 10^{-3} moles per liter for about a millisecond and then disappears by diffusion and by breakdown by a special enzyme. A chemical impulse follows the electrical impulse. This local, temporary increase in acetylcholine concentration ensures the rapid passage of the signal across the synaptic cleft.

Obviously, for this passage to be effective, the released acetylcholine must act on the other side of the synaptic cleft. There one can record an electrical wave significantly different from that of the nerve impulse (Figure 29), in that it does not travel along the membrane in an "all-or-nothing" way. It lasts three to five times longer, terminates more abruptly, and its amplitude is five to ten times lower. It originates in an increase in permeability that affects sodium and potassium ions simultaneously rather than sequentially—a simpler situation than in the case of impulse propagation. On the muscle side of the junction, only one category of channel is involved, not two. A crucial discovery was that when a "pulse" of acetylcholine is given locally through a micropipette, it creates an electrical wave in the postsynaptic membrane very similar to that brought about by stimulation of the nerve.[11] The ion channels in the postsynaptic membrane are opened by the acetylcholine but, unlike those involved in the propagation of the nerve impulse, they are not sensitive to changes in electrical potential. Modern high-resolution techniques permit the recording of the opening and closing of a *single* channel, events that take place very quickly. The minute wave that results lasts about a millisecond and has a characteristic square form (Figure 30): the ion channel can be only fully open or closed!

The release of acetylcholine by the nerve impulse converts the electrical signal into a chemical signal. The opening of the ion channels has the opposite effect: the conversion of a chemical into an electrical signal.

At the neuromuscular junction, the amplitude of the synaptic response is generally sufficient for the membrane potential to reach the threshold for the generation of an impulse in the muscle. Thus, each nerve impulse is followed by a contraction of the muscle fiber—a 100 percent efficient transmission. This is not always the case, however, particularly at synapses between neurons where the very small nerve terminals can only release single packets of neurotransmitters, and not 300 as at the neuromuscular junction, and not necessarily every time a nerve impulse invades the terminal.[12] Nevertheless, it is still true that the general pattern of chemical transmission at the neuromuscular junction applies to central synapses.

As we have seen, in the history of the neurosciences there has often

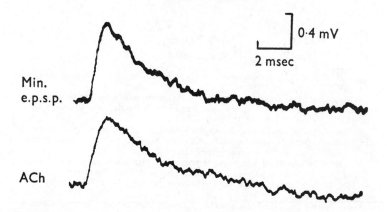

Figure 29. Electrical response in the postsynaptic membrane of a chemical synapse (in this case a neuromuscular junction) to a neurotransmitter (here acetylcholine). The shape and the properties of the wave differ from those of the propagated nerve impulse. The *upper* trace was recorded during the release of a "packet" of acetylcholine by the nerve terminal, and the *lower* during the local application of a high dose of acetylcholine (ACh) by a micropipette. The two traces can almost be superimposed. (From S. W. Kuffler and D. Yoshikami, 1975.)

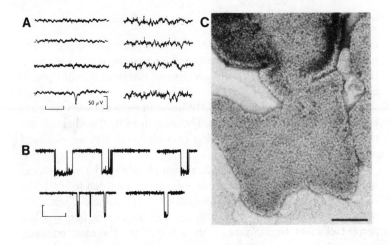

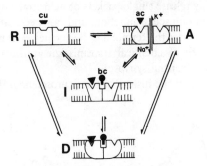

Figure 30. The postsynaptic electrical wave can be reduced to the collective opening of molecule channels.

A: Recording by an extracellular electrode of the spontaneous "noise" in the postsynaptic membrane. It is more marked in the presence of acetylcholine (on the *right*) than in its absence (on the *left*). (From B. Katz and R. Miledi, 1972.)

B: The postsynaptic results from the sudden opening and closing of a large number of ion channels, easily identifiable on this recording obtained by Alain Trautmann in cultured rat muscle cells. Horizontal bar: 100 milliseconds; vertical bar: 2 picoamps.

C: Electronmicrograph of a fragment of postsynaptic membrane, viewed from the nerve terminal. It shows the receptor molecules that contain the ion channel, whose opening and closing produces the fluctuations seen in A and B. Horizontal bar: 0.1 microns. (Micrograph by Jean Cartaud.)

Lower drawing: Very simplified, hypothetical representation of molecular transitions in the acetylcholine receptor. According to the model proposed here, the receptor molecule can exist in several interconvertible states or configurations (see the 1976 article by J.-P. Changeux et al., as well as the 1981 articles by R. Neubig and J. Cohen, and by T. Heidmann and J.-P. Changeux). These states include resting (R), stabilized by curare (cu); active (A), opened by acetylcholine (ac) —the only state that allows the passage of sodium (Na+) and potassium (K+) ions. The transition from R to A is very rapid—microseconds or milliseconds. In this drawing one can also see states in which the ion channel is closed: intermediate (I) and desensitized (D), stabilized by acteylcholine and accessible only slowly. Such states could be involved in short-term memory (see Chapter 5).

been a long delay between the discovery of a mechanism in the peripheral nervous system and the confirmation of its presence in the central nervous system. The evolution of our knowledge of neurotransmitters is an excellent example. Acetylcholine and adrenaline were recognized in the periphery in 1904 and 1905 by Elliott and Langley, but acetylcholine was identified in the brain only in 1941 by F. McIntosh and noradrenaline in 1954 by Marthe Vogt. These two neurotransmitters have become the honorary members of a club of chemical substances, which become more numerous every day. They include amino acids, such as glutamate, aspartate, and gamma-aminobutyric acid (GABA); the biogenic amines, such as dopamine and serotonin; and the polypeptides, such as the enkephalins, the endorphins, and substance P. One of the latest discoveries is VIP—not a Very Important Person but a vasoactive intestinal peptide. Indeed, it was first discovered in the intestine before being identified in the brain. Its case is not unique. Not only do the neurotransmitters used in the peripheral nervous system also serve in the central nervous system, but several of them play completely different roles elsewhere in the organism. Another example is somatostatin, a peptide that inhibits the release of growth hormone. Roger Guillemin and his collaborators showed that it was present in neurons of sympathetic ganglia and in the cerebral cortex, but it is also found in the pancreas, in the gamma cells of the islets of Langerhans, where it suppresses insulin secretion.[13]

Several of these neurotransmitters have been identified in the nervous system of very primitive animals such as the annelid worms, and they exist throughout the animal kingdom, particularly in such higher vertebrates as rats, monkeys, and humans. Their role at the chemical synapse is apparently just as universal as that of the nerve impulse in signal propagation in the axon. To date, no uniquely "human" neurotransmitter has been found.

Already, however, dozens of neurotransmitters have been counted in the brain, and the list is likely to grow longer in the future. This biochemical diversity contrasts with the uniformity of electrical signals. Sir Henry Dale thought that a single neuron produced and released only a single neurotransmitter. But there are noteworthy exceptions to this rule. A single neuron can, for example, contain a classic neurotransmitter like acetylcholine and a peptide like VIP.[14]

Recall that a single cerebral-cortex neuron may receive from tens of thousands of synapses and that these synapses employ various neurotransmitters. This diversity, both in the chemical nature of neurotransmitters and in their ionic effects, produces a "signal-combining device" with possibilities for calculations that a strictly "electrical" neuron would handle differently or not at all. As we shall see in Chapter 4, these capacities for local calculations have important consequences for the functioning of the neuron.

THE KEYS TO MOLECULE LOCKS

The chemical synapse plays a central role in communication between neurons. It channels the transfer of signals from cell to cell and, by polarizing the transfer, creates circuits and diversifies the activity of the neuron membrane. Its size is similar to that of a bacterial cell but obviously it does not possess all its properties; it is a specialized junction. On account of the strategic importance of the synapse in neuronal communication, the unraveling of its secrets is of considerable interest both theoretically and practically.

One way of approaching the study of the chemical synapse is to exploit the signals that it uses, the neurotransmitters or related substances, and the target molecules in the postsynaptic membrane upon which the neurotransmitter exerts its "electrogenic" effect.

At the end of the nineteenth century, Paul Ehrlich wrote: *Corpora non agunt nisi fixata* ("a body cannot act unless it is fixed"). How is this fixation achieved? Writing in the 1890s, Emil Fischer put forward a particularly striking image, which is still valid today. The cell contains a chemically active substance, which presents a geometrical configuration complementary to that of another substance, and which fits it "like a key in a lock." Working with the neuromuscular junction, John Langley in 1906 showed that this substance responded to nicotine and was blocked by curare, and that in adult muscle it was localized precisely where the axon terminated. He proposed that "the muscle substance which combines with nicotine and curare is not identical to the substance which contracts." He called it the "receptive substance," now more commonly known as the *receptor*. The binding of acetylcholine to this receptor "lock" in the postsynaptic membrane causes the opening of an ion channel associated with it.

For many years the receptor was considered mythical. Even Sir Henry Dale, who had gathered so many facts in support of the role of acetylcholine as a neurotransmitter, hesitated to use the term. Present in very small quantities, the receptor seemed to defy chemical identification. Two convergent strategies led to success.[15]

First, one had to find an organ containing much greater quantities of receptor than a muscle. The electric organ of the torpedo fish or the electric eel satisfied this condition (Figure 31). It can produce very powerful electric discharges. Three discharges of the electric eel (300 volts at 0.5 amperes) can kill a man. The discharges result from the simultaneous firing of billions of synapses with very similar properties to neuromuscular junctions. Schematically, the electric organ can be compared to a muscle whose synapses have proliferated after the contractile elements have been lost. This gigantic accumulation makes for an amplification of great utility to the biochemist.[16] As all these microscopic synapses have the same chemical composition, working with a kilogram of electric organ becomes practically the same as working with a single giant synapse of the same weight! The quantities of acetylcholine receptor available attain several grams. One need only separate it from the other components of the electric organ to identify its chemical nature. To do this it is necessary to mark it, for instance, by a radioactive tag that can be traced. One possibility is to label the neurotransmitter itself or an analog. When this experiment was tried, however, it failed, for the neurotransmitters (or analogs) bind nonselectively to too many molecules in addition to the specific receptor.

Once again, one must call upon the resources of the animal world. Certain snakes like the cobra or bungarum owe their terrifying reputation to the toxicity of their venom which, when injected into the bloodstream through their bite, kills their prey, including man, by paralyzing the respiratory muscles. It acts in some ways like the curare with which the Indians of the Amazon coat the tips of their arrows. The paralyzing substance in the venom of these snakes is a small protein, similar in size to insulin, called alpha-bungarotoxin.[17] This toxin binds almost irreversibly and very selectively to the synaptic site where acetylcholine binds. It is, in some ways, a wrong key that fits the right lock; once in the lock, it can no longer be removed, blocking the action of the receptor and paralyzing it. With radioactive tagging, it

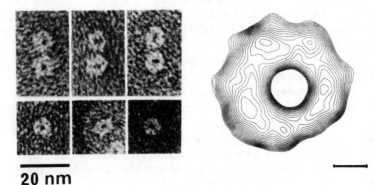

20 nm

Figure 31. The electric organs of the torpedo fish *(Torpedo marmorata)* contain many acetylcholine synapses and thus large quantities of acetylcholine receptor. In the drawing at the *top*, the electric organs are exposed after dissection of the two sides of the head. (From P. Savi, 1844.)

Below are several electronmicrographs of the acetylcholine receptor molecule by Jean Cartaud, as well as a reconstructed drawing obtained by computer analysis of these micrographs. The molecule has a central "hole" (could it be an ion channel?) and five subunits of different sizes. (From F. Bon et al., 1982.)

can serve as a very selective indicator of the receptor lock into which it fits.

Even if the torpedo fish and the bungarum snake have little chance of meeting naturally (although in the Sea of Japan one does find marine snakes that eat fish), their encounter in the test tube resulted in the isolation of the acetylcholine receptor. The snake's alpha-bungarotoxin effectively flags the abundant receptors of the electric organ.[18]

The receptor is a large molecule, a protein much bigger than the toxin. Under the electron microscope it looks like a rosette nine-billionths of a meter in diameter (see Figure 31). Its molecular weight is 275,000, or three and a half times that of hemoglobin. Like hemoglobin, it is made up of several chains, four of them different and one that is repeated twice. These five chains, firmly anchored in the post-synaptic membrane, cross it from one side to the other. The packing of the receptor molecules at the nerve terminal is so dense that the membrane appears to be made up almost entirely of these molecules side by side, joined together by a film of lipids (see Figure 30C). The postsynaptic membrane therefore has a remarkably simple biochemical structure, more so even than the membrane of a bacterial cell.

Through centrifugation, one can isolate the postsynaptic membrane from homogenates of electric organs. It forms tiny fragments, a micron in diameter (about the size of the synapse or even smaller). These fragments reseal to form vesicles, or tiny sacs, which one can fill with radioactive sodium or potassium ions. If acetylcholine is added to these vesicles, it triggers the opening of the ion channels. In the absence of a "natural" cellular environment, the vesicles respond to acetylcholine in a very similar way to the postsynaptic membrane of the living animal. This function, so important for intercellular communication, is preserved in the test tube.

The receptor protein forms the major part of these membrane fragments. Does it alone determine all the various features of the physiological action of acetylcholine? Where is the ion channel whose opening is controlled by acetylcholine? Is it part of the same macromolecule as the receptor itself? Weak detergents, like those used in housework, emulsify the vesicles without destroying the receptor. In their presence the receptor protein can thus be prepared in a pure and homogeneous form and reinserted in a lipid film of known chemical nature. This "reconstituted" membrane possesses all the known functional properties of natural vesicles and even of the natural postsynaptic membrane

(Figure 32). In particular it can accommodate the electrophysiological recording techniques used to detect the square wave-opening pattern of single channels. The form and properties of these recordings are

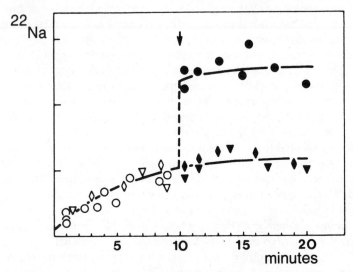

Figure 32. Reconstruction of an active membrane from chemically defined components: purified acetylcholine receptor and soy lipids. This mixture systematically forms small, closed vesicles (about a micron in diameter) that exclude, or retain, ions—in this case, radioactive sodium ($^{22}Na^+$). The addition of an analog of acetylcholine (arrow) triggers the opening of the ion channel in the receptor molecule and permits the entry of $^{22}Na^+$ ions. (From J.-L. Popot et al., 1981.)

identical to those observed at the neuromuscular junction in the intact animal. The receptor protein, with a molecular weight of 270,000, thus contains both the receptor site that recognizes acetylcholine *and* the ion channel that it controls.

Acetylcholine opens the channels by a mechanism similar to that already known for "allosteric" proteins.[19] These proteins are found in the cell at critical points in the biochemical pathways where, as Jacques Monod wrote in 1970, they "perform elementary cybernetic operations . . . playing the role of detectors and integrators of chemical information." They are subject to discrete, reversible transitions, all-or-none in nature, between distinct molecular states of activity or inactivity or, in the case of the receptor, open or closed channels (see Figure 30). The physiological reaction results from the stabilization by acetylcholine of the "open" state of the receptor channel. The postsynaptic wave recorded in the muscle fiber corresponds to the simultaneous opening of a large number of receptor channels. It represents the sum of discrete molecular events in the same way that the nerve impulse represents the opening of sodium channels and the resulting flow of ions in the axonal membrane.

The physiological response to acetylcholine, a critical stage in chemical synaptic transmission, is therefore fully determined by, and can be explained by, the properties of the receptor molecules. Like all cellular proteins, this molecule is made up of chains of amino acids (about 2,300), and its molecular properties are fully determined by the sequence of these amino acids and the spontaneous folding of this chain on itself. Each amino acid is composed of about ten to thirty atoms, which determine its chemical reactivity and its possibilities of bonding with other amino acids to construct a protein molecule. In our search for the mechanisms governing chemical communication between neurons, we have arrived at a molecular or even atomic explanation for this communication.

"PSYCHIC ATOMS" REEXAMINED

Similar methods led from EEG recordings to measures of the electrical activity in single neurons, from studies of the postsynaptic response to the opening of ion channels, itself based on changes in molecular configuration. At each stage, the level of organization is "reduced" to a more elementary level, from the population of cortical neurons to the cell or the synapse, from the nerve impulse or postsynaptic current to changes in single molecules. Each time, a seemingly single, continuous wave is "cut up" into discrete, elementary units, which are seen as together accounting for the wave, in the sense that the wave can be fully "reconstituted" from these discrete components. A global activity can thus be reduced to physico-chemical properties and can be described in the same terms as those employed by the physicist or the chemist. Admittedly, in practice, we do not use the complete chemical structure of the receptor molecule (which is known) to describe the postsynaptic response to acetylcholine, but it is certainly legitimate to do so.

In the final analysis, nervous activity, either evoked or spontaneous, and its propagation in the neuronal network, can be explained by *atomic* properties. Should we then reinvoke the notion of "psychic atoms" advanced by Democritus? The sodium and potassium ions that cross the channels of the axon or the postsynaptic membrane are the same in the neuron as in seawater. The molecules of the neurotransmitters and their receptors are composed of carbon, hydrogen, oxygen, and nitrogen, which in themselves are in no way specific to living organisms. The nervous system is made up of, and uses in its functional activity, the same "matter" as the inanimate world. Matter organizes itself into molecular building blocks, which contribute to communication between nerves in the same way that other molecules may regulate cell metabolism or chromosome replication. The proteins have a critical role to play, for enzyme pumps, ion channels, enzymes for neurotransmitter synthesis, and receptors are all proteins. Instead of readopting the term "psychic atoms," perhaps we should speak of "psychic molecules."

The most striking feature highlighted by present-day research on brain electricity and chemistry is that the mechanisms responsible for activity or, if one prefers, communication in the cerebral machine resemble those found in the peripheral nervous system and even in other organs. They are found equally in nervous systems of very simple organisms. What is true for the electric organ of the torpedo fish is also true for the brain of *Homo sapiens*. At the level of the elementary mechanisms of communication between nerves nothing distinguishes man from animals. No transmitter, no receptor or ion channel has yet been found to be specific to humans. We should therefore use the term "macromolecules responsible for communication between nerves" rather than psychic atoms. Gall secularized the anatomy of the human brain; let us secularize its activity.

4

Into Action

> Disturb the origin of the bundle and you change the
> animal.
> —Denis Diderot, *Le Rêve de d'Alembert*

We interact with our environment and communicate with our fellow human beings by moving our lips, eyes, and hands; by a set of motor activities that we call behavior. The study of these activities took shape in 1913, through a dynamic scientific movement initiated by John B. Watson—*behaviorism*. Concerned with eliminating the subjective from scientific observation, behaviorism restricted itself to considering the relationship between variations in the environment (the stimulus conditions) and the motor response that was provoked. It was enough to know the rules governing these relationships to explain behavior. Why should one be concerned about the contents of the "black box" inserted between the stimulus and the response? As one might have expected, the narrowness of this approach led the behavioral sciences, and with them many other human sciences, to an impasse.

The development of the neurosciences has brought another way of looking at behavior, in the tradition of Franz Joseph Gall and Paul Broca. The neuronal content of the black box can no longer be ignored. On the contrary, all forms of behavior mobilize distinct sets of nerve cells, and it is at their level that the final explanation of behavior must be sought. The comparison of the brain to a cybernetic machine or a computer may be useful in defining basic rules of behavior and specifying the relevant components of the machine. Because of the way it is constructed, the cybernetic machinery of the brain performs only a limited number of operations. Not everything is possible. As J. Z. Young commented in 1964, what it can do is determined by the extent to which it contains, or is itself, a "representation" of its environment. In other words, our interpretation of the external world and our responses to it depend on the internal organization of this "machine." The very simple nervous system of a mollusc does not analyze signals from the environment as profoundly as the nervous system of a monkey or a man, nor does it produce such a wide range of responses. The critical mechanisms lie in the central nervous system, where information is transmitted through a *code,* analyzed, and then processed. As a result of these computations, motor neurons go into action and command the contraction of muscles. Let us examine in detail the different forms of *internal coding* involved in going into action.

TO SING AND TO FLEE

Who does not remember a warm summer evening with the musky scent of flowers and the first songs of the cricket? Only the male crickets take part in this concert to attract and guide the receptive females to them. This call song is part of a very complex communication network that exists between partners of the opposite sex but also between the males. For the neurobiologist, the call song—because of its simple, repetitive character, stereotyped in nature but peculiar to a given species—constitutes a "schematic" behavior that is particularly useful for the analysis of "internal" mechanisms.[1]

The first pair of wings, or elytra, serve as a musical instrument. Their inner edge is the bow and the sawlike outer edge, the vibrating cord. When the male closes his wings, the bow rubs on the cord. The wing vibrates at about 5,000 cycles per second and produces the characteristic pure, flutelike sound. Powerful thoracic muscles control this closing movement. There is a close relationship between the contraction of these muscles and the production of a note. If one records the electrical impulses in the motor nerves with a microelectrode, they are also related: each impulse in the nerve corresponds to a note. One can hardly imagine a simpler form of coding (Figure 33).

The call song of the Polynesian cricket *(Teleogryllus oceanicus)* is composed of identical, repetitive phrases. They begin with a "chirp" of five notes, followed by ten "trills" of two notes. The rhythm of the impulses recorded in the motor nerves coincides exactly with that of the notes. The same rhythm is also found in the motor neurons of the thoracic nerve ganglia. It persists after section of sensory and motor

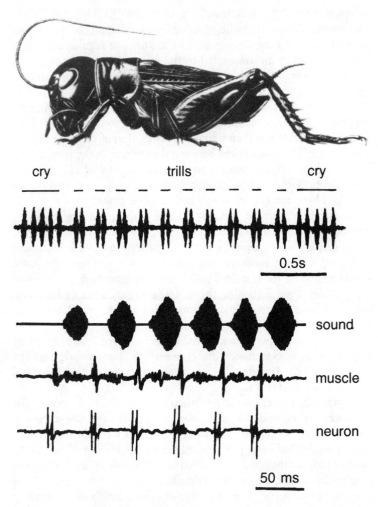

cry   trills   cry

0.5s

sound

muscle

neuron

50 ms

Figure 33. The song of the cricket is a simple example of a specific form of behavior directly related to the internal activity of a precise neuronal network. *Above* we see a drawing done by Finot in 1890 of the field cricket *(Gryllus campestris)*, now in the Museum of Natural History in Paris. *Below* is the recording, or sonogram, of the song of the oceanic cricket *(Teleogryllus oceanicus)*. The song consists of a phrase made up of a cry of five notes followed by ten trills of two notes. There is a perfect relationship between the nerve impulses propagated in the motor neurons, the contraction of the wing-closing muscles, and the emission of the sound resulting from the rubbing of the "bow" on the "string." (Redrawn from D. Bentley and R. Hoy, 1974.)

nerves, that is, after complete isolation of the ganglia. They must, then, contain spontaneous impulse generators (see Chapter 3), which produce all the characteristic features of the song in a regular, automatic fashion once they are connected to the necessary musculature.

The example of the cricket's song illustrates the two components of "going into action."

First, there are the *nerve connections*. Let us suppose that we connect the axons of the motor neurons in the wings to the muscles of the limbs. The cricket will then walk with the rhythm of the call song but will not sing. The connections between the neurons in the ganglia, and between these neurons and the muscles, define a set of cells, a stable network responsible for the production of the song—one that can be described by a mathematical structure I call a *graph*. [2]

Second, there are the *impulses*. Let us suppose that we artificially modify the membrane potential of one of the oscillatory neurons of the "song graph." The frequency of the impulses produced will change. The song will not have the same form. It will not have the same attractive pull on the female. The impulses spontaneously produced in this network thus determine the temporal organization of the notes according to a characteristic rhythm. They are responsible for the realization of the song.

In other words, two forms of coding are involved: the topology of the connections determines the geometry of the network, and the impulse pattern regulates the temporal expression of the associated behavior (see Figure 33).

It is possible to elaborate a mathematical model that permits the simulation or reproduction of a behavioral pattern and that therefore represents in a simplified, schematic manner its intrinsic mechanism. Such a model has been put forward for the swimming of the leech, where nearly all the neurons involved have been identified. [3] With the song of the cricket, we lack some details, but it is already clear that the conclusion will be the same, that this behavior is totally determined by a particular network—a graph of neurons—and the impulses within it. The cricket's song is particularly interesting because it is relatively independent of the outside world: once begun, it continues for hours.

Progressing from insects to vertebrates, we can undertake similar studies by taking recordings from identified neurons. Yet the number of cells is now so great that in order to implant an electrode in exactly the same neuron from one animal to another seems an impossible task.

Fortunately, there are situations in which such an experiment becomes possible, as in the case of a giant cell in the medulla of fish, the *Mauthner cell*, whose cell body and dendrites are half a millimeter wide.[4] What is more, a fish possesses only two of these cells, both of which are easily identifiable. They play a very precise role in the everyday life of the fish: they are involved in a reflex that permits it to escape from its predators. Let us observe a goldfish swimming calmly in an aquarium. If we tap on the aquarium or drop a golf ball in front of its glass wall, the fish suddenly turns around, its head moving to one side and its body changing orientation. It dodges, fleeing from the auditory or visual signal. The Mauthner cell has gone into action. It is not directly responsible for muscular contraction: hierarchically, it is above the motor neurons that command contraction; it coordinates and regulates their activity. If we make a recording of the Mauthner cell during the flight reflex, the generation of an impulse coincides exactly with the initiation of the reflex (Figure 34).

In contrast to the song neurons, the firing of the Mauthner cell is directly controlled by signals received from the outside world through the sense organs. Consider the case of the sound stimulus. The vibrations stimulate the inner ear, or lateral line, of the fish, which responds by bursts of impulses in the appropriate sensory nerve. These reach the Mauthner cell and cause a diminution of the membrane potential, as at the neuromuscular junction (see Chapter 3). If the threshold is reached, an impulse is triggered. The synapses of the auditory nerves on the Mauthner cell are *excitatory* (Figure 34D).

In other circumstances, for example, when the water is stirred up, there is no response: *inhibitory* synapses, also connected to the sense organs, block the effect of the excitatory synapses. Both types are chemical synapses,[5] but the effect of the neurotransmitter on the receptor is radically different in the two cases. Instead of decreasing the membrane potential, the neurotransmitter in inhibitory synapses has the opposite effect. It blocks the depolarizing effect of the excitatory transmitter and sometimes even shifts the potential in the other direction: it hyperpolarizes (Figure 34D).

What causes this difference? Is it due to the chemical nature of the neurotransmitter or to the ions that pass through the channels opened by the neurotransmitter (see Chapter 2)? The charge of the transported ion is determining. If the ion is positively charged and enters the cell, a depolarization occurs, causing excitation, as we have already seen in

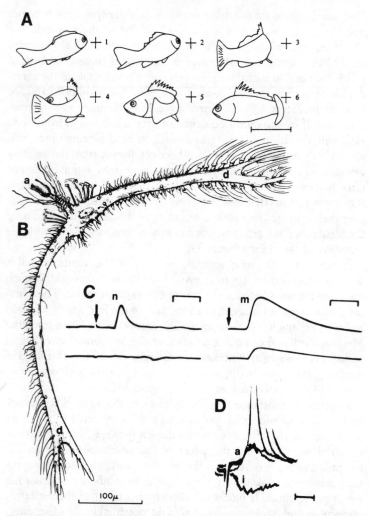

Figure 34. The firing of the Mauthner cell and the flight of the fish. *A:* These pictures show the fish every five milliseconds after a golf ball was dropped in front of the aquarium. (From R. C. Eaton et al., 1977.) *B:* This drawing of the Mauthner cell shows its giant dendrites (d) and the beginning of the axon (a). (From D. Bodian, 1952.) *C:* Here we see simultaneous recordings of the electrical impulse in the left Mauthner cell (n) and the contraction of the right trunk muscles (m). In the fish the left Mauthner cell innervates the right half of the body. (From G. Yasargil and J. Diamond, 1968.) *D:* The neuron membrane "calculates" the "activating" synaptic response (a) that triggers the nerve impulse (here cut off) and the inhibitory response (i) trying to prevent it. (From D. S. Faber and H. Korn, 1978.)

the case of the neuromuscular junction. If the ion is transported in the same direction but is negatively charged, like chloride, the electrical effect is obviously opposite in sign. There is inhibition. Cases also exist in which the receptor does not directly control the opening of a channel. It acts by the intervention of an "internal messenger," a sort of hormone that, rather than circulating from one cell to another, remains inside the neuron. The best known of these messengers is a cyclic molecule related to ATP, called cyclic AMP (cyclic adenosine monophosphate).

The neuron membrane behaves like an arithmetical calculator. It adds positive and negative signals. If the balance is on the plus side, the threshold is reached and it fires. If negative signals predominate, the neuron membrane remains silent. In the fish, the "decision" to take escape action thus results from an elementary calculation. The calculation is itself determined by receptors and ion channels in the neuron membrane and by the local ion environment. The flight of the fish in response to a stimulus from the outside world can thus be explained entirely by the connections of the graph to which the Mauthner cell belongs, by its impulse traffic, and, most important, by the molecular properties of its membranes that determine its "decision making."

TO DRINK AND TO SUFFER

The example of the Mauthner cell illustrates the antagonistic effects of excitatory and inhibitory synapses. Certain transmitters are specific for inhibition, others for excitation. Using the model of the Mauthner cell, and in a very schematic fashion, the excitatory transmitter becomes the escape substance in the fish. Indeed, it is tempting to give every behavioral pattern a particular chemical label. The temptation is even stronger when one considers the great variety of neurotransmitters found in the vertebrate brain, including that of man (see Chapter 3). Generally speaking, acetylcholine and glutamate are excitatory; others, like gamma-aminobutyric acid or glycine, are inhibitory. So why not a thirst substance and another for pain or for pleasure? In general terms, is there a chemical coding of behavior?

The case of thirst can serve as an example.[6] We drink when we have lost water—for instance, after physical effort. This water loss causes a reduction in the blood volume and a change in its salt concentration.

These variations in physico-chemical properties provoke a desire to drink, through the intermediary of the nervous system. Only a few neurons are involved. They are localized in a precise region of the brain —the hypothalamus, situated, as its name suggests, below the thalamus (see Figure 13). If this group of neurons is stimulated electrically in a rat, it begins to drink continuously. If the hypothalamus is removed, the rat will no longer drink. Just as the Mauthner cell stimulates the flight behavior of the fish, these hypothalamic neurons regulate drinking behavior in the rat, and also in man. Recording their activity has helped to identify the substance that stimulates them—a hypothetical "thirst transmitter." It is one of the numerous peptides that serve as hormones in some circumstances and as neurotransmitters in others. Called *angiotensin II,* it consists of a chain of eight amino acids. When it is injected into the blood or applied directly to the specialized neurons of the hypothalamus, bursts of impulses are released. Oscillating neurons, similar to those of the cricket or sea slug (see Figure 27), become active. Angiotensin II starts the "impulse clocks" of the hypothalamus and when its concentration passes a threshold, the animal will soon begin to drink.

Strictly speaking, angiotensin is not a neurotransmitter because it is not released by nerve terminals. Nevertheless, it informs the nervous system of the crisis provoked by the lack of water. As is well known, the kidney eliminates water in the urine, but it also has an informational role to play. What if the blood volume decreases following a loss of water? The kidney reacts by producing an enzyme that indirectly stimulates the release of angiotensin II in the blood. Its concentration in the circulation rises and becomes sufficient to excite the neurons in the thirst center. Angiotensin, therefore, acts as a chemical mediator for drinking. (It is not the only mechanism, by the way, that regulates drinking. An important role is also played by receptors sensitive to blood pressure in the great veins and the aorta.)

Pain is another example of how chemistry sheds light on the internal mechanism—in this case not of an action, but of a sensation. Pain can be relieved with an extract of the opium poppy and particularly with one of its constituents, morphine. The Sumerians in 4000 B.C. already knew of the effects of opium.

Like all sensations, pain arises from the stimulation of sensory terminals. They are found throughout most organs, but particularly in the skin and the viscera. These terminals are quite special: they consist of the end branches of dendrites, naked and highly forked, and they respond to various physical signals such as heat, cold, and pressure. But they also respond to certain internal chemical substances produced by the organism following irritation or a lesion. One of them, called *prostaglandin E2*, became famous because aspirin, one of the most widely used of all medicinal substances, blocks its synthesis and in this way attenuates certain painful sensations. These polyvalent nerve terminals "sound the alarm" by producing bursts of impulses that travel along the nerves to cell bodies situated in dorsal root ganglia connected to the spinal cord. In the spinal cord these "pain neurons" form synapses with relay neurons, which send their axons upward toward the brainstem and the rest of the brain.

The transmitter released in the spinal cord by these pain neurons is known. As in the case of thirst, it is a peptide, eleven amino acids long —*substance P*, one of the first peptides isolated from nerve tissue.[7] Substance P is present in the pain nerves, which extend from their peripheral sensory endings to the spinal cord.[8] Electrical stimulation of these nerves brings about its release. When it is applied locally to relay neurons in the spinal cord, it produces impulses that travel to the brain. Substance P may then well serve as the pain transmitter in the spinal cord.

So where does morphine act? On the periphery like aspirin or in the spinal cord at the substance P synapses? The isolation of its receptor has provided an answer to this question. As with the acetylcholine receptor (see Chapter 3), success came with the use of tracers—in this case, not snake venom, but a radioactive derivative of morphine, which exists in two mirror-symmetrical molecular forms (Figure 35).[9] Al-

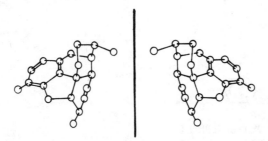

Figure 35. Formulas of levorphanol (on the *left*) and dextrorphan (on the *right*). The one is the mirror image of the other. Of these two optical isomers, only levorphanol binds to morphine receptors and stops pain.

105

though they are chemically composed of the same atoms, only the "levo" form (levorphanol) stops pain because it is a suitable key, fitting the physiological receptor lock, as opposed to the "dextro" form, which binds indiscriminately. The correct receptor is present in nerve tissue where we would expect it: in the spinal cord and, of course, the brain.

What is the use of this receptor? Morphine is prepared from a poppy, which, as far as we know, does not possess a nervous system and cannot suffer pain. Does morphine take the place of a natural substance present in the nervous system, a sort of "endogenous morphine"? Indeed, such substances have been isolated. Once again, they are peptides: very small ones, consisting of five amino acids, called *enkephalins*, [10] or longer ones, the *endorphins* (abbreviated from "endogenous morphine"). Enkephalins or endorphins bind with high affinity to the same receptor that recognizes the levo derivative of morphine. This may seem surprising because morphine belongs to a group of chemicals, the alkaloids, that differ radically from peptides. Yet if we look closer —using, for example, a physical method that reveals the shape of molecules—remarkable structural analogies appear (Figure 36). Their geometrical configurations in space are so similar that the enkephalin key and the morphine key fit and turn in the same receptor lock. [11]

How does the opening of the lock stop pain? The current hypothesis is that both endogenous and exogenous morphine block the pain message at the substance P synapses in the spinal cord. We know that a synapse can be blocked in several different ways: at the nerve terminal by suppressing the release of a transmitter or, on the other side of the

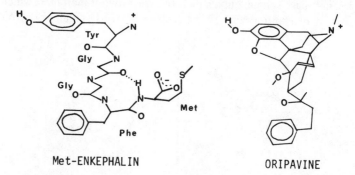

Met-ENKEPHALIN   ORIPAVINE

Figure 36. The structural analogy between an "endogenous morphine" synthesized by certain categories of neurons (met-enkephalin) and an opiate (oripavine). (From B. P. Roques et al., 1976.)

synaptic cleft, by inhibiting the receptor. In 1977 Thomas Jessel and Leslie Iversen showed that morphine uses the former mechanism; in effect, the opiates inhibit the release of substance P by the pain nerves. In the spinal cord the endogenous morphines, the enkephalins, play this role. A dual chemical "mediation" occurs: pain transmission by substance P, pain relief by enkephalins.[12]

Angiotensin II informs the hypothalamus about water loss in the organism and controls drinking. It sends signals from the *milieu intérieur* to the nervous system. Substance P transmits pain messages received from the skin or other organs toward the central nervous system, and the enkephalins control this transmission. Both examples demonstrate the intervention of chemical messengers specific to a particular activity or sensation. The hypothesis of a chemical coding is confirmed, but this in no way eliminates the two forms of coding already mentioned: one based on the geometry of connections, the other on the temporal succession of nerve impulses. Chemical coding complements the others. First, it permits a type of additional signaling, one that involves not the propagation of impulses along cables, but the diffusion of chemical signals over long distances using, for instance, the bloodstream. Above all, it creates a diversity in connections that otherwise have a similar geometry. Indeed, only a small fraction of sensory fibers' that enter the spinal cord, those specialized for pain, utilize substance P as a neurotransmitter. The others are engaged in the perception of heat and cold or tactile sensation and use different transmitters. Chemical labeling creates diversity. It allows finer and more precise relations between neurons and therefore between a particular behavior or sensation and a specific network of nerve cells.

TO ENJOY AND TO BE ANGRY

The capacity for enjoyment, like that for suffering, is inscribed in our neurons and synapses. Once again the hypothalamus plays an important role. Removing a particular area of the hypothalamus, as we have seen, stops drinking in a rat. The same operation in other parts of this essential brain center upsets the heartbeat or the body temperature; in yet other parts, it changes eating habits or copulation. As might be expected, electrical stimulation of the same areas has the opposite effect. On this hypothalamic map, each distinct "geographical" area is colored differently by its chemical signals. Most frequently these signals are peptides: drinking involves angiotensin II; eating, cholecystokinin; lovemaking, the hormone LHRH.

These small groups of neurons with their specific chemical labels regulate a variety of functions and behaviors that are so critical that we often call them "vital." Humans, like rats, devote a large part of their time, when they are not asleep, to drinking, eating, and copulating. A single cell, the Mauthner cell, allows the fish to escape from its predators. In man several thousands of neurons, in a precise part of the hypothalamus, make final decisions about the balance of energy and the survival of the species. The most fundamental behavioral patterns in our lives depend on no more than 1 percent of the total volume of the brain, and the triple coding—electrical, chemical, and by nerve connections—is involved in their determination.

But these behavioral patterns do not appear anytime or anyhow. The sensations of thirst or hunger or sexual desire do not immediately lead to drinking, eating, or copulating. Instead, a state of motivation is created that incites one to drink, eat, or make love; it disappears after these desires have been fulfilled. In 1855 Alexander Bain wrote in *The Senses and the Intellect* that "every state of pleasure replies to an increase, every state of pain to a decrease of part of or all the vital functions." Of course, Bain did not have our knowledge of the hypothalamus. In today's context, his remark takes on a new significance. Thirst corresponds to a desire to drink, which can become "painful," and drinking calms this thirst. Frustrated sexual desire is agonizing; its harmonious satisfaction appeases the anguish. Could "pleasure" regulate these vital behavioral patterns? Might there be in the hypothalamus a "pleasure center," which would concretize this link? How could it be identified?

Laboratory animals cannot use words to answer the experimenter's questions about sensations of pleasure or displeasure that they may experience. In 1954, in a very ingenious way, James Olds and Peter Milner succeeded in obtaining a reply from a laboratory rat. Suppose that we implant a stimulating electrode in a hypothetical pleasure center. An electrical current discharged from the electrode will create a sensation of pleasure. Let us now give the rat a device for stimulation so that by pressing a pedal it can induce a current. While exploring its cage, the rat may accidentally tread on the pedal. If the electrode is in the right place, the rat will enjoy this sensation and repeat the operation. It will stimulate itself.

Several self-stimulation points have been identified in the rat. They are found particularly in the hypothalamus, close to the various vital centers that play a key role in drinking, eating, and copulating. But the rat, even after satisfying its appetite for sexual activity, continues to self-stimulate. The self-stimulation points are therefore distinct from the vital centers. Other points of self-stimulation have been identified outside the hypothalamus, for example in the brainstem. Careful analysis of their geography reveals a remarkable coincidence. The self-stimulation points correspond to areas where cell bodies and processes contain a specific neurotransmitter —*dopamine.* Another remarkable finding: blocking the dopamine receptors by an antagonist such as pimozide or haloperidol stops the self-stimulation. Further, certain drugs that give humans a subjective sensation of pleasure or euphoria, such as cocaine or amphetamines, seem to act in a similar way to dopamine. In the hypothalamus and the brainstem, dopamine synapses can thus be regarded as "pleasure" or "hedonic" synapses, where "the cold information regarding the physical dimensions of a stimulus is translated into the warm experience of pleasure."[13]

The functional significance of these pleasure synapses is still not completely understood. Situated at the crossroads between sensory pathways and the vital centers of the hypothalamus, they regulate the expression of "vital" behaviors, sometimes by inhibiting them, sometimes by deciding to carry them out. Thus they participate in the development of motivational states that enable us to "go into action."

Do emotions, or what we care to call emotions, belong to these motivational states? Donald O. Hebb, in 1949, distinguished among the emotions "those in which the tendency is to maintain or increase the original stimulating conditions (pleasurable or integrating emotions)" and "those in which the tendency is to abolish or decrease the stimulus (rage, fear, disgust)." This distinction is based on the postulate of a close relationship between emotion and pleasure. Does the hypothalamus intervene once again? In the 1930s Walter Hess noted that the stimulation of discrete regions of the hypothalamus elicited not pleasure but "anger" in the cat, causing it to arch its back, make its fur stand on end, raise its tail in the air, and spit at and attack anything that moved. As soon as the stimulation stopped, the cat's rage stopped. Obviously, this attack of "rage" was very artificial. It represented only an external and partial manifestation of an affective state that can take on very diverse forms, particularly in man. Nevertheless, the hypothalamus once again plays a decisive role, as do other higher brain centers.

James Papez brought them to light in 1937 when examining patients suffering from rabies. They presented major emotional disturbances with anguish, rage, and terror, which he attributed to the lesions provoked by the spread of the virus. The virus attacks principally the hippocampus. This "old" cortex, as we saw in Chapter 2, corresponds to the cerebral hemispheres of reptiles and primitive mammals, which have moved to the interior with the expansion of the neocortex (see Figure 14). It is part of a group of structures called the "limbic lobe" by Broca, structures that are closely connected to the hypothalamus and contain the amygdaloid body and the septum. Continuing the tradition of Gall, or Fritsch and Hitzig, Papez proposed that the group of neurons that made up the anatomical substrate of the emotions was localized in this limbic system (Figure 37).

Almost at the same time, in 1939, Heinrich Klüver and Paul Bucy performed a striking experiment with a monkey. Removing a large part of the limbic system, as well as part of the nonlimbic cortex, provoked startling changes in behavior. The animal, normally wild and frightened, became placid and calm; it was tame. At the same time it developed curious oral behavior. It put anything it found in its mouth, even food it ordinarily did not like. It also showed exaggerated sexual activity, masturbating incessantly and copulating indiscriminately, even with individuals of the same sex or those of different species. Similar symptoms can be observed in humans, usually associated with a lesion of the amygdala, which, as we have said, is part of the limbic system.

Clearly, the genesis and expression of emotions do not depend on such simple mechanisms as do vital behaviors. The hypothalamus participates, but in conjunction with higher nervous centers like the limbic system. One cannot speak of an emotion center. A whole constellation of groups of neurons, a set of "integration foci," contributes. But each of these neuron groups is connected with the others in a specific way, with a precision comparable to that of the song neurons of the cricket

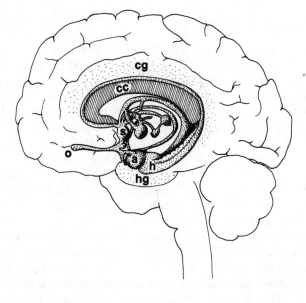

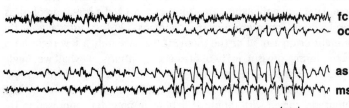

Figure 37. The limbic system. Inherited from primitive mammals, this complex ensemble of nuclei and nerve pathways is closely connected to the hypothalamus, the brainstem, and obviously the neocortex. It is involved in the genesis of emotions and related behavior. This explains the importance given to it by such authors as Paul MacLean and Arthur Koestler. *Above,* one sees the septum (s), amygdala (a), hippocampus (h), cingulate gyrus (cg), and hippocampal gyrus (hg). *Below* are EEG recordings from various parts of the brain during orgasm—the fronto-temporal cortex (fc), occipital cortex (oc), left anterior septal area (as), and right median septal area (ms). Slow, high-amplitude waves similar to those recorded during epilepsy appear, principally in the septum. Bar length: 1 second. (From R. G. Heath, 1972.)

or the Mauthner cell of the fish. To take up the comment of Denis Diderot in 1769, the connections of this graph form "a sort of skein of wool where the slightest thread cannot be broken, ruptured, displaced, or missing without serious consequences for the whole."

TO REACH ORGASM

Orgasm is for man, and perhaps even more for woman, the supreme ecstasy. From Saint Theresa of Avila to Simone de Beauvoir, whole libraries have been written about the quest for this intense wave of pleasure and emotion. Nevertheless, we lack precise descriptions of this "ineffable" state and our knowledge of its mechanisms is sketchy. The physiological manifestations such as local muscular contractions, changes in cardiac rhythm and blood flow, tell us little about the sensation of orgasm. They do, however, demonstrate that in woman the sensation precedes the purely physiological response by two to four seconds. In man, orgasm can take place even without ejaculation. Orgasm is then, above all, a cerebral experience and it is at the level of the brain that we must look for it.[14]

The few data available on its material nature stem from electrophysiological recordings and stimulation performed, as in many studies related to brain function, on subjects with serious neurological problems that only surgery can relieve. In sixty patients studied by Robert Heath in 1972, electrical stimulation of specific regions of the brainstem, lateral hypothalamus, and septum provoked a sensation of pleasure. Hedonic synapses do exist in humans! Do they intervene at the moment of orgasm? For the moment we have only a few recordings, taken during orgasm in two subjects. Contrary to what we might expect, they show no major change in electrical activity of the cerebral cortex. In one of the subjects, a man, spikes and slow waves of high amplitude, mixed with rapid oscillations in potential, appeared in the limbic system, in the septum, at the moment that he experienced orgasm. In form, these waves resembled those found during an epileptic seizure. They corresponded to the synchronous activity of a large population of neurons (see Chapter 3), and each slow wave was the result of thousands, if not millions, of elementary electrical impulses. Thus a mini-epileptic attack develops temporarily and locally in the septum. In the other subject, a woman, the same rhythmic phenomenon was recorded in the septum, but it spread to the amygdala and thalamic nuclei. But this discharge never invaded the neocortex. It remained limited to the limbic system and adjacent areas.

Our understanding of the chemistry of orgasm has not yet advanced as spectacularly as that of pain. Nevertheless, an important observation deserves to be reported. In 1972 Heath noted that the injection of acetylcholine in the septum of a female subject provoked an intense sensation of sexual pleasure, culminating in repeated orgasm. Acetylcholine induces orgasm in the septum. Could dopamine, and the pleasure synapses that contain it, be involved? Perhaps, but we have no data. The few additional observations available do not deal with the production of orgasm or its sensations, but with its consequences.

The Hottentots knew that stretching the vagina of a cow brought about the flow of milk. Oxytocin, a hormone released into the blood by the pituitary gland, acts on the mammary gland; once again, the hypothalamus controls this reflex.[15] Curiously, in woman, and also in man, a similar phenomenon takes place during the sexual act. Orgasm brings about a massive discharge of oxytocin. Why? We do not know, but at the same time other peptides are released into the blood and their importance is clearer.

In 1563 the Portuguese physician Garcia d'Orta noted that the use of opium diminished sexual activity and could even cause impotence. The administration of synthetic opiates (such as methadone) or natural peptides diminishes the number of copulations and the percentage of successful mountings in the male hamster. Drugs that block the effects of the opiates, such as naloxone and naltrexone, have the opposite effect. For instance, they provoke "irrelevant" erections in man as well as in the monkey. In addition, after orgasm the blood level of endorphin-type peptides increases markedly—in the hamster by at least four times after five ejaculations.[16] A similar release in the central nervous system probably accounts for the abolition of pain and the contented feeling that follows orgasm and also, quite conceivably, for the usually agreeable changes in one's mood that accompany it.

The release of endogenous morphines may also explain the diminishing of sexual appetite that usually follows orgasm. Could it be that the endorphins set up a feedback with the pleasure synapses of the hypothalamus or the brainstem? The hypothesis is seductive! We know that the hormone LHRH acts on a hypothalamic nucleus to induce copulation in both the male and the female. It has recently been discovered that the opiates block the release of LHRH and therefore inhibit copulation. The endogenous opiates then may serve as regulators of libido. A lack of opiates in the hypothalamus would engender a sensation of frustration and thus an increase in libido. On the other hand, their release at orgasm would temporarily extinguish sexual desire. Could the level of free endogenous opiates be a measure of what Sigmund Freud called, rather clumsily, "psychic energy"?

The example of orgasm was chosen for several reasons. Certainly this experience occupies an important place in the everyday life of human beings. But that is not our concern. In contrast to the other forms of behavior discussed so far, orgasm is not primarily manifested by an action clearly visible to the outside world; it is essentially a subjective sensation, experienced internally. We have no data to allow a precise, cell-by-cell and synapse-by-synapse description of the diverse electrical impulses and synaptic potentials responsible for it. Recordings from the septum and data on the effects of acetylcholine there nevertheless allow us to conclude that internal experiences like orgasm are similar in nature to behavioral patterns visible to the outside world. The little we do know of the electrical and chemical processes involved supports this conclusion.

Once again, we must not underestimate the importance of the diversity of the neurons involved, even if they constitute only a tiny fraction of all the neurons in the brain. The multiplicity of the chemical mediators strikingly illustrates this point. Acetylcholine, endogenous morphine, and dopamine distinguish some of these neuron groups. The chemical makeup of the cells that participate in a sensation as well defined as that of orgasm is closer to a canvas by Georges Seurat than a composition by Piet Mondrian.

A few years ago the discovery of chemical transmitters led us to believe for a moment that it would be possible to assign a specific chemical label to all forms of behavior or sensation. The example of the chemistry of orgasm shows that things are not so simple. One cannot say that there is one transmitter for singing, pain, or depression. One can simply state that the graph of neurons used in a particular behavior or sensation contains one or several critical links that use a specific neurotransmitter. A chemical "cut" in this link will certainly interfere with the expression of the behavior. But if the same transmitter exists in neurons of another network, there is a good chance that the chemical scalpel will also attack there. Morphine blocks pain messages from the spinal cord but causes impotence through its action on the hypo-thalamus. Hughlings Jackson's and Head's criticisms of a too narrow view of a "center" also apply to chemical coding. There is no transmitter for anger or pleasure, any more than there is an isolated center for them. So "organization is sufficient for everything? Yes, once again," as La Mettrie wrote—on the condition, of course, that one includes chemistry.

TO ANALYZE

As we saw in Chapter 2, the human brain is characterized by the privileged development of the neocortex. In the course of mammalian evolution, its area and the number of its neurons and synapses increased. On the other hand, lower structures—in particular the limbic system, the hypothalamus, and the brainstem—changed little. A cat deprived of its cerebral cortex at birth can walk, climb, feed itself, and even attack moving objects. In the same way, a baby born with no cortex wakes and sleeps regularly, feeds, sucks its thumb, sits up, yawns, stretches, and cries. It can follow a visual stimulus with its eyes and react to a sound. It pushes away unpleasant objects and is capable of voluntary movements. Thus, automatic behavior and some voluntary actions depend more on structures surrounded by the neocortex than on the cortex itself.

To hope to describe the functions of the cortex in terms similar to those used for the cricket's song or the rat's drinking behavior seems overly optimistic. However, a concrete way of going about it is to follow to the letter J. Z. Young's proposition that the organism is a "representation" of its environment. If this proposition applies to the neocortex, one should be able to discover these anatomical representations by exploring its surface; "reading these signs," if they exist, should help us define its role.

Since the end of the nineteenth century, through David Ferrier and Korbinian Brodmann, and more recently through David Hubel and Torsten Wiesel, we know that the sense organs project to distinct cortical areas after relay in the thalamus (see Figure 6). These areas are situated in the occipital lobe for vision, the temporal lobe for hearing, and the parietal lobe for touch. Each area thus "represents" a physical parameter to which the sense organ is sensitive. A first level of representation of the world in the cortex thus consists of territories distributed like continents, each corresponding to a major category of physical signal, reaching the organism through impulses in the sensory nerves.

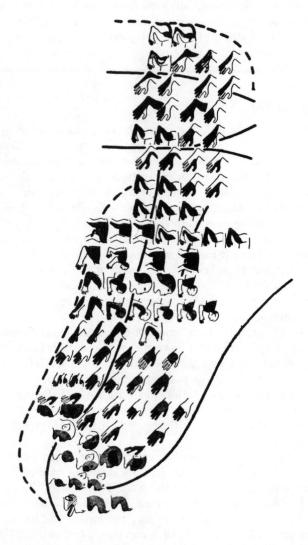

Figure 38. Map of the area involving touch in the macaque. Each little figure indicates a recording point on the surface of the cortex; the body part represented shows where the stimulation caused a response. Thus tactile stimulation of the tail causes a response in the dorsal region (at the top of the map); stimulation of the tongue, a response in the ventral region (at the bottom). (From C. N. Woolsey, 1958.)

Careful mapping of these cortical territories has revealed surprising details. Take the case of touch. The sensory receptors involved are found over the entire body surface and some are situated in deeper tissues. If we stimulate a monkey's thumb, for example, and try to record an evoked electrical response (see Chapter 3) in the cortical territory devoted to touch (areas 1, 2, and 3 of the parietal lobe), the first recordings are likely to be disappointing. When the electrode is randomly placed in this area, the chances are that no evoked response will be seen, however intense the stimulation. Let us, then, move the electrode systematically from one point to another over the cortical territory. Suddenly, an electrical potential appears. A few millimeters further on, the wave disappears. At this new position there is no longer a response from the thumb but from the index finger. Little by little, the map of a hand can be made out. If we pursue our exploration, the whole half of the body opposite the hemisphere being explored will appear. The figurine we are tracing on the surface of the cortex beings to look like a monkey (Figures 38 and 39). Working from the lower part of the hemisphere toward the top, we can recognize, in succession, the tongue, the head, the arm and the hand, the trunk, the leg and foot, and the tail.[17] Obviously, the resemblance is not perfect. First of all, the body occupies three dimensions but the figurine only two. The loss of one dimension distorts the projection. There are also discontinuities between contiguous regions of the body. The face, for example, is separate from the rest of the head. A striking feature is that the relative areas occupied by different body regions seem out of proportion. The hand, for instance, appears gigantic; its surface is almost equal to that of the rest of the body. If we move from the monkey to the rat or mouse, the map is no longer dominated by the hand, but by the snout and particularly the whiskers (see Figures 39A and 57). In man similar maps were drawn in 1950 by Wilder Penfield and Theodore Rasmussen from a large number of observations of patients suffering from epilepsy or discrete cortical lesions. The figurine, or sensory *homunculus,* possesses enormous lips, an immense hand, much smaller feet, and a ridiculously small trunk and sex organs. As in the monkey and the rat, the cortex occupied by the projection of different parts of the human body has little relation to the actual body surface area, but represents the importance of the organs to the sensory life of the individual: the whiskers in the rat, the hand in the monkey, the hand and the mouth in man. It is, in fact, directly proportional to the density of sensory endpoints on the body surface. It represents an image of the points of contact of the individual with the outside world (see Figures 38 and 39).

The ear and the retina also project on the cortex, but in a way that does not at all resemble the homunculus. In the case of touch receptors, the entire body serves in a way as a sense organ. With vision, the situation is different. One does not see with one's hands or one's lips.

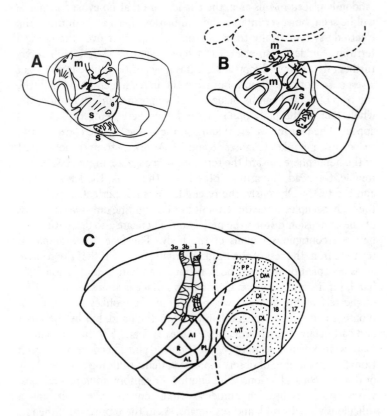

Figure 39. At the *top*, we see representations of the body in the motor (m) and somatosensory (s) areas of the cortex of the rat *(A)* and rabbit *(B)*. In the rat the area occupied by the snout, particularly the whiskers, is large, reflecting the importance in its life of sensation from this area. (From C. Woolsey, 1958.) *Below (C)*, we find that in the owl monkey *(Aotus)*, the number of sensory representations increases markedly. In the occipital region (dotted), the areas marked 17, 18, DL, DI, DM, PP, and MT each correspond to a map of the retina. (From J. H. Kaas et al., 1979.)

The cortical map reflects the distribution of the retinal neurons that line the fundus of the eye and receive the inverted image of the outside world as transmitted by the lens. The representation of the retina on the primary visual area (area 17) is nevertheless very distorted. It is divided into two so that the relationships between neighboring points are preserved only for each half-retina. The cortical map becomes difficult to read, but the relative simplicity of the division and the almost mathematical regularity of the projection of the retina on the cortex allow us to find our way.

Pursuing similar studies on different mammalian species, Jon Kaas and C. S. Merzenich and their collaborators drew more and more precise maps; they also made some fascinating observations.[18] In the territory concerned with the sense of touch in the monkey, they found that instead of a single figurine there were several, lined up side by side. Each figurine played a distinct role. One responded to certain skin receptors, a second responded to the skin but not to the same receptors, a third received the projection of sensory receptors in muscles, and a fourth responded to deep receptors of another sort. A similar situation is found in the visual system. In the monkey one can find up to *eight* representations of the retina, all placed closely together in the neighborhood of the primary area (area 17) and occupying the *association* areas of the cortex. Here again, it is not exactly the same aspects of the visual world that are analyzed in each representation. Certain projection areas are more specialized in recognizing orientation; others are concerned with direction; still others, with the identification of color (see Figure 39).

Is the same multiplicity of cortical representations found in all mammalian species? At least eight visual areas exist in the macaque, whereas in the hedgehog, a primitive insectivore, only two representations of the retina are known. In the same way the ear projects to two distinct areas in the squirrel but to three in the tree shrew (a primitive primate), four in the owl monkey, and six in the rhesus monkey. The number of representations increases as the neocortex increases its surface area. They have not yet been counted in man, but one would expect them to be even more numerous than in the monkey. The increase in number of these representations may coincide with the extraction of more and more varied and complex features from the environment. It is the basis, to recall Pavlov's remarks, of a more and more detailed *analysis* of the environment.

TO SPEAK AND TO DO

The cortex is not only an analyzer; it also plays an essential role in motor activity. Nevertheless, the surface devoted to motor command in the strict sense (mainly area 4) seems at first sight small compared with that responsible for analysis. It has approximately the same area as that involved in bodily sensation, but this is enough for it to control the contraction and relaxation of the muscles, which in the last analysis are responsible for all our interaction with the environment. In 1870 Gustav Fritsch and Edward Hitzig noted that electrical stimulation of this area caused movements, and that different limbs or parts of the body were involved depending on the location of the stimulation. Recent studies using local "microstimulation" of discrete parts of the surface of the motor area have confirmed Fritsch and Hitzig's initial observations. What is more, a figurine can be constructed that closely resembles those for the sensory areas 1, 2, and 3, although there are some significant differences. Again, in humans the area occupied by the representation of the muscles of the hand, as well as the mouth and larynx, is disproportionately large. Thus, alongside the sensory homunculus, lies an equally surprising motor homunculus. The cerebral cortex is covered with curious hieroglyphs, like those of a Mayan codex.

Does social communication involve a similar system of representation? Communication is in large part based on language, and a considerable part of the cortical surface is indeed devoted to language. The history of the discovery of these centers resembles the more general history of cerebral localization described in Chapter 1. Studies subsequent to those of Paul Broca, particularly recent studies with high-resolution X-ray techniques such as computer-assisted tomography, or CAT scans (Figure 40), confirm the presence of speech centers confined to one hemisphere, in more than 90 percent of cases the left hemisphere. "We speak with the left hemisphere," wrote Broca in 1861. A lesion that he described in area 44 of the frontal lobe causes characteristic speech disturbances, as we saw in Chapter 1. These patients speak slowly, distort words, and use mainly nouns and verbs in the infinitive. Their grammar is elementary. They have similar difficulties with writing, although they can sing quite well. So Broca's area cannot be simply a motor area for the muscles of the mouth and larynx.

A few years after Broca, Carl Wernicke showed that the destruction of area 22 in the left temporal lobe (near the auditory area) causes troubles of a different nature. These patients speak easily, stringing their words into perfectly structured sentences, but they speak nonsense. They cannot put words together to make meaningful sentences, and they also have trouble with writing. It is not simply an auditory deficit. Also in the left hemisphere, a lesion of a discrete area in the temporal lobe, the angular gyrus (area 39), creates difficulties in reading and writing without much disturbance of spoken language. This list is not complete, for the number of cortical areas known to be involved in the production and comprehension of language grows every day. This patchwork includes areas formerly defined as association areas. A particularly striking aspect of the human cerebral cortex is the large part of its surface devoted to social communication (see Figure 6).

More and more detailed exploration of the cerebral cortex is leading to the discovery of new features in the *terra incognita* of the association areas. Gall's first maps, divided into twenty-seven areas, seem very

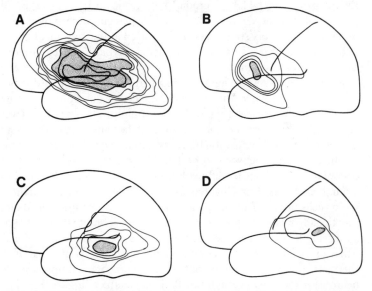

Figure 40. Cerebral-cortex lesions that cause language disturbances in humans as indicated by PET scanning. The contours define the sites of the lesions—in *A*, global aphasia; in *B*, Broca's aphasia; in *C*, Wernicke's aphasia, in *D*, so-called conduction aphasia. (From L. Vignolo, 1979.)

simple today. The geographical subdivision of the cortex continues,[19] and we are still coming across new towns!

The ultimate limit of this functional subdivision is the nerve cell itself. The cell-by-cell exploration of the cortex has already revealed remarkable functional specialization. In the visual cortex (see Chapter 2), for example, certain cells respond to a single eye, others to both eyes. Still other cells respond to bars of light oriented in a particular way or to spots moving in a specific direction. Moreover, in a given sensory homunculus, two neurons that respond in the same way to the same sensory signal still differ in that they are not in exactly the same position on the map and therefore are related to topographically distinct sensory cells on the surface of the body or in the retina. If one considers that there are about fifteen million neurons per square centimeter of cortical surface and that in man a single homunculus can have an area of several square centimeters, the set of singularities defined in Chapter 2 becomes enormous.

In the association cortex, things become even more complicated. The distinction between motor and sensory areas is lost. In area 5 of the monkey's parietal lobe, Vernon Mountcastle, in 1975, classified 90 percent of cells as sensory. The other 10 percent were motor cells, insensitive to sensory stimulation and involved in the movement of the arm toward a target. In area 7, considered a typical association area, certain neurons became active when the monkey fixated its gaze and others when it followed a light spot in a particular direction. Still other cells were active when the eye made rapid, low-amplitude scanning movements, or *saccades* (Figure 41). The number of cells sampled was very small, but as exploration continues it becomes clear that every neuron has its own singularity. In reality, there is very little redundancy.

The correlation between cortical cellular activity and the analytical operations carried out by different sensory areas is well established in a number of cases (see Chapters 2 and 3). This is also true for those motor cells of area 7 of the parietal lobe that, as just mentioned, are functionally related to precise eye movements. The situation is not at all as simple as in the case of the cricket's song or the fish's flight behavior. A *burst* of impulses replaces the single electrical signal. Furthermore, the superimposition of the recordings obtained from a single neuron for repeated eye movements is not perfect (Figure 41). The increase in frequency of the impulses, however, remains on the average the same from one saccade to another.

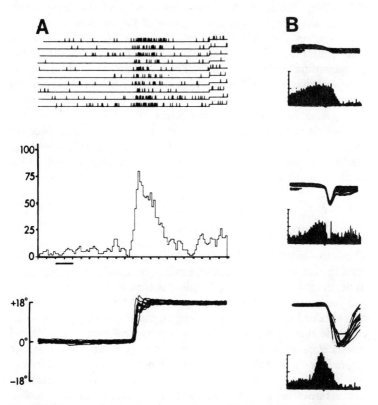

Figure 41. These recordings from a macaque show the activity of neurons in the cerebral cortex related to the control of eye movements (in area 7 of the association cortex, *left* figure) and hand movements (motor area 4, *right* figure). In *A*, activity in the same neuron was recorded when a rapid eye movement, or saccade, was triggered by a light signal. In the *top* example, each vertical tick corresponds to an impulse, and each horizontal line represents a recording made during a saccade. There is not an exact correspondence between successive recordings. The total number of impulses recorded per second is expressed as a function of time in the *middle* figure (bar length: 0.2 seconds). Activity in the neuron precedes the eye movement and continues during it. The movement is represented in the *bottom* figure by a continuous line. (From V. B. Mountcastle, 1975.)

In *B*, the activity of a neuron in motor area 4 was recorded during a movement of the hand (continuous line). The number of impulses per second is expressed as a function of time (the total length of the recordings is 1 second) as in the middle figure of A. The *top* diagram represents a fine rotation of the wrist; the *middle* one, the same movement disturbed by a forced rotation of the wrist; and the *bottom* one, a high-amplitude ballistic movement. In general, neuronal activity *precedes* the movement and continues during it. Note the decrease in activity in the middle of the disturbed movement. (From E. V. Evarts, 1981.)

Details on the connections among neurons in association areas are still lacking. We know more about the neurons of the motor cortex (area 4) that control the fine movements of the hand in the monkey. The axons of these giant pyramidal cells, the Betz cells, leave the cortex, enter the spinal cord, and contact the motor neurons that form synapses directly on the muscle. Their "hierarchical" position is in some ways like that of the Mauthner cell of the fish. In 1981 Edward Evarts recorded the activity of these neurons in the monkey when the animal made fine hand movements. Remarkably, these cells gave bursts of impulses not only during the movement but *preceding* it. For the moment we know little about the intrinsic neurotransmitters of the cerebral cortex, but a chemical coding similar to that seen in the hypothalamus and the spinal cord probably plays a critical role.

FROM STIMULUS TO RESPONSE

The behaviorists' search for phenomenological rules relating a stimulus from the outside world to a behavioral response has given way to more in-depth study, involving the decoding of electrical or chemical signals and the unraveling of neuronal networks and their connections. The data obtained so far, although fragmentary, are sufficient for us to safely conclude that all behavior, all sensation, is explicable by an *internal mobilization* of a topologically defined set of nerve cells, a specific graph. The "geography" of this network determines the specificity of the function. The examples of orgasm or emotions show that the neurons involved in a sensation can belong to several centers, such as the hypothalamus, the limbic system, and also the neocortex (see Chapter 6). For the cricket, going into action involves a network of only a few tens or hundreds of neurons. For humans, the simplest motor activity involves enormous sets of nerve cells simultaneously *at several levels.* This being the case it seems very artificial to dissect the brain into successive "skins"—reptilian, paleomammalian, and neomammalian[20]—or even to subdivide the cortex into a mosaic of distinct areas, unless one considers from the outset that they represent critical knots of "spider's webs," to use Diderot's metaphor, that spread both vertically from the spinal cord to the cortex and horizontally across the cortex, each characteristic for a given behavioral pattern or sensation.

Thus the neocortex allows the organism, and specifically man, to relate to the surrounding physical and social world, to analyze it in its multiple details and diverse organizational plans. The increase in the course of evolution in the number of physical representations, maps, figurines, and homunculi on the cortex permits the widening of our capacities for interaction and for grasping the broader aspects of the universe.

According to the classical notion, neurons that make up a particular network, related to a movement or a sensation, can be activated by receiving a stimulus from the sense organs. The oscillators in the sensory receptors (see Chapter 3) react with changes of frequency or number of impulses, or with silences, according to quite a small number of possible codes. If it were possible to connect the eye to the central end of the auditory nerve, one would "hear"—that is, one would have an auditory sensation—with the eyes. In other words, within the limits of the organism, the nature of a physical signal is coded by its connections, its intensity, and the evolution in time of the impulses it triggers. Finally, certain behavioral patterns, like the song of the cricket, have a temporal evolution that does not require continual interaction with the outside world. Spontaneous activity in oscillators makes such automatic behavior possible.

Chemistry brings a new dimension to internal coding. Released by specific neurons in quantities that depend on the number of impulses, neurotransmitters and hormones take over the coding begun by connections and impulse patterns. These chemicals can spread over great distances but are most frequently confined to the synaptic cleft. A neurotransmitter excites in some situations, inhibits in others. Computations become possible, and they become more and more sophisticated with progression from one neuron to the next.

All these observations and reflections lead not only to an explanation of the internal mechanisms of behavior but to the adoption of a deterministic point of view. In theory, nothing prevents us from describing human behavior in terms of neuronal activity. It is time that *neuronal man* entered on the scene.

5

Mental Objects

It is because something of exterior objects penetrates
in us that we see forms and that we think.
　　　　　　　—Epicurus, letter to Herodotus

I'll argue not only that there is no learning theory but
that in certain senses there certainly could not be.
　　　　　　　—Jerry A. Fodor

The human brain makes one think of a gigantic assembly of tens of
billions of interlacing neuronal spider's webs, in which myriads of
electrical impulses flash by, relayed from time to time by a rich array
of chemical signals. The anatomical and chemical organization of this
machine is fantastically complicated, but the simple fact that it can be
broken down into neuronal cogwheels whose movements can be recorded justifies the outspoken theories of the eighteenth-century mech-
anists. "Everything that happens in man's body is as mechanical as
what happens in a watch," wrote G. W. Leibniz. But the human brain
does not tell the time; at the end of the twentieth century, to liken it
to a watch may seem naive and much too reductionistic. We generally
prefer to think of the brain as a computer, whose capabilities are more
spectacular. Neither image is better. In both cases it is a question of
machines—that is the essential. But each of these machines possesses
its own particular properties, radically different from those of the cerebral machine.

The comparison with a computer, a cybernetic machine, has been
useful in introducing the notion of internal coding of behavior. The
disadvantage is that this image implicitly supposes that the brain functions like a computer. Such an analogy is deceptive.

In all man-made computers built so far one can distinguish the
hard-wired circuits from the programs, perhaps written on magnetic
disks. The human brain can hardly be conceived as simply executing

a program imposed by the sense organs. One of the characteristic features of the cerebral machine is, as we have seen, that its internal coding involves a topological system of connections described by a neuronal graph and a simultaneous coding by electrical impulses or chemical signals. In the brain, the classical distinction of hardware and software does not hold. Moreover, the human brain can develop strategies on its own. It anticipates coming events and elaborates its own programs. This capacity for self is one of the most remarkable features of the human cerebral machine,[1] and its supreme product is thought.

Thought exists in rudimentary form in nonhuman mammals. The large carnivores often employ sophisticated hunting strategies, and the chimpanzee will use a stick to dig for termites. Thought has progressively developed in the course of evolution, and its development coincides with that of the brain.

Is the brain a thought machine? In *Matter and Memory* Henri Bergson wrote that "the nervous system has nothing in the way of an apparatus to make or even to prepare representations." The thesis of this chapter is the exact opposite of Bergson's view. The human brain contains representations of the outside world in the anatomical organization of its cortex, and it is also capable of building representations of its own and using them in its computations.[2]

Let us try to examine the biological basis of these faculties, traditionally considered as belonging to the "psyche."

THE MATERIALITY OF MENTAL IMAGES

"The Mona Lisa visits Japan." Everybody will understand the meaning of this phrase: Leonardo da Vinci's famous painting has been taken to Tokyo for an exhibition. One can readily conjure up the image of this intriguing woman, with her enigmatic smile, her hands crossed in front of her. It is more difficult, however, to recall which of her two hands is placed on the other, and whether the background depicts fields or mountains. It is nevertheless true that when one hears "Mona Lisa" one has a *mental image*, an "inner vision" of Leonardo's painting, months or even years after having seen it at the Louvre. To recall this image is a personal, introspective event. Nevertheless, no one would question the reproducibility of this image. Someone who has seen the picture, and has a minimum of artistic ability, can redraw it from memory sufficiently well to communicate his inner experience to others. This fact should convince the most obstinate behaviorists that mental images do exist.

The ancients were already aware of mental images. Epicurus and Lucretius considered them simulacra, and Aristotle compared them to "the imprint left by a seal on a wax tablet." Interest in mental images continued during the classical era, through the empiricism of John Locke and David Hume in England and Etienne Bonnot de Condillac in France, and into the thinking of the associationists, in particular Hippolyte Taine, Alfred Binet, and Théodule Ribot in France toward the end of the nineteenth century. It was the Golden Age of the image. Images were promoted to the rank of basic elements of the human mind.

But a reaction against the image soon became apparent. In 1913 John B. Watson excluded from his behaviorist doctrine "all subjective terms such as sensation, perception, image." As a result of this censure, research on mental imagery came to a halt for nearly half a century. Fortunately, the balance has shifted once again in its favor.[3] Today the existence of mental images is no longer doubted. They can even be measured.

The method employed by Roger Shepard and his colleagues is very simple.[4] The subject sits in front of a television screen on which appear computer-generated objects and geometrical figures of various forms, such as assemblies of cubes in perspective (Figure 42). The subject is asked to compare two figures placed side by side, representing the same three-dimensional object but seen from different angles. By carefully observing the two figures, the subject can easily determine that they depict the same object, differing from each other simply by the degree

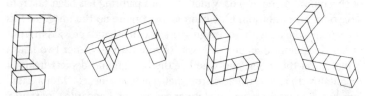

Figure 42. The human brain constructs "representations." Those studied the most are mental or memory images. In a series of ingenious experiments in 1971 and 1976, Shepard and his colleagues attempted to demonstrate their physical reality. For example, an object such as this set of cubes is presented to a subject, who is asked to decide whether or not the next object can be derived simply by rotation. The time taken for the subject to resolve the problem is measured. (From R. N. Shepard and S. Judd, 1976.)

of rotation. They are congruent. Some time, however, is needed to perform this mental operation. The experiment consists of measuring this time while varying the angle between the two figures. Each trial begins with a warning tone, followed half a second later by the presentation of a pair of objects. When the subject had verified their congruence, he presses a lever. The reaction time is short when the angle between the two objects is small; it is long when the angle is large. In general, the reaction time increases linearly with the angle of rotation. In the words of Shepard and his colleague J. Metzler, one can describe the determination of the identity of shape as a sort of "mental rotation in three-dimensional space," made at a speed of about 60 degrees per second. The subject mentally turns a *representation* of the object, a "mental image," which behaves as if it possessed a physical structure and even a measurable speed of rotation.

The material nature of these representations is also strikingly illustrated by an experiment involving the exploration of an imaginary island, reported by Stephen Kosslyn in 1980. He first asks the subject to draw the map of an island, like Treasure Island, with a beach, a hut, rocks, coconut trees, the treasure, and so on, dispersed in precise parts of the island. Then he takes away the map and asks the subject to explore the island in his imagination. At first the subject is on the beach, and the experimenter gives the instruction: "coconut tree." The subject searches mentally for the site of the coconut trees on the map and presses a button when he has found it. The time between the presentation of the words "coconut tree" and the response is measured. The experiment is then repeated with the hut, the treasure, and—as controls—places that are not on the initial map. A remarkable finding is that the duration of the mental exploration varies linearly with the real distances of the points the subject has marked on the map—from the beach, for example, to the coconut trees, the hut, or the treasure. The mental map thus contains the same information about distances as the real map.

Kosslyn has also asked subjects to undertake a mental exploration similar to that of the desert island, but using a familiar animal—an elephant. The subject must reply to a question, such as "How many nails in the foot?" by imagining the elephant. To do this, he has to use different scales, varying from a few centimeters to several meters to create his images. The smaller the scale, the longer is the time necessary for the subject to "see" the required feature. Often, after the experiment, the subject declares that he had to perform a mental "zoom" to examine details in very small images. Thus, the imaginary space has its *limits*. If it is already occupied by a large image such as an elephant, only something small, like a rabbit or a beetle, can fit in the remaining space.

All these experiments involve introspection on the part of the subject, but they allow measurements to be made that are reproducible from one subject to another. The material nature of mental images can hardly be doubted.

FROM PERCEPT TO CONCEPT AND THOUGHT

Mental images, as we have just defined them, arise spontaneously and voluntarily in the physical absence of the original object. They depend on memory. By definition, then, they are memory images, distinct from

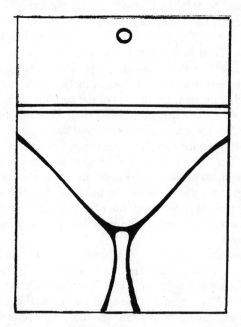

Figure 43. Ambiguous figure: glass of champagne or bikini? The same percept here evokes two distinct concepts. (From R. N. Shepard, 1978.)

130

sensations or perceptions, which are both experienced in the *presence* of the object. Until now, the term "sensation" has been employed purposely to describe the immediate results of activity in sensory receptors, reserving the term "perception" for the final stage, leading in the attentive subject to the recognition and identification of the object. The distinction between sensation and perception is particularly obvious when one examines an ambiguous figure such as that in Figure 43. What does the drawing represent? A glass of champagne or a bikini? It is sometimes one and sometimes the other. The visual sensation sent by the eye to the cortex is the same, but it gives rise to two distinct, irreducible perceptions. Each has a different meaning. Mental images usually evoke identified scenes or objects; they thus recall perceptions rather than sensations. If this is so, does the mental image have any relationship to the initial percept?

An experiment performed by C. W. Perky in 1910 strongly suggests that this is the case. He placed a subject in front of a translucent screen with a mark at its center. The subject had to fixate the mark and at the same time imagine a tomato. Meanwhile the experimenter, without the subject's knowledge, projected on the other side of the screen the outline of a tomato with a red light, but at an intensity below the threshold of perception. He progressively increased the intensity of the light until it was above the perceptual threshold. The subject, however, continued to assert that the tomato was purely imaginary. He confused his image and his perception of the object. The relationship between percept and image is obvious!

If this relationship exists, not only may percept and image be confused, but, if they concern different objects, they should be capable of competing with each other. Using a technique similar to that of Perky, in 1970 S. Segal and V. Fusella projected, not a tomato, but a white spot, whose luminosity they could vary. They then asked the subject to imagine a tree as they increased the intensity of the light spot. The intensity of light needed for the subject to perceive the spot was much greater in this situation than when no visual image was being evoked. On the other hand, the intensity needed was the same if the subject was asked to imagine a sound like the ringing of a telephone instead of a tree. There is thus competition between the percept and the image when both involve the same sensory modality, for there is a neural relationship, a material congruence between the percept and the memory image.

Let us return to the ambiguous figure perceived alternatively as a glass of champagne or a bikini. For each of these two perceptions, there is a different significance or *concept*. We are gradually leaving physiology to enter the domain of psychology and linguistics. Here biological data are critically lacking. We are thus reduced to formulating hypotheses. Let us hope that sooner or later they will be put to experimental proof.

First, we need to define what we usually mean by "concept." So let us take a walk together and look for antique chairs in the Boulevard Saint-German. In the first shop we see a Renaissance folding chair. In another there is a high-backed Louis XIII chair and in yet another a Louis XVI upholstered chair. In spite of distinct differences in form and style, we do not hesitate to call all of these "chairs." They all share certain features and have the same function, allowing us to group them under the same concept. We have however, excluded sofas. In creating the concept "chair," we bring together objects in the category "chair" and exclude *sofas*. This classification by categories overlooks differences in form and decoration between Louis XIII and Louis XVI chairs. By creating the concept "chair," we eliminate important details, we schematize and abstract. The concept becomes what Eleanor Rosch, writing in 1975, called a "prototype" of the object, bringing together in our case the characteristic features of different kinds of chairs.

This prototype concept is committed to memory. It can be recalled, for example, when one hears the word "chair," but also spontaneously, voluntarily, with no need for a sensory stimulus. Or it can be compared to a primary percept, such as a Louis XVI *ponteuse* or a sofa, and accepted or rejected. It thus possesses some of the properties of memory images. The concept is a simplified, formalized "skeletal" representation of the object in question, reduced to its essentials. A relationship begins to emerge between the percept, the image, and the concept; it is tempting to suggest that they share the same neural material base.

This way of seeing things is not new. It adopts certain aspects of classical empiricist and associationist theories on the nature of ideas. In his *Treatise of Human Nature,* David Hume wrote: "All the perceptions of the human mind resolve themselves into two distinct kinds, which I shall call impressions and ideas. The difference betwixt these consists in the degrees of force and liveliness with which they strike upon the mind. . . . Those perceptions which enter with most force and violence we may name *impressions. . . .* By *ideas* I mean the faint images of these in thinking and reasoning." In other words, for Hume, concepts are "faint" percepts or, perhaps better, *schematic* percepts. The hypothesis adopted here is that percept, memory image, and concept constitute different forms or states of the basic material infrastructure of mental representation, which we gather together under the general term "mental objects."

These remarks on the relationships between percepts, images, and concepts may be pertinent to a more general consideration of the nature of thought. The interest in images shown by Epicurus and Lucretius arose from the fact that they saw in images the "substance" of thought. Aristotle also wrote that thought was impossible without images. Much later, in 1870, Hippolyte Taine compared the mind to a "polyp of images." On the other hand, a more rationalist approach would minimize the importance of images. "We must consider that there are other things than images that can excite our thought, such as, for example, signs and words which in no way resemble the things they signify," wrote René Descartes in his essay on dioptrics. He also reflected, on the subject of a piece of wax: "The action by which we perceive it is not a vision, nor a contact, nor imagination, and has never been so whatever it may have seemed to be, but simply an inspection by the mind." At the beginning of this century, the Würzburg school even defended the thesis that thought could sometimes develop without the involvement of images. This was "imageless" thought. Closer to our time is the extreme view, expressed by Jerry Fodor in 1981, that there is no such thing as learning a conceptual system richer than the one that one already has. Concepts, he contends, cannot be learned through sensory experience with the outside world. They are innate.

My view is, rather, that the controversy ceases if we consider the following points. First, as we have seen, alongside very concrete *images,* which have considerable sensory content, there exist more schematic and abstract *concepts.* Even if in certain cases concepts may seem totally abstract and universal, we nonetheless regard them as "representations" and classify them with images in the category of mental objects. Furthermore, we must carefully distinguish the mental objects themselves from the operations and computations carried out *with* these objects. John Locke wrote that the two sources of all our knowledge are the impressions outside objects make on our senses and the workings of our spirit in relation to these impressions. The beads of an abacus cannot be confused with the calculations performed with these beads—although, of course, they are necessary to do the calculations! Finally, the brain is always spontaneously active (see Chapter 3) and may thus create internal representations without interaction with the outside world.

Mental objects do not generally exist in a "free state." As Ludwig Wittgenstein wrote in his *Tractatus*, they appear to be both independent and dependent in the sense that "we cannot imagine any object unrelated to the possibility of its liaison with others." The object possesses a form that limits its possibilities of combination with other objects.[5] Objects, according to Wittgenstein, "are linked together like the pieces of a chain," and the "irreversible" unraveling of this chain finally produces thought.

Wittgenstein goes further. For him, a logical proposition, a combination of mental objects, is an image. To decide whether it is true or false, it must be subjected to the test of reality. For him, "the proposition can only be true or false insofar as it is an image of reality." Deciding on the sense of a proposition thus returns to a direct or indirect comparison of an image—or, as we define it, a concept—with the original sensation or percept.

The cerebral machine is capable of performing computations with mental objects. It can evoke them and combine them, thus creating new concepts and "hypotheses" that can be compared among themselves. The brain functions like a "simulator," which, as Kenneth Craik wrote in 1943, gives to thought "its power to predict events," and to anticipate their sequence in time.

According to this scheme, language, with its arbitrary system of signs and symbols, serves as an intermediary between this "language of thought"[6] and the outside world. It translates stimuli or events into symbols or inner concepts and then, after the production of new concepts, retranslates them into actions on the outside world.

TOWARD A BIOLOGICAL
THEORY OF MENTAL OBJECTS

Apart from my introductory remarks, the word "neuron" has been avoided in this chapter. We have talked only of the cerebral machine and its capacity to handle mental objects. As the term suggests, these objects belong to the realm of thought and therefore imply a much higher level of organization than that of the nerve cell. But does this mean that we should consider them to be quite separate from the neuron? To the contrary, what we have learned in previous chapters leads us to reject such an idea. The cerebral machine is an assembly of neurons; our problem is to find cellular mechanisms that will allow us to pass from one level to another, to break down mental objects and then to reconstruct them from elementary activity in defined sets of neurons.

Mental images and concepts are memory objects. Ivan Pavlov, B. F. Skinner, and other behaviorists have led us to think of the *conditioned reflex* or, in more general terms, stimulus-response learning as the best, if not the only, basic model of learning. Can it serve as a point of departure in our attempt to explain the construction of mental objects?

Recently, in 1980, Anthony Dickinson submitted the notion of the conditioned reflex to a critical reexamination. Consider the well-known example of the laboratory rat exposed to a neutral stimulus such as a light, associated a few seconds later with a painful electric shock. After a number of trials, the experimenter notices that the rat's behavior changes: when the light goes on, *before* the shock is given, the rat stops moving and crouches. This is a sign of fear: the *freeze* reaction. For the behaviorist, the rat has simply learned a new response to the light.

The other, cognitivist interpretation—derived from Edward Tolman's basic work on cognitive maps in 1948—is radically different. The fear reaction is part of the rat's natural behavioral repertoire and will manifest itself in any unpleasant situation. It is not learned. The rat merely learns that the light precedes the electric shock. It anticipates the shock and forms a new mental structure, which is expressed indirectly in an automatic form of behavior. This interpretation becomes clear from the following experiment performed by R. Rizley and Robert Rescorla in 1972.

The rat was subjected to training sessions in which the light, instead of being associated with an electric shock, was paired with a neutral signal, a sound. The rat's behavior did not change. According to the behaviorists, the rat had learned nothing. Then the light was paired with an electric shock. When, later, the sound was produced, it provoked a fear reaction, although it had never been associated with a shock. During the first training sessions, an inner, behaviorily silent representation had been set up—a *concept* that related light and sound. When one of the components of this concept was associated with an electric shock, it became capable of provoking the fear reaction. Mental objects can, then, also be formed in the rat! A reexamination of animal memory leads to the same conclusion as research on mental images in humans. It also suggests that classical ideas on the conditioned reflex do not have the general validity once anticipated. They can hardly serve as a basis for the construction of memory objects.[7]

So how can we approach concretely the cellular mechanisms involved in the genesis of a mental object? One way is to return to the hypothesis of a physical relationship between mental image and percept. The "primary" percept is more accessible because it is directly coupled with activity in the sense organs. In monkeys and humans, a lesion of the primary visual cortex (area 17) causes blindness. In these species the primary visual cortex is indispensable to visual sensation, but we know from Chapter 4 that there are also multiple secondary representations of the retina (for instance, in areas 18 and 19 of the occipital lobe and in areas 20 and 21 of the temporal lobe). There are as many as eight of these maps in the rhesus monkey, and lesions of these secondary areas directly affect perception. The animal sees but does not recognize. In man, Henri Hecaen and Martin Albert in 1978 presented the case of a patient suffering from a lesion of areas 18 and 19. This man described a bicycle as bars with one wheel in the front and another at the back, but he could not identify it, name it. He was suffering from *agnosia,* a term coined by Freud when he was a neurologist to describe a defect in the ability to recognize a stimulus when there was no impairment of the primary sensory mechanisms. Various forms of visual agnosia have been identified. They result principally from localized lesions of the secondary visual cortex,[8] and include agnosia for objects (areas 18 and 21 on the left hemisphere), drawings and faces (the posterior part of the right hemisphere), and colors (the left occipital lobe). The formation of the "global" percept that gathers all these features together is thus the result of activity in *several* secondary areas. Various maps contribute to a single percept.

Knowing how these multiple areas are connected will help us to understand how the percept is formed. According to the classical scheme, the so-called secondary areas are activated only after the primary area. In other words, the primary area is hierarchically "above" the secondary areas in the analysis of the outside world and one assumes an anatomical "cascade" from the primary area to the secondary areas. In 1970 Edward Jones and Thomas Powell provided evidence for connections of this type. Their anatomical findings on the monkey's visual cortex showed that the connections of the primary area with the secondary areas followed a pathway going from the eye to area 17, then to area 20, and on to area 21.

This hierarchical organization no doubt exists, but it is not the only one. In 1981 Ann Graybiel and D. M. Berson demonstrated other pathways that may play an important role in the genesis of percepts. In Chapter 3 it was pointed out that fibers of the optic nerve coming from the retina relay in the thalamus before entering the cortex. From the thalamus, parallel pathways go directly and independently to areas 17, 18, 19, and 21. This being so, one could conceive of the formation of a primary percept as a result of the *simultaneous* activation, through these multiple parallel pathways, of primary and secondary representations in the cortex. The hierarchical pathways might then participate in bringing together these multiple representations of an object. Reciprocal interactions in these multiple areas would thus permit both analysis and synthesis at the same time. They would ensure the global nature of the percept.

We arrive at a notion of the percept that is both topological, for it involves specific sets of neurons, and dynamic, because it depends on their electrical and chemical activity. It therefore represents a logical consequence of the conclusions of Chapter 4. It is a new step to consider percepts as global "physical" entities, for a long tradition has assigned them to the psychological or mental world.

Pursuing and generalizing these reflections leads to theoretical propositions that, although still hypothetical, may be seen as attempting to bridge the gap that for many still separates the mental from the biological. They are in line with the work of Donald Hebb, Gerald Edelman, R. Thom, C. von der Malsburg, J. Hopfield, and A. Pellionisz and Rodolfo Llinás, as well as my own studies.[9] These ideas can be summarized as follows.

The *mental object* is identified as the physical state created by correlated, transient activity, both electrical and chemical, in a large population or "assembly" of neurons in several specific cortical areas.[10] This assembly, which can be described mathematically by a neuronal graph, is discrete, closed, and autonomous, but not homogeneous. It is made up of neurons possessing different singularities (see Chapter 2), laid down in the course of embryonic and postnatal development (see Chapter 7). The earmark of the mental object is thus initially determined or coded by the mosaic (or graph) of neuronal singularities and by a state of activity in terms of the number and frequency of impulses flowing in the circuits they form.

The *primary percept* is a labile mental object, whose graph and activity are determined by and dependent on interaction with the outside world. The neuronal graph associated with it is "fixed" by the encounter with the external object. The neurons utilized are recruited principally from the maps or homunculi of the primary and secondary cortex, which are projected by the sense organs (see Chapter 4).

The *image* is an autonomous and transient memory object, not requiring direct interaction with the environment. Its autonomy can be conceived only if there is a *temporally stable coupling* between neurons of the graph, which exists as a material trace before the image is evoked. To use von Malsburg's term, the "cooperativity" of this coupling between neurons is responsible for the invasive, all-or-none (or, rather, all-inclusive) character of their activation when the image is evoked.

The *concept* is, like the image, a memory object, but it contains only a small sensory component or even none at all, because it is the result of neuronal activity in association areas such as the frontal lobe (where multiple sensory or motor modalities are mixed) or in a large number of areas in different regions of the brain.

The *associative properties* of mental objects permit them to be linked together in an autonomous and spontaneous manner. Let us take up the analogy proposed by Bertrand Russell in 1918 between mental objects and atoms. Chemical bonding between atoms is based on a sharing of electrons. One can also imagine that mental objects are linked by the sharing, not of electrons, but of neurons. This supposes that a given neuron can take part in several graphs of different mental objects,[11] while conserving its own singularities, which existed before the formation of the mental object. However, the chemical bond between atoms is static, whereas the linking of mental objects is dynamic. A subpopulation, or contingent, of common neurons may then serve as a seed[12] and give rise to the sudden invasion of another "cooperative" neuronal assembly by a series of nerve impulses. New dynamic combinations could germinate spontaneously, and be passed on to neighboring assemblies in a seemingly more and more random manner the further one gets from the percept. Such linkages will lead to new *combinations* of neurons or existing neuronal assemblies. The rules governing these linkages and combinations will obviously be determined by the wiring pattern of the cerebral machinery, which will therefore impose its "grammar" on the linking of mental objects.

The *storage* of a mental object as a memory trace, in other words *learning*, occurs in an indirect manner.[13] It does not result from the "imprint" of a percept on the neuronal network, like a seal in wax. Nor does the interaction with the outside world simply trigger the activation of a fully prewired assembly of neurons. The key postulate of the theory is that the brain spontaneously generates crude, transient representations with graphs that *vary* from one instant to the other. These particular mental objects, or *pre-representations*, exist *before* the interaction with the outside world. They arise from the recombination of preexisting sets of neurons or neuronal assemblies, and their diversity is thus great. On the other hand, they are labile and transient. Only a few of them are stored. This storage results from a *selection!* Darwin helps to reconcile Fodor with Epicurus!

Selection follows from a *test of reality*. The test of reality consists of the comparison of a percept with a pre-representation. The test may involve "resonance" or, on the contrary, "dissonance" between the two neuronal assemblies.[14] Resonance manifests itself by potentiation of firing, dissonance by its extinction. A selection of the resonant percept "pregnant" with the outside world, and therefore "true," can thus take place. Obviously, this "comparator" will also work "internally," for memory objects: images and concepts.

The similarity in form, or *isomorphism*, of the percept with the external object results from the fact, already mentioned, that its graph is composed of neurons in a map or homunculus that is already a representation of the sense organ and thus of the world. Suppose we mark active neurons in black and the others in white: a "photograph" of particular aspects of an object will appear in each map. As just noted, storage of a pre-representation as a memory image occurs as long as it matches the percept. There is, then, a pruning of the sensory component, which brings about a loss of "vivacity" of the image and attenuates its realism, its isomorphism in relation to the object represented. Due to the diversity and transient nature of the pre-representations, only some features of the external object are stored and the features remembered may themselves vary from one experience to another. Isomorphism disappears as an abstract concept is selectively stabilized. The isomorphic component of the object is replaced by the algebra of neuronal combinations, which necessarily possess universal features. The creation of new concepts—imagination—arises from the linkage, combination, and selection of concepts, as well as images. Moreover, the "delocalized" character of the concept, in comparison with the percept or the image, and the fact that it can be formed in neurons in association areas, increases its capacity for linkage with other mental objects.

Language acts as a vehicle in the communication of concepts among individuals in a social group. The arbitrary nature of a system of signs[15] implies a "neutral" coupling of percept and concept, the outcome of a long apprenticeship during development (see Chapter 7). On the contrary, the "language of thought," permanently in contact with reality, will be much less arbitrary in nature than the language of words.

ASSEMBLING THE NEURONS

A biological theory has meaning only if it is based on the observation of natural objects and relates directly to them. One way of testing its validity is to examine the plausibility of the elementary mechanisms on which it is based.

Activation of specific sets of neurons was proposed in Chapter 4 to explain behavior and sensation. There is no particular difficulty in extending this idea to neuronal assemblies in the cerebral cortex. Nevertheless, the function associated with these assemblies may be expected to be different. Knowledge of the details of the intrinsic and extrinsic connections of the neurons of the cerebral cortex (Chapter 2) suggests concrete ways of assembling neurons to form mental objects.

Let us reconsider the description of the pyramidal cell, a basic unit of the cortex. Through its dendrites, in particular through its apical dendrites, it receives thousands or even tens of thousands of synaptic contacts from neurons converging on it. Through its axon, with its divergent branches, it is itself in contact with thousands of other neurons. The organization of the cerebral cortex in superimposed cellular crystals, as discussed in Chapter 2, allows local contacts to be established over several millimeters.[16] Besides these local relations, there are more distant contacts, made over several centimeters or more. Axon branches even link one hemisphere with the other. One characteristic of the neuronal graph of a mental object is that it is both local *and* "delocalized." The mental object rests, to use S. Atlan's expression of 1979, "between the crystal and the vapor." Neurons interact in a cooperative manner, as in a crystal, but are dispersed like vapors throughout multiple parts of the cortex, with no simple geometrical relationship.

This tentacle-like organization of mental objects suggests a form of linking that could serve as an outreach for the cooperative recruitment of new assemblies. It also allows for the large diversification of the assemblies in the human cerebral cortex. The number of neurons enlisted by a particular mental object is obviously not known. As an example, let us look at the percept. It may well use a significant fraction of the neurons present in several square centimeters of sensory cortex. If there are something like ten million neurons per square centimeter of cortical surface (see Chapter 2), and if only 10 percent of these cells contribute to the percept, one still has something like a million neurons recruited (close to the number of axons present in the optic nerve). If we now suppose that the pre-representations arise spontaneously from a similar number of neurons, then the number of possible combinations of a few million neurons scattered among tens of billions becomes enormous. Is it enough to explain the diversity of mental representations, images, and concepts?

We do not know exactly which cellular and molecular mechanisms are responsible for activating and stabilizing these neuronal assemblies. Given the present state of our knowledge, we must be content with proposing simple systems, at the neuronal or synaptic level, rather than looking to the overall cerebral cortex.

One of the first models to be mentioned was the *reverberating circuit*.[17] Let us suppose that neuron A sends its axon to neuron B and that B sends its axon back to A. The closed circuit A to B allows an action potential, once generated, to spread around it so that it oscillates. We know that such closed loops exist between the thalamus and the cortex, and that they are involved in the genesis of alpha waves (see Chapters 2 and 3). They may participate in the formation of mental objects by bringing cortex and thalamus into a solid relationship. Reciprocal connections also exist between cortical areas, and reverberating circuits of this type could directly contribute to the genesis of percepts.

Reverberating circuits are short-lived and cannot account for the process of cooperative growth, characteristic of memory objects. We must therefore look for alternative means of stabilization. To account for the diversification of mental objects, they make use of individual synaptic contacts. This immediately eliminates simplistic hypotheses such as the idea that "memory substances," such as nucleic acids or peptides, could transform whole populations of neurons whatever the mosaic of their neuronal singularities. The idea that one could transfer memory by placing an extract of an experienced brain in a naive brain, whether in a worm or a rat, is nonsense. The mechanism of the memory trace must therefore be looked for at the level of the neuronal connections themselves, that is, at the synapses.

In 1949 Donald Hebb proposed a synaptic mechanism for coupling that, although accepted by many in theory, has not yet been definitely proved experimentally. Nevertheless, his proposal deserves to be examined carefully in the light of our present knowledge of the synapse. According to Hebb, "when an axon of cell A is near enough to excite a cell B and repeatedly and persistently takes part in firing it, some growth process or metabolic change takes place in one or both cells, such that A's efficiency, as one of the cells firing B, increases." In other words, "repeated simultaneous excitation" of two cells modifies the efficiency of the synapses that link them. The *coactivation* of the two cells creates *cooperation* at the level of their contacts.

If we leave aside, for the moment, the "growth process" (which will be examined in Chapter 7), the "metabolic change" that may increase the efficiency of a chemical synapse can be envisaged at at least three levels.

1. *The release of the neurotransmitter.* The arrival of an electrical impulse in a nerve terminal causes the release of one or several "packets" or *quanta* of neurotransmitter. In 1979, using the sea slug *Aplysia*, with its very simple nervous system (see Chapter 3), Eric Kandel recorded changes in the efficiency of a synapse located between a pair of identified neurons: a sensory neuron of the siphon and a motor neuron of the muscle used to retract the gill. When the synapse was stimulated repeatedly, it habituated—that is, the number of quanta of neurotransmitter released decreased. Kandel discovered that if the head of the sea slug was rubbed, the synapse lost its habituation, and the release of quanta increased. This recovery was stimulated by neurons with their cell bodies situated in the head of the sea slug and their axons directly in contact with the nerve terminal that habituated. The synaptic reactivation seems to be due to a chain of chemical reactions,

including the synthesis of cyclic AMP (see Chapter 4), the phosphorylation of membrane proteins (which changes their charge), and the transport of calcium. The entry of calcium into the nerve terminal may regulate the efficiency of the synapse by increasing the probability of the release of quanta of neurotransmitter.

2. *The concentration of the neurotransmitter in the synaptic cleft.* In certain synapses, but not in all, the synaptic cleft contains an enzyme that destroys the neurotransmitter. The best-known example is that of acetylcholinesterase, which splits acetylcholine and limits the temporary concentration of the neurotransmitter in the cleft during transmission of the nerve signal. Blocking the enzyme causes an increase in the concentration of acetylcholine in the cleft and prolongs the electrical response. No known endogenous substance in the nervous system can modify the activity of this enzyme, but man has invented nerve gases that kill by doing this.

3. *The action of the neurotransmitter on the receptor.* The receptor for the neurotransmitter in the postsynaptic membrane is the target of many forms of regulation that modify the efficiency of synaptic transmission. One of them has attracted the attention of pharmacologists for many years. It is known as *desensitization* and has been analyzed in detail at the neuromuscular junction,[18] but it also exists in the central nervous system. Administration of concentrated acetylcholine at the motor endplate in brief impulses lasting about a millisecond causes the opening of the ion channel associated with the receptor. But if the acetylcholine, even at a low concentration, is applied to the receptor for much longer, the ion channel does not open and the receptor no longer responds to the transmitter. It becomes desensitized. The molecular mechanism of this regulation is known.[19] In the presence of even a low concentration of acetylcholine, the receptor molecule is slowly and reversibly converted from an "activable" to a "nonactivable" form. The calcium present in the interior of the cell accelerates this allosteric transition. Depolarizing potentials have the opposite effect. The change in the ratio of the activable to the nonactivable form of the receptor is a forceful regulator of synaptic efficiency.[20]

Any of these forms of regulation could be involved in coupling neurons and thus might take part in a mechanism such as that proposed by Hebb. Although nothing has been demonstrated yet, desensitization has been suggested as a mechanism in the storage of memory traces;

this proposal is particularly attractive on account of its simplicity. Consider two neighboring synapses A and B, making contact with the same target. Activity in synapse B could change the ratio of the activable to nonactivable forms of the receptors in synapse A and thereby modify its efficiency over a period of up to several minutes in at least three different ways.

As a first possibility, suppose that A and B use the same neurotransmitter: it could diffuse in low concentration on the *outside* of the neuron from B to A and make the receptor in A nonactivable. Thus activity in B would cause an inactivation of synapse A. The same effect would be observed if calcium were used as an *internal* communication signal between B and A. When B functioned, the ion channel in the postsynaptic membrane would open and calcium would enter the cell. From there it would diffuse inside the neuron to synapse A. If, as is the case for the acetylcholine receptor, calcium accelerated desensitization, it would again stabilize the receptor in a nonactivable state. Third, the membrane potential can also regulate desensitization: at the neuromuscular junction, decreasing the electrical potential slows desensitization. Thus, according to Hebb's idea, the genesis of impulses by a neuron could modify the efficiency of the synapses the neuron receives.

The final effect on the neuron—the production of an action potential—would also depend on the excitatory or inhibitory nature of synapses A and B. If, for example, A was inhibitory, its inactivation by B would facilitate an action potential. Various, combined coupling mechanisms could develop at each of the neurons that constituted the "nodes" of the assembly.

Similar models could also be worked out on the basis of forms of regulation other than desensitization. In any case, the time scale of the molecular processes involved would determine the stability of the coupling. With desensitization, we are dealing with short-term, reversible coupling, for tenths of a second, seconds, or minutes. Longer-term regulation would occur if, for example, the back and forth between activable and nonactivable states became stuck in one or the other state due to a chemical reaction modifying the receptor for days or weeks. The stability of the modification would itself be limited by the stability of the molecules making up the synapse, such as the neurotransmitter receptor. The receptor molecule does not last forever (see Chapter 7). After its "death," it could be replaced by another molecule with different properties. Such changes could be controlled by the activity of the neuron, by the intermediary of, for example, cyclic AMP or calcium. A long-term regulation of synaptic properties would follow. A stable graph could then be set up, perhaps for a lifetime.

In any case, our present knowledge of the chemistry of the synapse allows us to make plausible suggestions about mechanisms by which assemblies of neurons could be selectively stabilized in the short or long term.

Finally, the earlier, theoretical discussion of the storage of mental objects emphasized a critical operation in their selection—the test of reality. As R. Thom has proposed, resonance or dissonance of mental objects may take place. Can one imagine a cellular mechanism responsible for resonance in neuronal assemblies?

In Chapter 3 we saw that the nerve cell may behave as an oscillator. Two sorts of "slow" ion channels suffice to create oscillations in the membrane potential. This spontaneous activity could, of course, be at the origin of the "internal" genesis of mental objects and their linking together without interaction with the outside world. However, oscillations do not always reach the threshold for impulse release. They may remain latent. The convergence of two oscillations of this type on the same neuron would result, if they were in phase, in an amplification of the latent oscillations, leading to a burst of impulses. If they were not in phase, there would be an attenuation, manifested by a complete absence of impulses.

PROBLEMS OF CONSCIOUSNESS

Conjuring up an image, like that of the Mona Lisa, produces an inner experience, one we are aware of. While we are awake and attentive, we appreciate and pursue the formation of percepts and concepts. We can store and recall mental objects, link them together, and recognize their resonance. We are conscious of all this in our unending dialogue with the outside world, but also within our own inner world, our "me."

At the level of integration we are now discussing, what we might call *consciousness* can be defined as a kind of a global regulatory system dealing with mental objects and computations using these objects. One way of looking at the biology of this regulatory system is to examine its different states and identify the mechanisms that guide the change from one state to another.

145

The first example we shall use is that of *hallucinations.* In this case, as F. Morel indicated in 1947, an awake subject "experiences a modification of his relations with the outside world without appropriate [external] stimulation." He perceives mental images that are produced spontaneously and involuntarily, without an external source. Hallucinations are frequent in schizophrenics and even serve as a diagnostic feature.[21] These patients may hear voices speaking to them in the third person or commenting on their thoughts, repeating them, judging them. They may also hear their own thoughts spoken aloud like an echo. The hero of the *Iliad,* the prophets of the Old Testament, and, closer to our time, Joan of Arc, Joseph Smith, and numerous mystics, fell prey to auditory hallucinations, whose symbolism has deeply marked Western culture. In addition to these auditory disturbances in the schizophrenic, one may observe visual hallucinations such as scenes of heaven and hell, although these are less frequent. From the Burning Bush to the most recent apparitions of the Virgin, religions have accepted these "visions" as revelations of supernatural forces. In reality, hallucinations have a solid biological basis.

In the awake nonschizophrenic subject, electrical stimulation of precise parts of the cerebral cortex, such as the primary visual area 17, causes very simple hallucinations: bright spots, flashes of light, or "seeing stars." If, instead of the primary visual cortex, one stimulates secondary areas, like area 19, more complex hallucinations appear. The patient thinks he sees a butterfly and tries to catch it, or he sees his dog coming, whistles to it, and becomes annoyed with the doctors who do not see it.[22] Thus, electrical stimulation, or sometimes lesions, of cortical areas that we know are responsible for the formation of percepts can cause hallucinations. That is, mental images can be evoked spontaneously by direct stimulation of cerebral tissue, in circumstances totally outside the subject's control. The subject has an inner vision of the images, but their recall and even their linking together are no longer governed by the intentional component of his consciousness.

Certain hallucinogenic drugs like mescaline or LSD also produce hallucinations, particularly visual ones. For centuries, the Huichol Indians of the mountains of Mexico have known of the "transcendent" virtues of the mescal cactus, or peyote. They eat peyote buttons on their annual pilgrimage to the Wirikuta, where they rediscover paradise and "become like gods." The hallucinations they experience are rarely set down in words. They prefer to represent them by remarkable yarn pictures or rugs with flamboyant geometrical designs; with arrows, feathers, and abstract shapes—all vividly colored in blue, yellow, and red. In 1888 Louis Lewis isolated the active ingredient of peyote. It was the alkaloid mescaline, but it needed to be administered in much higher doses than a substance later synthesized by Albert Hofmann: lysergic acid diethylamide (LSD), whose effects Hofmann himself accidentally experienced the day of its synthesis. Mescaline and LSD provoke visual hallucinations that are always vividly colored but relatively shapeless. When taken in repeated large doses, these drugs provoke disturbances that resemble acute schizophrenia. The chemical mechanisms of these hallucinations seem similar to those of schizophrenia itself.

With LSD, as with morphine, the target is a synaptic neurotransmitter receptor (see Chapter 4). This receptor, however, has not been so unequivocally identified as the opiate receptor. LSD binds to the same sites as serotonin, but it also binds to the receptor of dopamine (a cerebral transmitter already mentioned in connection with "pleasure synapses" and discussed again at the end of this chapter).[23] Recalling images from memory is thus subject to neural control involving one or several specific categories of chemical synapses, which transmit messages from the "intentional" consciousness of the subject.

The hallucinogenic drugs act as a chemical "scalpel" dissecting away the intentional part from the perceptual component of consciousness. Other regulatory mechanisms can also affect consciousness selectively. Hesiod, in the eighth century B.C., called sleep the "brother of death." It is like "becoming unconscious without entirely losing consciousness," accompanied by the "suspension of complex sensorimotor relationships, which unite the being to his surroundings."[24] Sleep causes a lowering of the level of consciousness, but is totally unrelated to death. It is an active process, composed of a complex sequence of cerebral activities, which can be recorded by electroencephalography (see Chapter 3). When one falls asleep, the rapid alpha and beta rhythms, characteristic of the waking state, progressively disappear and give way to slow waves of high amplitude—the delta waves—characteristic of *slow-wave sleep.* At regular intervals, approximately every ninety minutes, there are short "brain storms" —*paradoxical sleep*— accompanied by rapid eye movements, as well as erection in the male. (Due to the rapid eye movements, paradoxical sleep is also known as *REM sleep.*)

In 1893 Friedrich Goltz noted that removal of the cerebral hemispheres in a dog did not interfere with the cycle of waking and sleep. In the same way, anencephalic babies, who have no cerebral cortex, go to sleep and wake up like normal infants. The cortex does not control sleep rhythms. A group of nuclei situated in the brainstem between the spinal cord and the thalamus is responsible for this. Some of these neurons provoke slow-wave sleep; others, paradoxical sleep; still others are responsible for waking. Anatomically, they are part of a complex network of neurons and connections in the brainstem called the *reticular formation* (Figure 44).[25] Morphologically, these neurons are quite unusual. Although their cell bodies are located in the brainstem, in groups of several thousand cells, their axons spread widely throughout the brain (see Figures 11 and 44). Some send axonal branches to almost the entire cortex. Through this fanlike divergence of their axons, these very small groups of cells can exert their influence on a large part, or even all, of the brain.

As noted in Chapter 1, a team of Swedish scientists has shown that each of these small groups of neurons uses a particular neurotransmitter.[26] The *locus coeruleus* is responsible for waking the cortex with noradrenaline and shares this activity with a group of cells releasing acetylcholine. Another nucleus, containing serotonin, puts the cortex to sleep. Yet another induces paradoxical sleep. However, as we have already seen in connection with drinking (Chapter 4), it is always difficult to associate a particular neurotransmitter with a function. Noradrenaline is not *the* transmitter for waking, nor is serotonin *the* transmitter for sleep. Each marks a pathway containing several relays, one of which has recently been discovered to use neuropeptides.

In 1913 Henri Piéron knew nothing of neurotransmitters and peptides, but he performed an experiment that is still of great significance today. His hypothesis was that a chemical substance, a "hypnotoxin," accumulated during the day. By evening it had reached a high-enough concentration to cause sleep; it was then destroyed during the night. To test this idea, Piéron kept dogs awake for several days by tying them up during the day and taking them for walks at night. He took samples of cerebrospinal fluid when they were exhausted from their lack of sleep and injected it in the cerebral ventricles of other, wide-awake dogs, which immediately went to sleep for several hours—even during the day. This experiment has since been repeated with rabbits and cats.[27] Hypnotoxins *do* exist. Several neuropeptides, different from the endor-

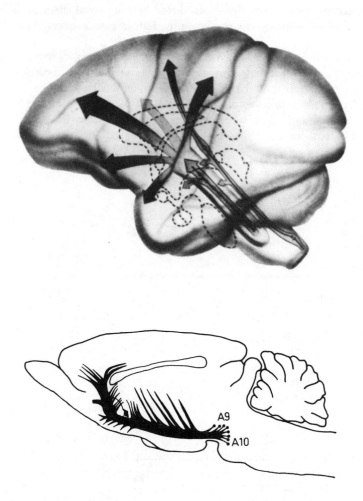

Figure 44. The reticular formation of the brainstem controls global aspects of cerebral functioning. In the 1950s it was thought that the reticular formation was a diffuse set of neurons, as shown in the *upper* figure, which depicts the brain of a monkey. (From H. W. Magoun, 1954.) Today we know that it is, rather, a host of discrete nuclei, which can be distinguished essentially by the neurotransmitter they synthesize. In the *lower* figure, in the brain of a rat, nuclei A9 and A10 are marked to indicate the neurons synthesizing dopamine. (From O. Lindvall and A. Björklund, 1974.) Their axons project to diverse regions of the brain, in particular the frontal cortex (see A.-M. Thierry et al., 1973).

phins and enkephalins, may be involved. The divergent activity of brainstem neurons may thus be mediated by a hormonal effect, with a "bath" of neuropeptides regulating the state of consciousness of the cortex.

How is the cortex awakened or put to sleep by these control systems? One might imagine that during slow-wave sleep the activity of cortical neurons decreases and that it increases again on waking or during the short periods of paradoxical sleep. This is not the case. In 1981 M.S. Livingstone and David Hubel managed to record the same visual-cortex cell in a cat for several hours while the animal was asleep and awake

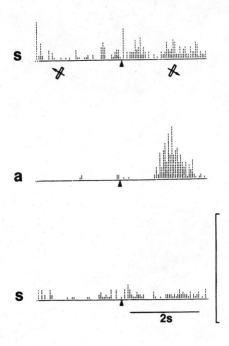

Figure 45. The consequences of waking on the activity of single neurons in the visual cortex of the cat. From *top* to *bottom,* the recordings were obtained during slow-wave sleep (s), when the cat was awake (a), and once again during slow-wave sleep (s). For each state, the activity of the recorded neuron is represented. Each vertical line indicates the frequencies of the impulses (scale: 100 impulses per second). Waking suppresses the background noise and reveals the neuronal response to the movement of a light stimulus in the direction indicated in the upper figure. (From M. S. Livingstone and D. H. Hubel, 1981.)

(Figure 45). They observed that during slow-wave sleep, neurons were not electrically quiet. On the contrary, they exhibited considerable spontaneous activity, usually in the form of regular bursts coinciding with the peaks of the slow delta waves. Waking caused these bursts to disappear, or desynchronize. It also reduced the frequency of the impulses. Livingstone and Hubel also observed that during slow-wave sleep stimulation of the eye by light evoked a response from visual-cortex neurons. However, the frequency of the recorded impulses was generally lower than in the waking cat; moreover, the spontaneous activity was very pronounced. Waking the cortex thus improves the signal-to-noise ratio; it increases contrast, as if the cells were in a state of quiet wakefulness, preparing themselves for interactions with the outside world and thus assuring each neuron the opportunity to express its own singularities, participate in the formation of conscious percepts, and integrate its activity in an assembly of neurons.

Consciousness, then, corresponds to a regulation of the overall activity of cortical neurons and, more generally, of the entire brain. A few small groups of neurons in the brainstem, with their cell bodies centrally situated, exert a "global" influence, thanks to the divergent nature of their axons. The regulation of states of alertness thus relies on anatomically and chemically simple mechanisms.

ATTENTION

As we saw in the example of hallucinogens, in pathological or artificial circumstances, the production of mental objects may escape the control imposed by one's will. This control is also lost, as is the perceptual component of consciousness, when one falls asleep. The "wholeness" of consciousness breaks down into elementary regulatory mechanisms. Until now we have considered only the formation of images and concepts and their linking together in the alert, awake subject. When one falls asleep, images do not cease; on the contrary, they take on the exuberant forms of the dream, an imaginary and unreal form of thought. Once again the perception of mental objects becomes dissociated from their intentional production.

In 1965, in an attempt to identify objective signs of dreams, William Dement woke sleeping subjects at different EEG stages of sleep and asked if they were dreaming. He found that during paradoxical (or

REM) sleep the majority of replies were positive, but that a considerable number reported dreams during slow-wave sleep. The dreams during slow-wave sleep, however, had a factual content, concerning tax declarations or scientific problems, for example; in other words, they were relatively close to conscious thought. They differed from the dreams of paradoxical sleep, which were filled with vivid images and lively narratives. As with hallucinations, during dreaming, images and concepts form and link together without significant interaction with the outside world, but this imagery develops in the fog of slow-wave sleep and only rarely reaches consciousness. This mental activity, then, belongs to the "non-conscious" or, if one prefers, the unconscious. Nevertheless, to take Sigmund Freud's view that the dream is "the royal road to the unconscious" or the disguised expression of a repressed wish teaches us little about its functions or, even more important, the mechanisms that regulate this spontaneous production of mental objects.

A remarkable experiment performed in 1979 by Michel Jouvet and his colleagues is particularly instructive in this context. The storm of paradoxical sleep is so violent that one might expect it to involve motor centers and consequently cause the sleeping subject to move. In reality, this does not happen. Movements are blocked in the spinal cord at the level of the motor neurons that govern muscular contraction. A specific brainstem nucleus, the locus coeruleus alpha, paralyzes the motor neurons. If it is destroyed, the paradoxical activity is "freed" and can give rise to a behavioral pattern. Imagine that this center is damaged in a cat—will it then show spastic, disordered movements, as if having an epileptic fit? Not at all. On the contrary, Jouvet observed that the sleeping cat manifested organized behavior. It explored its territory, licked and washed itself, attacked an imaginary prey, and showed signs of "anger," but all without any particular logical order. Normal elementary behavioral patterns were thus linked together in a haphazard fashion. Automatic behavior, which we know is controlled by subcortical centers, was observed, but it occurred randomly, without meaningful coordination. The generator of paradoxical activity, which is responsible for this behavior, thus has the role of evoking mental objects and linking them together according to patterns already recorded in the form of stable graphs. But it does not really organize them. Another form of regulation, necessitating that the cat be awake, is essential to link them together in a meaningful behavioral pattern.

The reason for the periodic appearance of paradoxical activity during sleep is not known. It has stimulated many hypotheses. During the course of evolution, development of paradoxical sleep parallels the expansion of the cortex, and it seems reasonable to relate the two. Could paradoxical activity play a role in the way the cerebral cortex treats mental objects? Could it serve to "rehearse" mental objects and patterns so they will not be lost during the night? Could it be responsible for continuing during sleep the stabilization of neuronal graphs begun during the day?

It is a big step from understanding the significance of paradoxical activity in cats to the interpretation of dreams. Obviously, major differences exist between the "exteriorized" behavior of the operated cat and dreams. In particular, the experimental cat never shows signs of sexual activity, which occupies such a large part of our human dreams. And yet, the sequences of unrelated events in our dreams remind us of the apparently random behavioral "collages" of the operated cat. But should we go as far as adopting Jacques Lacan's idea that the dream, like the unconscious, is "structured like a language"? That depends on which language we are talking about—that of a normal person or of a mad one?

As early as 1824, Pierre Cabanis noted that "the way in which the state of sleep produces images perfectly resembles that in which the phantoms of delirium and madness are produced." Some years later, in 1855, M. Moreau de Tours wrote the following memorable phrase: "Madness is the dream of the waking man." In delirious states the intentional and perceptual components of consciousness persist, as in hallucinations, but the "dialogue" with the outside world and with one's self is disturbed. The delirious person pursues an autonomous discourse that, as in a dream, is not directly bound to his interactions with the environment. He is no longer open to persuasion; he is the victim of an inner imagery that replaces his representation of the real world. The conscious control mechanism that normally deals with comparing perceived and conceived objects functions poorly, if at all. An understanding of the organic causes of this state might give us some idea of the essential components of consciousness, but our knowledge is still far too fragmentary to permit definitive answers.

Let us examine some of the features that characterize delirious speech.[28] Typically, it is disorganized, with ideas and words strung together in an illogical way. In a single sentence one finds contradictory themes and words, whose meaning does not fit the context. Concepts are no longer used correctly as tools of reasoning. A *random component* appears in speech and even in the formation of words. There is a clear analogy to Jouvet's operated cat and to the series of images in a dream. But at what level is the disturbance? Is the initial thought disorganized so that the delirious person can no longer compare it with reality, or, on the contrary, does a defect in the ability to compare things make the thought become disorganized? There are probably several answers to this vexing question!

In any case the cerebral comparator no longer functions normally. Comparisons with the outside world use the sense organs for access to essential regulatory mechanisms, particularly *attention,* which manages the relationships of the brain with the environment.

Watch a cat exploring an unfamiliar room. It walks about calmly, looking around, moving its ears from left to right and sniffing. If it finds nothing attractive, it sits down, continuing to look around, before finally falling asleep. Now introduce a mouse in a transparent box: the cat suddenly gets up, turns its head toward the box, raises its ear, and fixes its eyes on the mouse. This is the *orientation* reaction. Both Ivan Pavlov in 1910 and E. N. Sokolov in 1963 described it as the body's first response to any type of stimulus, allowing the animal to use the appropriate analyzing instrument to assure optimal conditions for perceiving the stimulus. If it is a fake mouse, the cat's response will evolve: when we take the mouse away for a few minutes and then put it back, the cat's response is less pronounced than the first time. In the end the cat no longer responds. It will *habituate.* If, however, we now present a real mouse, the cat again reacts as it did the first time. It *dishabituates.* These varied reactions ensure an efficient exploration of the environment. The orientation reaction is used for a first, detailed examination and an initial focusing of attention; the situation is then constantly updated by the cycle of habituation and dishabituation.

The same process obviously applies to humans. We face continual challenges in our everyday life, whether we are crossing a street or listening to a Bach fugue, in which shifting tonalities and voices, subjects and countersubjects, "dishabituate" constantly. This process may not be obvious on the outside, in a particular form of behavior or attitude, but it can be recorded as an EEG trace. As we saw in Chapter 3, when a subject fixes his attention, desynchronized beta waves replace the regular alpha waves. If he habituates, the alpha waves reappear.

But one's attention can be directed more selectively toward a particular sensory modality. Stephen Hillyard and his colleagues recorded the variations in evoked potentials (Chapter 3) in the temporal or occipital regions when the ear was stimulated by a click or the eye by a flash of light.[29] The subjects were asked to fix their attention on one eye or one ear just at the moment that the click or the flash appeared. A marked change in the form of the recorded wave was noted depending on whether the subjects fixed their attention on the right or left ear or eye. Fixing the attention increased the amplitude of the principal slow waves significantly. It created a "hyperarousal" of the particular cortical area selected by the subject (Figure 46).

The mechanism for this spotlighting of a particular sensory area has been investigated in the cat at the cellular level. Once again the reticular formation plays a critical role. In 1979 Wolf Singer followed the

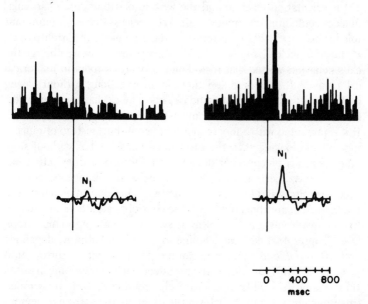

Figure 46. EEG recordings comparing the effects of attention on the activity of individual neurons in the posterior parietal cortex of the monkey *(above)* and on the evoked potentials, recorded at a similar level, in man *(below)* in response to a flash of light. In the recording on the *left*, the subject was inattentive; on the *right*, attentive. Focusing attention increases the amplitude of the evoked response and improves the signal-to-noise ratio. In the upper recordings, the vertical bars indicate the frequency of the impulses. (From R. Galambos and S. A. Hillyard, 1981.)

propagation of electrical impulses in the cat from the optic nerve to the cortex via the thalamus. When the cat was awake, the impulses traveled normally. But if the reticular formation (close to the locus coeruleus alpha, which is responsible for paradoxical sleep) was stimulated just as the impulses were passing, the transfer of the signals to the cortex was markedly facilitated, as judged by a rise in the amplitude of the cortical evoked potential (see Figure 46). This rise results from the removal of an intrinsic inhibition, which makes a given "channel" work at a low yield during rest. Acting as a neurotransmitter, acetylcholine can inhibit an inhibition and thereby activate. The nucleus of the reticular formation that contains this neurotransmitter acts as a regulator of the visual channel.

Nuclei in the reticular formation regulate the passage of sensory messages. They also participate in more global forms of control, such as the orientation reaction and the fixation of attention. A particular nucleus containing dopamine—the A10 nucleus—plays an important role in this respect.[30] Let us return to the example of the attentive cat. If the A10 nucleus is removed and a few months later we observe the cat's behavior, we see that it no longer explores a room in its normal calm way.[31] It goes here and there in all directions, without paying particular attention to details and objects. The cat has completely lost its attentive attitude; it has become hyperactive and is easily distracted. If it is presented with a mouse in a transparent box, instead of remaining still and looking at it, the cat walks around the box without stopping. When a precursor of dopamine, DOPA, or a drug acting like dopamine is injected, this abnormal behavior disappears: the cat becomes calmer and seems more attentive. Thus dopamine neurons in the brainstem are concerned with the control of attention, in addition to their involvement in the "pleasure synapses" that control motivation (see Chapter 4). Like acetylcholine in the visual pathway, dopamine acts as an *inhibitory* neurotransmitter in the cerebral cortex. It is possible that this inhibition in turn affects an inhibitory mechanism, thus leading to facilitation, selectively arousing cortical areas innervated by these neurons. Whatever the situation, the dopamine neurons of the A10 nucleus are involved in regulating the *selective contact* of the brain with the outside world.

This brings us back to delirium. The first psychiatrists to describe schizophrenia, Emil Kraepelin in 1896 and Eugen Bleuler in 1911, already attributed considerable importance to the disturbances in attention, particularly the orientation of attention, that afflict some of these patients. Recent research has confirmed their point of view.[32] When tested, schizophrenics generally reveal significant disturbances in attention. Their reaction times are long and variable. They are easily distracted and their exploration of both the outside world and their own inner world seems slow. Their difficulties with thought and language can also be interpreted as defects in attention, involving both poor selectivity (in that they cannot exclude irrelevant internal or external stimulation) and excessive fixation of attention. Most drugs that attenuate the symptoms of schizophrenia are related to the dopamine receptor.

Clearly the operated cat and the schizophrenic differ in many respects. Malfunctioning of the A10 nucleus in the brainstem cannot alone explain the disease. Nevertheless, this work emphasizes the critical role of the brainstem nuclei as "regulators." Some of the dopamine neurons control the orientation of attention, just as certain acetylcholine neurons control the visual pathway. They exercise a very selective control over exchanges between the brain and the outside world and maintain a permanent dialogue between inner thought processes and the real world outside. Other groups of still poorly identified neurons are concerned in an "internal" focusing of attention on memory images or concepts. One might expect that they impose their rules, their specific "grammar," on operations carried out on mental objects, their linking together, and, of course, their exchange with the environment.

The different groups of neurons in the reticular formation receive signals from the sense organs. They are closely tied to the cranial nerves and have direct access to the outside world. As they know what is going on outside, they can activate or extinguish either large parts of the brain or very precise cortical areas, even particular parts of an area. These brainstem nuclei do not perform detailed analyses. That is the job of the cortex. But they control the pathways that permit this analysis. They act in some ways as "pilots" or, if one prefers, as the console of the cortical "organ," selecting a particular keyboard or set of pipes particularly suited to the formation and treatment of specific mental objects. For this piloting to give the organism the autonomy it needs, the brainstem neurons must themselves be informed of the analysis performed by the cortex on mental objects; indeed, pathways do exist from the cortex to the brainstem. These *reentries* close the loop.[33] A confrontation is possible between the outside world and one's inner world. The regulatory system evaluates resonance and dissonance between concepts and percepts. It becomes a mechanism for the perception of mental objects, for the surveillance of their linking. The different groups of neurons in the reticular formation inform each other of their mutual activity. They form a system of hierarchical, parallel pathways in permanent *reciprocal* contact with the other structures of the brain. A holistic *integration* between various centers results. From the interplay of these linked regulatory systems, consciousness is born.

THE CALCULATION OF EMOTION

The most fundamental social motivations, according to Harry Harlow, are the different forms of love and affection. Within a social group, emotions are communicated through attitudes, gestures, and, even more important, facial movements, without necessarily having recourse to words. As we saw in Chapter 4, the emotions involve neurons in the hypothalamus and the limbic system, which are important not only for an individual's motivation to look for food or sexual partners, but also for "togetherness." If one accepts Jean-Paul Sartre's view, "emotion is a form of existence of consciousness . . . a state of consciousness." Indeed, emotions are perceived internally by the conscious subject, but percepts elicited from the outside also engender emotions. There is continual traffic between the cerebral cortex, the limbic system, and the hypothalamus.

The involvement of the frontal cortex, the most forward part of the cortex (see Figure 6), in emotional behavior was suggested by an observation dating from the time of Paul Broca. It concerned the famous case of Phineas Gage, a railroad worker in New England, cared for by Dr. John Harlow for many years until his death.[34] Gage was twenty-five years old when, while filling a hole in a rock with gunpowder and tamping it with a pointed iron bar, the charge exploded and the bar was blown out. The point penetrated the left angle of his jaw, came out of the top of his skull in the frontal region near the sagittal suture, and was picked up some distance away covered with blood and pieces of brain. Less than an hour after the accident, Gage climbed a staircase and told the story of his accident to a surgeon! He survived for twelve years but with serious behavioral disturbances, which Harlow described very precisely and which still serve as criteria in the diagnosis of lesions of the frontal lobe: "He is fitful, irreverent, indulging at times in the grossest profanity (which was not previously his custom), manifesting but little deference for his fellows, impatient of restraint or advice when it conflicts with his desires, at times pertinaciously obstinate, yet capricious and vacillating, devising many plans of future operation, which are no sooner arranged than they are abandoned in favor of others that he finds more practical." Since the beginning of the century, other cases of frontal lobe lesions have been reported, and a wide variety of consequences have been noted. The disturbances are either "psychopathic," as in Gage's case, or "depressive." The patient becomes apathetic and indifferent and cannot express his emotions; he speaks little or not at all. It is obvious that the frontal lobe plays a role in regulating emotional states. Its intimate anatomical relationships with the limbic system account for this role.

As the case of Gage shows, lesions of the frontal lobe do not cause only emotional disturbances. There is also a very specific aphasia, due to the fact that Broca's area is situated in the extreme posterior part of the frontal lobe (see Chapter 4 and Figures 6 and 40). Moreover, disturbances of short-term memory occur. The patient "forgets to remember." He is easily distracted and shows difficulty in concentrating, in attention. He also has little appreciation of the past or the future, as can be seen in an inability to formulate projects and to realize them. The frontal lobe is the zone where a large number of cortical areas converge. In particular, many secondary sensory areas project to it, while it projects on noncortical motor centers such as the basal ganglia (see Figure 13). In this way it can intervene in the execution of programmed movements and in their adaptation to external as well as internal events. Lesions of the frontal lobe also cause disturbances in the orientation of an individual toward his own body, his self.

It is a region with many capabilities, participating in the elaboration and execution of the most complex mental activity; "constructive activity, verbal intelligence, discursive thought, and logical reasoning."[35] It is exceptionally well developed in humans, in whom it occupies 29 percent of the cortical surface area, compared with only 17 percent in chimpanzees and 7 percent in dogs (see Figure 6). To use the terms introduced in the theoretical part of this chapter, mental objects are linked and combined in the frontal lobe, and "programs" of motor action and representations of the space in which future movements will be carried out are constructed. *Intentions* are built up and "materialize" as images or concepts, themselves "composites" of other images or concepts involving strategies for future behavior. The frontal cortex is an "organ of civilization"—calculating, anticipating, foreseeing.

This anticipatory function has recently been demonstrated at the cellular level in the monkey. The demonstration was based on a relatively simple learning test, developed by C. Jacobsen for the chimpanzee: the "delayed-response" task.[36] One puts two identical overturned bowls in front of an alert monkey. A piece of apple is placed under one of the bowls, but the monkey cannot reach it. A few seconds or minutes later, the monkey is allowed to choose one of the overturned bowls. If, on its first attempt, it indicates the bowl under which the apple is hidden, the response is considered positive and the monkey is allowed to eat the apple. Obviously from one trial to another the apple is placed randomly under either bowl. After a few trials the monkey learns to give the correct answer regularly. Jacobsen showed that removing the frontal lobe caused a major deficit in the performance of this test. In the light of these results, in 1980 J. M. Fuster recorded electrical activity of single neurons in the frontal lobe of a macaque while the delayed-response test was being performed. He distinguished several types of cellular response. Some neurons were active upon presentation of the bowls, or during the execution of the response. Others discharged impulses during the entire experiment. The most interesting neurons were less active during the presentation of the stimulus and the execution of the response but showed a marked increase in discharge rate *during the intervening delay.* They did not respond if the bowls were presented again without the apple, if the monkey had not learned the task, or if it was distracted during the task. The response of these neurons is therefore related to the storage of visual information and to the elaboration of an appropriate motor act. It is true that only a small number of the total neurons in the frontal lobe behave in this way. Yet the simple fact that they *can* be recorded by an electrode passing through the cortex suggests that they are not rare. A neurophysiological model of anticipation becomes possible.

To return to patients with lesions of the frontal lobe. Almost all, A. R. Luria indicated in 1978, suffer from an appreciable reduction of their critical faculties: they cannot correctly evaluate their behavior or judge their own actions. The role of the brain as a comparator necessitates that the frontal lobe be intact. We have already emphasized the importance of the role played by attention in the constant dialogue between the brain and the outside world, whether physical or social.

It is no great surprise to find that the frontal cortex is greatly influenced by the dopamine, A10 nucleus in the brainstem, which, as we have seen, is involved in regulating attention. A rat, in which this nucleus has been removed, fails the delayed-response test, as if the frontal lobe were missing. The A10 nucleus, then, acts as a "regulator" of the frontal lobe. It permits the internal focusing of attention on this brain area and allows it to act as a comparator.

The immediate result of comparison, in the terms of our theoretical discussion, is to bring out the resonance and dissonance between mental objects. What will the consequences be? It has already been emphasized that lesions of the frontal lobe cause both emotional and cognitive disturbances. Even if different, though overlapping, parts of the lobe are preferentially engaged in one or the other of these behaviors, they may become linked or "associated" at the cortical level. One might envisage that resonance between mental objects on the cognitive plane is communicated to the neighboring emotional part of the frontal cortex, releasing bursts of impulses that travel to the limbic system and the hypothalamus with a consequent pleasurable effect—or, if there is dissonance, a depressive effect. It becomes easy to understand the seriousness of the emotional disturbances that a delirious person will suffer if such resonance is missing or inadequate. One can also understand how a single word could evoke resonance or dissonance with a memory image, thus provoking joy or distress.

The dialogue between the cortex and the limbic system and hypothalamus does not always end in the same way. Resonance between rational concepts is pleasurable, but as Blaise Pascal said, "the heart has its reasons that reason does not know." In other words, the limbic system and the hypothalamus (together, the "heart") have enough autonomy vis-à-vis the cortex that, under the pressure of particularly strong sensory stimulation, motivation may increase to such an extent that the subject "goes into action" even if the cortical resonance ("reason") says "no" to the act in question.

SEEING MENTAL OBJECTS

Emotions are transmitted from one individual to another by facial expressions or bodily gestures. The conceptual or imagistic content of this communication is, however, limited. No television transmits mental concepts or images directly from one brain to another! Communication of mental objects is usually accomplished through the symbols of language, a heavy and cumbersome coding system, not necessarily well adapted to the "language of thought."

The organization of the cortex reflects the difficulty of communicating mental objects from one individual to another with the means at our disposal, with the mouth, ears, hands, and eyes. As we saw in Chapter 4, the left hemisphere governs the spoken language. But as John Hughlings Jackson wrote in 1868, "the two brains cannot simply be double." Patients with Broca's aphasia sing quite well, but lesions in the right hemisphere have been described as causing professional musicians to lose their ability to perceive and produce music. Lesions of the right hemisphere are also accompanied by major defects in tests of mental imagery, such as those described at the beginning of this chapter.

The specialization of each hemisphere in different communications tasks is also illustrated by the well-known studies of Roger Sperry on patients in whom the *corpus callosum,* the fiber bundle that unites the two hemispheres, had been cut.[37] After this operation, both hemispheres remain connected to the sense organs, but, because half the fibers in each optic nerve cross, the right hemisphere sees the left half of the visual field and the left hemisphere the right half. It is thus possible to communicate separately with each hemisphere. Sperry asked N.G., a California housewife, to tell him what she saw on a screen, which was divided vertically down the middle and upon which different images were projected on the left and right sides. He asked her to fixate a point in the middle of the screen. When a picture of a cup was presented on the right, she replied, "I saw a cup." When a spoon was projected on the left half of the screen, she replied that she had seen nothing. Yet, with her left hand, she chose a spoon from a pile of objects in order to indicate what she had seen. When she was asked to name the object in her hand, she said, "Pencil." The dialogue continued. A photograph of a naked woman was projected on the left of the screen. She blushed a little and laughed behind her hand. "What did you see?" asked Sperry. "Nothing, just a flash of light," she replied. "Why are you laughing, then?" "Oh, doctor, you have some machine!" The patient was capable of verbally naming an object (like the cup) presented in the right visual field, and therefore to the left hemisphere. She was not able to name an image presented to the right hemisphere.

Nevertheless, she recognized the spoon and reacted emotionally to the photograph of the naked woman. The right hemisphere analyzes and produces images whereas the left hemisphere is specialized in verbal and abstract operations.

Let us reconsider the theoretical notions discussed at the beginning of this chapter. Various results suggest that mental objects with a realistic component, like pictures, preferentially mobilize neurons in the right hemisphere, while those with a more verbal or abstract content—concepts—recruit neurons in the left hemisphere. This conclusion is, however, relative, for each hemisphere contains functional sensory areas. For example, the visual areas of *both* hemispheres contribute to the vision of an object in space and thus to the formation of a spatial percept. Assemblies of neurons working in cooperation must then be distributed through both hemispheres. Their interrelationship is possible through the 200 million, or more, axons of the corpus callosum. The continual to and fro of percepts and concepts might then correspond to a right-left oscillation. This recruitment of masses of active neurons is accompanied—for the "logic" of linkages and for their emotional charge—by "movements" in another direction: with the involvement of the frontal lobes, the activity of assemblies of neurons will swing back and forth from the front to the back of the brain.

These movements in the activity of large groups of neurons are not purely imaginary. Recent advances in the techniques used to explore the brain, whose full impact is still unknown, already permit us to "see" these movements through the skull. The technique is based on a visualization of the energy expenditure that results from nervous activity. As we saw in Chapter 3, the production of an electrical impulse uses energy, resulting in an increased consumption of glucose, the basic source of energy in the body. The metabolism of glucose produces carbon dioxide, which, when released, acidifies the blood and causes the capillaries to dilate. As the overall circulation increases, more blood flows in the tiny blood vessels around active neurons.[38] In the skin one sees this as a reddening. In the cerebral cortex a local increase in blood flow cannot be seen unless one has a way to "see through" the tissues, and particularly the skull. Such a technique is available: positron-emission tomography, or *PET scanning,* which uses radioactive isotopes. When injected in the blood traveling to the brain, these isotopes serve as markers of blood flow, which is directly related to brain activity.

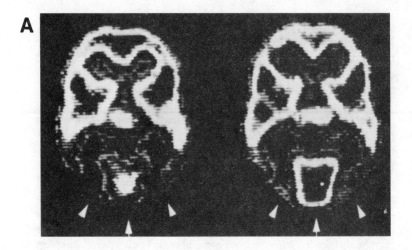

Figure 47. "Internal" states of activity of the human brain observed through the skull by PET scanning, using a positron camera and the radioactive tracer ^{18}F-fluorodeoxyglucose. In *A*, the subject has his eyes closed (on the *left*), then opens them (on the *right*). The visual cortex in the occipital lobe "lights up" (arrows). (From a color photograph by M. E. Phelps et al., 1981.)

B shows the effect of the complexity of the visual scene on the activity of the visual cortex (arrows). On the *left*, the subject has his eyes closed; in the *center*, they are open but see only a uniform white background; on the *right*, the subject is looking at a wooded park near the laboratory. In this photograph, the intensity of the black is directly proportional to activity. (From M. E. Phelps et al., 1982.)

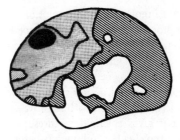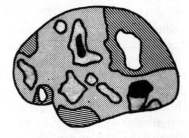

Figure 48. Differences in cerebral blood flow indicated by a positron camera (using the radioactive isotope Xenon 133) in a normal subject without any obvious mental disturbance (*left*) and in a schizophrenic patient (*right*). At rest the radioactive landscape shows a relative hyperactivity in the frontal lobes (in black) in the normal subject, which is not found in the schizophrenic patient. (From D. H. Ingvar, 1982.)

They cause, not an actual reddening, but a radiation, visible to a camera sensitive to gamma rays (Figures 47 and 48).

The isotopes used (xenon 133, carbon 11, or fluorine 18) do not themselves give off gamma rays. Rather, they emit positively charged particles —*positrons*— which travel over distances of a few millimeters before colliding with a negative electron. There is then a tiny "explosion," releasing two photons, or particles of light, that fly off in opposite directions. The camera used detects these two photons simultaneously, thanks to a battery of photosensitive cells around the object under study, in this case a person's skull. A computer connected to the camera performs a series of triangulations to locate the point at which the photons were emitted. The results are represented point by point on a video screen as a two-dimensional image. The regions that are richest in isotopes appear brightest on successive computer "slices" of the brain. They represent areas of greatest blood flow, that is, those with the highest metabolism and therefore the greatest electrical activity. The positron camera allows us to see the state of activity of neurons inside the skull. In this light, David Ingvar in 1977 called this technique *ideography.*

As this is a very recent technique, it still has severe limitations. First of all, in space. The blood capillary network is much larger than a nerve

C shows the effect of auditory stimulation. On the *left,* the subject's ears are blocked; in the *center,* he is listening to a Sherlock Holmes story, and, on the *right,* to one of the Brandenburg concertos by Johann Sebastian Bach! There is increased activity in both the temporal lobes, where the auditory cortex is situated, in the frontal lobes. (From a color photograph by J. C. Mazziotta et al., 1982.)

NB: When black and white reproductions are made from color photographs, there is no linear relationship between the intensity of the black and the activity.

cell. Measures of the local blood flow cannot attain the resolution of a single neuron. For this reason other procedures have been developed. For instance, in 1977 Louis Sokoloff and his colleagues demonstrated that deoxyglucose, a molecule closely related to glucose, is taken up by active cells. Unlike glucose it is not burned up by cell metabolism, but accumulates inside a neuron. In theory, it should permit us to follow the state of activity of a single neuron. When tagged with fluorine 18 and studied with a positron camera it gives splendid pictures (see Figure 47). Unfortunately, the positron travels a few millimeters before producing the two photons. There is thus an unavoidable "graininess" to the PET scan pictures; their resolution is poor, no better than a square centimeter. Time factors also impose limits on such analyses. The radioactively labeled substances used take some time to reach the nerve tissue and accumulate in large-enough quantities for maximum contrast. The recording and the computer analysis also take time. To obtain a readable image by PET scanning still requires several minutes.

Nevertheless, amazing results have already been reported. A proof of the validity of the method is that the "radioactive landscape" is different when subjects are awake and when their level of consciousness is reduced. The alert state is characterized by a higher blood flow or glucose metabolism in the frontal cortex than in the rest of the cerebral cortex: a *hyperfrontal* distribution. When consciousness is lost, this difference diminishes or disappears.

The stimulation of a particular sense organ causes an accumulation of the radioactive tracer in the related sensory area. In the case of vision, in 1981 and 1982, M. E. Phelps and his collaborators noticed marked differences in the distribution of deoxyglucose in the cortex depending on the scene before the subject. If the eye was stimulated with white light, the main response involved the primary visual cortex (area 17). On the other hand, when the subject looked at a checkerboard of black and white squares, there was a greater accumulation in area 17 but also activity in the secondary visual areas 18 and 19. Furthermore, if the subject looked at a complex environment, such as the wooded park around the laboratory, the intensity of the reaction was even greater in both primary and secondary areas. These results reinforce the idea, put forward at the beginning of this chapter, that the formation of a visual percept involves secondary areas as well as the primary visual cortex.

In 1982 Ingvar also showed that when a subject speaks, the blood flow increases in the parts of the motor cortex devoted to the mouth and in the auditory cortex. This is most marked in, although not exclusive to, the left hemisphere. A purely mental activity, one with neither sensory stimulation nor motor activity, changes the radioactive landscape of the cortex with the blood flow increasing particularly, as we might expect, in the frontal lobe.

Studies in three different laboratories in the United States and Sweden have revealed a clear difference in the distribution of blood flow in normal subjects and chronic schizophrenics. In the latter, no hyperfrontal activity is seen; blood flow in the frontal cortex is quite low. Rather, there is a *hypofrontal* distribution, with peaks of activity in the temporal and parietal regions. One possible interpretation is that schizophrenics have a dormant frontal cortex, but they also exhibit other anomalies (see Figure 48).

PET scanning allows us to study the internal functioning of the brain. Its clinical applications are already of great importance. Temporal and spatial resolution, although still poor, will probably improve in the future. Other methods are being developed. It is not overly optimistic to envisage one day the appearance on the screen of the image of a mental object.

One essential question, however, remains. PET scans reveal states of activity in groups of neurons. Can one find the trace, or *engram*, that persists between two evocations of a mental image? Is there a cerebral "organ" that preserves some elements of an image as the seed for the development of cooperation within the neuronal assembly? Or, on the other hand, does the entire cerebral cortex participate in the storage of mental objects? Certain cerebral lesions in humans selectively affect the use of memory. The temporal lobe and the "old" cortex, the hippocampus, certainly play a role. There is, however, no proof that the engram is localized in either. Indeed, is their tiny surface area sufficient to account for the huge capacity of human memory? In harmony with our conclusions about the genesis and stabilization of assemblies of neurons, it seems, on the contrary, more reasonable to envisage the memory trace as spread throughout the cortex and maybe even through a large part of the rest of the brain. As Keith Oatley wrote in 1978: "The ability to learn is a fundamental property of the nervous system of mammals which is not limited to one of its parts."

THE SUBSTANCE OF THE SPIRIT

The theme of this chapter—to destroy the barriers that separate the neural from the mental and construct a bridge, however fragile, allowing us to cross from one to the other—carries great risks and can be criticized. It is based on relating mental activity to states of physical activity in neuronal assemblies. The term "mental objects"—used as the title of this chapter—concretizes this notion by pairing the noun "object" with the adjective "mental." The main risks are oversimplification, failure to account for all mental processes, and partiality. Certainly, the experimental data are still too fragmentary for us to go much further. Indeed, the problem is not to explain everything, but rather to place a ladder against the wall of this mental Bastille. "Spiritualistic" alternatives have often been put forward. In contrast to these, the interpretation here is open to experiment and will, it is hoped, stimulate research.

The proposed hypothesis, or model, has the advantage of taking into consideration both psychological information and data gathered from anatomical observations and physical measurement, whether electrophysiological or chemical. This explains the continual back and forth in this chapter between what one might call the subjective and the objective. Such an effort is open to criticism of its methodology, unless one day—a day I hope is close—it leads to real progress in our knowledge of the brain and its functions.

The concept of assemblies or cooperative groups of neurons leads directly from one level of organization to another, from the individual neuron to a population of neurons. The number of neurons engaged in the graph of a mental object is not known: hundreds of thousands, millions maybe. It is conceivable that these assemblies possess some kind of autonomy, and that within them new properties can appear, explicable in terms of intrinsic properties of the neurons—just as the properties of a molecule can be explained on the basis of those of its atoms. Clearly identified synaptic and molecular mechanisms make such assemblies of neurons quite plausible, for individual neurons can easily be integrated into larger units that permit passage from one level to another.

The correlated states of activity that make up the graph of a mental object have not yet been measured. Only states of activity of cortical regions or of generalized parts of the human brain have been observed with the positron camera. But I have high hopes that this technique, or others in the future, will allow us to follow mental objects themselves in spite of their fleetingness and their dispersion throughout the brain.

To do this, it will be necessary to identify large populations of neurons distributed over wide regions of the cortex and probably other parts of the brain. Those mental objects that are images will probably be derived partly from the homunculi in the primary or secondary sensory areas; those that are concepts, from the association areas, such as the frontal cortex, that have no particular sensory or motor bent. The figurative or abstract nature of these representations will thus depend on the proportions of neurons involved that are in preexisting cortical homunculi, compared with the proportion of cells in other cortical areas. The neurons participating in assemblies of concepts will be both dispersed and multimodal, or perhaps amodal. This should bestow on them very rich "associative" properties, allowing them to link together and above all to combine. Thus, it becomes plausible that such assemblies, made up of oscillatory neurons with high *spontaneous* activity, could recombine among themselves. This recombining activity would represent a "generator of hypotheses," a mechanism of diversification essential for the genesis of pre-representations and subsequent selection of new concepts. In a word, it would be the substrate of imagination. It would also account for the "simulation" of future behavior in the face of a new situation. In order for a system to organize itself, it is obvious that there must be more than simple creation of diversity. A *selection* is possible, as we have seen, by the comparison of mental objects in terms of their resonance or dissonance.

Operations on mental objects, and above all their results, will be "perceived" by a *surveillance system,* composed of very divergent neurons (such as those in the brainstem) and their reentries. The existence of regulatory loops with reentries at several organizational levels of the brain could lead to high-amplitude oscillations. (The alternation of mania and depression and the periodic appearance of delirious states characteristic of certain mental disturbances could be explained in this way.) These linkages and relationships, these "spider's webs," this regulatory system would function *as a whole.* Can one say that consciousness emerges from all this? Yes, if one takes the word "emerge" literally, as an iceberg emerges from the water. But it is sufficient to say that consciousness *is* the functioning of this regulatory system. Man no longer has a need for the "Spirit"; it is enough for him to be Neuronal Man.

6

The Power of the Genes

Heredity is law.
—Charles Darwin

The cerebral machine constructs mental representations because it contains, in its anatomical organization, in its neurons and synapses, representations of the world around us. This organization is characteristic of a given species. According to Carolus Linnaeus in 1770, the description of a species relies on those "parts that are not subject to variation." Its scientific name often refers to these characteristic traits in abbreviated or symbolic form. Thus, modern man designated himself *Homo sapiens sapiens,* doubtlessly to emphasize a property that he feels characterizes his brain.

The definition of the species *Homo sapiens sapiens* depends just as much on the form of the brain as on the form of the skull, the hands, or the spinal column. Recall the reproductions of the human brain from Vesalius during the Renaissance (Figure 2), Willis in the classical age (Figure 3), and Leuret and Gratiolet in the nineteenth century (Figure 5). If we compare them with modern photographic atlases, we find the various pictures differ more in the way they are drawn and reproduced than in the actual form of the brain. Allowing for differences in artistic style and the technique of reproduction, the brain seems to have remained *invariant* since the sixteenth century, in spite of tremendous changes in the social and cultural environment.

The stability of the brain's gross anatomy, which serves as a basis for the neurobiological definition of the species (Figure 49), is also found in its microscopic details. Medical students have to learn a precise and rich nomenclature for the nuclei, tracts, and convolutions of the human brain. The very existence of this nomenclature is a measure of the invariance of the detailed anatomy. When Santiago Ramón y Cajal drew the neurons and fibers that make up the brain centers, he was

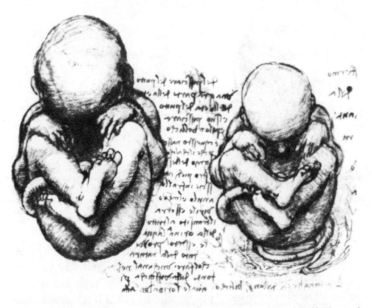

Figure 49. Drawings of the human fetus made by Leonardo da Vinci (around 1510). The number of neurons and the major anatomical features of the human brain are set at birth. The power of the genes ensures the "cerebral unity" of the species. (From L. da Vinci, selected by P. Huard, 1961.)

unconcerned that his tissue samples came from different individuals. This indifference would have been a grave mistake if the cellular organization of the brain varied greatly from one individual to another. Macroscopically as well as microscopically, the anatomy of the nervous system seems basically reproducible within a given species and between generations. How can one explain this?

ANATOMICAL MUTATIONS

One way of trying to understand how a power exerts itself is to challenge it and analyze its reactions to the attacks. Are there exceptions to the invariability of the nervous system? If so, is its organization subject to variations that are perpetuated from one generation to another, inscribed in its *genome?* Or, on the other hand, are the variations eliminated in subsequent generations, thus belonging to the *phenotype?*

171

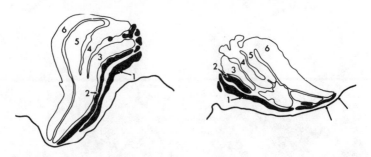

Figure 50. The albino mutation causes a major reorganization of the lateral geniculate nucleus in the thalamus, which relays the visual pathways on their way to the cortex in man and several mammalian species. On the *left* is a normal human; on the *right,* an albino. There is abnormal fragmentation and fusion in layers 2 through 5. Bar length: 2 millimeters. (From R. W. Guillery et al., 1975.)

We have already discussed the differences in brain weight in man (see Chapter 2). Recently, in 1979, Terry Hickey and Ray Guillery reexamined the histological variability of the human brain in a reasonably large sample of fifty-nine people who had died from causes independent of the nervous system. In their postmortem examinations, they studied the lateral geniculate nucleus, the relay between the retina and the visual cortex (see Chapter 4). They noticed a significant variation in the stratified pattern of this area from one case to another. Certain segments were missing, others were fused together. A surprisingly wide anatomical variability does exist between individuals. Is it hereditary (genotypic) or, on the contrary, unstable from generation to generation (phenotypic)?

Some answers were obtained from one particular case among the fifty-nine, that of an albino who died of uremia.[1] The reorganization of the lateral geniculate nucleus was amazing. Instead of a regular layered pattern, there were scattered groups of cells, sometimes fusing one layer to another (Figure 50). Similar major anatomical variations are also found in other mammalian species subject to albinism, such as the Siamese cat, the white mouse, the Himalayan rabbit, and the white tiger.[2]

Albinism affects about one person in 17,000 and its genetics are well known. The disease is transmitted from generation to generation as a recessive trait according to simple Mendelian laws. It can also appear spontaneously, although rarely, in populations not having an "albino" gene. The albino trait results from an abrupt change in genetic makeup, transmissible by heredity, which we call a *mutation.* [3]

The principal target of the albino mutation is known. Strangely, the affected molecule has nothing to do with the central nervous system, at least at first sight. One or several enzymes responsible for the synthesis of the skin pigment—melanin—are lost, causing a lack of melanin and thus the white skin and hair characteristic of albinos. Also, the eyes appear red, for they are no longer lined by a dark layer of pigmented cells. Careful study of the anatomy of the central nervous system has shown that the lesion is not restricted to the lateral geniculate nucleus. It is present in the eye or, more precisely, in the optic nerve. In the normal individual, optic nerve fibers divide into two bundles, one of which "crosses" so that half the fibers coming, say, from the left eye project to the right geniculate nucleus, while the other half in the same optic nerve remain on the same side of the brain. In the albino, the fibers do not cross in the same way: some that ought not to have crossed do in fact go to the geniculate nucleus of the opposite side, where they become mixed up with those that are projected there normally. This explains the fragmented appearance of the layers of the lateral geniculate nucleus. But that is not all. Neurons of the lateral geniculate nucleus normally send their axons to the visual cortex. This is also the case in the albino, whatever the origin of the optic nerve fibers, which means that the information sent to the cortex is not correct. Thus the whole visual pathway is reorganized in a "chain" from the eye via the lateral geniculate nucleus to the cerebral cortex.

The albino mutation is in many ways typical of mutations that affect the nervous system. A single change in one gene can simultaneously modify *several* characteristics, as different as the color of the skin or the fundus of the eye and the organization of the visual pathways. What is more, an anatomical defect in a specific part of the nervous system has secondary effects in other, directly or indirectly related centers. In genetics the term *pleiotropism,* derived from the Greek, is used to designate the multiplicity of effects of a single mutation. Mutations of the nervous system are very frequently pleiotropic.

The neural targets affected by genetic mutations vary considerably from one mutation to another. An extreme case is that of anencephaly, which in man, as in the mouse, involves the absence of the cerebral cortex. It is relatively frequent, affecting one to five births in a thousand.

The impact of well-defined gene mutations has been carefully analyzed in the cerebellum.[4] As we learned in Chapter 2, the cerebellum is made up of a small number of cell categories, organized quite regularly in layers of granule and Purkinje cells, and other layers containing the branchings and synapses of these cells (see Figures 21 and 51). In the mouse the *reeler* mutation affects this stratification: most of the Purkinje cells are grouped in amorphous cellular masses in the center of the cerebellum; they no longer form regular cellular "crystals." The *Purkinje cell degeneration* mutation, as its name suggests, involves the loss of almost all Purkinje cells in the cerebellum. The *weaver* mutation is characterized by the disappearance of the granule cells. In all these cases, the lesion involves members of the same cell category. The *staggerer* mutation affects the synapses that link the granule cells and the Purkinje cells in the normal cerebellum. Similar genetic disorders also occur in man. They demonstrate unequivocally that the major features of the brain's anatomy—such as the distribu-

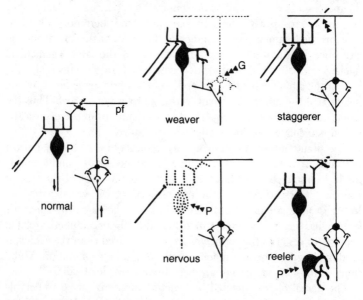

Figure 51. Highly schematic diagram of the effect of genetic mutations on the organization of the cerebellum in the mouse. The "nervous" mutation causes the death of Purkinje cells (P). In the "weaver" mutation the granule cells (G) disappear. In the "reeler" mutation the Purkinje cells migrate abnormally, while in the "staggerer" mutation synaptic contacts between the granule cells and the Purkinje cells are not formed. (From J.-P. Changeux and K. Mikoshiba, 1978.)

174

tion of the main cell types, their differentiation into categories, and the formation of the principal connections and pathways linking them together—can vary as a consequence of genetic mutations and are therefore subject to the authority of the genes.

A large number of mutations occur in man. More than 2,000 have been described, resulting from changes in different genes. Among these, at least 300 affect the central nervous system and result in various anatomical lesions. In addition to these "localized" mutations, more drastic changes can occur in the *chromosomes,* which carry the genetic material. Their number and their length can change. A fragment can be lost (deletion) or transported from one chromosome to another (translocation). A well-known example of a disorder of the nervous system related to a change in the chromosomes is mongolism. It is found in humans and monkeys when three number 21 chromosomes are present instead of two: thus, it is called *trisomy 21.* [5] Nevertheless, chromosome defects and mutations are rare events. On average, a given gene mutates in each generation between once in a hundred thousand and once in a million times. The rarity of mutations, and their equally rare reversion, means that most genes persist without modification for generations. This stability of the genetic material ensures the invariance of the characteristics of the species, in particular the invariance of the anatomy of its nervous system.

HEREDITY AND BEHAVIOR

Individuals with hereditary anatomical lesions, such as those just described, inevitably show important changes in behavior. Siamese cats squint; reeler, weaver, and staggerer mice, as their names suggest, have great problems in walking. They move slowly and hesitantly, falling over and getting up again with great difficulty—symptoms characteristic of cerebellar lesions. These defects do not improve with age. Indeed, if we remove the cerebellum of a normal mouse at birth, when it grows up it has fewer behavioral problems than the "weaver" mouse, which has no granule cells. As a consequence of the mutation, synapses form abnormal circuits, which can hardly be modified or compensated for by experience. Genes are powerful dictators!

There are subtler behavioral changes consequent to mutations, ones that do not cause obvious anatomical defects in the nervous system, sense organs, or motor apparatus. A relatively simple example is found in the fruit fly *(Drosophila)*, with which Thomas Hunt Morgan and his collaborators established the basis of modern genetics in 1923. As noted, mutations are rare events, and the geneticist is confronted with a major experimental problem: how to isolate and select mutants involving a given function.

Seymour Benzer developed a very ingenious method of "concentrating" behavioral mutants in the fly.[6] He treated populations of *Drosophila* as if they were solutions of proteins. He suspended a mixture of normal and mutant flies in a test tube, forcing them to the bottom of the tube and then letting them move freely toward a source of light at the mouth of the tube. The normal fruit flies moved spontaneously toward the light and tried to escape; the others remained at the bottom of the tube. Thus, the population of flies was progressively divided. Those that consistently did not move toward the light were collected. Many were abnormal for obvious reasons, perhaps being blind or paralyzed. But some were of interest to us: they showed clear behavioral problems without major reorganization of their anatomy. The *shaker* mutant, for instance, beats its wings vigorously when it is anesthetized. The *nap* mutant becomes paralyzed when it is warmed to 35° Centigrade. The *bang-sensitive* mutant dies in a few seconds after a mechanical shock. What is the origin of these defects?

Electrophysiological study of the propagation of the nerve impulse and its transmission at the neuromuscular junction has supplied the answer.[7] In the shaker mutant, the postsynaptic wave is abnormally long due to a prolonged release of neurotransmitter, which in turn is due to a change in the potassium channel. In the nap mutant, propagation of the action potential along the nerve is disturbed due to a defect in the sodium channel. Although not yet definitely established, it is probable that the bang-sensitive mutation involves the enzyme pump responsible for maintaining differences in sodium and potassium concentration inside and outside the nerve cell (see Chapter 3).

Thus each of these mutations affects one of the proteins involved in maintaining the membrane potential or propagating the nerve impulse (the sodium and potassium channels and the enzyme pump). They probably affect the "structural" genes that code for these proteins. The behavioral effect can thus be explained simply by a defect in the propagation of nerve signals or by the absence of these signals.

These first examples will probably not satisfy ethologists and psychologists, who find the behavior of these mutant fruit flies totally uninteresting. It is true that generalized paralysis is too crude a model for studying normal behavior. They would perhaps be more interested in the genetics of the cricket's song. As noted in Chapter 4, the song of the male is made up of specific phrases, consisting of a chirp followed by ten trills of two notes (see Figure 33). Raising the larva in isolation and even making it deaf does not change this behavior: it is totally innate. On the other hand it differs from one species of cricket to another (Figure 52). In the Australian cricket *Teleogryllus commodus*, the number of notes in the trill is much greater than that in *Teleogryllus oceanicus*. If these two types are crossed, the first-generation hybrids have a different song from either of their parents. There is a clear hereditary element in the song of the cricket. If these hybrids are

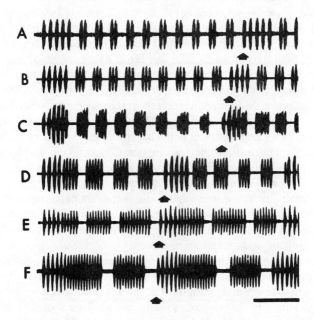

Figure 52. The heredity of the song of crickets of the genus *Teleogryllus*. In *A* and *F*, we see the songs of the male *T. oceanicus* and *T. commodus*, species capable of interbreeding. From *B* to *E*, we see the songs of various hybrids obtained by crossing the two species and their descendants. The case of hybrid B is particularly interesting. Each trill contains three notes instead of two. Bar length: 100 milliseconds. (From D. Bentley, 1971.)

coupled with one of the parents—for example, a mother *Teleogryllus oceanicus*—the new hybrids have a remarkable song. Their trill has exactly and systematically one note more (that is, three), than the trill of the *Teleogryllus oceanicus* (Figure 52). How can we explain such a subtle difference? We know that oscillating neurons determine the form of the trill. We also know that a few proteins determine the rhythm of these biological clocks (see Chapter 3). Differences in the few genes that code the structure of these proteins may thus suffice to cause distinct differences in the structure of the song.

The cricket does not learn to sing. The fruit fly is capable of learning, but not to sing! It can distinguish two odors innately. If, during training sessions, one odor is associated with an electric shock, but not the other, it progressively learns not to be trapped by the odor associated with the shock. Benzer and his collaborators managed to isolate mutants that were "unconditionable" for an olfactory stimulus coupled with an electric shock. They had not lost their sense of smell or become insensitive to the shock, nor were they paralyzed. They simply learned poorly or not at all.[8] The *amnesiac* mutant loses its memory four times more quickly than the normal fly. The half-life of its memory is only fifteen minutes. The *dunce* mutant seems unable to store information, while the *rutabaga* mutant can store but not use it. We still do not know the exact nature of the biochemical defects in these mutants. Nevertheless, in the dunce mutant, an enzyme that breaks down cyclic AMP is missing.[9] This finding agrees with that in the experiment of "cellular learning" performed on the sea slug (see Chapter 5) in which cyclic AMP seems involved in the long-term modification of synaptic properties, perhaps by regulating the efficiency of the release of the neurotransmitter by nerve terminals. The basic coupling mechanisms between neurons in the fruit fly, sea slug, and probably man may be determined by a few structural genes, just like the propagation of the nerve impulse and synaptic transmission.

Our next example involves man. From the genetics of behavior in the fruit fly to that in man is quite a leap, one that may elicit cold silence or even violent opposition. The severity of these reactions is easy to understand for many reasons, including ideological ones. Political exploitation of genetics has led to racism and thereby discredited the objectives of this discipline. Also, methodologically, the great genetic heterogeneity of human populations, together with often insuperable problems in performing experiments on humans, makes the collection of data and their interpretation difficult. Yet despite the limitations imposed by ideological conflicts that have falsified its objectives, and despite the technical difficulties involved, the study of human genetics has made considerable progress.[10]

Some mental diseases that at first glance do not seem to be associated with an anatomical disturbance of the brain have been the subject of genetic analysis. Firm results have been obtained only in a few cases so far. The best-documented example is that of so-called bipolar manic depression. In the nineteenth century, Étienne Esquirol and Emil Kraepelin emphasized the hereditary character of the disease, but objective proof of this has obtained only been recently.[11] As a first step, one can compare the mental state of identical twins (who come from the same egg and are therefore genetically identical) with that of nonidentical twins. Such a comparison shows that the signs of the disease appear in both identical twins in between 50 and 92 percent of cases with a mean of 69 percent, whereas for nonidentical twins there is from 0 to 38 percent incidence in both members, with a mean of 20 percent. A second piece of evidence comes from studies of family genetics. Close relatives have a 20 percent risk of suffering from the same disease (which is ten times the risk in a normal population). The risk is the same whether the person was raised in his own biological family or adopted. Within a given family, the incidence of the disease can be followed from one generation to another, but it is also possible to follow certain genetic "markers," totally unrelated to the psychosis, such as the absence of color vision or glucose-6-phosphate dehydrogenase deficiency. These markers are situated close together on the map of the X chromosome and have a high chance of being transmitted together from one generation to another. They are *linked*. Analyses of many family trees have shown the linkage of at least one well-defined type of manic depression with these genetic markers within a family. The contribution of heredity in predisposing to this serious mental illness cannot be doubted. The most likely explanation of these genetic findings is that one or several dominant genes on the X chromosome are concerned. The physiological or biochemical disturbances brought about by these genes are not yet clear. Noradrenaline and acetylcholine seem involved, as well as, not unexpectedly, the hypothalamus and the limbic system (see Chapter 4). No particular anatomical lesion seems present. Is it again a question of the regulation of a biological clock, perhaps in the midbrain "regulatory" nuclei?

These few examples are necessarily limited both in their variety and in their importance, but they illustrate the role of genetic factors in the anatomical organization of the nervous system, in the genesis and propagation of nervous activity, and in such sophisticated behavior as learning and affective states. The power of the genes is omnipresent.

THE SIMPLICITY OF THE GENOME AND THE COMPLEXITY OF THE BRAIN

Recognizing the power of the genes in no way forces us to submit to their supreme authority. Charles Darwin wrote, "Heredity is law," and Noam Chomsky, in 1980, claimed that a genetically determined capacity for language specifies a certain class of humanly accessible grammar. But we need not adopt an unconditional allegiance to their views. First, where are the Tablets of this Law, calling on us to respect it? And, further, does this supreme power really possess all the means to apply its Law?

Since the experiments of O.T. Avery, Colin MacLeod, and M. McCarty in 1944, we know that the material of heredity is *deoxyribonucleic acid,* or *DNA.* Made up of nucleotides in two complementary "strings of pearls," wound together in a double helix, it is duplicated without error during cell division, and thus forms the "fundamental biological invariant."[12] The sequence of its nucleotides completely defines the sequence of the amino acids of all the proteins in an organism, whether an *E. coli* bacterium or a human being; a structural gene codes for every protein in the organism. The Tablets of the Law are inscribed in the DNA of the chromosomes.

In order to understand the genetic determination of cerebral organization, we must first be able to decode DNA and understand how it is expressed in proteins. The neurobiologist must become a molecular biologist. But the molecular genetics of the brain are still in their early days. We must satisfy ourselves with examples taken from simple systems, such as a bacterial cell, the oviduct of the chicken, or the abdominal ganglion of the sea slug. With these, we can describe the level of analysis reached so far in our understanding of the molecular biology of cerebral organization.

The research conducted by François Jacob, Jacques Monod, François Gros, and collaborators on *E. coli* showed that the DNA of the genes does not directly code the amino acid sequence of a protein.[13] Another molecule — *ribonucleic acid,* or *RNA* — serves as intermediary. Although possessing the same fibrous shape as DNA, it is chemically different. In the chromosome, DNA is transcribed into *messenger RNA,* which passes into the cytoplasm and there is translated into the sequence of amino acids.[14]

At a given moment in the life of a cell, not all genes are transcribed into messenger RNA and expressed as proteins. A certain "management" is involved in the expression of genes. This genetic "husbandry" is subject to *regulation,* which can be illustrated by two examples: one from *E. coli,* the other from the chicken.

E. coli lives in our intestines. It digests milk sugar, or lactose, by using the enzyme beta-galactosidase. Obviously, since we do not drink milk all the time, the bacterium has to adapt to our diet. It only synthesizes the enzyme when lactose is present. Between meals the synthesis of the enzyme is suppressed, but after a meal containing lactose, the sugar stimulates the synthesis of the enzyme in the bacterium. This stimulation involves the chromosome. The structural gene for beta-galactosidase is "silent" when there is no lactose but becomes "active" when it is present. The lactose, although not directly attached to it, causes the structural gene to be transcribed into messenger RNA. A protein rather like the acetylcholine receptor — a *repressor* — is involved. This molecule "lock" recognizes the sugar "key" just as the receptor recognizes the neurotransmitter. But it is not in a membrane and does not open an ion channel. It attaches to a particular locus, or position, on the chromosome. When it is bound to (or detached from) this locus it suppresses (or induces) the transcription of the gene. The repressor thus plays the role of intermediary agent between the outside world, represented by the lactose, and the genes of the chromosomes. It regulates the activity of the genes at the chromosomal level. The reactions of this allosteric protein, like those of the acetylcholine receptor, are totally predictable. They are determined by the amino acid sequence of the protein, itself coded by a specific gene that, because of its function, is designated a *regulatory* gene.[15]

Another form of regulation is found only in higher organisms with large ensembles of cells, grouped into tissues. Each tissue is specialized for a particular function, determined by a number of critical proteins. For example, blood corpuscles produce hemoglobin; the skin, a pigment (melanin), which we have already discussed. We have also mentioned that in the nervous system some neurons synthesize acetylcholine as a neurotransmitter, others noradrenaline, and yet others a neuropeptide. In this light the concept of a neuron *category* was put forward to describe cells possessing the same set of active genes—genes that can be expressed as proteins (see Chapter 2). This set contains proteins common to all cell types and indispensable for basic cell processes such as metabolism, production of ATP, and protein or membrane synthesis. In addition to these shared proteins, there are others, unique to a particular tissue or cell type. The activation of their structural genes constitutes a kind of regulation, but it differs from that involved in the synthesis of beta-galactosidase by *E. coli.*[16]

In the chicken the proteins of the white of the egg are synthesized by the oviduct when the "real" egg—the yolk—passes from the ovary into the cloaca. These proteins coat the egg as its passes. They are produced only during the laying season. Hormones, such as estrogen and progesterone, regulate this production just as lactose regulates the synthesis of beta-galactosidase in *E. coli.* They increase messenger RNA about 3,000 times. The hormones act only on a "target organ," with little or no effect on other tissues such as skeletal muscles or the liver. Each tissue possesses a characteristic "sensitivity" to a particular hormone. In other words, it contains a set of genes *ready to respond* to that hormone.[17]

The mechanisms of gene activation, which allows a tissue or a group of cells to respond to a hormone, are still incompletely understood at the chromosomal level. We simply know that it is accompanied by modifications in the physical state of groups of genes, of chromosomal "domains." This can be seen, for example, in the vulnerability of DNA to certain enzyme attacks. One enzyme that can break down DNA attacks the structural gene of ovalbumin, but not that of hemoglobin, when the DNA is prepared from the oviduct. On the other hand, it will break down the gene of hemoglobin but not of ovalbumin if the DNA is extracted from the bone marrow. It is thought that the packing of the genes, perhaps even their chemical composition, changes when, during development, an embryonic cell differentiates into a red blood cell, a muscle fiber, or a neuron.

Obviously the brain is more complicated than the oviduct. Nevertheless, both are composed of differentiated cells. So far, few major differences have been found between the basic mechanisms of this differentiation in various tissues. It is likely that the gene activation follows the same, or similar, rules in the oviduct of the chicken, the nerve ganglia of the sea slug,[18] and the human brain.

It has often been said, following Jacques Monod, that "what is true for *E. coli* is also true for the elephant." Recent work on the structure of genes in higher organisms, however, has led us to modify this proposal. Without doubt, DNA is the material support of heredity and the genetic code is universal. So it came as a huge surprise to find that in higher organisms the length of certain structural genes seemed unreasonably great compared with the length of the protein coded for by these genes. The ovalbumin molecule, for example, consists of 386 amino acids; as three nucleotides code for one amino acid, one would expect the ovalbumin gene to be 1,158 nucleotides long. But the ovalbumin gene reaches about seven times this length—7,900 nucleotides![19] How can this enormous difference be explained? If one compares the sequences in the chromosomal DNA with those in the proteins, only certain fragments of the gene can be identified in the protein. The sequences that code for the protein are split up, scattered among other DNA sequences not coding for any known proteins. The number of these intervening sequences can be very high. There are seven in the ovalbumin gene, but up to fifty-one in the genes of other proteins. Thus a large part of the DNA of chromosomal genes does not code for any known protein. Why such a waste?

Here, again, the answer is not clear. We simply know that in the case of split genes, like the ovalbumin one, most of the DNA, whether coding or not, is transcribed into RNA, which is then cut up and the coding fragments spliced end to end (in the same sequence as the original, with no mistakes) to yield a "mature" messenger RNA, which can be directly translated into protein. Recently, in 1979, D. Hamer and P. Leder showed that if one interferes with this cutting up and splicing together again of the initial messenger RNA, it becomes unstable, disappears from the cell, and is thus not available for translation and protein synthesis. An attractive hypothesis is that this cutting up and splicing together is part of a third type of control mechanism, one concerned with the *stability* of the initial messenger RNA. In this light the expression of a structural gene in a higher organism would undergo a chain of regulatory steps, with, first, the unwinding of the gene, then its transcription into an initial messenger, then the cutting up and splicing together of the RNA into the final messenger, and finally the translation of the messenger into a sequence of amino acids.

The amount of stable messenger RNA present in the cytoplasm of a differentiated cell reflects the population of active genes synthesizing proteins. It can be used to identify this population. How does the brain compare with other organs in this matter? How large is its set of active genes? Does it differ significantly from that of the oviduct or the lens of the eye? The findings so far are still preliminary, but highly suggestive. The techniques used give information on both the *diversity* and the *abundance* of messenger RNA. In principle, the diversity reflects the number of genes transcribed into stable messengers, while the abundance is related to the state of activity of a gene. The more active a gene is, the more protein it produces and the greater the abundance of its messenger. The lens of the eye produces a very small number of proteins but in large quantities. It has about 3,000 different messengers, but the number of each is high. In the oviduct of the chicken there is greater diversity—at least 13,000—but the abundance is moderate. The liver and the brain have at least 20,000 different types of messenger RNA in common. According to W. Hahn and his collaborators, there are another 40,000 unique to the brain, but this is probably a low estimate.[20] The number of different messenger RNA molecules produced in the brain and unique to this organ may be in the neighborhood of 150,000. Their abundance, on the other hand, is low. In other words, there are many genes that are turned on, but their levels of activity are relatively low. These figures accord with the great diversity of cell categories and neurotransmitters in the brain.

Thus, the brain takes pride of place among all the organs in the body for the richness of its messenger RNA and the number of its active genes. This was to be expected. But what is the relationship of this genetic "fortune" with the total number of genes in the genome? Does the brain reserve for itself almost all the DNA available in the chromosomes?

The total quantity of chromosomal DNA limits the maximum number of genes. In the nucleus of the fertilized mouse egg there are six millionths of a microgram (a millionth of a gram) of DNA. If we arbitrarily cut this strand of DNA into medium-sized segments (corresponding, for example, to a gene coding for a protein with a molecular weight of 40,000), we find approximately two million such segments. The maximum number of genes that we could hope to find with this quantity of chromosomal DNA cannot be greater than this number. In fact the number of coding sequences is much lower. We have already mentioned that intervening sequences are not translated into proteins. (Structural genes lose four-fifths of their DNA in this way.) In addition, a large portion of DNA consists of sequences repeated many times. This redundant part can hardly be considered as structural genes. Further, the structural gene of a single protein may be repeated several times. Thus, the number of structural genes available represents only a minute fraction of the total chromosomal DNA.

Estimates of the maximum number of structural genes are still very approximate, but in the mouse the range is between 20,000 and 150,-000. The latter figure seems quite possible. It is of the same magnitude as the "diversity" of messenger RNA found in the brain. This would suggest that the brain "capitalizes" on most of the structural genes available in the chromosomes.

Is this considerable genetic capital sufficient to cover the complexity of the brain and account for the genetic determination of its organization? The reply must obviously be yes, but that raises an enormous problem. Compared with the extreme diversity and complexity of the anatomy of the brain, the initial capital seems small. To begin with, let us see how the total DNA content per cell nucleus has evolved from bacteria to man.

E. coli bacterium	0.01	$\times$	10^{-6} micrograms
Fruit fly *Drosophila*	0.24	$\times$	10^{-6} micrograms
Chicken	2.5	$\times$	10^{-6} micrograms
Mouse	6	$\times$	10^{-6} micrograms
Man	6	$\times$	10^{-6} micrograms

There is a moderate increase in DNA content from bacteria to mice. Not surprisingly, the egg of the fruit fly *Drosophila* contains twenty-four times more DNA than *E. coli* and the mouse twenty-five times more than the fruit fly. Very approximately, the nervous system of the fruit fly contains 100,000 neurons and that of the mouse of fifty to sixty times more. When we pass from the mouse to man, we encounter a paradox. The number of cerebral cells jumps from some five or six million to several tens of billions. The level of organization and performance of the brain increases spectacularly, while the total quantity of DNA in the nucleus of the fertilized egg does not change significantly. Within 10 percent, it is the same in mouse, ox, chimpanzee, and man, pointing to a remarkable *nonlinearity* between the DNA content and the complexity of the brain. The paradox becomes even more striking when one looks more closely at man. What are a mere 200,000 or even a million genes compared with the number of synapses in the human brain or even the number of different types of neurons identifiable in the human cerebral cortex? No simple relationship exists between the complexity of organization of the genome and that of the central nervous system. The aphorism "one gene—one enzyme" coined by George Beadle and Edward Tatum in 1941 can in no way become "one gene—one synapse." So how can we explain that the very complex organization of the central nervous system of higher vertebrates can be built up, in a reproducible way, from such a small number of genetic determinants? The way this complexity emerges during embryonic development—the "mechanics of development" cited by Wilhelm Roux in 1895—provides an answer.

THE AUTOMATON CELL

Looking at a section of cerebral cortex cell by cell under the microscope or even—if we have the courage!—synapse by synapse, we easily forget that these tens of billions of neurons and their synapses are derived from a single egg cell with its two sets of chromosomes. When we think about it, we see a serious problem. What guiding mechanism plans and directs the evolution of generations of cells from this single egg to form the body's most complex organ? It is very tempting to invoke the intervention of obscure but omnipotent forces in the execution of this task. A Herculean labor of description and analysis becomes necessary to avoid this trap. To understand the brain is no longer enough. One has to consider, in addition, the temporal pattern of all the successive stages between the egg and the adult (Figure 53).

Everything begins with the meeting of the unfertilized ovule and the sperm in the mother's Fallopian tubes. This contact leads to a doubling of the set of chromosomes, followed—about thirty-six hours later in humans—by the first division into two cells (see Figure 53A). The cells continue to divide until, four days after fertilization, a hollow *morula* (or mulberry-shaped mass) of fifty-eight cells forms (see Figure 53B). Not all these cells will be used to make the human embryo. After implantation in the wall of the uterus, the cells on the surface establish contact with the maternal tissues to ensure the nutrition of the embryo.

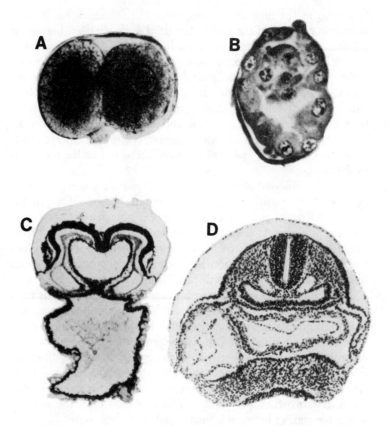

Figure 53. Various stages in the development of the human egg and embryo. *A:* One and a half days after fertilization, the egg undergoes its first division. *B:* After four days, there are fifty-eight cells, with some outside the cell mass and others inside. Only the internal cells will produce the embryo, which will be implanted in the uterus a few days later. *C:* Around the twentieth day, in the dorsal region, the embryonic outer layer (or ectoderm) thickens into a plate, which will form the nervous system. *D:* At thirty-two to thirty-four days, the neural plate closes to form the neural tube. (From R. O'Rahilly, 1973; G. L. Streeter, 1951.)

The other cells gather inside the morula and proliferate to form the real embryo.[21]

At this stage the embryo still has no nervous system. It is made up of a compact ball of cells, in which cavities quickly form and which splits into concentric layers. The innermost layer participates in the formation of the digestive system, while the outermost has a more noble future. Toward the end of the third week after fertilization, it consists of a single layer of cells, but then thickens and differentiates so that its dorsal region forms a plate from which most of the nervous system derives. This is the *neural plate* (see Figure 53C). In the formation of this embryonic organ, two major factors decide which embryonic cells will differentiate into nerve cells: first, they must remain on the surface of the embryo and, second, they must be in the dorsal region. Thus, the relative position of cells in the embryo determines their future and, particularly, their setting out on the royal road to the brain.

Once it is differentiated, the neural plate forms a groove, the edges of which subsequently close into a tube (see Figure 53D). On the twenty-fifth day of embryonic life, the tube is still open at its two ends, but later it closes. At the front, three vesicles develop that will form the brain, with the rear part becoming the spinal cord. Between four and six weeks after fertilization, the nervous system of the human fetus roughly resembles that of a fish (see Figure 13).

The nature of the cellular transformations that yield neurons from the egg cells is still poorly understood. We must call on theoretical models to grasp a reality that is difficult to approach experimentally.

In 1975 L. Wolpert and J. Lewis proposed that the behavior of an embryonic cell resembled self-reproducing mathematical entities described by John von Neumann as "automatons." The principal property of these automatons is that they can arrive at several "discrete" states, toward which they evolve. This evolution takes the form of successive choices between a small number of these states.

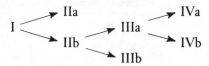

For instance, in the above example, the route is from I to IIb, IIb to IIIa, etc. The choice between one or the other of these states is regulated by a very simple signal: yes or no. Once the choice is made it determines the possible options in the next decision. At all times the past history of the automaton decides its future behavior. The main interest of this model is that even with only a small number of signals (for example, 20), we reach a very high number (2^{20}, or a million) of different ways of directing the automaton toward its final state. This model guarantees a considerable diversification with a minimum number of signals.

Leaving the vocabulary of the theoretician for that of the embryologist: the automaton can be likened to an embryonic cell and each of its states related to a state of cell differentiation described in principle by the repertoire of active chromosomal genes. Even if this repertoire is limited to a maximum of 200,000 genes in mammals and encumbered by a few tens of thousands of fundamental genes, there is still enough information to determine a large number of final states. If each state is defined, for example, by 1,000 active genes and if these 1,000 are taken from a total of 200,000, the number of possible states becomes 10^{2700}! The combination of a limited number of genes and signals yields an enormous number of cell types. This principle provides a first solution to the paradox already mentioned concerning the simplicity of the genome versus the complexity of the adult brain. The automaton model is thus compatible with the demands of real embryonic development. Does it allow us to go further in interpreting available experimental data?

Amazing mutations, which remained puzzling for many years, are found in the fruit fly *Drosophila* and several other insects. In the adult they may be seen in such astonishing monstrosities as the replacement of an eye by a wing, (ophthalmoptera) or an antenna by a limb (aristapedia). The term *homoeotic* is used for these mutations.[22] How can the single mutation of a chromosomal gene explain the sudden exchange of one body part for another in a place where one would not at all expect this part to appear? To answer this question, we must return to the first stages of embryonic development. The eyes, antennae, limbs, and wings develop from disklike cell clusters in the nymph before its metamorphosis into a fly. If these disks are transplanted from one larva to another, the corresponding organ will grow. They contain all the information necessary for producing an eye, an antenna, a limb, or a wing; and the adult fly is built up from these disks as from a Lego set. When are these disks formed? They appear very early in development and already possess their distinctive character. Three hours after fertilization the embryo still has only a very small number of cells, yet some are already forming minute disk precursors. At this stage the homoeotic genes become active. They decide which type of organ will form from a given disk after metamorphosis. Each disk precursor, made

189

up of ten to forty cells, is thus confronted with a choice between a small number of states, for instance as follows[23]:

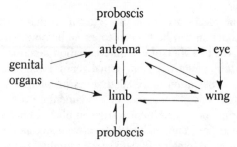

These precursors then behave much like the automatons of Wolpert and Lewis's model, with homoeotic genes controlling the transitions. The homoeotic genes here act as major regulatory genes in embryonic development, making decisions that determine entire organs, including, of course, the nervous system.

No one has seen a mutation that caused a hand to take the place of an eye in man or other mammals. Nevertheless, certain homoeotic genes found in the fruit fly have counterparts in mice and even in humans. In addition, mutations have been identified in the mouse that selectively alter the formation of the nervous system. Several of these mutations are found on T chromosomes, modified forms of chromosome 17, and several combinations are already known.[24] All of these affect embryonic development, but at different stages and to different degrees. A mutation may, for instance, have a minor effect, as when a mouse has a short tail, or no tail at all, but survives nonetheless. Sometimes, however, the effect is so dramatic that it completely stops embryonic development. The blockage occurs in the cell lines destined for the nervous system, but at very different stages, according to the combinations of T mutations. Late blockage, at fifteen to twenty-one embryonic days, is manifested by a severe change in the forebrain and by the absence of eyes. Earlier blockage, at eleven embryonic days, interferes with the closing of the neural tube; the brain may even be completely absent. Still earlier, on the eighth embryonic day, the outer layer of the embryo, including the neural plate, does not form. If the block is between the second and the eighth day, the embryonic cell mass itself does not appear. According to Wolpert and Lewis's model, these genetic alterations, like homoeotic mutations, would effect transitions of automatonlike cells each time they had to make a choice on their way to forming a brain. At every fork, the "road to the brain" can be blocked by a mutation like that of the T chromosomes. Thus, in the same way as a homoeotic gene, a group of genes can control the temporal evolution of cellular transitions leading to the formation of the brain.

Homoeotic genes in the fruit fly and T chromosomes in the mouse illustrate how the genes exercise their power over the development of the nervous system. To begin with, they do not have to be numerous to have great power. On the contrary, only a few are needed to make a decision of such consequence as the disappearance of the brain. The earlier these decisions are made during embryonic development, the greater their effect. Time plays an important role in the formation of the embryo, and the brain. The sequential opening of a few genes in the course of development creates a diversity sufficient to explain, at least in part, how the general organization of the brain develops.

THE EMBRYO SYSTEM

In the regularity of its timing and its reproducibility, the development of the embryo fascinated the first molecular biologists, who, in the 1960s, began to apply to embryology the knowledge they had gained of the biochemical genetics of the *E. coli* bacterium. They began to write about a "genetic program" controlling the development of the embryo in time. Were they thinking of a program for a play, or of a magnetic disk, the software that serves to program a computer? In *The Logic of Life* (1970), François Jacob wrote: "A bacterium represents the translation of a nucleic sequence about a millimeter long and composed of some twenty million signs. Man is determined by another nucleic sequence, about two meters long, and containing several billion signs. Organizational complication then corresponds to a lengthening of the program." DNA is the magnetic disk containing the program. Recently, in 1981, another molecular biologist, Gunther Stent, questioned this notion, as did the theoretician S. Atlan in 1979. The concept of an individual program, clearly developed from cybernetics, may just apply to the bacterial cell. To use it in the context of the development of a multicellular organism can be contested from several points of view.

First of all, DNA is a linear structure and the development of an egg occurs in three dimensions. There must exist other geometrical reference points that are not in the program. Further, the concept of a program implies a single control center. If chromosomal DNA contains this program, the only time it exists in a unique form is in the fertilized egg. The first division of the egg breaks this unity. Each cell receives a complete set of chromosomes, and yet, as Jacob wrote, "although containing the whole of the program, each cell translates only fragments of it." So where can we find this genetic program if it is "delocalized" in the course of the first developmental stages of the embryo? To get around this, we must abandon the concept of the organism as a cybernetic machine. But with what should we replace this concept? Wolpert and Lewis's model enables us to understand the diversity of the cellular pathways leading to the formation of the principal adult organs. It does not explain, in its simplest form, the temporal coordination that exists between the different pathways, a coordination that points to the unitary and global nature of some hypothetical program.

The systems theory proposed by Ludwig von Bertalanffy in 1973 gives us an answer in principle. Once again it is a formal mathematical theory, but this time it leads to a very concrete experimental situation. The basic idea is that the "holistic system" is made up of elements, which can easily be, for example, the automatons already mentioned. A system will then be defined by the number of these elements, by their different classes (if these exist), and above all by the relation in space and time of the elements and the rules governing their interactions. The formal notion of a program is replaced by an exhaustive description of properties, elements, geometry, and a communication network. The global behavior of the system is worked out from elementary local data. If we abandon, once again, the theoretician's vocabulary for that of the embryologist, the "embryo system" can be broken down naturally into automatonlike elements represented by the embryonic cells, whose number, state of differentiation, position, and so on evolve with time. The rules of interaction are laid down by the exchanges of signals between cells and, more particularly, the relationship between intercellular signaling and the position of these cells in the embryo. The genes of each embryonic cell no longer constitute independent units. The communication network established between the cells continuously coordinates their expression. Adopting the embryo-system model makes us describe reality more precisely and in more detail. It emphasizes the importance of interaction between cells in the formation of the complex adult organization. It also offers a way of interpreting the paradoxical effects of certain mutations involving the nervous system.

When we described the albino, we emphasized the fact that this mutation, qualified as pleiotropic, concerns both pigmentation and the visual pathway from the eye to the cerebral cortex. Why? We must examine the first stages of the development of the visual pathways and remember that the retina is black because of a layer of pigment cells containing melanin. Albinos have red eyes; the melanin is missing from the eyes, as well as from the rest of the body. In the normal embryo the pigment appears in the eye very early, when the retinal neurons whose axons will form the optic nerve are dividing for the last time. At this stage embryonic neurons and pigment cells are in close contact. Quite probably there is an exchange of signals between these cells, and the pigment, or something derived from it, is implicated in these signals. Whatever actually happens, when the pigment is present, the neurons send their axons in the correct direction; when it is absent, they go in the wrong direction. The rules of interaction between neurons and pigment cells at this critical stage of development determine the direction taken by the axons on their way to the lateral geniculate nucleus. Things do not stop there, for the lateral geniculate neurons themselves contact neurons of the visual cortex, where considerable reorganization takes place. Interactions between pigment cells and retinal neurons give way to interactions between retinal neurons and lateral geniculate neurons, then between these and cortical neurons. As predicted by the embryo-system model, a disturbance at any point of the cellular interaction network gives rise to a wave of effects, extending as far as the cerebral cortex. It explains the pleiotropic impact of single gene mutations if they disturb the communication network between developing cells.

A small number of genes, which we shall call "communication" genes, suffice to determine and control this network.[25] Like the automaton model for embryonic cells, the embryo-system model makes the relative poverty of the genome compared with the wealth of the adult central nervous system less paradoxical.

Our understanding of the chemistry of the factors involved in the interactions between cellular elements of the embryo system is in its early stages. We still do not know what the T chromosomes produce or what the "inducer" of the neural plate is. There is no lack, however, of candidates; indeed, there is a veritable treasure trove of diverse molecules. Among them, we may mention cyclic AMP, which we discussed in relation to the efficiency of the release of neurotransmitters during learning. In addition, retinoic acid has recently been suggested,[26] for in the test tube it stimulates multipotential embryonic cells to take a particular pathway, for example, toward the intestine. But is it involved in the same way in the embryo during development? Later in the embryo and in the newborn better-known factors become involved—better known because they are some of the hormones of the adult, such as the sex hormones.

Indeed, sex marks the anatomy of the brain and many of its functions. As we know, sex is determined by a different chromosome composition in the male (XY) and in the female (XX). But it seems that these chromosomes are not directly expressed at the level of the target organs, such as the external genitalia or the brain. "Liaison agents," the sex hormones, serve as intermediaries diffused among the embryonic cells. They are synthesized in the endocrine glands of the embryonic ovary and testicle and act at some distance from their site of production.

The activity of hormones in establishing sexual behavior has been best studied in the developing rat.[27] During copulation the male mounts the female, but the female never mounts the male. The receptive female adopts a characteristic position. She stands on her four feet with her head pushed forward and back arched, so that her rear quarters are lifted up, exposing the opening of the vagina. She also turns her tail to one side to facilitate penetration by the male. This posture of the female constitutes the *lordosis* reflex. It is sufficiently characteristic that it can be quantified. In the adult rat, removal of the ovaries abolishes lordosis. The female no longer responds to the male. But lordosis reappears soon after the injection of female hormones. They are necessary for the carrying out of this behavior.

Hormones play an even more striking role during postnatal development. Removal of the testicles in the newborn rat leads to the appearance of lordosis when the male reaches adulthood. Although genetically male, the castrated animal adopts female behavior. The male hormones produced by the newborn's testicles block the female lordosis behavior and the characteristic mounting behavior of the male appears.[28]

We still do not know the anatomical basis of lordosis. On the other hand, there are clear morphological differences between males and females in those parts of the hypothalamus that control ovulation. The volume of the preoptic area, one of these centers, is eight times larger in the adult male rat than in the female. But a particular type of synapse on the preoptic neurons has been found to be 30 percent more frequent in the female than in the male, and castration of a male at birth increases these synapses until, as an adult, he has about the same number as a female. Thus, hormones act on the anatomical sexual differentiation of specific centers in the brain of rats and logically also in humans,[29] although here the data are still fragmentary. Hormones are probably responsible for sex differences in the mean weight of the brain mentioned in Chapter 2 and also in the shape and area of the corpus callosum connecting the two hemispheres (its posterior part is wider in females than in males).[30]

Sex hormones control the activation and expression of genes in the target cells through the intermediary of receptors—molecule "locks" that selectively bind the hormones. Unlike the neurotransmitter receptors discussed in Chapter 3, hormone receptors are not bound to the cell membranes; instead, like genetic repressors, they are attached to the chromosomal genes. In both mouse and man, mutations are known that affect the structural genes of these molecule locks. When this happens, all tissues, including the brain, lack these receptors and therefore cannot respond to the hormone in question.

Sex differentiation, including that of the brain, is controlled by a hormonal communication network, itself under genetic control.[31] The hormones participate in interactions that coordinate the expression of genes in the very diverse cells and organs of the embryo and the newborn. Other, still poorly understood chemical factors could play a similar role during the division of embryonic cells and their migration and differentiation. The embryo-system model thus allows us to drop the holistic and pointless idea of a genetic program; it emphasizes the contribution of intercellular interaction in the development of the organism and in the establishment of the complex adult organization.

THE GENESIS OF THE CORTEX

The cerebral cortex· begins to form before the brain differentiates sexually. Already at the sixth week of human embryonic life, the most forward vesicle of the neural tube divides into two compartments, each of which will form a cerebral hemisphere (Figure 54). Initially, the wall of the neural tube is made up of a single layer of contiguous cells. They divide very actively and in a few months produce several tens of billions of cells. At times they produce up to 250,000 cells per minute. As the

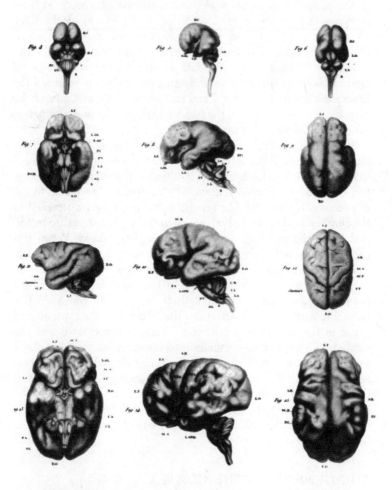

Figure 54. This nineteenth-century engraving describes the development of the human brain. The three *upper* drawings are of a fetus of fourteen weeks. The *next* three show a fetus aged four and a half months. *Below* this, on the *left* and the *right*, the brain of an adult squirrel monkey is compared with that of a five-month-old human fetus, in the *center;* the resemblance is obvious. The three *bottom* figures depict a human fetus, aged six months. The principal fissures and convolutions of the cortex are already present. (From F. Leuret, 1839; L. Gratiolet, 1857.)

divisions take place, two phenomena are observed. First, the area of the cerebral vesicles increases. This expansion is quite spectacular in humans; it is much more marked than in monkeys. At the same time the vesicle walls thicken and the first "layer" appears. The deepest cells continue to divide, forming a proliferation zone. Then they migrate to the surface to accumulate in a differentiation zone or *cortical plate*, which will become the cerebral cortex in the adult (Figure 55).[32]

Sixteen to twenty weeks after fertilization, nerve cell division probably stops. Thus the maximum number of cortical neurons is attained well before birth. We are born with a brain in which the number of neurons can only diminish.

The cortical plate progressively thickens and the neurons produced in the generating zone accumulate. Layers I to VI gradually become distinguishable. The piling up of neurons in the cortical plate could proceed in two different ways. In the adult, layer I is the most superficial, layer VI the deepest (see Chapter 2). As the proliferation zone is even deeper, logically one would expect the layers to be formed like sediments, with layer I being the furthest away and layer VI the nearest to the zone of generation. This is not what happens. Curiously, the

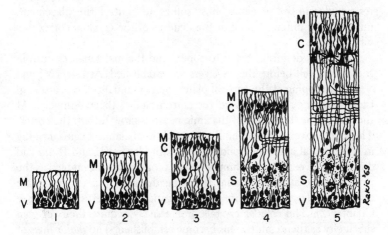

Figure 55. Schematic drawing of five stages in the embryonic development of the cerebral cortex from the wall of the neural tube. Precursors of neurons and glial cells proliferate in that part of the neural tube in contact with the ventricle (V). Then the cells migrate toward the periphery (M), where they accumulate to form the cortical plate (C), which will give rise to the major part of the adult cortex. (Drawing by P. Rakic, from R. L. Sidman, 1970.)

opposite occurs.[33] To observe this, one must mark the cells at the moment that they divide for the last time, using, for example, a radioactive precursor of DNA. They can then be identified, in the adult, in the cortical layer in which they finally arrive. It is clear that the neurons of layer VI, the closest to the generating zone, are laid down first, then those of layer V (which must thus cross the already-established layer VI in order to reach their final position). The process continues until layers III and II are formed, after a long passage through the already-formed cortex. Thus successive layers are set one inside the other like Russian dolls. The oldest are on the inside and the more recent on the outside.

The rules for the multiplication, migration, and placement of the cellular "crystals" corresponding to each successive layer of the cortex seem to be the same throughout the cortex, with few exceptions. This explains the remarkable uniformity noted by Thomas Powell and his collaborators in the organization of the adult cortex (see Chapter 2). There is always approximately the same number of neurons in a vertical core below a given surface area, and the proportion of pyramidal and stellate cells is the same. Whatever the area, the rules of development are the same. In other words, the same genetic command applies. A restricted number of genes must suffice to control the placement, number, and differentiation of the neurons of the cerebral cortex (see Chapter 8).

Axons and dendrites begin to appear and the first synapses form in the cortex well before the six layers are established. As layers VI and V are developing at the cortical plate, the pyramidal-cell precursors in them send their axons toward the corresponding thalamic nuclei. At the same time, the axons of thalamic neurons grow toward the cortex. The loop between the cerebral cortex and the thalamus begins forming in a reciprocal and synchronous way, before layers III and II are laid down.[34] The cerebral machinery is thus progressively assembled as the parts become available. Axons from the thalamus initially terminate diffusely in layer IV, before they reorganize into vertical slabs (see Chapter 2). The cellular crystals progressively acquire their regional specificity as their connections become established. The *major* lines of connection in the cerebral cortex, in both monkey and man, are in place *before birth.*

The human infant is born with a brain weighing about 300 grams —20 percent of the weight of the adult brain—whereas the chimpanzee's brain already reaches 40 percent of its adult weight by birth. One of the major features in the development of the human brain, then, is that it continues well after birth, for about fifteen years (compared with a gestation period of only nine months). The increase in brain weight does not contradict the fact that the neurons of the cerebral cortex have stopped dividing several weeks *before* birth. It reflects the growth of axons and dendrites, the formation of synapses, and the development of myelin sheaths around the axons.

In 1910 Santiago Ramón y Cajal described the amazing increase in complexity of the dendritic trees of pyramidal cells after birth in man (Figure 56). More recently, these studies have been extended in monkeys and humans.[35] Not long after their formation in the cortical plate, pyramidal cells show a very simple form. There is a smooth apical dendrite, another dendrite derived from the cell body, and the axon, which has already left the cortex. Then new dendrites appear at the base of the cell body, horizontal branches form on the apical dendrite,

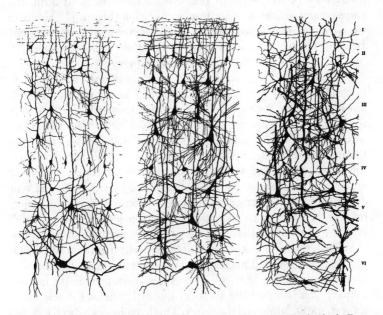

Figure 56. Growth of the dendritic trees of cerebral-cortex neurons in man after birth. From *left* to *right:* infants of three, fifteen, and twenty-four months. These sections from the superior temporal cortex were stained by the Golgi method. (From J. L. Conel in J. Altman, 1967.)

and the cell body takes on a more pyramidal shape (see Figures 56 and 77). These dendrites, at first "bald," become "hairy" and then covered with spines.[36] Brian Cragg estimated in 1975 that in the cat the mean number of synapses per cortical neuron increased from a few hundred to about 13,000 between the eighth and the thirty-seventh day after birth. This increase is just as great, if not greater, in monkeys and especially humans.

During this period the different maps, including homunculi, are drawn in the cortex as the thalamic fibers penetrate it and form synapses. One particularly well-studied example of the development of a cortical "homunculus" (body map) found in the somatosensory cortex in the mouse. As already noted, it is characterized by the large area devoted to the representation of the whiskers (see Figure 39). Tangential sections of the somatosensory cortex reveal rows of "barrels" from 200 to 400 microns in diameter, each barrel corresponding to a whisker on the mouse's snout.[37] These barrels appear progressively after birth in layer IV of the cortex. If one whisker is destroyed at birth, the corresponding barrel does not form in the adult (Figure 57). How can the periphery of the body project to the cortex with such precision? Between the whiskers and the cortex there are at least two synaptic relays, one in the thalamus. What happens there?

If the corresponding thalamic nucleus is cut in serial sections, rows of small barrels or "barreloids" appear, which also correspond to rows of whiskers. When one whisker is destroyed the day after birth, neither the cortical barrel nor the thalamic barreloid form. The map of the whiskers is preserved from the snout to the thalamus and from the thalamus to the cortex. When a whisker is destroyed four days later, the cortical barrel does not appear but the thalamic barreloid develops normally. The thalamic barreloid is stabilized between one and four days after birth; the cortical barrel, later—after four days. The projections of the whiskers are therefore laid down sequentially in a "chain" from the snout to the thalamus, then from the thalamus to the cortex.

What is the mechanism responsible for preserving the relative position of the whiskers through this chain of projections? The simplest hypothesis is that the geometry is never lost; it is present in the nervous pathways that connect the snout to the thalamus and in the axons between the thalamus and the cortex. This hypothesis has been tested in the visual system where, as with the whiskers, the retina projects point by point on the lateral geniculate nucleus of the thalamus.

Let us follow the axons of the optic nerve. As they leave the retina, they could perhaps be randomly mixed. However, anatomical studies and recordings of the activity of retinal neurons and their axons in different parts of the optic nerve show that this is not the case.[38] The topographic relationship of neurons in the retina is maintained in the

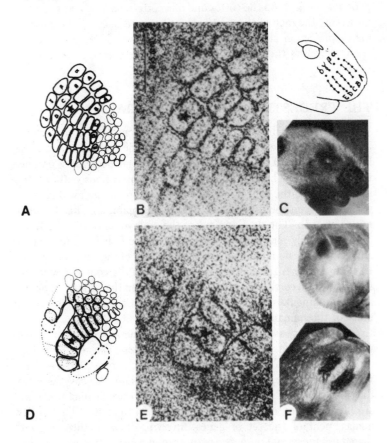

Figure 57. The importance of peripheral sense organs in the development of maps in the cerebral cortex. Here we see the projection of the whiskers in the mouse. *A, B,* and *C* represent the normal adult. In layer IV of the cortex (B) the neurons are organized in "barrels," each barrel corresponding to a whisker of the mouse (C). In A, the whole cortical map of the whiskers is reconstructed. The star indicates the same whisker in A, B, D, and E. In the mouse in *F,* several rows of whiskers were destroyed at birth; in *D* and *E,* we see that the corresponding barrels are missing in the adult cerebral cortex. (From H. Van der Loos and T. Woolsey, 1973.)

optic nerve axons, which remain grouped together in bundles. In other words, the map of the axons reproduces that of the neurons. There is a preservation of the geometrical relationship of neurons from the retina to the optic nerve and from the optic nerve to the lateral geniculate nucleus. From this simple process, we can see how the periphery projects on the cortex and one cortical area on another while preserving the map of the relationships between neurons. This principle of projection allows for a considerable diversification of cortical areas, as well as the neurons that make up these areas.

THE PREDESTINATION OF THE BRAIN

When a human baby is born, the cortical neurons have stopped dividing. Their maximum number is thus fixed. In the event of a lesion, the lost neurons cannot be replaced. Neurons can only decrease in number throughout life. The main features of the connections between the sensory organs, the central nervous system, and the motor organs, as well as between the principal centers in the brain, are already determined at birth. The development of the embryo, and later the fetus, follows a highly reproducible pattern from one individual to another and from one generation to another. The power of the genes is obvious. Individual differences are small compared with the consistency in the major lines of cerebral organization. Whatever the ethnic, climatic, and environmental differences, the authority of the genes ensures the unity of the human brain within the species.

This power is based on a small number of genetic determinants, and yet it makes itself felt. To this end, the genetic oligarchy employs distinct methods. The first is *economy*. We know from Chapter 3 that several intestinal peptides can be found in the brain. We have also seen that in the albino a single gene may intervene in two distinct functions at different times, during development and in the adult. This thrifty management of the set of genes, involving their reutilization and shared use for several purposes, permits solid construction with a minimum of structural elements. Rather than a helter-skelter accumulation, a limited capital is put to economic use.

Genes diversify their action in another way, by *combining their effects in time and space*. The automaton model of an embryonic cell suggests how a large number of distinct cellular states can be obtained with a minimum number of signals, and this applies equally to nerve cells. With the embryo-system model, one realizes how a few genes involved in communications between embryonic cells could coordinate the expression of sets of genes spread throughout several different parts of the embryo and its developing nervous system.

A small number of genes is enough to control progressively and sequentially the division, migration, and differentiation of the neurons forming the cerebral cortex. The laying down of its regular, uniform crystalline structure of cells can be completed with a minimum expenditure of genes. Yet this regular structure will undergo diversification from area to area thanks to the projection of maps of the periphery, after relay in the thalamus, on corresponding regions of the cortex. Multiple representations of the body, the organs, and even the nervous centers will be inscribed in the cerebral cortex during development. The mechanisms involved in these projections are poorly understood, but it seems likely that geometrical relationships between growing axons are preserved. Here again, very few genetic determinants are necessary. An interweaving of the map of thalamic axons and cortical cellular crystals will allow for considerable diversification between cortical areas. Furthermore, the map of one cortical area may project to another area by associational or commissural axons. This can be the basis for a combination, or interaction, between cortical maps.

All these methods, with others to be discussed in the next chapter, make the disproportion between the total number of genes and the complexity of the organization of the central nervous system less paradoxical. One solution may thus lie in multiple combinations of gene activity in time and space. The consequences are important. Obviously, one may speak of the "genetic determinism" of the functional organization of the central nervous system. But this term will cover very different processes, depending on whether it refers to the primary structure of a protein, such as a neurotransmitter receptor, or very highly integrated faculties, such as human language. In the first instance, there will be a direct and unequivocal relationship between the sequence of the nucleotides of the structural gene and the sequence of amino acids in the protein. In the second instance, we are dealing with a cerebral function that utilizes large cellular groupings whose layout has been determined progressively with time and not necessarily synchronously. It is no longer possible to think of a gene coding for a given structure or function. The gene for madness, language, or intelligence does not exist. We know that it is not possible to assign an integrated cerebral function to a single center or a single neurotransmitter; it belongs, rather, to a system of "transit stations," where different states of electrical and chemical activity are integrated. In the same way the actions of genes overlap, are integrated and linked. The actions of many genes "converge" on a given brain structure, and a single gene may have "divergent" effects on several different structures. Genes express themselves sequentially and differentially during development, permitting the creation of the human brain organization. The reproducibility of the temporal and spatial unfolding of these gene expressions ensures the *invariance* of this organization.

7

Epigenesis

> One can doubtless possess at birth a particular dispo-
> sition for features that one's parents transmit by their
> organization, but it is certain that, if one does not
> exercise strongly and habitually the faculties that such
> a disposition favors, the particular organ that executes
> the acts would not develop.
>
> —Jean-Baptiste de Lamarck,
> *Zoological Philosophy*.

The assembly of a car, like that of a computer, follows a plan, a program, that defines precisely the position of all the bolts and welds in the machine. The slightest error in the details in carrying out this program can have catastrophic consequences. From the outset the assembly is done with the greatest precision. As we have just seen, building the human brain does not follow a particular program. Certainly the power of the genes exists, but does it extend to the finest details of organization, to the precise form of every nerve cell and the exact number and geometry of the synapses? Or, on the contrary, do the genes simply control the main features of the cerebral "body work" in the embryo system? Can one say that a strictly genetic determinism *entirely* accounts for the structural complexity of the human brain?

First of all, the word "complexity" should not mislead us. As S. Atlan emphasized in 1979, it connotes above all the fact "that one does not understand a system. It reveals an order of which one does not know the code." Faced with a reality that is so difficult to approach, the only healthy way to react is to allow our scientist's brain to construct "representations," to imagine the extent of this complexity and how it develops. Obviously we must remain on our guard, recognizing that these are only "model images," whose validity will be decided only by a confrontation with reality.

Several "combining" mechanisms could, in principle, generate the enormous complexity of the human brain. Some have already been introduced and discussed in the last chapter. The differential expression of genes, as we saw, permits the creation of a large number of cell categories, but can this mechanism be applied to the topology and connections of nerve cells? Does it explain the very great diversity of neuronal singularities in the human brain? A very simple observation makes one hesitate. Once a nerve cell has become differentiated it does not divide anymore. A single nucleus, with the same DNA, must serve an entire lifetime for the formation and maintenance of tens of thousands of synapses. It seems difficult to imagine a differential distribution of genetic material from a single nucleus to each of these tens of thousands of synapses unless we conjure up a mysterious "demon" who selectively channels this material to each synapse according to a preestablished code! The differential expression of genes cannot alone explain the extreme diversity and the specificity of connections between neurons.

A combining mechanism of a different nature has been proposed—an *epigenetic* one, which does not require any modification of the genetic material.[1] It does not act on a single cell but on a higher level, on groups of nerve cells. It is based not on a single "ID card" derived from the genes expressed by a given neuron, but involves the topology of entire networks of connections established between neurons during development. It enlists the multitude of transient geometrical figures drawn up in three dimensions during the formation of the network. Let us look at the nature and the limits of this *epigenesis by selective stabilization of synapses*.

DIFFERENCES BETWEEN IDENTICAL TWINS

It is well known that identical twins, who develop from the division of the same fertilized ovum, bear a much more striking resemblance than twins developed from different eggs. They are genetically identical, but do they possess exactly the same brain? The answer to this question is essential to our argument. Let us suppose that the answer is yes. This would mean that the genes exercise an absolute power on every one of the 10^{15} or 10^{16} synapses in the human cerebral cortex. If this is not the case, our answer should allow us to define the limits of the power of the genes and the anatomical level at which we might expect to find epigenetic factors at work.

We have already discussed identical twins in relation to research on the hereditary components of certain mental diseases (see Chapter 6). What can we say about the detailed anatomy of the brains of identical twins? Adopting our usual methodology, this analysis must be made at the level of the neuron and its synapses. To do it, we must find *exactly the same cells* in the same area of the same hemisphere and compare the details of their "trees" to see whether they are as similar as the wrinkles of the face or the lines of the hands. How can we isolate the same cells from so many millions? A first approach is to examine the nervous system of simple organisms.

Cyrus Levinthal and his collaborators chose a small crustacean, familiar to aquarium owners: the water flea, or daphnid *(Daphnia magna).* [2] This organism presents several advantages. It is easily reared and the females reproduce without the intervention of a male—that is, by parthenogenesis. They give birth to *clones*— asexually reproduced offspring who are genetically identical, or *isogenic.* That is, they produce a population of identical twins. Another advantage of the daphnid is that its nervous system, like that of the sea slug or the leech, is made up of a small number of cells, individually identifiable under the microscope. It thus becomes easy to study in detail the differences between identical twins once one has gone to the trouble of mapping all the nerve cells and all their synapses. This is possible only with the electron microscope. A nervous center, such as the eye, is cut into hundreds of thin sections, all of which are saved and observed, section by section, through the microscope. Each neuron is then reconstructed, with the details of its cell body and its branches (Figure 58).

The first finding of such a study is that from one isogenic daphnid to another the number of cells does not vary. In all individuals examined, the single, cyclopean eye is made up of exactly 176 sensory neurons, neither more nor less. What is more, these 176 cells establish synaptic contacts with exactly 110 neurons of the optic ganglion. Nor is there any qualitative variation in the connections between these cells. Each sensory neuron, taken individually, terminates on the same neurons in the optic ganglion. For example, the sensory neuron D2 systematically terminates on neurons L1 and L4 of the ganglion. The general organization of the eye and of the optic ganglion is preserved from one isogenic individual to another. The genes see to that.

Nevertheless, if the clones are more closely examined, we find *variability* between individuals—for instance, in the exact number of synapses and the precise form of the axonal branches. The number of synapses between neurons D2 and L4 may be fifty-four for specimen number 1, sixty-five for specimen number 2, twenty for number 3 and forty for number 4. An axonal branch may fork three times in individ-

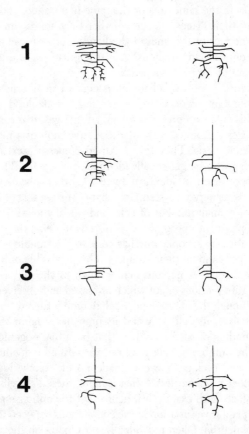

Figure 58. Variability in neuronal organization in identical twins. Here the terminal branches of the axon of corresponding neurons in four different, genetically identical daphnids are compared. Two examples of this particular neuron are present in each animal, on each side of the plane of symmetry. The variability of the axonal branching is greater from one genetically identical individual to another than between the left and right side in the same individual. (From E. R. Macagno et al., 1973.)

ual number 1, but only once in number 4. The eye, like the optic ganglion, is symmetrical. Each neuron present on the left also appears on the right. There is variability between the right and the left, but much less than that between one individual and another. Although genetically identical, the daphnid twins are not anatomically identical. The number of cells and the major features of their connections do not vary, but there is a fluctuation, a "graininess," in the details of their branches and connections.

What is true for the daphnid is probably also true for the sea slug and the fruit fly. Is it true for the fish as well? The number of nerve cells is greater in vertebrates than in invertebrates. Comparison becomes more difficult. Levinthal has exploited the fact that in the fish some neurons, like the Mauthner cell (see Chapter 4), are huge and only one or two of them are present. He chose the Müller cells, motor neurons situated close to the Mauthner cell and also easily identifiable. The fish called *Poecilia formosa,* like the daphnid, reproduces without the intervention of a male and gives birth to female clones genetically identical to their mother. It was found that from one individual to another among these clones, the dendritic tree of the first Müller cell has *approximately* the same form in its branches and synapses but with variations in the details. The findings on the daphnid thus apply to at least some neurons in the fish.[3]

What is the situation in a mammal like the mouse? The number of cells is much greater. There are no longer isolated, easily identifiable giant cells but rather categories of cells (see Chapter 2); within a single category, such as the Purkinje cells of the cerebellum, one finds a large number of individual neurons. The ideal would be to compare the details of the dendritic and axonal trees of the same neuron taken from such a population in two isogenic individuals. But is this even theoretically possible? The first point to remember is that it is not easy to obtain identical twins in the strict sense of the term. One must be satisfied with consanguineous mice, which have a large number, if not all, of their genes in common due to interbreeding for fifty years or more. It is thus possible to compare individuals with almost identical genomes. On the other hand, to find the *same neurons* within the same cell category poses serious problems. In the daphnid, the sea slug, and to some extent the fish, this identification is possible. Is the same true in the mouse? The answer is no.

First, the number of neurons is not fixed. In counting them in a particular part of the brain, such as the hippocampus, one finds a significant variation (several percent) from one consanguineous individual to another.[4] Yet this variation, though of the same order of magnitude, is still less than that between individuals from genetically different lines. But there is another problem: it is not possible to number the neurons according to their position, simply because they are not laid down in a perfectly regular and reproducible way during development.

The cells of the sea slug's abdominal ganglion or the daphnid's eye are identifiable because they come from embryonic stem-cells, which divide a fixed number of times and are laid down in specific places during development. In the mouse, the places they occupy are less rigidly dictated. This can be easily demonstrated if the fate of embryonic cells is traced to adulthood using what are known as *chimeras*. [5]

What do we mean by a chimera? Do we mean a cross between a lion and a goat with a serpent's tail? Obviously not. We mean a composite mouse, a mosaic in which cells from two different individuals are placed side by side. In order to produce such a chimera,[6] two lines of mice are chosen whose cells differ in terms of the concentration —*high* or *low*— of a "neutral" enzyme: beta-glucuronidase, which is closely related to beta-galactosidase (discussed in Chapter 6). It will serve as an internal marker. It can easily be identified in sections of nerve tissue by using a red stain. In "high" mice the Purkinje cells absorb the color, but in "low" mice they do not; they remain unstained. One can produce a chimera by mixing the cells of a "high" embryo with those of a "low" embryo. A new, mixed but viable embryo is formed. It is rather special in having *four* parents. Let us now try to find the Purkinje cells from the "high" embryo and those from the "low" embryo in the cerebellum of this chimera (Figure 59). If the precursors of the Purkinje cells divide in a regular way and are distributed according to a definite geometric plan in the cerebellar cortex, the red-stained cells in the adult mouse should form a regular, segmented configuration like the stripes of a zebra or the squares of a checkerboard. This is not the case. We find a patchwork of Purkinje cells, in which red and white (unstained) cells are mixed up in an apparently (although not strictly) random manner. The division and the migration of the precursors of the Purkinje cells are thus not subject to as rigorous and precise a determinism as the laying down of neurons in the daphnid or sea slug. The mélange is such that it becomes illusory to try to label and number each individual neuron. It is not, in principle, possible to make comparisons between "identical" neurons. With the increase in the number of cells, the variability in the construction of the nervous system also increases. Whereas in daphnid and sea slug, this variability is seen

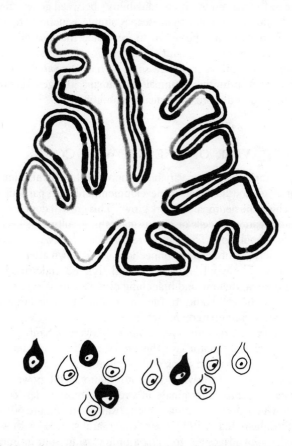

Figure 59. Mouse chimera demonstrating the variability in the distribution of Purkinje cells in the cerebellum. The *upper* figure shows a section taken from a composite or "mosaic" mouse, "made" from the fusion of two embryos at a stage when they consisted of only a few cells. The chimera embryo thus possesses four parents. In one of the two fused embryos, the Purkinje cells were stained in red, and we see them here (in black) on the chimera's cerebellum distributed irregularly among the Purkinje cells of the other embryo (in gray in the top figure and in white in the *lower*, detailed figure). There is a mixing up of the embryonic precursors of the Purkinje cells during the development of the cerebellum. (From M. L. Oster-Granite and J. Gearhart, 1981; D. Goldowitz and R. J. Mullen, 1982.)

only in the branching of the neurons and the number of synapses, for a given area or center in the mammal, it is already apparent in the number and the distribution of the nerve cells.

The evolution of the nervous system is thus accompanied by an increase in the margin of "irreproducibility" between genetically identical individuals, a margin that escapes simple genetic determinism. From this view, it may be useful to introduce the idea of a *genetic envelope* to delimit the invariant characteristics subject to strict genetic determinism and others that show some phenotypic variability. As one progresses from primitive mammals to humans, the genetic envelope opens to more and more individual variability.

THE BEHAVIOR OF THE GROWTH CONE

The significant phenotypic variability found in the organization of the adult brain obviously reflects its developmental history, particularly the way in which the neuronal network grows. This growth does not involve the multiplication of cells or organisms, as in a culture of bacteria or an animal population. There is no replication of DNA. On the contrary, the network of nervous connections is laid down after replication has stopped. The word "growth" should thus be understood in the sense of the lengthening and branching of nerve fibers, which eventually connect the cell bodies to each other (and to their targets) after the cells are differentiated and set in place.

A very curious structure—yet another discovery of Santiago Ramón y Cajal—acts as a "motor" for this growth. In fixed and stained sections of the three-day-old chick embryo, Ramón y Cajal observed that the rudimentary axons leaving the motor neurons and growing toward the developing muscle terminate in swellings, more or less conical in form, to which the name *growth cones* was given (Figure 60). In the spinal cord, he noted in 1909, their "edges [are] studded with winglike or lamellar appendages . . . forming a protoplasmic spur insinuated in between the cells or epithelium." Some are "extremely flat . . . recalling the form of a webbed foot." Others take "the form of a giant club, held up in full swing." "It loses its roughness as soon as it has left the spinal cord; its form is then that of a spindle, a grain of wheat." Cajal concluded: "From the functional point of view, one can say that the growth cone is a sort of club or battering ram, possessing an exquisite chemical sensitivity, rapid amoeboid movements, and a certain driving force that permits it to push aside, or cross, obstacles in its way . . . until it reaches its destination." At about the same time, in 1907 and 1908, Ross Harrison cultured nerve cells for the first time and, by direct microscopic observation, studied the elongation of nerve fibers and the behavior of the growth cone (see Figure 60). The growth cone appears on appendages that will become either axons or dendrites. Extremely mobile, it advances and retreats, pushing out fine prolongations, or *filopodia*, that expand and retract up to 10 or 20 microns. These exploratory movements are accompanied by the progression of the growth cone at a speed of 15 to 20 microns per hour.

The growth cone navigates "visually," steering itself by the cells it meets. Nevertheless, in spite of its "tacking," it generally heads toward a precise target. Apart from a few fibers that get lost, the axons coming from the motor neurons of the spinal cord, for instance, grow toward the embryonic muscles and not toward the skin or the skeleton. The mechanisms of this orientation have not yet been completely elucidated.

In 1975 Rita Levi-Montalcini discovered and purified a chemical substance, a protein, that stimulated the elongation of axons coming from neurons in the sympathetic ganglia. She called it *nerve growth factor*, or NGF. *In vitro*, this protein attracts axons by their growth cone, which orients itself toward a target producing NGF.[7] Does this chemotaxis, this orientation toward a chemical agent, also operate in the embryo *in vivo?* It probably does, but it does not explain everything. Other experiments suggest that the substrate on which the growth cone moves is "palpated" by it and thus plays a role. The two possibilities are not mutually exclusive. In both cases, the growth cone is oriented toward its target. On its way it meets different obstacles, and there is very little chance that the obstacles will be exactly the same for two neurons of the same category, let alone for two neurons in two different individuals, even if they are isogenic. The growth cone, with its "homing" head, is the only really mobile part of the neuron. As it moves forward, it leaves behind it a fixed segment, which in a way marks where it has passed. It zigzags, so that its comings and goings are difficult to predict, but are reflected in the topology of the final nervous connections.

Under the electron microscope, a growth cone looks somewhat like a tiny amoeba which has lost its nucleus and remains attached to the

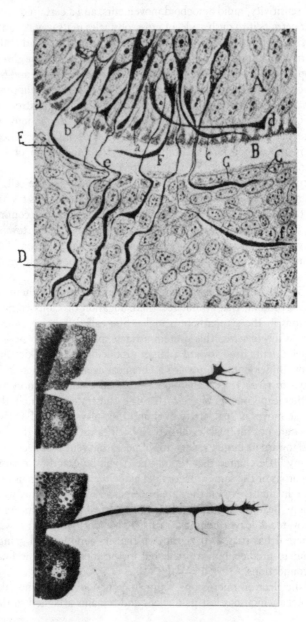

neuron cell body. Although it lacks chromosomes, it divides by fission, producing with each division a branch and thus gradually building up the axonal or dendritic tree. The rules for fission of the growth cone, like those for its budding, determine the general appearance of the "tree" that will be recognized in the adult as, for instance, a pyramidal or a stellate cell (see Chapter 2). The exact point of branching is rarely defined, nor is the exact orientation of each trajectory. The behavior of the growth cone thus determines the variability of the geometry of axons and dendrites in the adult.

When the growth cone reaches its target, its behavior changes drastically. Its incessant movements suddenly cease. The weblike formations disappear and its filopodia retract. The immobilized cone is transformed in a few hours into a nerve terminal, which gradually takes on the appearance of a mature synapse. The same reaction occurs with all the target cells of a given category. The growth cone does not distinguish between individual cells of the same category.

The amazing behavior of the growth cone should not disguise the fact that it obeys only a few simple rules. Certain principles, such as the amoeboid movement, are common to most growth cones. Others, like the recognition of the targets, appear to be characteristic of a given cell category. In no case does the behavior of the growth cone reflect the diversity of neuronal singularities. It simply ensures the invasion of all target cells belonging to a particular category of neuron, and that is already quite something. The genetic cost is modest, but the result is the possibility of great variability in the arrangement of the first contacts with the target. There is very little precision in the assembly of the network. Epigenetic factors are then needed to tune it up and create the final set of neuronal singularities.

Figure 60. In these drawings made by Ramón y Cajal in 1909 (*top*) and Harrison in 1908 (*bottom*), we can see the growth cones at the tips of growing embryonic axons. Ramón y Cajal's figure shows, in the intact embryo, axons leaving the spinal cord (A) and crossing the space that separates the cord from the surrounding muscles, as well as the penetration of growth cones (D to G) into the developing musculature. Harrison's figure illustrates the changes in shape and the progression of a growth cone in *in vitro* cultures of fragments of embryonic nerve tissue taken from a frog. Two stages of the progression of a growth cone are shown, drawn at an interval of fifteen minutes.

REGRESSION AND REDUNDANCY

In considering the development of the nervous system, and particularly the brain, one obviously looks first for constructive mechanisms, such as cell duplication and differentiation, or the proliferation of connections, which will lead to the formation of this gigantic assembly of neurons and synapses. However, one must accept the idea, at first rather surprising, that development is accompanied by regressive phenomena, which attack the emerging cellular assembly, sometimes quite forcefully.

At the beginning of the century, in 1906, R. Collin noticed that in sections of embryonic nerve tissue, certain nerve cells didn't stain normally; they appeared to be degenerating, as if about to die. Cell death has since been observed in many areas and is found systematically during the development of the nervous system. One of the best analyzed examples is that of the motor neurons of the spinal cord of the chick embryo. In 1975 Viktor Hamburger persevered and counted the neurons along the entire length of a major motor nucleus of the

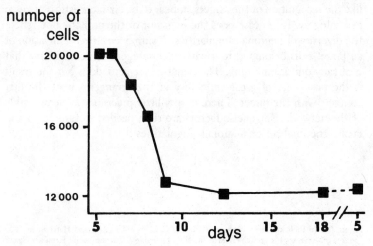

Figure 61. Spontaneous death of motor neurons of the spinal cord during development of the chick embryo. On the x axis: days of development in the egg (after the break, days after hatching). On the y axis: the total number of cells in a lateral motor column. Forty percent of neurons die in a few days. (From V. Hamburger, 1975.)

cord. In an embryo five and a half days old, he found over 20,000 neurons on one side whereas the adult has only 12,000. Between the early embryo and the adult, then, 40 percent of the neurons die (Figure 61). Most of these cells die during the sixth and the ninth days of embryo life, but cell death continues later at a much slower rate. This neuronal "sacrifice" is part of normal development; indeed, it constitutes one of its critical phases.[8]

Most frequently, neuron death affects only some of the neurons in a given category. However, in one case, described by Ramón y Cajal, a whole category of cells dies. These particular neurons of layer I, the most superficial layer of the cerebral cortex, characteristically have axons and dendrites oriented parallel to the cortical surface rather than perpendicular to it, like the pyramidal cells. These cells were first observed in the human fetus but have since been found in other mammals. Purely and simply, they disappear in the adult.

After the crisis of cell death, a more selective regressive phase takes its place, with consequences that are nonetheless important. It affects only the terminal branches of axons and dendrites. Ramón y Cajal noted that at the very first stages of nerve growth a few fibers "lose their way," missing their target and finally degenerating. He also observed that in the neonatal cerebellum, Purkinje cell axons had twenty to twenty-four collateral branches whereas in the adult human only four or five remained.

This process of regression seems to be quite general. It is found in the peripheral as well as in the central nervous system. It has been studied in detail in skeletal muscle. Using high-resolution electrophysiological techniques, it is possible to count active nerve terminals during development.[9] In the adult each "fast" muscle fiber is only innervated near its midpoint. In the newborn rat, however, each fiber has four or five active nerve terminals. As the rat begins to walk, the number of these functional terminals progressively decreases, until in the adult only one is left. During this time the number of motor neurons and muscle fibers changes very little. The regression affects only the axonal branches and synapses. At the same time the total field of muscle fibers innervated by each neuron decreases. At birth, in addition to hyperinnervation of muscle fibers, there is also overlap of the innervated fields. The system is both *redundant* and *diffuse*.

The final result is that each muscle fiber is innervated by a single axon terminal and each neuron innervates a fixed number of muscle fibers—about a hundred in the case of the soleus muscle. The innervation becomes simple and precise. The redundancy was temporary. The elimination of active nerve terminals leads to an increase in the *order* of the system.

Although the phenomenon is widespread, it has been possible to analyze it only in situations where the number of synaptic contacts is small enough to measure. In the cerebellum of adult mammals, each Purkinje cell receives a single climbing fiber. The situation is like that found in the muscle. Newborn rats or mice have a certain redundancy in the cerebellum, for each Purkinje cell receives four or five climbing fibers (Figure 62).[10] In the ensuing weeks, the adult organization develops and a single climbing fiber becomes stabilized while the others degenerate. In the cerebral cortex, each pyramidal cell receives and forms thousands of synapses. To count them during development is a long and difficult task that only a few, highly motivated anatomists have had the courage to undertake. In the macaque, as we know from Chapter 6, the dendrites of pyramidal cells, at first "bald," become covered with spines. Eight weeks after birth they reach a stage described in 1977, by Jennifer Lund and her collaborators, as "supraspiny." During the first few months or years of life, the number of these spines decreases by at least a factor of two. Similarly, in humans, a net decrease in visual-cortex spines and synapses has been noticed in the first years of life (Figure 63).[11]

The territory innervated by the axons of some pyramidal cells has also been studied in the cortex.[12] It is known that some of these cells, whose cell bodies lie principally in layers II and III, send axonal branches to the other hemisphere through the corpus callosum. This territory can be regarded as the cortical homologue of the group of muscle fibers, or motor unit, innervated by a single motor neuron. In the cortex, as in the muscle, this territory is much larger at birth than in the adult. It shrinks with the maturation of the cortex, as axonal branches are eliminated. Regression of nerve terminals is thus an integral part of the development of connections in the adult cerebral cortex. The succession of a phase of synaptic "exuberance" by a phase of regression of axonal and dendritic branches thus marks a critical period in the development of the nervous system. It seems legitimate to consider it a characteristic process in the epigenesis of neuronal networks.

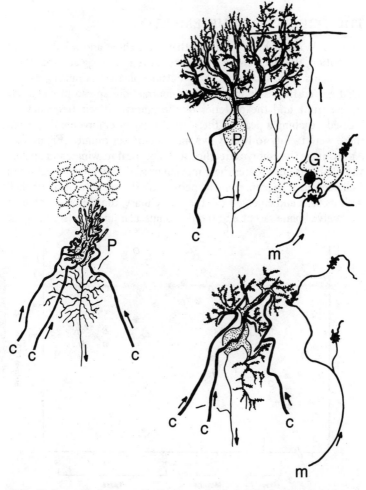

Figure 62. Regressive phenomena attack synapses during their development. Here we see a schematic representation of the formation of synaptic contacts in the cerebellum of the mouse and rat after birth. Whereas the dendritic tree of the Purkinje cell (P) becomes more complicated by successive branching, the number of climbing fibers (c) that form functional synapses with the Purkinje cells diminishes in the normal mouse (*upper right* figure). In the neonate there are at least three functional contacts per Purkinje cell (*left* figure). In the adult, only one remains. In the "weaver" mutant, where the granule cells (G) disappear, multiple innervation of Purkinje cells persists in the adult (*lower right* figure). The mossy fibers (m), which normally form synapses with the granule cells (G), grow as far as the Purkinje cells. (From J.-P. Changeux and K. Mikoshiba, 1978.)

THE DREAMS OF THE EMBRYO

In 1885 William Preyer noticed that after three and a half days of incubation, the chick embryo began to move in the egg and that these movements were independent of outside physical stimulation. The head moved from side to side, then contractions spread progressively to the trunk and the posterior of the embryo. Their frequency increased, reaching a peak on the eleventh day of embryonic life, when there were twenty to twenty-five movements per minute (Figure 64). At this stage the embryo stretched its limbs, beat its wings, and opened and closed its beak. Later these movements became linked together in a characteristic sequence, finally permitting the chick to break its shell with its beak and emerge from the egg. Curare, the poison that blocks the acetylcholine receptor at the neuromuscular junction (see Chapter

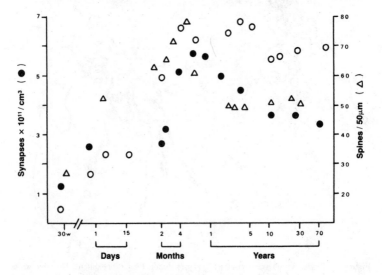

Figure 63. Graphs of the number of spines (shown as triangles) on a segment of the apical dendrite of pyramidal cells in the human visual cortex (area 17), compared with the density of synapses (solid dots) in the visual cortex at various ages from fetuses to adults. The volume of area 17 is also plotted (open circles), from less than one cubic centimeter in the late fetus to a maximum of about 7 cm³ reached by the end of the first year. This measure of volume allows the total number of synapses to be calculated. Thus we see an overshoot in both spine and synapse production, especially during the first two years after birth. Before adulthood almost half the spines and synapses are lost. (From L.J. Garey, 1984, and P.R. Huttenlocher et al., 1982.)

3), stops these movements, paralyzing the embryo. Thus, the first neuromuscular contacts already contribute to the movements of the embryo and transmit signals in a manner similar to adult synapses. Even growth cones release neurotransmitters!

If a microelectrode is placed in the embryonic spinal cord, intense spontaneous electrical activity can be recorded.[13] At three and a half days, when the first movements appear, rhythmic activity is detected. Later, bursts of impulses develop, first localized in precise parts of the spinal cord and then spreading throughout it. The recorded electrical activity coincides exactly with the movements of the embryo. Without doubt, the embryonic motor activity is nervous in origin. It results from the spontaneous activation of the neuron oscillators found initially in the spinal cord and then in the brain of the embryo.

Every mother recalls with great emotion the day she felt her baby's first movements inside her. These movements are astonishingly similar to those of the chick embryo. In the human embryo, the heart begins to beat three to four weeks after fertilization. Around the tenth week, the first spontaneous movements of the trunk and limbs appear, but the mother feels them only about seven weeks later. They are, of course, accompanied by electrical activity. In 1969 R. Bergstrøm recorded this activity in the brainstems of human fetuses born by cesarean section at two months of age. This activity continues and increases from the third month onward. A few weeks before birth, the EEG recording shows signs of an alternation of wake and sleep.[14] Periods of sleep are interrupted by episodes of intense electrical activity very similar to paradoxical sleep. Is it possible that the fetus can dream before birth? Perhaps, although the recorded activity differs from the paradoxical activity seen in an adult (see Figure 23C). It is accompanied by violent body movements in the fetus, something like the behavior seen in Michel Jouvet's operated cats, discussed in Chapter 5. Perhaps the brain centers that inhibit the actualization of paradoxical behavior have not yet developed at this stage. If this is true, the spontaneous movements of the fetus might well reflect the content of its "dreams." Their content seems very limited! The fetus seems to dream only of the first movements it will have to make after its birth: cling to its mother, suck her breast, and several months later, walk. But can one really speak of dreams in this context?

One thing is certain. There is, very early on, intense spontaneous activity in the nervous system of the embryo and the fetus, and it

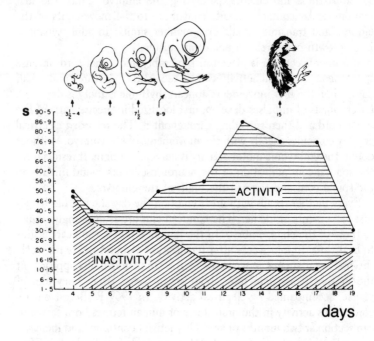

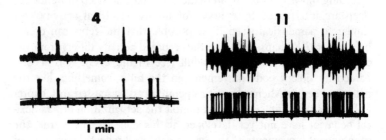

Figure 64. Spontaneous activity in the developing chick embryo's nervous system. In the upper figure, the average duration of periods of motor activity or inactivity in seconds is expressed as a function of the number of days of development. After three and a half days, the embryo is subject to spontaneous movements, while still in the egg. (From V. Hamburger, 1970.)

The *lower* figure shows the coincidence of these movements (*bottom* line) with the generation of electrical impulses in the spinal cord (*top* line) in an embryo of four days (*left*) and an embryo of eleven days (*right*). (From K. L. Ripley and R. L. Provine, 1972.)

continues throughout its development. At the same time the sense organs are developing.[15] Around the sixth month of pregnancy, the organs of hearing have most of their adult features. Touch receptors have already matured, and the visual system is not far behind. All the adult sensory functions are laid down well before birth, and they are spontaneously active very early. Their performance is not yet that of the adult, but evoked responses can be demonstrated, mixed in with the embryonic "dreams." These responses become more and more frequent during the stages of development that, as we know from Chapter 6, will continue after birth.

It is plausible to think that spontaneous nervous activity and then evoked activity contribute to the epigenesis of neuronal and synaptic networks. As this activity spreads through the network, it permits interaction between elements of the embryo system, such as the sense organs, brain centers, and motor organs. Because of the divergence of the axonal branches and convergence of inputs to the dendrites, this activity leads to both diversification and integration. Electrical and chemical signals can combine in the developing neuronal network, allowing for new possibilities of computation and organization. The cost in structural genes is once again very small. As we know from Chapter 3, a few proteins forming ion channels are enough to produce an electrical oscillator. This modest cost bears no relation to the enormous potential for interaction and combination that results.

BUILDING THE SYNAPSE

The final tuning of the adult neuronal network takes place at the ultimate communication channel between neurons—the synapse. It is thus important to know how the synapse is put together if we wish to understand the molecular mechanism of epigenesis. In Chapter 3, we saw that, although the synapse is about the same size as a bacterial cell, it is chemically simpler. On the presynaptic side, there is no nucleus, only a few mitochondria, and just a few vesicles; on the other side of the synaptic cleft, a rather homogeneous membrane. In synapses of the torpedo's electric organ or the neuromuscular junction, the set of molecules making up the postsynaptic membrane is fairly well established. It consists of a few proteins, embedded in a lipid base, of which the two principal ones are the acetylcholine receptor and an "assembly" protein with a molecular weight of 43,000. The packing density of the receptor molecules is so high—10,000 to 20,000 molecules per square micron—that they touch each other (see Figure 30C), forming a sort of irregular, two-dimensional crystal, internally stabilized on the cytoplasmic side by the assembly protein.[16]

Is this remarkable molecular arrangement present over the entire surface of the muscle fiber? If we examine the length of the fiber, as we get further from the nerve terminal, the density of the receptors falls sharply. A few microns from the terminal, the density is already a thousand times less. Soon after, we can find no more receptors, for they are present only in the region of a nerve ending, where the neurotransmitter is released (Figure 65, part 4).

In the embryonic muscle fiber, this specific arrangement of the receptors does not exist. But the receptors are present *before* the growing nerve fibers arrive, before any interaction between the growth cone and its target. They are spread uniformly over the entire surface of the muscle but at low density, about a hundred times less than at the adult nerve terminal. Nevertheless, the surface of the embryonic fiber is so large that, compared with that of the adult synapse, we find many more receptors than are necessary for the formation of the synapse (Figure 65, part 1).

Another difference in the membrane of the embryonic muscle fibers is that the receptor molecules "move," diffusing like molecules of a gas. In the adult synapse, on the other hand, they are completely fixed beneath the nerve terminal. Like all molecules in living organisms, the receptor molecules have not been given eternal life; they are very mortal. Whereas the neurons of a human brain can survive for more than a hundred years, the life of synaptic molecules is much shorter. In the adult neuromuscular junction, the half-life (easier to measure than the total lifespan of the receptor) is about eleven days. But those molecules that disappear are immediately replaced by other, newly synthesized ones. The molecular architecture of the adult synapse is constantly renewed so that its organization remains stable. In the embryonic muscle fiber, the situation is even more fluid. The half-life of the receptor is very short, only eighteen to twenty hours. The embryonic receptor is very labile.[17]

Major differences exist in the surface of the muscle fiber before the arrival of growing axons and after the formation of the adult synapse. In the embryo, the acetylcholine receptor is distributed *diffusely* over

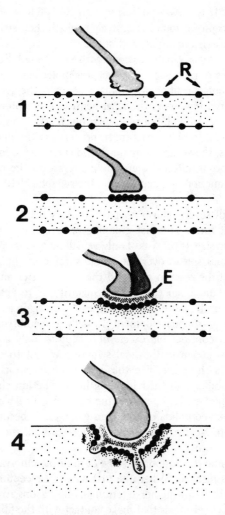

Figure 65. Schematic diagram of the formation of the molecular components of a synapse between a nerve and a skeletal muscle during embryonic development and after birth in the rat. *1:* Arrival of the growth cone at the surface of the muscle fiber, where the acetylcholine receptor (R) is diffusely distributed. *2:* Immobilization of the growth cone and localized accumulation of receptor molecules beneath the nerve terminal. *3:* Temporary multiple innervation and localization of acetylcholinesterase (E) with disappearance of receptors outside the synapse. *4:* After birth, maturation of the motor endplate with stabilization of the receptor and change in the mean opening time of ion channels.

the whole fiber. It is *mobile* and *labile*. In the adult neuromuscular junction, the receptor is found exclusively beneath the nerve terminal; it is densely packed, *immobile*, and *stable*.

The formation of a synapse begins with the immobilization of a growth cone on a muscle fiber. The receptor molecules, which at first appear throughout the fiber, accumulate beneath the terminal and become fixed. In a few hours the local density of receptors increases more than tenfold. A "blob" of receptors thus marks the synaptic site (Figure 65, part 2). Impulses pass from the nerve to the muscles. The muscle contracts, the synapse functions, and the enzyme for breaking down the neurotransmitter—acetylcholinesterase in the case of the neuromuscular junction—is deposited in the synaptic cleft (Figure 65, part 3).[18]

There are still several stages to pass through before the synapse reaches its adult form. The first grouping of receptors is only a few square microns in size. It consists of only a small percentage of the stock receptor molecules spread over the whole surface of the embryonic muscle fiber. All the receptors beyond the synaptic site must now be removed. As a consequence, the total quantity of receptors in the muscles falls abruptly, more than ten times. Once again a spectacular regression occurs during development. Initially, the embryonic muscle fiber produces a considerable excess of receptors; only a small, but critical, fraction remain in the final synapse. At first these receptor molecules have a short life, like the embryonic receptors, but they progressively stabilize and their life lengthens. The ion channel also changes its properties. Its opening time shortens. The blob of post-synaptic receptors consolidates and then enlarges. It becomes folded like an accordion. Nearly three weeks are necessary for the synapse to acquire its adult form.[19]

In the meantime the temporary stage of multiple innervation, mentioned earlier, is reached. When the first patch of receptors becomes stabilized beneath a growing nerve terminal, other axons arrive nearby. Of the four or five terminals that make contact with the fiber, the one that persists in the adult synapse is not necessarily the one whose growth cone marked the synapse initially. The putting together of the synapse consists of a chain of chemical reactions and molecular interactions. From simple beginnings, the synaptic complex develops a sophisticated architecture. Initially labile, it becomes progressively stable. Processes of *stabilization* take over from those of assembly.

THE THEORY OF EPIGENESIS
BY SELECTIVE STABILIZATION OF SYNAPSES

The observations described in this and the preceding chapter show that:

1. The principal features of the anatomical and functional organization of the nervous system are preserved from one generation to another and are subject to the determinism of a set of genes that make up what I have called the *genetic envelope.* This envelope controls the division, migration, and differentiation of nerve cells; the behavior of the growth cone; mutual recognition by cell categories; the formation of widespread connections; and the onset of spontaneous activity. It also determines rules governing the assembly of molecules in the synapse and the evolution of this connecting link.

2. A phenotypic variability is found in the adult organization of isogenic individuals, and its degree increases from invertebrates to vertebrates, including humans, parallel to the increase in brain complexity.

3. During development, once the last division of neurons has taken place, axonal and dendritic trees branch and spread exuberantly. At this critical stage there is redundancy, but also maximal diversity in the connections of the network. This redundancy is temporary. Regressive phenomena rapidly intervene. Neurons die, and a considerable portion of the dendritic and axonal branches are "pruned." Many active synapses disappear.

4. Impulses travel through the neuronal network even at very early stages of its formation. They begin spontaneously, but are later evoked by the interaction of the newborn with its environment.

The theory proposed here takes into account the observed data and complements them with the following hypotheses (Figure 66).[20]

1. At the critical stage of transient redundancy and maximum diversity, the embryonic synapses, excitatory and inhibitory, can exist in at least three states: labile, stable, and degenerated. Nerve impulses can be transmitted only in the labile and stable states. It is possible for transitions to take place between labile and stable states (stabilization), labile and degenerated states (regression), and stable and labile states (labilization).

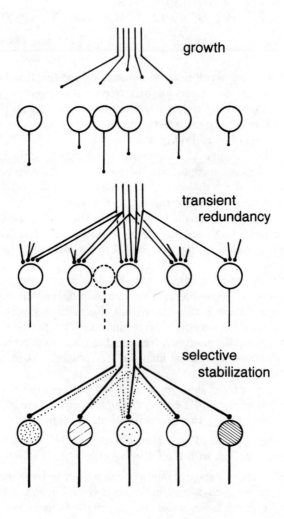

growth

transient
redundancy

selective
stabilization

Figure 66. Hypothesis of epigenesis by selective stabilization. Spontaneous or evoked activity in the developing neuronal network controls the elimination of excess synapses formed during the stage of transient redundancy.

2. The evolution of the connective state of each synaptic contact is governed by the overall message of signals received by the cell on which it terminates. In other words, the activity of the *post*synaptic cell regulates the stability of the synapse in a *retrograde* manner.

3. Epigenetic development of neuronal singularities is controlled by the activity of the developing network. It commands the selective stabilization of a particular set of synaptic contacts from within the total set present during the stage of maximum diversity.

These concepts have been brought together in the form of a mathematical model, which is, of necessity, simplified and schematic, but autonomous with regard to biological reality. It then becomes possible to reconcile this formal representation with experimental data.

The theory that has just been formulated has two important applications on biological grounds. The first is to give a plausible explanation for the recording of a temporal sequence of nerve impulses as a stable pattern of connections described in terms of a specific synaptic geometry. Adult structure depends on the effects of activity on a preexisting anatomical organization. Certain preexisting connections are selected by activity or "experience" without inducing any synthesis of new molecular species or structures. The second consequence, which has been the object of a rigorous mathematical proof, is that the same afferent message may stabilize different arrangements of connections, which nevertheless result in the same input-output relationship. This variability in patterns of connection may account for the phenotypic variability seen between isogenic individuals. It also takes into account the diversity of neuronal singularities within a single category of neurons, without necessitating some genetic "combining" mechanism.

THE EXPERIMENTAL TESTING OF EPIGENESIS

Mathematical theories can stand on their own, but this feature is also their weakness. In the natural sciences, particularly in biology, theories are limited by many more constraints than in mathematics. Obviously, a theory must be internally coherent and satisfy mathematical logic, but it must also accurately reflect external realities. A biological theory is useful only if it is representative of natural objects or phenomena and can thus be directly tested by experimentation. Numerous biological theories have collapsed and disappeared from the scientific literature; many others will suffer the same fate because, in spite of infallible reasoning and convincing mathematics, they fail the test of reality.

How does our theory of the epigenesis of neuronal networks by selective stabilization fare? Experimental data are still limited. Rigorous testing first demands a description of the graphs of developing neurons. It also requires knowledge of the nervous activity in the embryo or newborn. Very few neural systems are suited to such analyses. The few data we possess concern the neuromuscular junction of the chicken and the rat and the mammalian cerebral cortex.[21]

As we have seen, the chick embryo is capable of considerable spontaneous movement. What happens if the movements are blocked—for instance, by injecting curare or the snake's alpha-bungarotoxin in the embryo? These poisons act selectively on the acetylcholine receptor at the neuromuscular junction. They do not interfere with the heartbeat or other vital processes, so the embryo will survive. The initial accumulation of receptors under the growth cone still takes place. Thus, the activity of the neuromuscular junction does not govern the formation of the first patch of receptors on the muscle. On the other hand, this activity has an effect on the storage of acetylcholinesterase, the enzyme for the breakdown of acetylcholine, at the synaptic site. The muscle must be active for this enzyme to accumulate. The same is true for the disappearance of receptors outside the neuromuscular junction, which does not occur in paralyzed embryos.[22] Muscular activity is necessary to eliminate them. It does not accelerate the breakdown of the receptor; it simply blocks its synthesis. Thus, the labile receptor disappears. Embryonic nervous activity controls the expression of the genes that determine the synthesis of acetylcholine receptor at the muscle fibers. It also controls several, but not all, critical stages in the molecular organization of the postsynaptic side of the neuromuscular junction.

Does nervous activity also act on the other side of the junction, on the motor neuron and its axon? Ron Oppenheim took up Viktor Hamburger's observations on the death of motor neurons in the spinal cord, but using embryos paralyzed by snake toxin.[23] There were two surprising results. First, although the toxin acted on the postsynaptic side of the synapse, on the acetylcholine receptors, an effect was observed on the presynaptic side, on the motor neuron and its axon. There was a transfer of some sort of signal backward across the synapse, in the opposite direction to the propagation of nerve impulses. The second surprise was that if, under standard conditions, the paralysis took place between the fourth and the sixth day of embryonic life, the embryo possessed an *increased* number of motor neurons compared with normal embryos (Figure 67). Paralysis led to more motor neurons! Did it affect their replication? No, the paralysis interfered with the process of neuron death, which is known to take place around the fifth day. It allowed the neurons that would have disappeared without the paralyzing agent to survive. This initially paradoxical finding is in agreement with the hypothesis of selective stabilization, as is the already-mentioned fact that an excess of receptors persists in paralyzed embryos. The artificial situation created by the paralysis shows that in normal conditions spontaneous activity leads to the death of a large number of neurons as well as to the disappearance of receptors outside the synapse.

A similar phenomenon occurs at the nerve terminal once the phase of neuron death is over. At the critical stage of multiple innervation of muscle fibers, the paralysis of the motor nerve, or indeed of the muscle (Figure 67), prolongs the temporary state of redundancy.[24] On the other hand, electrical stimulation of the spinal cord or the muscles accelerates the elimination of the excess terminals.[25]

The biochemical mechanisms of the competition that results in the stabilization of certain nerve terminals at the expense of others are not yet completely understood. A simple hypothesis is based on the production of some kind of nerve growth factor by the muscle.[26] Growth factors produced by embryonic muscle fibers could act in a retrograde way, crossing the synapse from the muscle to the nerve in the opposite direction from the nerve impulse.[27] They would attract motor nerve endings and lead to multiple innervation of the muscle fibers. If at this stage of maximum redundancy, the synthesis of these factors stopped, the stock would become depleted and the survival of the nerve terminals would be related to the rate of utilization of the factor. If we suppose the more active the terminals are, the more they utilize, it becomes plausible that one might receive a sufficient quantity to become stabilized, while the others would "starve" and be eliminated.

Expressed mathematically, this competition model predicts the selective stabilization of one motor terminal per muscle fiber and the innervation of a fixed number of fibers by a motor neuron.[28] It also predicts a considerable variability in the final innervation of a muscle.

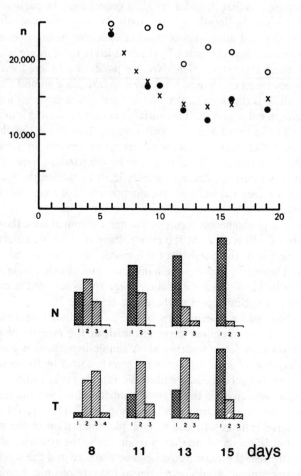

Figure 67. The effects of embryonic or neonatal activity on two regressive phenomena: cell death in the chick embryo *(top)* and the elimination of multiple innervations of muscle fibers in the rat *(bottom)*. In the *upper* figure, the evolution of the total number of motor neurons (n) is shown as a function of the number of days of development. Chronic paralysis by the alpha toxin in snake venom causes a larger number of neurons to survive (open circles) than in normal controls (black dots and crosses). (From N. Laing and M. Prestige, 1978.)

In the same way, in the *lower* figure, sectioning the tendon of a leg muscle in the newborn rat paralyzes the muscle and slows the elimination of excess innervations. In these diagrams the height of the column indicates the percentage of muscle fibers with one, two, three, or four functional synapses in the normal rat (N) and the rat with the operated tendon (T). In the young rat, each muscle fiber receives three or four functional motor terminals. In the adult, there is normally only one. (From P. Benoît and J.-P. Changeux, 1975.)

For example, imagine that we can number a set of muscle fibers from 1 to 300 and that these fibers are innervated by a pool of fifteen motor neurons. At the end of their development, the neurons would share the population of muscle fibers approximately equally. There would thus be about twenty muscle fibers per neuron. However, and this is the essential point, none of the twenty fibers would show any obvious numerical order. Each neuron would participate in a "lottery" for the numbers of the fibers it is to innervate in the adult, although each neuron would "win" the same number of fibers. Thus, motor neurons would innervate a fixed number of muscle fibers, distributed without any particular geometrical regularity among the different neurons. Nor would there be any regularity in the distribution from one isogenic individual to another. The model reflects both the regularity of the innervation of a muscle and phenotypic variability.

This model also explains the "conservative" effect of the paralysis of a muscle on the evolution of multiple innervation. We need only suppose that the state of activity of a muscle controls the synthesis of the retrograde growth factor. In the embryo the muscle produces the factor. Muscle activity, especially intense during the stage of multiple innervation, stops it. Paralyzing the muscle removes this block and the factor is produced in excess. Without competition, multiple innervation persists.

The formation of the neuromuscular junction, then, depends on epigenetic regulation, in which activity plays an important role at several critical moments. In this respect it must be stressed that the regulatory mechanisms used are similar, whatever the muscle fiber, even whatever the muscle. A small number of genetic determinants within the genetic envelope are sufficient to explain how the innervation of muscles develops. Once again, economy is effected by their being shared.

Can the findings from the neuromuscular junction be applied to other systems, such as the cerebral cortex? The available data are more fragmentary but already indicate that cortical development is at least partially regulated by activity. In Chapter 2, we discussed at length the organization of the cerebral cortex into "stripes," or slabs. In the visual cortex, neurons in alternate columns respond to stimulation of one or the other eye. This characteristic organization is due, as we saw, to the way in which the thalamic axons project to the cortex. Pasko Rakic, in

1976 and 1977, and David Hubel and Torsten Wiesel, in 1977, showed that this organization did not yet exist in the fetal monkey during the third and fourth months of gestation. The axons were distributed diffusely, with those responding to the right or left eye mixed together. Segregation into columns began around the fifth fetal month and continued for several weeks after birth. Cells that had responded to both eyes gradually came to respond to one only. Although the synaptic mechanism is not yet established, the evidence suggests that cortical neurons in layer IV initially receive axons from both eyes but later become innervated by axons from one eye only.

Is the segregation of the ocular-dominance columns controlled by visual experience just as experience controls the innervation of muscles? In a series of classical experiments, Hubel and Wiesel showed that closing one eye by suturing the eyelids during the first six weeks of postnatal life had long-lasting effects on the adult monkey.[29] The columns, or "stripes," corresponding to the closed eye became narrower while the stripes corresponding to the other eye widened (Figure 68). If an eye was closed at birth and opened three weeks later, the width of the stripes recovered. Similar experiments in the adult had no

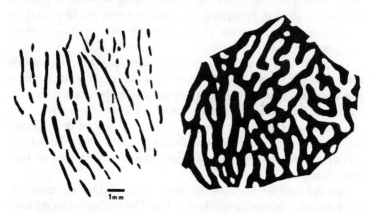

Figure 68. Consequences of closing an eye on the left and right ocular-dominance columns in the visual cortex of the macaque. In the *left* figure, one eye had been surgically closed in a two-week-old monkey and the pattern examined eighteen months later by an anatomical method similar to that mentioned in Figure 20. The bands corresponding to the closed eye (in black) have narrowed, compared with those corresponding to the open eye. In the *right* figure, the same experiment was performed on an adult monkey. There is no effect on the normal organization of the bands (From S. LeVay et al., 1980.)

effect. There was a *critical period* during which abnormal activity in the visual system caused an irreversible lesion. Balanced activity in the visual pathway is necessary for the development of a normal adult network.[30] In humans similar effects to those produced by the experimental lid suture arise naturally from congenital cataracts, when the lens of the eye is opaque at birth. The resulting amblyopia, or loss in the sharpness of vision, can be interpreted as a disturbance of visual-cortex innervation.

How the synaptic mechanisms are affected by these changes in nervous activity is not yet completely elucidated. It seems as if the target neurons initially receive functional terminals from both eyes and that lack of activity in one eye results in the retraction of the corresponding nerve terminals, leaving in place the fibers coming from the other eye. However, experimental confirmation of this interpretation in terms of selective stabilization is still lacking.

As already mentioned, during cortical development the nerve fibers that connect the two hemispheres via the corpus callosum are also subject to regression. In 1979 G. M. Innocenti and D. O. Frost showed that the occlusion of an eye, or even experimental strabismus, could change the course of development of callosal innervation. Once again, "inactivity" causes the preservation of redundant connections. Thus cortical development is subject to significant epigenetic regulation through nervous activity, and many features of this control are compatible with the hypothesis of selective stabilization. But how far does the influence of this epigenetic regulation extend? It seems probable that it intervenes particularly in the intrinsic differentiation of a given cortical area, that it participates in the development of its synaptic "micro-organization." But does it influence the development of relationships between different cortical areas?

HEMISPHERIC SPECIALIZATION—A GENETIC OR EPIGENETIC PROCESS?

Especially in man, one finds a remarkable series of areas specialized in what Colwyn Trevarthen in 1982 called "cooperative understanding" between individuals of a social group. Among others, one can obviously point to the language areas, usually localized in the left hemisphere (see

Chapters 1, 2, and 5). Does this hemispheric specialization result from active epigenesis or, on the contrary, is it the result of strict genetic determinism?[31]

Research into this problem has often been confused with research on the preferential use of the left or right hand. Contrary to what might be expected, the same hemisphere is not necessarily responsible for both handedness and spoken language. Not all left-handed people speak with their right hemisphere. This observation was an early result of a very discriminating test developed by Juhn Wada and Theodore Rasmussen in 1960. Each cerebral hemisphere is fed by one carotid artery. When a barbiturate, such as Amytal, is injected in one carotid, the corresponding hemisphere is temporarily anesthetized. If this hemisphere is the one responsible for language, the subject temporarily loses his speech. If the other hemisphere contains the language centers, speech is preserved. It has been found that 5 percent of right-handers speak with their right hemisphere and 70 percent of left-handers with the left hemisphere! This means that handedness is not necessarily associated with the hemisphere controlling speech. The two phenomena are regulated quite differently.

First, let us consider handedness, before turning to the problem of speech. Irrespective of culture, about 90 percent of human beings use the right hand for writing and difficult manual tasks. This preference was already present in prehistoric man. The "negative" handprints outlined on the walls of caves formerly inhabited by Cro-Magnon man are left hands in 80 percent of the cases. Thus, the people who outlined them must have used their right hands to apply the color. They also used their right hands to attack their victims with the primitive weapons that they manufactured. Could this already have been a reflection of their cultural environment? Cro-Magnon man's symbolism remains mysterious, but a long historical tradition has given negative attributes to the left. In French, apart from its meaning as an orientation in space, *gauche* has a pejorative sense, which has even been adopted in English. According to Christian tradition, at the Last Judgment, the good will be with the lambs at the right hand of the Son of God and the evil with the goats on his left. Could it be that a strong cultural heritage was sufficient to impose a "right-handed" epigenesis, or is it that tradition has simply accentuated an innate feature?

Let us look at the heredity of handedness. Its familial incidence does not obey simple laws. Families of left-handers do exist, but there are right-handers in left-handed families and left-handers in right-handed families. Statistics derived from a large sample of families show the following proportions for right-handed children: 92 percent when both parents are right-handed, 80 percent when one parent is right-handed and the other left-handed, 45 percent when both parents are left-handed.[32]

Can these observations be interpreted on the basis of a genetic model? The simplest model imaginable would be based on the hypothesis that handedness is determined by a single gene present in two forms: a dominant one (R) for right-handedness and a recessive one (L) for left-handedness. This model would predict that all children of left-handed parents (LL) should be themselves left-handed, but this is not the case. Such children are often right-handed. We must therefore look for another mechanism.

In 1972 Marian Annett proposed a more satisfactory genetic model, which also involves a single gene but invokes a very simple additional hypothesis. Individuals possessing at least one active form of the gene would all be right-handed; those who did not would have an equal chance of being right- or left-handed. This model would explain the fact that half the children of left-handers are right-handed. But it would remain in the realm of theory if there did not exist a very illustrative natural example found in the mouse and even in man.

This is the *situs inversus* mutation (iv).[33] This mutation, which affects only one individual in 10,000, does not involve handedness or hemispheric specialization, but the arrangement of the viscera. Affected individuals have their heart on the right, the liver on the left, and the intestines the wrong way around. In other words, their viscera present a mirror image of those of a normal individual. There is a noteworthy analogy with the heredity of handedness: the descendants of "inverted" mice are half normal and half inverted. It would seem as if mice that have two copies of the mutant gene (iv/iv) have one chance in two of being inverted. Mathematically the results agree with Annett's model. Normally, the embryo is curled up in the uterus in a "left-handed" spiral. But in the uterus of an iv/iv mother fertilized by an iv/iv father, half the embryos are curled toward the left and the other half to the right (Figure 69). The number of embryos forming "right-handed" spirals coincides exactly with that of inverted adults. The experimental data thus confirm the theoretical model.

What is the mysterious mechanism by which a single mutation of

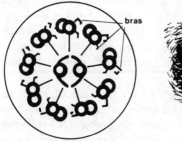
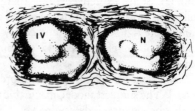

Figure 69. The inverted viscera mutation suggests a genetic model for the determination of the asymmetry of the cerebral hemispheres. Individuals with this mutation have the heart on the right and the liver on the left. The *right* figure shows that in the mouse with this mutation (IV) the embryo is curled in the uterus in the opposite direction from the normal embryo (N). (From Layton, 1976.) This mutation causes a paralysis of the flagella, shown schematically in a section viewed under an electron microscope in the *left* figure. We see that there is a loss of the "arms" that hold together the tubular elements (black circles), essential for their movement. (From B. A. Afzelius, 1976.)

a chromosomal gene can invert the arrangement of a whole set of organs? In 1976 B. A. Afzelius made a remarkable observation. Examining three patients with a total inversion of their viscera, he noticed that they showed curious symptoms of chronic sinusitis and bronchitis, apparently unrelated to the inversion of their organs. Moreover, their sperm were straight, stiff, and motionless. In the cells of these patients, cilia and flagella were completely paralyzed, and consequently the mucus was not eliminated from the respiratory pathways by the ciliated epithelium of the bronchi. When examined under the microscope, the flagella had an unusual structure. Normally, a flagellum contains nine pairs of very fine microtubules held together by hooklike "arms," but in these patients the hooks were missing (Figure 69). The microtubules could no longer move in a coordinated fashion; cilia and flagella were paralyzed.

What could be the relationship between changes in flagella movements and the arrangement of body organs? A probable hypothesis is that when the embryo consists of only a few cells, the movement of groups of these cells determines the left or right orientation of the organs that will be derived from them. Movements of cilia or flagella permit the cells to reach their definitive position. In the absence of these movements, the cells are arranged haphazardly on the right or the left. Thus, an apparently insignificant event, the paralysis of cilia and flagella, can provoke a complete change in the symmetry of the viscera, if it interferes with an early stage of development.

Left-handers are not particularly more susceptible to bronchitis than right-handers. Handedness does not depend on the structure of flagella! But it might very well be explained by a mechanism similar in principle to that determining the arrangement of the organs. What, in this case, might the early effect of the gene be? In 1968 Norman Geschwind and Walter Levitsky reexamined some of the very detailed research of nineteenth-century anatomists and made an important discovery. Using simply a camera and a ruler, they showed that, in humans, there were characteristic anatomical differences between the hemispheres. On the upper surface of the posterior temporal lobe is an area called the *planum temporale.* It had a larger surface area on the left in sixty-five out of a hundred brains they examined and on the right in eleven (Figure 70). The slope of the Sylvian sulcus was also steeper and the frontal lobe more rounded on the right than on the left. As was established later, these differences exist in the human fetus before birth.[34] The planum temporale was larger on the left in most fetuses and neonates examined at ten to forty-eight weeks after conception (54 to 77 percent). Anatomical asymmetry between the hemispheres thus

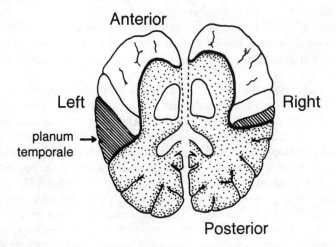

Figure 70. Anatomical differences between the right and left hemispheres in man. The planum temporale of the temporal lobe is larger on the left than on the right in the majority of brains examined. (From M. LeMay, 1982.)

precedes any form of "education." It is determined by genetic factors, perhaps influencing the tangential proliferation of the neurons in the planum temporale so that they divide for a longer time on the left than on the right.

In reality, however, it is not so simple. Any strictly genetic model predicts, as we have seen, a much greater concordance between identical twins, whose chromosomes are identical, than between twins developed from different eggs. Yet, as far as handedness is concerned, no major difference can be observed between identical and nonidentical twins. Even more surprising is the fact that twice as many left-handers are found among twins, identical or not, than among nontwins.[35] Could intrauterine experience reverse the effect of the genes? That is not yet known, but we do know that neurological disorders are more frequent in twins of either sort than in the general population. Perhaps crowding in the uterus provokes minor trauma, which cancels out the initial interhemispheric differences and forces the balance in the other direction!

Clinical observations on the development of language areas in children can be useful in studying hemispheric dominance. Before discussing this problem, we should remember that language areas are different from those concerned with handedness and that they do not necessarily develop in the same hemisphere.

Circumscribed lesions of the cerebral cortex in children provoke language difficulties, similar to those observed by Paul Broca in the adult. But are these lesions mainly in the left hemisphere, as in the adult?

In the 1960s a study of about sixty cases led to the suggestion that in children aphasia could result from damage to the right hemisphere as well as to the left. In addition, it was believed that the aphasia was entirely reversible. In other words, there was an *equipotentiality* of the cerebral hemispheres at birth, with their specialization appearing only when language was acquired.[36] Later proposals evolved in the opposite direction, and today a subtler view is held.[37] In 1983 A. Roch-Lecours focused on a group of very special aphasias, those that affect right-handers after a lesion of the *right* hemisphere. They are very rare in the adult, appearing in only 0.4 percent of cases, but in children, although still rare, they are ten times more frequent. In the early stages of development, the right hemisphere thus has a certain potential that is lost in adult life. Other clinical data support this interpretation.

In a fortunately small number of newborns, serious epileptic crises or invasive tumors make it necessary to remove one hemisphere totally. In most known cases, this operation does not interfere with the acquisition of language,[38] but it is very clear that nine or ten years later these children do not possess all the linguistic abilities of a normal child. Removal of the left hemisphere causes problems with the understanding and production of sentences with complex syntax. After surgical removal of the right hemisphere, deficits in the performance of visual and spatial tasks are observed. Well-studied cases are still sparse, but probably, as Roch-Lecours indicated in 1983, we are born with *two* language areas, but the left area, because of its innate properties, is ready to dominate and will do so immediately or within a year after birth.

In conclusion, an innate predisposition, based on a genetic model such as that proposed by Marian Annett, weights the balance in favor of one of the hemispheres, usually the left. For a certain time during the first stages of development, the other hemispheres can take over at least some of its functions, as, for instance, after minor trauma or, more dramatically, after the total ablation of one hemisphere. Epigenetic regulation thus intervenes in the differentiation of language areas. It seems as if at a certain critical moment similar, if not strictly identical, neural structures exist in both hemispheres, but are lost selectively on the right or on the left during the long period of apprenticeship leading to adulthood. We are still a long way from a cellular or molecular analysis of hemispheric specialization in humans, but the data we possess are obviously compatible with the hypothesis of selective stabilization. We have already seen that in animals there is a significant loss of fibers in the corpus callosum linking the two hemispheres during postnatal development. Could this process participate in hemispheric specialization? Could this be an important piece of evidence in favor of the hypothesis of selective stabilization?

THE CULTURAL IMPRINT

The brain's capacity to produce and combine mental objects, to remember them, and to communicate them is seen most vividly in humans. Mental representations are propagated in different coded forms from one individual to another and perpetuate themselves through generations, without requiring any sort of genetic mutation. A new form of memory is born outside the individual and his brain. Signs and symbols that evoke mental objects are recorded on substrates containing neither neurons nor synapses—on stone or wood, paper or magnetic disks. A *cultural tradition* is formed.

A remarkable feature of the development of the human brain, already pointed out, is that it continues long after birth (see Figure 56). As we have seen, brain weight increases by a factor of 4.3 up to adulthood. Most of the synapses of the cerebral cortex are formed *after* birth. The fact that synapses continue to proliferate postnatally permits a progressive "impregnation" of the cerebral tissue by the physical and social environment. How is this cultural imprint acquired? Does the environment "instruct" the brain by leaving its imprint, as a bronze seal does in a piece of wax? Or, on the contrary, does it simply selectively stabilize successive combinations of neurons and synapses as they appear spontaneously during development?

In 1968 the eminent linguist Roman Jakobson studied the way in which the babbling of children is transformed into spoken language. According to him, the child "can accumulate sounds that are never found in a single language or even a group of languages." The child produces an abundance of "wild sounds," of which only a few are found in adult language.[39] This phenomenon does not seem restricted to humans. In 1982 P. Marler and S. Peters found the same thing in the learning of song by the swamp sparrow *(Melospiza gregaria)*. Like the song of the cricket (see Chapter 4), that of the sparrow can be analyzed quantitatively from two-dimensional graphic recordings, or *sonograms*, with frequency on the y axis and time on the x axis. The song of the adult male in captivity is very simple: it never consists of more than two types of syllable. In contrast, before the "crystallization" of the adult song at about 335 days of age, the number of different syllables produced is always greater. Forty to fifty days earlier there are four to five times more! Marler was even able to record nineteen different syllables in one fledgling. As the twittering of the young bird changes into the song of the adult, there is a marked decline in the number of types of syllables produced (Figure 71). What is more, the two types that persist in the adult may differ from one individual to another. There is both elimination of syllables ("syllabic attrition") and variability in the definitive song of the adult. The crystallization of the song looks as if it might represent the selective stabilization of syllables!

Sparrow fledglings produce a great variety of syllables spontaneously, but they are also capable of imitating "model" songs synthesized by a computer. They invent and improvise but also imitate. Are such imitations incorporated in the adult song during the attrition process? Yes, imitated syllables can be used in the two syllables of the male's song. Marler and Peters found about fifty types of different syllables in the songs of all their "educated" sparrows; among these nineteen, or 42 percent, were imitations. Thus education can lead to a considerable artificial diversification of the song.

The young sparrow does not imitate just any model song. If exposed, for example, to the song of a related species of sparrow—the song

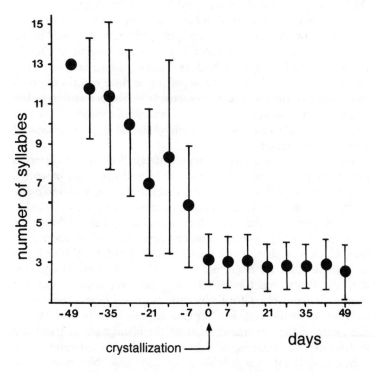

Figure 71. The song of the young swamp sparrow *(Melospiza melodia)* consists of a repertoire of about fifteen syllables and sometimes more. The "crystallization" of the adult song is accompanied by the loss of more than three-quarters of the syllables produced by the young. There is "syllabic attrition." (From P. Marler and S. Peters, 1982.)

sparrow *(Melospiza melodia)* —young swamp sparrows will imitate only a few of the syllables of the song sparrow. As adults, they incorporate even fewer of them in their definitive song. There is thus an elimination of foreign syllables both during imitation and attrition. The capacity to learn is limited by the genetic envelope peculiar to a given species.

For humans, the process of learning speech is certainly more complex than the learning of song by the sparrow, but there are several common features.[40] As infant babbling becomes real language, it is quite probable that there is an "attrition" of spontaneous or imitated syllables. Obviously, the nervous centers involved in the production of the bird's song are different from language areas, but common rules at the cellular and synaptic levels could have similar effects.

The phenomenon of attrition can also be seen in man in language perception. In Japanese, for example, the phonemes "ra" and "la" do not exist, in contrast to Western languages like English or French. Japanese adults have great difficulties in distinguishing between them. On the other hand, Japanese babies of two or three months can do it easily, just like their Western counterparts.[41] The acquisition of language, then, is accompanied by a loss of perceptual capacity. These few, very limited data can again be easily explained by the concept of selective stabilization.

The invention of a *written* representation for mental objects is incontestably a cultural phenomenon. But the identification of written signs and their combination requires that they be committed to memory beforehand. The percepts evoked by these signs must be linked to concepts. Obviously, the human brain was capable of all this *before* the invention of writing. The use of writing necessitates a long apprenticeship, which is much easier for the child than the adult. Writing leaves an impression on the brain, but where? Our lack of knowledge here does not allow us much room for speculation. We might expect that many areas are involved. First, obviously, the visual areas—the primary and particularly the secondary (see Chapter 6)—must be used. We are also aware of the importance of the right hemisphere in visual and spatial tasks. But neurological data are often hard to interpret; moreover, experimentation is difficult, if not impossible. Nevertheless, the diversity of human culture provides fantastically rich material, and there are a few rare situations where nature has carried out its own experiments, even providing controls!

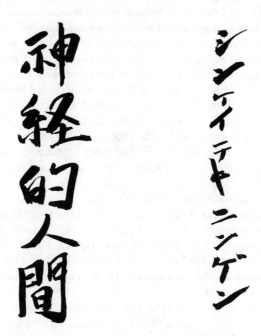

Figure 72. "Neuronal man," written in Kanji (on the *left*) and in Kana (on the *right*). Different parts of the brain are used to interpret the ideograms of Kanji and the phonetic signs of Kana. (Calligraphy by Shigeru Tsuji.)

Japanese writing uses two systems of signs. *Kana,* rather like an alphabet without being one, is made up of sixty-nine symbols, each corresponding to a distinct sound. Kana is phonetic and combinative. *Kanji,* on the other hand, is not phonetic but ideographic. As in Chinese, each sign has a specific meaning, but the relationship between the sign and its sound is quite arbitrary. The number of Kanji signs is, of course, much greater than that of Kana characters, (3,000 are necessary to read a newspaper); their form is also more varied and complex. In school, Kana is taught first, with Kanji being introduced only at the end of the first grade (Figure 72).

Do these two forms of writing use different regions of the brain? Since the beginning of the century Japanese neurologists have realized that localized vascular lesions in the cortex can cause difficulties with spoken and written language in Japanese, just as in Western, patients.[42] Certain lesions in the left hemisphere, in Broca's or Wernicke's areas, may have a greater impact on the use of Kana than Kanji. Other lesions of the same hemisphere cause selective difficulties in writing and reading Kanji, whereas the use of Kana seems normal. When Kana or Kanji characters are presented to the right or left hemisphere through one or the other visual field, the results also suggest that the left hemisphere is more specialized for Kana and the right for Kanji, particularly in the case of nouns.[43] This difference between the hemispheres in the use of Kana and Kanji agrees well with what we already know about their respective roles from Chapter 5. The formal, abstract, combinative nature of Kana suits the left hemisphere well. In contrast, recognition of Kanji characters appeals more to the particular capabilities of the right hemisphere in processing and storing images.

The precise geography of the cerebral territories receiving the imprint of the two systems used in Japanese writing, or even alphabetic writing in general, is still a *terra incognita* whose exploration must await the future. Nevertheless, present observations indicate that a significant variability in the organization of the cortex is related to the cultural environment.

Certain authors even go as far as to think that the differentiation of language areas varies between illiterate and educated people. It has been noted that aphasia following left-hemisphere lesions is less frequent in illiterate patients than in patients who can read and write. Other authors, however, have been unable to confirm these results.[44] Tests of differential listening through each ear suggest that the right ear is more efficient than the left in illiterate subjects, while in literate subjects the efficiency of the two ears is about equal.[45] Is this enough to conclude that the epigenesis of cortical organization can be influenced by reading and writing? It is possible, but a convincing demonstration remains to be seen.

"TO LEARN IS TO ELIMINATE"

The "complexity" of the human brain needs no emphasis; S. Atlan is right to insist that the use of this term usually reveals our ignorance. The development of new techniques for anatomical and functional exploration should allow rapid progress in this field and help to fill some of the more obvious gaps in our knowledge. Such methods will, however, encounter fundamental difficulties. An organization can be described only to the extent that it is reproducible from one individual to another. As we saw in Chapter 6, the power of the genes perpetuates the major organizational features, such as the shape of the brain and its convolutions, the organization of its areas, and the general architecture of the brain tissue. But considerable variability, as seen in identical twins, remains, despite the genes' power. It becomes obvious as soon as our analysis reaches the cellular or synaptic level. In the water flea, or daphnid, this variability is limited to the geometry and number of synapses, but in mammals it affects the number and distribution of neurons. In humans it even influences our hereditary tendency to use the right hand. This phenotypic variability is intrinsic. It is the result of the precise "history"[46] of cell division and migration, of the wandering of the growth cone and its fission, or regressive processes and selective stabilization, which cannot be exactly the same from one individual to another even if they are genetically identical. The way in which the brain of the higher vertebrates, especially humans, is constructed introduces a basic variability. The human brain cannot be compared to a compilation of a million sea slugs' abdominal ganglia, in which most of the neurons can be numbered and labeled.

The theory of epigenesis by selective stabilization of neurons and synapses during development takes variability into account. Indeed, this is one of its major advantages. The formal mathematical approach used in this context is intended as a rigorous demonstration that "different learning inputs may produce *different* connective organizations and neuronal functioning abilities but the *same* behavioral capacity . . . in spite of the totally deterministic character of the model."[47] In other words, according to this scheme, experience—which is never the same from one individual to another—leads to a similar behavioral performance, although based on different neuronal and synaptic topology. Individuals who speak with their right hemisphere do not use a different language from those speaking with the left hemisphere. The behavioral code is, to use Gerald Edelman's expression, "degenerate." Epigenesis ensures the *reproducibility of function* despite anatomical variations resulting from the way in which the machine is built.

Several observations converge in support of this theory. The number, topology, and connections of neurons are all affected by regression, as are the types of syllables learned by sparrows, and probably also by man!

Regression affects the peripheral as well as the central nervous system, suggesting that it is a generalized phenomenon, related to the development of neuronal networks. The very early activity of the nervous system in the embryo, together with the role of its spontaneous or evoked activity in regulating various formative stages of a synapse and its evolution up to adulthood, also supports the theory. The facilitating effect of nervous activity on certain cellular or synaptic regressive processes lends additional support. Nevertheless, it still remains to be shown that this theory can be applied strictly to the development of neuronal graphs in the central nervous system.

The laying down of "redundant" and "variable" neuronal or synaptic topologies—the substrates of epigenesis—costs much less in genetic information than would a point-by-point coding of the diverse neuronal singularities found in the adult. The genes that make up the genetic envelope, in particular those that determine the rules of growth and stabilization of synapses, can be shared by all neurons in the same category, perhaps by several categories of neurons. The number of genes necessary for epigenesis through selective stabilization is also relatively low.

Another advantage of the theory of selective stabilization is that it takes into consideration a unique and characteristic property of the nerve cell—that of establishing thousands of discrete, individual contacts with other cells through its synapses. Convergence at the dendrites and divergence through axonal branching create a possibility of "combining" connections, not only for the cell but also for the neuronal "system." Selective stabilization involves populations of nerve cells. As we saw in Chapter 5, the properties of convergence and divergence permit combinations of nervous activity. In this way mental objects can participate in the epigenesis of the brain, with percepts becoming associated with concepts. Future developments in neurobiology will, it is hoped, permit us to discover to what extent mental exercise, either spontaneous or evoked, contributes to the fine tuning of cerebral-cortex connections, including those of the language areas.

According to this scheme, culture makes its impression progressively. The 10,000 or so synapses per cortical neuron are not established immediately. On the contrary, they proliferate in successive waves from birth to puberty in man. With each wave, there is transient redundancy[48] and selective stabilization. This causes a series of critical periods when activity exercises a regulatory effect. If we consider that the growth of axonal and dendritic trees is innate and that selective stabilization defines acquired characteristics, the innate can be differentiated from the acquired only by detailed study at the synaptic level. This study is made difficult by the intimate association of growth and epigenesis, and their alternation over time. One has the impression that the system becomes more and more ordered as it receives "instructions" from the environment. If the theory proposed here is correct, spontaneous or evoked activity is effective only if neurons and their connections already exist before interaction with the outside world takes place. Epigenetic selection acts on preformed synaptic substrates. To learn is to stabilize preestablished synaptic combinations, and to *eliminate* the surplus.

Finally, the theory takes into account the paradox dealt with in the preceding chapter: the nonlinearity, noticeable during evolution, between the complexity of the genome and that of cerebral organization. Let us consider this in the light of the still intriguing problem of the evolutionary origins of the human brain.

Anthropogenesis

> The universe did not give birth to life nor the biosphere to man. Our number came up in a game at Monte Carlo. It is not surprising that, like the man who has just won a million, we still feel the strangeness of our condition.
> —Jacques Monod, *Chance and Necessity*

The earliest writings bear witness to the deep anxiety human beings have always experienced concerning their origins. In Genesis we read that "from the clay of the ground the Lord God formed man, breathed into his nostrils the breath of life, and made man a living person." The clay referred to by the scribes of the desert is composed of atoms, and only atoms. So is man. Had the scribes already realized the material nature of man? Their knowledge was still too limited for them to explain the metamorphosis of clay into a living being. But mental images and concepts came together and were combined in their brains. It was a sculptor who had realized the unprecedented in giving life to a clay statue. This symbolic vision, this mental object, calmed the anxieties of a large segment humanity for several thousands of years.

Since the era of the *Encyclopedia,* that most important landmark in the history of ideas, observed data have accumulated. Comparative anatomical studies of living creatures suggested to Jean-Baptiste de Lamarck his theory of an evolutionary "descendance" of species. In geological strata, the fossil remains of extinct species, and later those of the direct ancestors of man, were found. New techniques became available to date these "documents" of the past objectively. Molecular biology revealed differences and similarities in the ultimate material of heredity, DNA. The slow and erratic progress of biological evolution, conforming prosaically to the laws of thermodynamics, replaced the vision of the sculptor's gestures and his imaginary life-giving breath.

In the light of our current knowledge, the very recent differentiation of *Homo sapiens* stands out as a veritable planetary "phenomenon," to use Pierre Teilhard de Chardin's word. For an observer who wishes to be objective, the phenomenon is certainly not the descent of some "spirit" into the brain of a distant ancestor of man, but the gigantic transformation of the earth's surface accomplished by a single, unique animal species. Swarming over all dry land, this species has disrupted and destroyed in a few thousand years virtually the entire environment that gave birth to it. This power of domination "of the fishes in the sea, and all that flies through the air, and all the living things that move on the earth," including obviously his fellow beings, is due to man's brain. Let us examine the process by which, over a few million years, this "phenomenal" development of *Homo sapiens* came about.

MONKEY CHROMOSOMES

In 1809 Lamarck ended the first part of his *Zoological Philosophy* with "some observations relative to man," in which he suggested that "during a series of generations . . . an ordinary race of quadrupeds" was "transformed into bipeds." About fifty years later, in 1863, Thomas Huxley, a zealous neophyte of the newly emerging Darwinist school, took up this idea in the light of Darwin's own *Origin of Species,* published in 1859. The storm broke loose. Man was descended from the monkey! Two centuries earlier, Father Vannini had been burned alive in Toulouse for stating the same thing. Today, the idea is no longer so fearsome. We limit ourselves prudently to stating that humans and monkeys have common ancestors. Their chromosomes bear undeniable witness to this, just as much as the shape of their skulls or their brains.

It is not very difficult to observe the chromosomes of a human being or a monkey under the microscope. A blood sample is taken and the white cells cultured. They divide, and their chromosomes separate into well-defined rods. Once dispersed they are easily stained and identified. In American monkeys the diploid number varies from twenty to sixty-two. It is much more consistent in Old World monkeys. The most closely related to humans—the orangutans, gorillas, and chimpanzees —all have forty-eight chromosomes. Humans have only forty-six. Does this mean that we have a pair of chromosomes less than the apes? Not at all (Figure 73). High-power examination of stained chromosomes brings out an alternating pattern of light and dark bands, whose thickness and distribution varies from one segment of the chromosome to another. Altogether there are almost a thousand bands that can be compared in these various species. An early discovery was that the

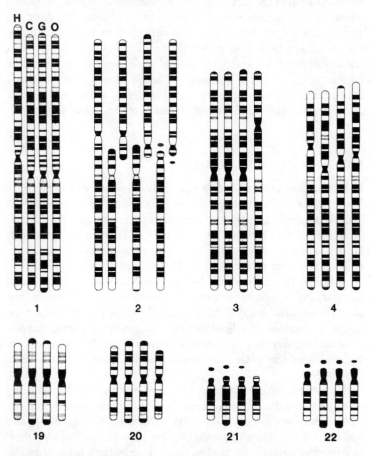

H C G O

1   2   3   4

19   20   21   22

Figure 73. Comparison of selected chromosomes (numbers 1 to 4 and 19 to 22) in humans (H), chimpanzees (C), gorillas (G), and orangutans (0). The chromosomes were stained to demonstrate their banding. The similarity in the distribution of the bands is striking. In humans, chromosome number 2 results from the fusion of two chromosomes (2p and 2q) present in chimpanzees, gorillas, and orangutans. Only differences in detail distinguish the four species. (From J. J. Yunis and O. Prakash, 1982.)

pattern of these bands is strikingly constant in the orangutan, gorilla, chimpanzee, and man.[1] The chromosomal relationship between the four species cannot be doubted. A second finding was that humans had not lost any chromosomes. The characteristic bands of *two* chromosomes of the ape could be found in a *single* human chromosome, number 2, which results from the end-to-end fusion of the 2p and the 2q chromosomes of the ape. Five chromosomes seem completely identical in the four species. The others differ slightly, mainly by the inversion of certain chromosome segments, as if some fragment had broken away and become reincorporated the other way around. More rarely, small chromosome fragments actually disappear.

A comparative map of these structural alterations can be drawn. The presence of the same transformation in two different species signifies a common ancestry. On this basis the orangutan seems the furthest from man and the chimpanzee the closest. A genealogical tree grows up. The central trunk groups the chromosomal characteristics common to all four species. It represents a long-disappeared "hominoid" ancestor. Then there are diverging branches for first the orangutan, then the gorilla, the chimpanzee, and finally man (Figure 74).

The order of the branches of this hypothetical genealogical tree is still the subject of lively debate. This does not matter. The species alive today represent only a few typical specimens of a flourishing, multiple

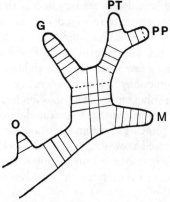

Figure 74. Genealogical tree, drawn on the basis of chromosomal differences between the orangutan (O), gorilla (G), two chimpanzee species —*Pan troglodytes* (PT) and *Pan paniscus* (PP)—and modern man (M). Each line represents a chromosomal change. (From B. Dutrillaux, 1981.)

ascendancy. The striking analogies of their chromosomes are very significant. In spite of the reorganizations just mentioned, their genetic content is very similar. Since the work of Thomas Hunt Morgan on the fruit fly *Drosophila* (see Chapter 6), we know that each band represents a gene or a well-defined group of genes.[2] Here, on chromosome number 1, we find the structural gene of the enzyme enolase 1; there, on chromosome number 11, that of the enzyme lacticodehyrogenase A. In this way almost 400 genes have been located on the human set of chromosomes. Comparisons with the great apes have been made for about only forty genes, but so far they have practically all been found on the same chromosomes.[3] These striking similarities have been confirmed by other biochemical data.

For example, DNA, the genetic material, has been compared in chimpanzee and man using a molecular hybridization technique.[4] The DNA molecule is made up of two complementary strands in the form of a double helix (see Chapter 6). Under the right conditions, they dissociate and reassociate spontaneously *in vitro*. When strands taken from a chimpanzee are mixed with strands from a human being, they reassociate to form hybrid "man-monkey" molecules, differing from the natural DNA of each parent in only about 1 percent of their length. Some researchers have even proposed that the homology between nonrepetitive DNA sequences in the chimpanzee and man is virtually complete!

Logically, these homologies are repeated in the proteins coded for by DNA. The complete amino acid sequence of six proteins, including the alpha and beta chains of hemoglobin, is *exactly* the same in chimpanzees and humans. One substitution is found in delta-hemoglobin and myoglobin and a few more (three to eight) in much larger molecules such as carbonic anhydrase or transferin. In 1975, after examining forty-four proteins using rapid, high-resolution techniques, M. C. King and A. C. Wilson estimated that the mean difference between amino acid sequences in proteins of chimpanzees and humans did not exceed 0.8 percent. The well-known A, B, and O blood types used by anthropologists in their studies of human groups are identical with those of the chimpanzee, as is the Rh factor.[5] Based on structural data of this type one can estimate, at least on an empirical level, the genetic distance between chimpanzees and humans. It is only twenty-five to sixty times greater than that between human populations of Caucasians, Africans, and Japanese!

Everyone therefore agrees that, genetically speaking, the chimpanzee and man are very close. However, their brains and, above all, their cerebral functions differs markedly.

FOSSIL PUZZLES

From the shrew to man, the weight of the brain relative to that of the body increases spectacularly (see Chapter 2). If we arbitrarily set the index of encephalization at 1 in the shrew, it is 11.3 in the chimpanzee and 28.7 in man. The neocortex develops even more rapidly. Its progression index, set at 1 in insectivores, jumps to 58 in the chimpanzee and 156 in man. Other regions of the brain do not follow the same evolution. Indeed some, like the olfactory bulb, move proportionately in the opposite direction. How has this "corticalization" of the brain come about?

The only "documents" available are fossils. During fossilization, the soft tissues, particularly the brain, disappear. Only the bones are preserved. We must revert to Franz Joseph Gall's cranioscopy, discussed in Chapter 1, and examine the skull and the imprints of the blood vessels in it, to reconstruct the cranial cavity and assess its volume, which fortunately is always quite close to that of the brain. We are, however, far from direct observation of the brain and its convolutions.

Since the discovery of *Pithecanthropus* in 1891 by the young military physician Eugene Dubois, the remains of "fossil man" or the hominids have been grouped into three genera: *pre-Australopithecus*, *Australopithecus*, and *Homo*. Recent authors further distinguish two species of *Australopithecus* and three of *Homo*: *Homo habilis*, *Homo erectus*, and obviously *Homo sapiens*. [6] Before discussing this subject, it is important to note that this nomenclature is based on a limited number of individuals. Only eleven *Australopithecus* skulls have been measured, five of *Homo habilis*, and twenty of *Homo erectus*. Already the boundaries between these species are contested because of a few intermediate specimens. Future discoveries will probably lead to revisions, but the known specimens provide enough of a yardstick to draw a preliminary genealogical tree of our fossil ancestors.

Many species of primates were abundant in Africa during the thirty million years before our era. The first hominids appeared in the same regions about four million years ago or, according to certain authors, perhaps five or even seven million years ago! These predecessors of *Australopithecus* already used their hind limbs for walking. Their faces showed the first signs of becoming more "delicate" than those of the apes and their molar teeth were less incisive; above all, their cranial capacity, at 400 cubic centimeters, was comparatively enormous, although it remained less than that of a chimpanzee. Later came the real *Australopithecus,* whose features were even less apelike. Their height was between 1 and 1.5 meters (depending on the species), and their cranial capacity—from 400 to 550 cubic centimeters—began to overtake that of the chimpanzee and approach that of the gorilla. They first appeared about three and a half million years before our era and disappeared only about a million years ago.

At about the same time, three to four million years ago, the oldest known members of the genus *Homo* appeared. These members of *Homo habilis* were completely bipedal and were larger than *Australopithecus.* Their teeth were adapted to omnivorous eating habits. Their cranial capacity was, on average, about 650 cubic centimeters, but occasionally reached 750. About one and a half million years ago, these skillful ("habile") hominids were succeeded by *Homo erectus*—the *Pithecanthropus* whose existence had been predicted by Ernst Haeckel in 1874 (he had invented the name before the species was discovered). The cranial capacity of *Homo erectus* was between 800 and 1,200 cubic centimeters, or even more for those specimens still surviving less than half a million years ago. His hands were like those of modern man.

Then, as Yves Coppens described it in 1981, *"Homo sapiens* arrived inconspicuously, so inconspicuously that the boundary between *Homo erectus* and himself varies and even varies a lot according to different authors!" The capacity of his skull ranges in various specimens from 1,200 to 1,400 cubic centimeters and reaches a mean value similar to that of modern man (see Chapter 2). Meanwhile, Neanderthal man, considered a subspecies of *Homo sapiens,* appeared in Europe and in the Near and Middle East. Curiously enough, the internal volume of his skull—from 1,550 to 1,690 cubic centimeters— is slightly more than the mean value found for modern *Homo sapiens.*

Within a few million years, the brains of man's ancestors tripled in volume. Did the complexity of their cerebral organization increase proportionately, or, on the contrary, did it evolve independently?

Careful examination of the skulls of fossil man brings to light morphologial transformations that reflect a profound evolution in the organization of the brain within. There is an increase in the height of the brain above the cerebellum, a preferential development of the frontal lobe, and a proliferation of the grooves and folds corresponding to the cortical convolutions. In addition, the imprints left by the blood vessels on the inner surface of the skull show a marked enrichment in the vascularization of the meninges, the membranes that enveloped the brain, and thus of the brain itself (Figure 75).

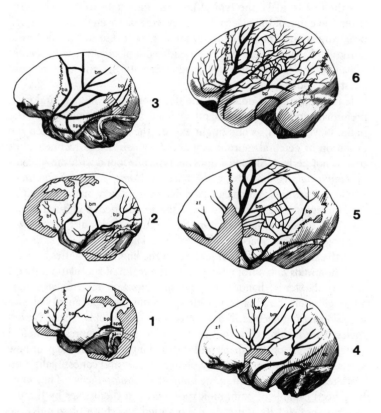

Figure 75. Casts of the inside of the skulls of man's fossil ancestors permit the reconstruction of the blood vessels that irrigated the membranes enveloping the brain—the meninges. The pattern becomes markedly more complicated from *Australopithecus africanus* (1) and *Australopithecus robustus* (2) to modern man, or *Homo sapiens sapiens* (6), after progressing through *Homo habilis* (3), *Homo erectus* (4), and *Homo sapiens neanderthalensis* (5). (From R. Saban, in Y. Coppens, 1981.)

The "industries" of our ancestors also bear witness to their cerebral functioning. The oldest known stone tools, discovered in Ethiopia by Chavaillon in 1969, date from two or three million years ago. These broken quartz fragments, with a few artifactual finishing touches, have been found near the remains of *Australopithecus*, who seems to have been responsible for making them. *Homo habilis*, as his name indicates, developed the manufacture of stone tools, cut to form a sharp edge. He built stone shelters and made use of red ocher. *Homo erectus* was the first to make the typical bifacial stone tools called Acheulean (from the name of the place where they were discovered, Saint-Acheul, near Amiens in France). He also knew how to use fire for domestic purposes. Finally, there came a rapid cultural advance with *Homo sapiens* — the first to bury his dead systematically and thus to pose questions about his own nature.

It is comforting to note that the development of human, and even prehuman, industries went hand in hand with the evolution of the brain. Nevertheless, as one might expect, the correlation between the evolution of cerebral morphology and advances in the technology of tools is not perfect. Shaped stones are typically found with the remains of *Homo habilis*, but also with those of *Homo erectus*. Sometimes *Homo sapiens* used Acheulean axes, like those usually manufactured by *Homo erectus*. Was biological evolution in advance of cultural evolution as Coppens suggested? Or did certain peoples already show a technological conservatism? Will we ever know?

In the same way, any commentary on the linguistic abilities of these fossil hominids falls automatically into the realm of speculation. As we saw in Chapter 7, handedness and specialization for language *can*, although rarely, be situated in different hemispheres. Manual skill and precision are not necessarily associated with the use of language. Nevertheless, the making of a tool of a specific shape requires a "mental representation" of that shape and the working out of a strategy of how to realize it. Thus, the faculty involving imagery and conceptualization was already well developed in the brain of *Australopithecus*. They must have been capable of communication between themselves by the use of signs, but did they already use a varied repertoire of sounds, the rudiments of the first spoken language?

THE WINKS OF THE YOUNG CHIMPANZEE

The phenomenal development of the cerebral cortex in man's fossil ancestors is just one more illustration, although a very spectacular one, of the paradox of the nonlinearity between the evolution of the genome and that of the brain (see Chapters 6 and 7). This paradox takes on its true dimensions if one recalls recent discoveries in molecular genetics. Not only are most structural genes of the chimpanzee also found in man, as we have just seen, but equally in cats and mice. Moreover, their spatial relationship on the chromosomes is preserved from cat to man.[7] It seems that we must admit that this evolution took place on the basis of a relatively small number of genetic mutations and chromosomal reorganizations. Obviously, no major disruption of the genetic material accompanies the development of the human brain.

So what happened? Clearly, we cannot go back in time to find out, but must we therefore abandon our search for traces in the genes of the evolutionary process? Ernst Haeckel, whose importance in the history of ideas is comparable to that of Charles Darwin, showed us in 1874 that one way of proceeding is to understand the link between the evolution of a species, or *phylogeny,* and an individual organism's embryonic development, or *ontogeny.* According to him, the "connection between the two is not external or superficial but deep, intrinsic and causal." It does not matter whether phylogeny caused ontogeny, as Haeckel suggested, or the opposite.[8] Probably it went both ways. More important are the openings offered by present and future developments in molecular genetics toward an understanding of Haeckel's "connection." One approach is through a comparison of the modes of gene expression during ontogeny.

Karl von Baer in 1828, and later Haeckel, quite rightly drew attention to the striking resemblance of the first developmental stages of the fetus from the tortoise to man (Figure 76). The major differences appear in the final stages of development. From reptiles to primates, these are mainly expressed in the enormous expansion of the neocortex. This observation led to the quite legitimate hypothesis that the evolution of higher vertebrates took place through the addition of extra stages in their ontogenetic development. To the extent the initial stages persisted, there was a "recapitulation" of the evolution of the species during the embryonic development of the most evolved organ-

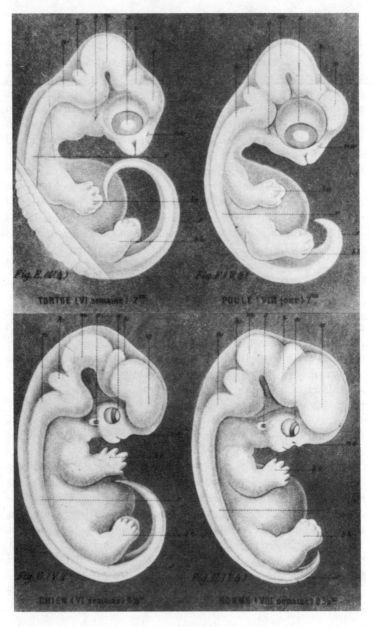

Fig. E. III (4)
TORTUE (VI semaine) 7ᵐᵐ

Fig. F. IV (4)
POULE (VIII jour) 7ᵐᵐ

Fig. G. IV.4
CHIEN (VI semaine) 8½ᵐ

Fig. H. IV. 4
HOMME (VIII semaine) 8½ᵐ

isms. Thus, the mammalian embryo would pass through "fish" and "reptile" stages.

This law is subject to exceptions. Stephen Gould turned his attention to cases in the animal kingdom suggesting an evolution in the opposite direction. The evolution of the skull and the face in higher primates and man seems to be one of these exceptions. The head of a young chimpanzee and that of the human child are similar. Even more astonishing is the resemblance between an *adult* man and a *young* chimpanzee, whose simian features develop only as it grows older (Figure 77).[9] Should one conclude that the chimpanzee has undergone a final addition of a monkeylike face to a more humanlike common ancestor? Does the chimpanzee descend from man? Or, on the contrary, has there been a final deletion in the adult human, due to an arrest of skull development, thus leading to the persistence of fetal features? The known fossil remains of man's direct ancestors, *Australopithecus* or *Homo habilis*, are unquestionably pithecoid. The adult simian features gradually disappeared, and the similarity with the young chimpanzee became more striking. It seems as if its features became transformed into those of man, as if what is a transitional stage in the ontogeny of other primates became a terminal stage in man.[10] As far as the shape of the body, especially that of the skull, is concerned, man resembles the fetus of a chimpanzee suddenly become adult. He is "neotenic."

Is this theory enough to explain the transition from the head of a monkey to that of man? Obviously not. Another characteristic feature of the development of the human skull and brain is that it continues long after birth. This rule is quite independent of the previous one. The "morphological" development of the skull stops when its proportions are similar to those of a fetal chimpanzee, but absolute growth in size continues. The cranial capacity of the chimpanzee increases by only 60 percent after birth. In contrast, that of man increases more than fourfold. In *Australopithecus*, values intermediate between those of chimpanzee and man have been estimated.[11]

Although the gestation periods for chimpanzees and humans are very similar (respectively, 224 and 270 days), the volume of the brain reaches 70 percent of its final value during the chimpanzee's first year, whereas this percentage is reached only after about three years in

Figure 76. Comparison of the embryonic cerebral vesicles in four vertebrate species. From *left* to *right, top* to *bottom*, we see the tortoise (sixth week), the chicken (eighth day), the dog (sixth week), and man (eighth week). The resemblance is clear. (From E. Haeckel, 1874.)

humans.[12] Thus, the volume of the brain continues to increase long after birth in man.

Can the evolutionary development of the human brain be completely explained by neoteny and prolonged maturation? The reply is still no. The development of the brain, particularly of the cerebral cortex, must not be confused with that of its bony case. The similarity in the proportions of the skull or the face of the newborn chimpanzee and the adult human is totally unrelated to the content inside. No one will argue that the brain of the newborn chimpanzee is closer to an adult human brain than the brain of its own parents. Nor does the prolonged postnatal increase in cranial capacity suffice to make a

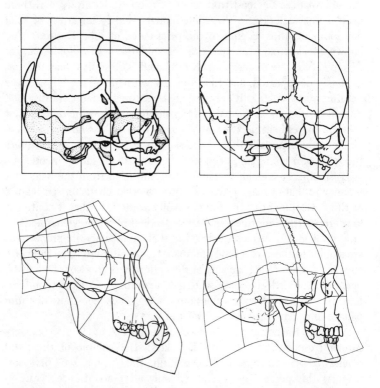

Figure 77. Comparison of skulls of the chimpanzee (on the *left*) and modern man (on the *right*) in the fetus (*top*) and the adult (*bottom*). The fetal skulls are much more similar than the adult ones. But the adult skull is much closer to the fetal skull in man than in the chimpanzee. (From D. Starck and B. Kummer, 1962.)

man. In the rat it increases 5.9 times, which is more than in man!

Anatomical observation shows that the cortical surface area increases from 500 square centimeters in the chimpanzee to more than 2,000 square centimeters in man. All cortical neurons are formed before birth in the chimpanzee as in man. Man differs from the great apes in having a large additional contingent of neurons, and this feature is genetic. In the same way, the relative surface area of the frontal cortex (whose importance in the genesis of mental objects was discussed in Chapter 5) increases from chimpanzee to man, and this is already determined before any contact with the outside world.

These anatomical facts are supported by behavioral observations. The gestures and expressions of the young chimpanzee are astonishingly similar to those of the young human infant.[13] The monkey manifests the same six stages of sensorimotor development that Jean Piaget and his followers have described in children.[14] Like children of two to four years, chimpanzees in the zoo play construction games with cubes of different shapes and colors, but they do not progress much further. In humans, development continues through a series of successive stages, during which the child elaborates patterns of reasoning, initially concrete and then progressively more and more abstract and universal. These operations on mental objects are over and above the cognitive development of the chimpanzee.

At the same general level one can include the oft-cited example of the young baby's smile. The monkey grimaces but does not smile. The human baby smiles, but this smile is not simply an imitation of the mother's smile. A natural experiment provided by premature babies proves this. They develop in a perinatal environment that is very different from the mother's womb. They come into contact with the outside world much earlier than infants born at term. Do premature babies smile at their "legal" age or, on the contrary, at their real biological age? The observations are unambiguous. They smile at the same biological age as full-term infants.[15] The child's smile is biologically determined.

It is true that the skull of an adult human resembles that of the young chimpanzee. But this neoteny cannot explain the extension of the cortex, the prolonged postnatal development, or the cognitive development of the newborn baby. All these features can be considered as a series of *final additions* to the monkey's ontogeny. How can they be explained genetically?

GENES FOR COMMUNICATION AND
SELECTIVE STABILIZATION

The "comparative anatomy" of DNA is still too incomplete to enable us to discern with certainty the set of genes that participates in the final phylogeny of the brain. In Chapter 6, when we discussed the power of genes, we saw that during ontogeny sets of genes were expressed differently from one cell to another and from one tissue to another in the embryo. Communication between cells plays a critical role in the coordination of this genetic expression in the "embryo system." This communication is itself under the control of genes that have no equivalent in unicellular organisms like bacteria. Their activity provides a vehicle for intercellular communication and sooner or later intervenes in the internal regulation of all embryonic cells. In the end, these "communication genes" are the regulating genes of regulatory genes! Insofar as neurotransmitters and hormones control the expression of genes in developing nerve cells, the genes controlling the synthesis of these chemicals are communication genes. The same is true of genes that govern the development of cell lines into nerve tissue or those that ensure firm contacts between cells of the first embryonic morula.[16]

Mutations of these communication genes can have such important morphological effects that the brain can be completely suppressed (see Chapter 6)! Can we see in them the "connection" that Haeckel suggested between ontogeny and phylogeny? It seems legitimate to propose that the evolution of the brain in our ancestors involved differential activity in the genes of embryonic communication.[17] Considering that their effects would be amplified, mutations in some of these genes could account for a dramatic morphological evolution.

Can one go further in defining these genes? Let us return to the more general problem of the evolution of the nervous system, not only in vertebrates but in the entire animal kingdom. The nineteenth-century evolutionists had the *sang-froid* to draw up genealogical trees of all living species on the basis of simple morphological criteria (which must obviously have counterparts at the level of the genome). The common ancestor of invertebrates and vertebrates was often imagined as a sort of worm, resulting from a repetition of identical fragments, or metameres. At the dawn of evolution, a few communication genes must have been enough to stimulate the development of a *redundant* organization of this type from a single metamere. Such an organization is still found today in annelid worms, like the earthworm, whose nervous system consists of a series of cellular aggregates, or ganglia, all identical. As we progress from worms to mollusks and insects, redundancy is gradually lost. The final result, as we saw in the sea slug *Aplysia,* is a nervous system in which practically every neuron differs from its neighbors in its state of differentiation, in the "map" of the genes expressed (see Chapters 2 and 5). Thus, in invertebrates, the evolution of the nervous system has passed through successive stages of redundancy and diversification. Present-day species, in testimony to this evolution, have each successive stage fixed in their genes.

In the vertebrates, the evolution of the nervous system took a different direction. It began with an accident. Instead of forming from a solid chain of cells, as in the invertebrates, the nervous system developed from a hollow tube. This "discovery" may seem insignificant, but it influenced subsequent events. A hollow tube can "swell" by increasing the surface area of its walls, something that cannot happen in a solid cylinder. The neural tube of vertebrates indeed expands into successive vesicles, found from fish to man (see Figures 13 and 76). Some of these vesicles become much larger than the others. The most anterior one forms the cerebral hemispheres; the most posterior, the cerebellum. Both undergo an explosive development in the primates, accounting for almost all the cranial content in man. This increase in surface area can be compared to the stage of redundancy at the beginning of the evolution of the nervous system of the invertebrates. There are, however, differences in detail. There is no longer a repetition of ganglia in a linear chain, but rather a two-dimensional development of "cellular crystals" (see Chapters 2 and 6), which grow along their edges without changing in thickness. The example of the cerebellum is particularly significant in this respect. As we have seen, it is made up of five major categories of neurons organized in three distinct layers. Although the number of cell categories and their layered organization does not change as we progress from rat to man, the total number of neurons in the Purkinje cell category increases from 0.35 to 15 million. An enormous increase in cell redundancy accompanies the increase in area.

There is no shortage of genetic models for this evolutionary step. In the mouse, the "dwarf" mutation causes an impressive reduction in body size, with a 70 percent loss of weight without a change in body proportions.[18] The brain is also affected, losing a third of its weight and a fifth of its cells. The defect is due to an extremely low level (a thousand times less than normal) of growth hormone, or somatotropin. But the brain seems relatively protected. The receptor "locks" in the brain (see Chapter 3) seem to be more efficient in "capturing" this hormone than the rest of the body. Logically, one might imagine that, if the level of growth hormone remained normal, such an increase in receptor efficiency might lead to a differential increase in the size of the brain and perhaps of the neocortex.

Certain congenital malformations in humans provide an example of how this differential growth could take place. Some children at birth have a brain weighing between 18 and 60 grams, or ten to twenty times less than that of a normal infant, born at term.[19] These "microbrains" have the same convolutions as the normal brain, and the cortex has the normal six layers of cells. Even the number of neurons in a vertical column of the cortex is the same as in normal infants. However, the number of these columns *across* the the cortex is greatly reduced. It seems that the tangential proliferation of embryonic neurons in the walls of the cerebral vesicles is affected, leading to a dramatic reduction in cortical area. Obviously, if we contemplate the opposite effect, the result would be an increase in the area of the cortex. A few mutations in communication genes, or chromosomal changes,[20] might then be sufficient to elicit a spectacular increase in redundancy in a given species.

An increase in surface area would of course have repercussions on the axonal and dendritic trees of cerebral and cerebellar cortical neurons. Already in 1909 Ramón y Cajal mentioned that in man these trees developed principally during the first few years after birth. At the time language develops, this growth is not yet finished. Because of the relative length of the period of synaptic proliferation in humans, compared with cats or monkeys, the number of branches of neuronal trees increases. Here again, in both the real and figurative sense of the expression, there is "terminal" addition of new branches. Ramón y Cajal's well-known drawing, which compares the development of a pyramidal cell during vertebrate phylogeny and human ontogeny, clearly illustrates this point (Figure 78).

From the higher vertebrates to man, and particularly from the monkey to man, more and more synapses are produced during development, thus increasing the number of possible connections in the adult. With each wave of synaptogenesis, a number of excess connections form. Synapse redundancy amplifies cellular redundancy. Again, the prolonged production of some hormone or nerve growth factor could explain this ultimate stage of embryogenesis on the basis of a few mutations in communication genes (see Chapter 7).

This increase in cell and synapse redundancy, more marked in humans than in primitive mammals, is only temporary. As we saw in Chapter 7, cell death, synapse elimination, and selective stabilization help to give individual "singularities" to each neuron. But the stage of diversification is not fixed in the genes and, in this respect, differs from the transition of the nervous system of the worm to that of the sea slug. With each generation, interactions with the outside world regulate the elimination of this redundancy. The development of the brain becomes

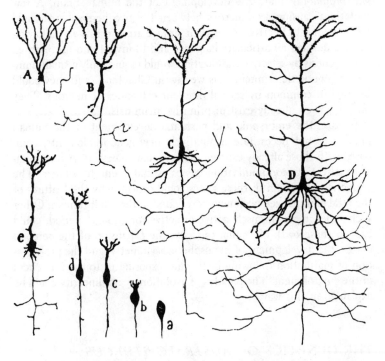

Figure 78. The phylogenetic and ontogenetic evolution of the pyramidal cell. The *top* line shows the phylogenetic development through the history of different species: the frog (A), lizard (B), rat (C), and man (D). The *bottom* line represents, from *right* to *left*, ontogenetic development in the mouse embryo: embryonic neuron or neuroblast (a), beginning of the dendritic branching (b), elongation of the apical dendrite (c and d), growth of basal dendrites and collateral branches (e). (From S. Ramón y Cajal, 1909.)

subject to the environment, which, in a way of speaking, takes over from the genes. As we have seen, the period of this interaction is exceptionally long in man. The contribution of the outside world to the building of the brain thus increases. The sequential steps in synaptic growth and selective stabilization, as well as the succession of "critical periods" proper to each step, create finer and finer interweaving between the anatomical complexity of the human brain and the effects of the environment. The impressions left by environment become linked together and superimposed. Even if each affects only a small number of preestablished synaptic contacts, as long as there is communication between the various superimposed "strata" of influences, they will *profoundly* mark the development of the human brain. A few mutations causing asymmetries between the two hemispheres could favor the most effective use of their surface area, in this way allowing man to develop an articulate language and to invent and use writing.

Epigenesis by selective stabilization would require only a small number of genetic determinants, as we saw in Chapter 7, and they could be used in common by several different categories of neurons. They probably even already exist in primitive mammals.

In sum, the embryonic and postnatal development of the human brain does not necessitate qualitatively new genetic elements, compared with those already existing in our simian ancestors. A few mutations affecting communication genes would seem to suffice. The extinction of certain of these genes could explain why the features of the fetal chimpanzee become incorporated in the adult human. Other such genes, more intensely active or active for a longer period, could explain the growth of cranial capacity, the expansion of the cerebral cortex, the development of hemispheric asymmetry, and the prolongation of maturation following birth, thus exposing us to the influences of the environment. The paradox of evolutionary nonlinearity could be explained in this way.

THE GENETICS OF *AUSTRALOPITHECUS*

In his work *Animal Species and Evolution* (1963), Ernst Mayr recalled that the eminent geneticist J. B. S. Haldane stressed the fact that the extraordinary increase in size of the human brain was an unprecedented evolutionary transformation. The transition from *Australopithecus* to *Homo habilis*, like that from *Homo habilis* to *Homo sapiens*, was probably achieved over a period of about a million years, or 50,000 generations. Many features apart from those involving the brain distinguished these species, including their stature and the shape of their limbs and teeth. It must be admitted, however, that evolution has expressed itself primarily in changes involving the brain. Equally notable is the fact that this evolution stopped with the splitting off of *Homo sapiens sapiens* a few tens of thousands of years ago. Since then, the scatter of individual variations in cranial volume has increased, but the mean has not changed. The genetic mechanisms underlying this sudden acceleration, and equally sudden arrest, will always remain conjectural. We shall never know the population genetics of *Australopithecus*, *Homo habilis*, or *Homo erectus*. The historical question, however, is quite clear. Which environmental factors were responsible for the maintenance, throughout generations, of those mutations or chromosomal reorganizations affecting the development of the brain, particularly the neocortex?

An important point should be considered. "Corticalization" is not restricted to primates and certainly not to man. It has existed since the beginning of the evolution of mammals. Proportionately, there is just as spectacular a "divergence" from platypus to the shrew as from the chimpanzee to man. Present-day primitive mammals, who bear witness to this evolution, do not have a particularly well developed social life. But any "genetic experiment" that causes a differential growth in the area of the neocortex brings a simultaneous increase in learning capacity and "representational" ability. As a consequence, the organism expands its field of exploration in its environment. Its chances of survival improve. If such a genetic experiment succeeds, the genetic alterations or chromosomal reorganizations that formed its basis will be stabilized in the hereditary patrimony of the species.

In view of these considerations, it seems probable, although obviously still hypothetical, that the development of social bonds, so marked in the higher primates, should initially be the *consequence*, not the *cause*, of the growth of the neocortex. However, one should not exclude the possibility of a reciprocal contribution from the social environment on the genetic evolution of man's direct ancestors, in particular *Australopithecus*, *Homo habilis*, and *Homo erectus*. Diverse hypotheses have been proposed on this subject: all plausible but all difficult to verify! They vary according to the image each author has of his own species. Haeckel already considered human language the decisive step that man made to break away from his animal ancestors. The result, Jacques Monod wrote in *Chance and Necessity,* was "the intense pressure of selection that forced the development of the power of simulation and of language that explained its operations."

More down-to-earth hypotheses concern the eating habits of our first ancestors. Chimpanzees and gorillas are mainly vegetarians, but occasionally they catch a gazelle and eat it. During the warm period that followed one of the last ice ages, did our ancestors develop hunting because gathering food had become more difficult? Cooperation became necessary to catch the large mammals of the African plains. It was necessary to develop tools to kill them, as well as to teach the young to share their food, just as young chimpanzees learn from their mothers.[21] As Mayr wrote, "The reward of a successful hunt was a strong selective pressure in favor of an improved brain, increased possibilities of planning, preservation of information (memory), and, most important, refined communication techniques."

Another, rather "machistic" mechanism, which has seduced many an enlightened mind (in practice if not in theory), concerns "polygamy of the chiefs"! Promoted to the ranks of "Grand Homme"[22] as a result of his cerebral superiority, the chief alone would mate with a large number of the tribe's females. In this way, his chromosomes were distributed through the social group.[23] Anthropological data are still too contradictory to support such a thesis, which would, however, be very advantageous, genetically speaking. Equally plausible is the "feminist" concept that the competence of the mother in rearing her puny, clumsy, defenseless newborn, in understanding the necessity of educating it and accomplishing this with tenderness and efficiency, played a decisive role in the evolution of our ancestors.[24]

With the development of their memory capacities, individuals in a social group could recognize each other and distinguish themselves from members of neighboring groups. They defined friends and enemies. Intraspecies battles between present-day monkeys, such as baboons, are usually inoffensive play. Did *Australopithecus* and the first *Homo* deliberately misdirect the aggressiveness stemming from their limbic system toward their fellows when they realized that they could kill them? Were the first Acheulean stones of *Australopithecus* really weapons of war, as much as hunting tools or farming instruments? Obviously, those able to outwit the strategies of their enemies had the greatest chance of survival. A frightening thought is that the genetic evolution of the human brain may be a consequence of the ability to murder one's fellows. Is Jesse's tree rooted in the tradition of the sons of Cain rather than those of Abel? Clearly, there is no objective answer to this question. For Coppens, the increase in cranial volume "changed gear" and accelerated with the appearance of *Homo erectus*. Coppens also noted systematic artificial fractures in skulls of *Homo erectus* and the intentional widening of the opening at the base of the skull.[25] Were these the first vestiges of religion, or simply signs of a ferocious intraspecies struggle, accompanied by cannibalism?

The genetic mechanisms that gave rise to modern man's brain appear to have stopped several tens of thousands of years ago. Did this arrest coincide with the separation of a species that was the first to bury its dead? Did the image that their brains allowed them to have of themselves and of their nature lead to the establishment of a system of social regulation, a morality, which forbade the continuation of a path that had so far led to the evolution of their brains? It seems probable. But have all the aspects of this path disappeared in modern man? Did the sudden stop in evolution suppress them all? It is quite legitimate to ask this question. The continual development of more and more sophisticated weapons of war, regardless of society, religion, philosophy, or culture, suggests that they have not all disappeared. Perhaps the neocortex has not expanded enough to cause modern man to stop this belligerent and biologically absurd behavior. But, one can hope that the human cortex has reached a sufficient level of development for us to understand that making bombs and using them represents a "fossil" activity of our brains.

THE "PHENOMENON OF MAN" RECONSIDERED

As our knowledge of neurobiology, molecular genetics, and paleontology advances, the "phenomenon of man" seems less prodigious. From mouse to man, the cerebral cortex is made up of the same cell categories and the same elementary circuits. The area of the cortex progressively increases, as do the number of cells and their connections. Obviously, the input and output pathways of the cortex follow a similar evolutionary process, and so do the connections between the different parts of the cortex. This continuity of the anatomical evolution of the brain is accompanied by at least an equal continuity in the evolution of the genome. Indeed, the genome varies much less than the brain. We are within striking distance of an explanation for the paradox of an increase in cerebral complexity with a constant set of genes.

One proposal invokes mutations or chromosomal reorganization affecting embryonic communication genes, for this could quite simply account for the increase in the number of cortical neurons and the proliferation of axonal and dendritic branches. An active epigenetic process of selective stabilization introduces new diversity in an organization that would otherwise become redundant. An opening to the outside world compensates for this relaxation of a purely internal determinism. Interactions with the environment contribute to the formation of a more and more complex neural organization, despite the meager evolution of the genetic inheritance. Each generation renews this selective shaping of the brain by the environment. It is accomplished very rapidly compared with the geological time scale of the genome's evolution. Epigenesis by selective stabilization saves time. The Darwinism of synapses replaces the Darwinism of genes.

The genetic mechanisms underlying this evolutionary thrust will probably remain beyond our comprehension for a long time. We may ask whether the transitions from *pre-Australopithecus* to *Australopithecus* and then to the first *Homo habilis* came about as a sudden, abrupt break. In contrast, were there gradual hybridizations between genetically heterogeneous groups in the move from *Homo erectus* to *Homo sapiens* or from Neanderthal to modern man? We should like to have a precise answer, but will this ever be possible?

One of the advantages of the evolutionary divergence that led to *Homo sapiens* is, of course, the increased capacity of the brain to adapt to its environment, with an accompanying increase in the ability to form and combine mental objects. Thought develops and communication between individuals becomes richer. Social bonds intensify and, during the postnatal period, imprint every brain with an original, largely indelible mark. An individual, epigenetic variability in the organization of neurons and synapses is grafted onto existing genetic differences. Neuronal singularities blend with genetic heterogeneity and mark every human brain with features specific to the particular environment in which it has developed.

The Brain—Representation of the World

> Men judge things according to the organization of their brain.
> —Benedict de Spinoza, *Ethics*, I

> Experience and reason accord to establish that men believe themselves free only because they are conscious of their actions and not of what determines them.
> —Benedict de Spinoza, *Ethics*, III

Jacques Monod took pleasure in drawing on reminiscences of the famous physicist Leo Szilard, who, toward the end of his life, abandoned physics to devote himself, with a newcomer's ardor, to the study of the brain and learning mechanisms. One day they were both present at a seminar where the speaker, after expounding at length on a vague and pretentious theory of the brain, tried with more or less success to reply to the questions with which Szilard pursued him. The tension mounted. Finally, Szilard was so irritated that he concluded the debate. "This theory is just good for *your* brain!" he shouted.

Any work that attempts to reflect on the brain is undeniably limited both by the fact that the author is restricted by the aptitudes of his own brain and by the current state of knowledge. Readers of my book must judge for themselves whether the theories I am proposing can be applied to the brain of this author! As to the limits imposed by the state of present-day research on the nervous system, remember that this research has undergone tremendous expansion in the last few years. The neurobiological revolution has just begun and has not yet achieved its major objectives. Many questions remain unanswered, and that is why observed data frequently lead to hypotheses and theoretical discussions. Perhaps we should be silent when we lack data. I have deliberately taken the risk of entering into theoretical discussions, but they have always been clearly demarcated from descriptions of experimental findings. One should not forget that what was hypothesis yesterday may tomorrow be obsolete or, on the contrary, promoted to the rank of fact. Readers must carefully define the limits for themselves.

On some topics, there are only a few observations; on others, there are many. Inevitably, in selecting my examples, I have given only a "partial" view, in both senses of the word, of a much richer and more diversified reality. I trust that the most rigorous minds will be indulgent toward my effort and attribute the gaps, inexactitudes, and imprecisions, which they will certainly find, to my "pedagogic" desire to communicate to a nonspecialized audience the chief features of a research effort that is in constant flux.

The severest criticism that can be leveled concerns the very idea of a project involving the subject of my title. Some people will see my attempt to build a bridge over the gulf that separates the humanities from the neurobiological sciences as an abusive, even an illegitimate impertinence. Perhaps I should have restricted myself to the brain itself —its anatomy, physiology, or biochemistry—excluding anything that is even remotely related to what we might call "psychology." Perhaps that would have been wiser. Sigmund Freud, in 1920, provided one answer to such a criticism, which was cited by A. Bourguignon in 1981 in his consideration of epistemological questions posed by psychoanalysis: "Biology is really a domain with unlimited possibilities. We must expect to receive from it the most surprising enlightenment and we cannot guess what replies it will provide in a few years to the questions we are asking of it. Maybe the replies will be such that they will cause the whole artificial edifice of our [psychoanalytic] hypotheses to collapse."

In the course of these chapters, the reader has learned that the human brain is made up of billions of neurons, linked together by an immense network of fibers and connections, in which electrical and chemical impulses circulate—all of which can be described in molecular or physico-chemical terms—and that all behavior can be explained by an internal mobilization of a topologically defined set of nerve cells. The last proposition was extended, in a hypothetical way, to those "private" processes that are not necessarily manifested by behavior visible to the outside world, such as sensations or perceptions, the elaboration of memory images or concepts, and the linking together of mental objects into "thought." Although we are far from possessing the techniques that would permit us to establish which neuronal assemblies contribute to a particular mental object, the positron camera already offers the possibility of glimpsing them through the walls of the skull. Thus, to consider mental processes as physical events is not to take an ideological stand but simply to adopt the most reasonable and, more important, the most generative working hypothesis. As John Stuart Mill wrote: "If it is materialistic to look for the material bases of mental operations, all theories about the mind must be materialistic or insufficient." And to those who hesitate to accept the simplicity of this hypothesis, Paul Valéry responds: "There is no virgin forest, no clump of seaweed, no maze, no cellular labyrinth that is richer in connections than the domain of the mind." We are in the midst of a historic moment reminiscent of the one in which biology found itself before the last World War, when vitalist doctrines predominated, even among scientists. Molecular biology has destroyed them. We must assume that the same will happen to spiritualistic theses and their various "emergentist" derivatives.

The combinational possibilities provided by the number and diversity of connections in the human brain seem quite sufficient to account for human capabilities. There is no justification for a split between mental and neuronal activity. What is the point of speaking of "mind" or "spirit"? It is only that there are two "aspects" of a *single* event, which one may describe in terms taken from the introspective language of the psychologist or from the language of the neurobiologist. The philosopher J. M. Zemb recognized the validity of this point when he wrote in 1981: "The neurophysiologist can doubtless keep his distance and state philosophically that his reductionism is not a wager against what he cannot see but a way of saying what he can see." It seems quite legitimate to consider that mental states and physiological or physicochemical states of the brain are identical.

Such a conclusion still leads to reticence in certain circles. The debate on the "mind-body" problem can exist only insofar as one denies that the functional organization of the nervous system corresponds to its neural organization.[1] It is remarkable that some contemporary psychologists have resurrected old Bergsonian theses. Why?

A first answer can be found when one considers the insistence with which several of them proclaim that psychology must be accorded the status of a "special science."[2] This insistence is comprehensible when used to defend the "social status" of a discipline, to emphasize the value of its methods or define the content of a teaching course. But the development of knowledge has nothing to gain from such isolationism. On the contrary, in the course of the history of science, the fertilization of one discipline by another has repeatedly fostered progress. We can think, for example, of the application of the methods and concepts of physics to physiology in the nineteenth century with Hermann von Helmholtz or Emil Du Bois-Reymond, or of the marriage of genetics and biochemistry that has recently given birth to molecular biology. To set aside psychology as a "special science" benefits neither psychology itself nor the neurosciences.

Another, deeper reason put forward by those who contend that the psychological cannot be reduced to the neurological is that "the nervous system of higher organisms characteristically achieves a given psychological end by a wide variety of neurological means."[3] In other words, mental states seem largely "independent" of physiological states of the nervous system. If this is the case, what is the point of relating the one to the other?

This attitude is not new. As we saw in Chapter 1, in the nineteenth century Pierre Flourens was its faithful defender, expressing his "spiritualistic" point of view publicly. More recently, in 1929, Karl Lashley repeated Flourens' experiments and removed large parts of a rat's cerebral cortex without major disturbance to the animal's performance in a maze. His experiments had a considerable impact but were the target of severe criticism. Without questioning the results, what did they signify? One must ask whether the maze test that Lashley used was sufficiently discriminatory to demonstrate all the defects caused by a lesion. Further, we know quite well that the cerebral cortex is much more differentiated in man than in a rat! Indeed, decades of research on patients suffering from cortical lesions and recent observations with PET scans demonstrate that, as Franz Joseph Gall suggested, the human cerebral cortex is divided into many areas, each of which is functionally specialized (see Chapters 4 and 5). As we look back, it is quite clear that searching for the anatomical substrate of a cerebral function has, time and again, been a source of progress.

One must, however, emphasize that the genesis of a mental object, as postulated in Chapter 5, involves numerous, topologically dispersed populations of neurons, whose functional characteristics, or "singularities," can be highly variable (if the hypothesis of selective stabilization is correct). As we saw in Chapter 7, it is unlikely that the brains of identical twins are strictly identical. Thus, mental objects are constructed in one individual or another, and probably from one moment to another in the same individual, from similar neuronal populations, which, however, differ in detail. The resulting behavioral performance will nevertheless be more or less the same. As was discussed at length, this variability does not exclude a neuronal determinism; on the contrary, it simply makes its analysis more difficult.

The fundamental capacity of the brain of the higher vertebrates, particularly humans, involves the construction of "representations," either as a result of interaction with the environment or spontaneously by an internal focusing of attention. If one adopts the theory put forward here, these representations are built up by the activation of neurons, whose dispersion throughout multiple cortical areas determines the figurative or abstract character of the representation. A mental object is by definition a transient event. It is dynamic and fleeting, lasting only fractions of a second. The singularities of the neurons that form it, however, are much more stable; they are built up during development by mechanisms involving internal genetic expressions and regulations stemming from a chain of reciprocal interactions with the environment. Thus, the epigenetic component of neuronal singularities itself constitutes a "representation," written in the "wiring" between the nerve cells. This imprint of the physical and sociocultural world remains stable for many years, even throughout the life of an individual. It is renewed from one generation to another, and this relearning imposes an important temporal constraint on the evolution of individual behavior patterns and, of course, the social milieu. We are born with a brain whose maximum number of cells is already fixed. With its aid, we can achieve levels of cerebral functioning that neither the monkey nor, quite obviously, the sea slug can attain. The major features of the organization of the brain, which ensure the unity of humankind and are subject to genetic constraint, also constitute a representation of the world, built up over generations by the evolution of the genome of our fossil ancestors.

Consequently, the human brain contains, or produces, at least three major categories of representations of the world. The kinetics of the formation of these representations and their stability encompass time scales ranging from tenths of a second to hundreds of millions of years.

Each of these modes of representation widens the horizon of the world represented. The "rigidity" of a brain determined entirely genetically would, from the very beginning, impose a limit on the number of possible operations. The capability of constructing labile representations opens the organization of the brain to the social and cultural environment. These "new worlds" can evolve on their own—limited, however, by rules that are determined by the overall performance of the cerebral organization.

If the hypotheses put forward in Chapters 5 and 7 are correct, the formation of each of these representations, although using different elements and various levels of organization, obeys a common rule, inspired by Darwin's original hypothesis. A process of selective stabilization takes over from diversification by variation. The mechanisms associated with the evolution of the genome have already been the subject of much discussion.[4] Chromosomal reorganization, duplication of genes, recombinations and mutations, all create genetic diversity, but only a few of the multiple combinations that appear in each generation are maintained in natural populations. During postnatal epigenesis, the "transient redundancy" of cells and connections and the way in which they grow produce a diversity not restricted to one dimension like the genome, but existing in the three dimensions of space. Here again, only a few of the geometric configurations that appear during development are stabilized in the adult. Much more speculative is the hypothesis of the genesis of mental objects, especially concepts. The suggestion that there is a spontaneous diversification through recombinations within neuronal assemblies, followed by a selection through resonance, is attractive—but does it correspond to reality? Does such a model apply for the more "creative" aspects of our thought processes? Is it also valid for the acquisition of knowledge?

In exploring the world, scientists also proceed in two stages. They focus their attention on an object, build—with more or less success— a model of this object, and agree to consider it as a simplified and formalized representation of the independent, real object. But as we all know from bitter experience, not all the models envisaged at a given moment necessarily survive. When confronted with experimental results, a model is sometimes validated but sometimes destroyed!

For example, does the proposed model apply to an invention that changed the face of the world, that of writing? We possess very few samples of man's first attempts to make written signs. It seems, however, that in the beginning they were images, "thing-signs" or *pictograms*, and that progressively they grew more and more stylized and simplified, losing all schematic resemblance to the object and becoming "word-signs" or *ideograms*. We have much more documentation concerning the evolution of this system of ideograms into an alphabet, in which the letters no longer represent ideas but the sounds, or *phonemes*, into which a language can be decomposed. This transition took place between 1800 and 1500 B.C. in the Near East, at Ugarit in Syria, and was based on cuneiform writing, but a similar transformation took place in the Sinai, on the basis of Egyptian hieroglyphics. In both cases, alphabetic writing took over at a moment when ideographic writing "became heavy and complicated . . . in the hands of more and more scholarly scribes, elaborating more and more complex traditions."[5] The development of signs flourished, but the major event was the mixing in with these ideograms of the first alphabetical signs associated with sounds. When a scribe used them, he conveyed his meaning not by a single sign, but by a combination of signs. The system of writing became mixed (Figure 79). It resembled that used today in Japan, where Kanji and Kana coexist (see Chapter 7). After this phase of diversification, which occurred in both Mesopotamia and Egypt, there came a stage of "selective stabilization." Ideograms disappeared while alphabetical signs remained. At the same time the alphabetical characters were simplified. Their number progressively diminished. There was no "attrition" of syllables (as in Chapter 7) but an attrition of alphabetical characters! It is interesting that this segregation of the alphabet from a mixed system of writing did not take place where the alphabetical signs first appeared. The conservatism of the scribes saw to this. It occurred not at the sites where the signs had been invented, but around their borders. Was there a form of "geographical isolation" of the alphabet by wandering merchants eager to employ a practical system of writing closely related to the arithmetic they used for their accounting? The analogy with the evolution of species and the selective stabilization of synapses is striking. But of course it remains only an analogy.

It is nevertheless worth noting that in the history of ideas "instructive" hypotheses have most often preceded selective hypotheses. When Jean-Baptiste de Lamarck tried to found his theory of "descendance" on a plausible biological mechanism, he proposed the "heredity of acquired characteristics," a tenet that advances in genetics would eventually destroy. One had to wait almost half a century before the idea of selection was proposed by Charles Darwin and Alfred Wallace and validated in principle, if not in all the details of its application. In the same way the first theories about the production of antibodies were

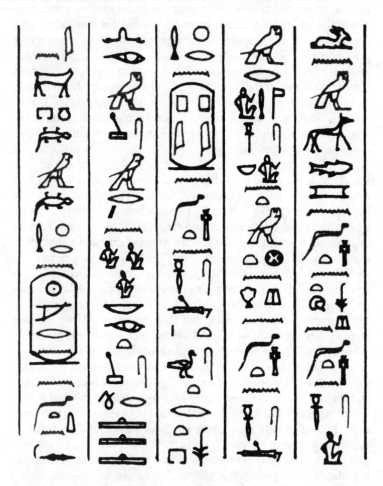

Figure 79. Mixture of alphabetical signs (in gray) and ideograms (in black) on an Egyptian inscription of the Sixth Dynasty, around 2300 B.C. In Western forms of writing, only the alphabet has survived. (From B. André-Leicknam and C. Ziegler, 1982.)

originally based on instructive models before selective mechanisms replaced them. It could conceivably be the same for theories of learning.[6] To understand the reasons for this temporal succession, we must obviously examine the functioning of the scientist's brain. An instructive concept consists of only one step. It is the simplest possible approach. Moroever, whether we like it or not, it contains an "egocentric" component. "Nature directs forms" much as the sculptor models clay into a statue. The image of human behavior that first occurs to the scientist's brain is transposed into elementary mechanisms that have nothing to do with it and are situated at a completely different level of organization. The concept of selection, on the other hand, implies further reflection. It involves two steps, and it satisfies the quest for a material mechanism totally devoid of "intentional" aspects. It is natural that this more complicated procedure, more difficult to execute, should have systematically appeared in second place throughout the history of scientific thought.

With the development of writing, an extracerebral memory was available to fix images and concepts in a more stable material than neurons and synapses. It could be used to consolidate and complete an already broad range of events and cultural artifacts, of symbols, customs, and traditions, relearned by each generation and perpetuated without genetic influence. Mental images and concepts were thus able to survive much longer than the brain that had produced them in fractions of a second. How does this cultural memory work? To answer this question is beyond the scope of this book. It involves the fascinating but still little explored realm of the links between the neurosciences and social anthropology and ethnology.

The general problem of the temporal stability of cultural and biological events and objects brings us to a more directly cerebral subject, that of the relationship between what we commonly call structure and function. In discussing mental objects, we saw how correlated activity in sets of neurons could lead to their coupling through changes in synaptic efficiency, explained in terms of the regulation of molecular properties in the synapse. In the same way, during the epigenesis that follows birth, activity in a developing network governs the stabilization of some synapses and the elimination of others. A fleeting functional activity thus leaves a structural trace; it becomes a structure itself. As A. D. Ritchie wrote in 1936: "The notion of structure appears when we consider the organism in an abstract instant of time. Abstraction is valid because in the history of the organism there are relatively stable events that do not change much and these are called structure. On the other hand, there are unstable events and these are called function. Finally, the distinction is quantitative and depends on the time scale that we use."

Does this conclusion challenge the distinction usually made between organic and functional disturbances of the nervous system? This question deserves to be considered. The very diversity of neurological or "mental" disturbances, however, does not allow us to give one answer, and we must restrict ourselves to a few very general observations on a subject that, once again, is beyond the scope of the present work. Of all the organs of the body, the nervous system is unusual in that its total number of cells is fixed at birth. Any neurons that are destroyed are never replaced. Nevertheless, axons and dendrites preserve a remarkable capacity to regenerate even in the adult. After a lesion, new growth cones form and reinvade the territories formally occupied by the damaged nerves. The possibility of restoring function is quite high in the young but gradually declines with age.[7] In a few cases that have been studied in detail, such as the neuromuscular junction, regeneration involves a stage of transient redundancy followed by selective stabilization, just as in normal development.[8] The state of activity of the system once again controls this evolution and contributes to the recovery of function, even if this is only partial. Not all forms of activity are effective. Certain impulse frequencies will facilitate the effect, but others will inhibit it. The same situation is found during development. "Pathological" environmental factors can break down neurons and synapses in a normal individual. The possibility of recovery exists, but it declines over time. Modification of synaptic efficiency will obviously be easier to reverse than a loss of synapses, but, once again, *only* as long as the activity within the network permits it.

This brings us once more to an examination of the reciprocal interactions between the social and the cerebral in man. The brain of *Homo sapiens sapiens* probably differentiated in the African plains, in populations of a few hundred thousand individuals. Today, billions of these people have invaded almost the entire planet and are even trying to travel beyond it. Are the organization and the flexibility of the human brain still compatible with the evolution of an environment that it can control only very partially? Is a profound disharmony being established

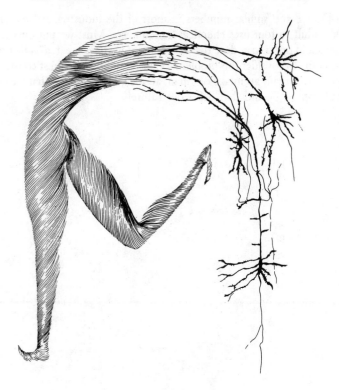

Figure 80. "Neuronal apocalypse," with the brain of man being torn apart by the environment it has created. (Original drawing by S. Carcassonne.)

between the human brain and the world around it? We may well ask. The forms of architecture we enclose ourselves in, the working conditions we endure, the threats of total destruction with which we menace our like, the malnutrition we inflict on the majority of our fellows— do all these favor a balanced development and functioning of our brain? It is very doubtful. After having destroying our environment are we not now destroying our own brains? A single statistic indicates the urgency of the problem, one reflecting the consumption of some of the most widely sold drugs in world: the benzodiazepines. These minor tranquilizers act on the cerebral receptor of an inhibitory neurotransmitter: gamma-aminobutyric acid. They enhance its effects, calming anxiety and easing sleep. Seven million packets are sold every month in France and similar numbers in most of the industrialized nations. One adult in four uses chemical tranquilizers. Must we put ourselves to sleep in order to endure the environment we have created? The time has come to consider this problem seriously. But first we must construct within our brain an image of "man, an idea, like a model, that we can contemplate,"[9] and that befits our future!

Glossary

Acetylcholine: one of the first neurotransmitters discovered; its effect at the neuromuscular junction is blocked by curare.

Adenosine triphosphate (ATP): small molecule produced by cell metabolism and used in storing and transferring energy.

Agnosia: a defect in the recognition of sensory stimuli that is not due to a change in the body's basic sensory mechanisms or to a lowered state of attention.

Allosteric protein: regulatory protein (enzyme, gene repressor, or pharmacological receptor) carrying at least two distinct categories of binding sites, which interact, indirectly, via discrete conformational transitions of the protein molecule.

Amino acids: organic compounds containing amino and carboxyl groups that form the essential structure of proteins and are also active as neurotransmitters. Some examples are glutamic acid, aspartic acid, and gamma-aminobutyric acid (GABA).

Aphasia: a defect in the production and/or comprehension of written and/or spoken language due to a brain lesion (see Figure 40).

Aplysia: the sea slug, a mollusk of the gastropod class whose very simple nervous system has been the subject of important studies at the cellular level (see Figure 26).

Axon: a single fiber growing out of a neuron, along which impulses travel from the cell body to the axon terminal. It is the output channel of the nerve cell and terminates in branches, at the end of which synapses form (see Figure 8).

Basal ganglia: a large group of neurons in the floor of the forebrain (see Figure 13).

Brainstem: an important part of the brain from the medulla to the midbrain.

Catecholamines: a family of chemical substances with a catechol nucleus to which an amine group is attached. Several of them act as neurotransmitters—for example, noradrenaline and dopamine (see Figures 11 and 44).

Category: the smallest possible grouping of cells of the same morphology and biochemical type (see Figure 15).

Cellular crystal: an ensemble of nerve cells of the same category organized in a regular pattern, such as the Purkinje cells of the cerebellum (see Figures 21 and 22).

Cerebellum: an outgrowth of the hindbrain that is specialized for motor coordination; it contains only a small number of neuron categories, including Purkinje and granule cells (see Figures 3, 13, and 21).

Cerebral cortex: the layer of gray matter forming the outer shell of the cerebral hemispheres; it is highly developed in mammals, particularly the *neocortex* (see Figures 3, 13, 14, 15, and 16).

Chromosome: a rodlike body in the cell nucleus containing DNA and visible by microscopy during cell division (see Figure 73).

Clone: an individual (or cell) derived from a single individual (or cell) by asexual reproduction (see Figure 58).

Corpus callosum: the large fiber bundle connecting the cerebral hemispheres (see Figures 3 and 5).

Cortical areas: distinct zones of the cortex characterized by their cellular architecture and function (see Brodmann's maps in Figure 6). Classically, one distinguishes the primary *sensory* areas, responsible for receiving input from the sensory organs; the *motor* areas, dealing with motor commands; and the remaining *association* areas.

Cyclic AMP: a small cyclic molecule derived from ATP and used as an internal signaling mechanism in the cell.

Dendrites: multiple, branched outgrowths of a neuron that receive numerous synaptic contacts from axon terminals, thus collecting signals and transmitting them to the cell body (see Figure 8).

Deoxyribonucleic acid (DNA): the molecular basis of heredity, made up of linear chains of nucleotides, themselves formed of an organic base, a sugar (deoxyribose), and phosphate. Usually two complementary DNA chains form a double helix.

Dopamine: a catecholamine neurotransmitter that is implicated in one theory of schizophrenia (see Figure 44).

Enkephalin: a peptide neurotransmitter that acts like morphine. There are two types: leu-enkephalin and met-enkephalin (see Figure 36).

Gamma-aminobutyric acid (GABA): an amino acid that acts as an inhibitory neurotransmitter.

Gene: a segment of the chromosome composed of DNA and with a defined function. Structural genes code for proteins, while regulatory genes govern the activity of structural genes (see Chapter 6).

Genome: all the genetic material (DNA) of a cell.

Genotype: the genetic constitution of an individual.

Graph: a mathematical expression providing a rigorous description of the geometry of a network.

Hippocampus: a cortical structure in the medial part of the mammalian temporal lobe; it results from the infolding of an "old" cortical area found in reptiles and primitive mammals. It does not have the typical six layers of the neocortex (see Figures 14 and 37).

Homoeotic: describes genes whose mutation (in invertebrates) causes the replacement of one organ by another; for example, in the *ophthalmoptera* mutation a wing appears in the place of an eye.

Hypothalamus: a cluster of neurons in the forebrain beneath the thalamus. Despite its small size, it plays an important role in "vital" functions, including feeding, drinking, sexual behavior, sleep, temperature regulation, emotion, and hormone balance (see Figure 13 and Chapter 4).

Ion: an atom or molecule carrying an electrical charge, such as sodium (Na^+) or chloride (Cl^-) ions.

Ion channel: the pore through which ions cross the cell membrane. There are several categories, defined by their ion specificity and their electrical sensitivity. The propagation of a nerve impulse involves sodium-selective channels (see Figure 30).

Isogenic: describes individuals with the same genotype, like identical twins (see Figure 58).

Lateral geniculate nucleus: thalamic nucleus relaying the visual pathways (see Figure 50).

Limbic system: a group of primitive structures important for the control of emotional behavior, including the hippocampus, parts of the thalamus and hypothalamus, and related nuclei of the septum and amygdala (see Figure 37).

Locus coeruleus: nucleus in the central part of the brainstem whose neurons contain noradrenaline (see Figure 11).

Mauthner cell: a giant neuron; only two are situated in the medulla of fish. It is involved in the flight reflex (see Figure 34).

Membrane: a continuous lipid and protein film delimiting and enveloping all cells, including nerve cells. Among its constituent molecules, there are molecule channels, enzyme pumps, and neurotransmitter receptors.

Membrane potential: the difference in electrical potential across the cell membrane due to a difference in concentration of ions inside and outside a cell.

Mutation: a spontaneous or induced modification, transmissible by heredity, of the genetic material, the DNA.

Myelin: the lipid substance forming a sheath around certain nerve fibers.

Neocortex: see **Cerebral cortex.**

Neuron: the nerve cell, formed of a cell body (or soma) containing the nucleus, and outgrowths of two types: dendrites, converging toward the cell body, and a single axon leaving it (see Figure 8).

Neurotransmitter: a chemical substance involved in the transmission of the nerve signal at a chemical synapse. There are probably dozens of such transmitters in the brain (see Figure 11).

Noradrenaline (norepinephrine): a catecholamine neurotransmitter with multiple functions in the central and peripheral nervous systems (see Figure 11).

Peptide: a linear chain of amino acids, like a protein, but shorter (up to twenty amino acids). Some examples are enkephalin, substance P, and LHRH.

Phenotype: the cluster of apparent, observable characteristics of an individual resulting from the interaction between the genotype and the environment in which the individual develops.

Planum temporale: a cortical area near the auditory cortex (see Figure 70).

Pleiotropic: describes the capacity of a gene to influence several distinct characteristics in the phenotype; for example, the albino gene affects both skin pigment and the anatomical organization of the visual pathways in the brain (see Figure 50).

Postsynaptic: on the "downstream" surface of a synapse, the part usually formed by a dendrite, a muscle, or a gland (see Figures 9, 17, and 30).

Presynaptic: on the "upstream" side of a synapse, normally formed by an axon terminal (see Figures 9 and 17).

Protein: the fundamental cell component; it is a "macromolecule" formed of linear chains of a large number of amino acids (sometimes more than a thousand). The amino acid sequence is characteristic of each type of protein. Enzymes, receptors, molecule channels, and antibodies are all proteins (see Figure 31).

Pump: an enzyme that uses ATP to actively transport ions and create a concentration gradient across the cell membrane.

Purkinje cell: a neuron characterized by its bushlike dendritic tree; it is the principal cell category in the cerebellar cortex (see Figures 21, 51, and 62).

Pyramidal cell: the main cell category in the cerebral cortex, out of which it sends its axon (see Figure 15).

Receptor: a term for two different receivers: (1) the sensory *cells* of the sense organs (e.g., the rods and cones of the retina) and (2) the *molecules* that recognize specific substances such as neurotransmitters or hormones (e.g., the acetylcholine receptor; see Figure 31).

Repressor: an allosteric protein regulating the expression of structural genes as proteins.

Reticular formation: groups of cell bodies in a bed of nerve fibers in the ventral part of the brain, from the medulla to the thalamus. In fact the groups are discrete; the best known contain catecholamines like noradrenaline or dopamine (see Figures 11 and 44).

Ribonucleic acid (RNA): a linear macromolecule related to DNA and important in transcribing and translating DNA to produce proteins.

Septum: a group of neurons related to the limbic system (see Figure 37).

Serotonin: a neurotransmitter derived from an aromatic amino acid, tryptophan.

Singularity: the distinguishing characteristic of each cell in a given category based on the precise set of connections that it gives and receives.

Soma: the cell body of a neuron, containing the nucleus and cytoplasm, together with mitochondria and other organelles (see Figure 8).

Stellate cell: a cortical neuron whose axon remains within the cortex (see Figure 15).

Substance P: a peptide neurotransmitter involved in the handling of pain messages in the spinal cord.

Superior colliculus: a paired nucleus in the roof of the midbrain responsible for certain visual reflexes.

Synapse: the junction between neurons or between neurons and other cells, such as muscles and glands. At a synapse the membrane of the axon terminal and that of the postsynaptic surface are juxtaposed, but not fused. There exist electrical synapses, where electrical signals are transmitted directly, and chemical synapses, which use a transmitter to cross the intercellular cleft (see Figures 9 and 17).

Thalamus: a group of nuclei in the forebrain, beneath the cortex. Most pathways entering or leaving the cortex relay in the thalamus, and it receives fibers from the cortex in turn (see Figures 3, 13, and 18).

Notes

Complete publishing information for the citations in both the text and the notes is contained in the Bibliography. Only names and dates are given here.

Preface

1. Although Freud's *Project* was written in 1895, it was not actually published until 1954. On Freud's neurological background, see F. J. Sulloway (1979).
2. See G. M. Edelman and V. B. Mountcastle (1978).
3. E. Morin and M. Piatelli-Palmarini (1974).
4. B. Pascal, *Pensées*, 51:434.

1 The "Organ of the Soul"

1. J. H. Breasted (1930); C. A. Elsberg (1945).
2. For details on the history of our knowledge of the brain from antiquity to modern times, see J. Soury (1899); E. Clarke and C. D. O'Malley (1968); E. Clarke and K. Dewhurst (1972); H. Hecaen and G. Lanteri-Laura (1977); A. R. Luria (1980); M. A. B. Brazier (1984).
3. For an in-depth analysis of the work of Gall and his successors, see R. Young (1970); H. Hecaen and G. Lanteri-Laura (1977). See also H. Hecaen and J. Dubois (1969); H. Hecaen (1978).
4. For a historical analysis and references, see H. Van der Loos (1967); E. Clarke and C. D. O'Malley (1968); M. A. B. Brazier (1978)
5. Translation by S. Hoole.
6. G. E. Palade and S. L. Palay (1954); J. D. Robertson (1956).
7. For references to the history of the brain's electrical activity, see M. A. B. Brazier (1984); J. C. Eccles (1964).
8. F. McIntosh (1941); W. Feldberg (1948).
9. B. Falck et al. (1962); A. Dahlström and K. Fuxe (1964).

2 The Component Parts of the Brain

1. See S. J. Gould (1981).
2. P. V. Tobias (1975).

3. See G. von Bonin (1937).
4. T. Meynert (1867, 1874); W. B. Lewis and H. Clarke (1878).
5. S. L. Palay (1978).
6. E. G. Jones (1975, 1981); see also S. Ramón y Cajal (1909).
7. J.-P. Changeux (1980, 1983a).
8. N. Brecha et al. (1979, 1981); B. Zipser and R. McKay (1981).
9. K. Brodmann (1909); C. von Economo (1929).
10. E. G. Gray (1959); J. J. Sloper et al. (1979); M. Colonnier (1981).
11. J. J. Sloper et al. (1979).
12. C. D. Gilbert and T.N. Wiesel (1981); E. G. Jones (1981).
13. V. B. Mountcastle (1957, 1976).
14. See D. H. Hubel and T. N. Wiesel (1977).
15. See S. LeVay et al. (1980).
16. D. H. Hubel et al. (1978).
17. J. C. Eccles et al. (1967).
18. H. Wässle et al. (1981).
19. J.-P. Changeux (1980, 1983a).

3 Animal Spirits

1. E. D. Adrian (1946).
2. M. Jouvet (1979).
3. J. E. Desmedt (1977).
4. J. C. Eccles (1964).
5. E. R. Kandel (1976).
6. I. Prigogine and R. Balescu (1956); I. Prigogine (1961).
7. F. Strumwasser (1965); M. J. Berridge and P. E. Rapp (1979); R. Meech (1979).
8. A. J. Hudspeth and D. Corey (1977).
9. V. P. Whittaker et al. (1964); N. Morel et al. (1977).
10. B. Katz (1966); S. W. Kuffler and J. G. Nicholls (1976).
11. Ibid.
12. H. Korn et al. (1981).
13. For references, see R. Acher (1981); F. E. Bloom (1981).
14. T. Hökfelt et al. (1980).
15. J.-P. Changeux (1981a). For references, see also A. Karlin (1983); R. Stroud (1983); J.-P. Changeux et al. (1984).
16. D. Nachmansohn (1959).
17. C. Y. Lee and C. C. Chang (1966).
18. J.-P. Changeux et al. (1970).
19. J. Monod et al. (1963, 1965).

4 Into Action

1. Y. Leroy (1964); D. Bentley (1971); D. Bentley and R. Hoy (1974).
2. J.-P. Changeux et al. (1973).
3. G. S. Stent et al. (1978).
4. See D. S. Faber and H. Korn (1978).
5. The Mauthner cell also receives electrical synapses, mixed with chemical ones.
6. See E. M. Stricker et al. (1976); B. I. Rolls and E. T. Rolls (1981).
7. U. von Euler and J. Gaddum (1931).
8. T. Hökfelt et al. (1980).
9. C. B. Pert and S. H. Snyder (1973); E. J. Simon et al. (1973); L. Terenius (1973).
10. J. Hugues et al. (1975).
11. B. P. Roques et al. (1976).
12. J. L. Henry (1980); L. Terenius (1981); J. M. Besson et al. (1982).
13. R. A. Wise (1980).
14. J. M. Davidson (1980).
15. C. Fox and G. Knaggs (1969); C. Fox and B. Fox (1971).
16. M. R. Murphy et al. (1979); M. R. Murphy (1981).
17. C. N. Woolsey (1958).
18. J. H. Kaas et al. (1979, 1981).
19. See H. Hecaen and M. Albert (1978); B. Kolb and I. Q. Whishaw (1980).
20. P. D. MacLean (1970).

5 Mental Objects

1. S. Atlan (1979); A. Bourguignon (1981b).
2. J. A. Fodor (1975, 1981a, 1981b).
3. M. Denis (1979); S. Kosslyn (1980).
4. R. N. Shepard and J. Metzler (1971); R. Shepard and S. Judd (1976).
5. See J. Bouveresse (1979).
6. J. A. Fodor (1975, 1981a, 1981b).
7. J. M. McGaugh (1973).
8. See H. Hecaen and M. Albert (1978); A. Luria (1980).
9. D. O. Hebb (1949); G. M. Edelman and V. B. Mountcastle (1978); R. Thom (1980); C. von der Malsburg (1981); C. von der Malsburg and D. Willshaw (1981); J. Hopfield (1982); A. Pellionisz and R. Llinás (1982); J.-P. Changeux et al. (1973); J.-P. Changeux (1981b, 1983a, 1983b); see also W. Little and G. Shaw (1975, 1978).
10. See D. O. Hebb (1949).
11. G. M. Edelman & V. B. Mountcastle (1978).

12. See R. Thom (1980).

13. J.-P. Changeux et al. (1973); J.-P. Changeux (1981b, 1983a, 1983b); G. M. Edelman and V. B. Mountcastle (1978).

14. R. Thom (1980).

15. F. de Saussure (1915).

16. R. A. Fisken et al. (1975).

17. R. Lorente de Nó (1938); E. R. Hilgard and D. Marquis (1940).

18. B. Katz and S. Thesleff (1957).

19. J.-P. Changeux (1981a).

20. T. Heidmann and J.-P. Changeux (1980, 1982).

21. C. Pull and M.-C. Pull (1981).

22. H. Hecaen and M. Albert (1978).

23. On serontonin, see S. Peroutka and S. Snyder (1979). On dopamine, see D. Burt et al. (1976); P. Whitaker and P. Seeman (1978).

24. H. Piéron (1913); H. Ey et al. (1975).

25. G. Moruzzi and H. W. Magoun (1949); H. W. Magoun (1954).

26. B. Falck et al. (1962); A. Dahlström and K. Fuxe (1964); T. Hökfelt et al. (1980).

27. M. Monnier and L. Hösli (1964); M. Sallanon et al. (1981).

28. P. Boyer (1981); S. Schwartz (1982).

29. S. A. Hillyard et al. (1978); R. Galambos and S. A. Hillyard (1981).

30. For references, see U. Ungerstedt (1971); A.-M. Thierry et al. (1973); H. Simon (1981).

31. J. J. Bouyer et al. (1980); P. Buser (1980).

32. J.-P. Mialet (1981).

33. G. M. Edelman and V. B. Mountcastle (1978); G. M. Edelman (1981).

34. See D. Ferrier (1880); B. Kolb and I. Q. Whishaw (1980).

35. A. R. Luria (1980).

36. C. Jacobsen (1931); C. Jacobsen and H. Nissen (1937).

37. R. W. Sperry (1968); M. Gazzaniga (1970); S. Springer and G. Deutsch (1981).

38. S. Kety and C. Schmidt (1945); N. Lassen (1959).

6 The Power of the Genes

1. R. W. Guillery et al. (1975).

2. R. W. Guillery (1974).

3. H. de Vries (1901).

4. V. S. Caviness and P. Rakic (1978); J.-P. Changeux and K. Mikoshiba (1978); C. Sotelo and A. Privat (1978); P. Rakic (1979).

5. J. Lejeune et al. (1959); J. Lejeune (1977); F. Gullotta et al. (1981).

6. See S. Benzer (1967, 1973).

7. J. Hall (1978); Y. N. Jan and L. J. Jan (1978).

8. W. Quinn et al. (1974); Y. Dudai (1981).

9. D. Byers et al. (1981).

10. W. Bodmer and L. Cavalli-Sforza (1976).

11. J. Mendlewicz et al. (1979, 1980); J. Mendlewicz (1980).

12. J. Monod (1970).

13. F. Gros et al. (1961); F. Jacob and J. Monod (1961).

14. For references, see J. Watson (1976).

15. F. Gros et al. (1961); F. Jacob and J. Monod (1961).

16. See J. Gurdon (1974); L. Hood et al. (1975).

17. P. Kourilsky and P. Chambon (1978); R. Breathnach and P. Chambon (1981).

18. R. Scheller et al. (1982).

19. P. Kourilsky and P. Chambon (1978); R. Breathnach and P. Chambon (1981).

20. W. Hahn et al. (1978); J. van Ness et al. (1979).

21. See F. Jacob (1979).

22. T. R. Wright (1970); J. Postlethwaite and H. Schneiderman (1973); P. A. Lawrence and G. Morata (1983); see also W. McGinnis et al. (1984).

23. E. Hadorn (1967, 1968).

24. D. Bennett (1975); H. Shin et al. (1982).

25. R. Goldschmidt (1940); C. Stern (1954); A. Garcia-Bellido (1981).

26. S. Strickland and V. Mahdavi (1978).

27. S. Levine (1966); C. Aron (1974); B. McEwen (1976); R. A. Gorski (1979); Y. Arai (1981).

28. S. Strickland and V. Mahdavi (1978).

29. On the rat, see S. Levine (1966); C. Aron (1974); B. McEwen (1976), R. A. Gorski (1979); Y. Arai (1981). On man, see E. Sullerot (1978).

30. C. de Lacoste-Utamsing and R. L. Holloway (1982); see also P. V. Tobias (1975); R. Holloway (1980).

31. For references, see D. W. Pfaff (1980).

32. For references, see P. Rakic and P. Goldman-Rakic (1982).

33. J. B. Angevine and R. L. Sidman (1961); P. Rakic (1974).

34. C. J. Shatz and P. Rakic (1981).

35. On monkeys, see J. S. Lund et al. (1977); R. Boothe et al. (1979). On humans, see J. L. Conel (1939–1963).

36. J. S. Lund et al. (1977); R. Boothe et al. (1979); L. J. Garey (1984).

37. H. Van der Loos and T. Woolsey (1973).

38. J. H. Scholes (1979); N. Bodick and C. Levinthal (1980); K. A. C. Martin and V. H. Perry (1983).

7 Epigenesis

1. J.-P. Changeux (1972, 1983a, 1983b); J.-P. Changeux et al. (1973); G. Stent (1973); J.-P. Changeux and A. Danchin (1976); W. M. Cowan (1979); see also S. Ramón y Cajal (1909).
2. See E. R. Macagno et al. (1973).
3. F. Levinthal et al. (1976).
4. R. E. Wimer et al. (1976).
5. B. Mintz (1974).
6. R. Mullen (1977); M. L. Oster-Granite and J. Gearhart (1981); D. Goldowitz and R. J. Mullen (1982).
7. R. B. Campenot (1977).
8. W. M. Cowan (1979); R. Pittman and R. W. Oppenheim (1979).
9. P. A. Redfern (1970); M. R. Bennett and A. G. Pettigrew (1974a, 1974b); P. Benoît and J.-P. Changeux (1975, 1978); M. C. Brown et al. (1976); J. -L. Gouzé et al. (1983).
10. F. Crepel et al. (1976); J. Mariani and J.-P. Changeux (1981); J. Mariani (1983).
11. P. R. Huttenocher et al. (1982); L. J. Garey (1984).
12. G. M. Innocenti (1981a, 1981b); D. O'Leary et al. (1981); G. O. Ivy and H. P. Killackey (1982).
13. V. Hamburger (1970); K. L. Ripley and R. R. Provine (1972).
14. D. Jouvet-Mounier (1968); C. Dreyfus-Brisac (1979).
15. R. Marty and J. Scherrer (1964).
16. For references, see J.-P. Changeux (1981a).
17. For references, see D. M. Fambrough (1979); J.-P. Changeux (1981a); M. J. Dennis (1981).
18. A. Michler and B. Sakmann (1980); C. G. Reiness and C. B. Weinberg (1981); J. Steinbach (1981).
19. For references, see G. D. Fischbach et al. (1976).
20. See also J.-P. Changeux et al. (1973).
21. For references, see J.-P. Changeux (1981a, 1983a); W. A. Harris (1981); P. G. Nelson and D. E. Brenneman (1982).
22. G. Giacobini et al. (1973); S. Burden (1977a, 1977b); J.-P. Bourgeois et al. (1978).
23. R. Pittman and R. W. Oppenheim (1979); R. W. Oppenheim and R. Nuñez (1982).
24. P. Benoît and J.-P. Changeux (1975, 1978); W. Thompson et al. (1979).
25. R. A. D. O'Brien et al. (1977, 1978).
26. J.-L. Gouzé et al. (1983).
27. See C. E. Henderson et al. (1981); C. E. Henderson (1983).
28. J.-L. Gouzé et al. (1983).

29. For references, see S. LeVay et al. (1980); T. N. Wiesel (1982).

30. See also M. Imbert and P. Buisseret (1975); Y. Frégnac and M. Imbert (1984)—for the effects of activation on the development of orientation selectivity in visual-cortex neurons (Chapter 2).

31. See C. Trevarthen (1973, 1980); S. Springer and G. Deutsch (1981).

32. D. C. Rife (1940); M. C. Corballis and M. J. Morgan (1978); M. J. Morgan and M. C. Corballis (1978).

33. K. Hummel and D. Chapman (1959); W. Layton (1976).

34. J. G. Chi et al. (1972); D. Teszner et al. (1972); J. A. Wada et al. (1975).

35. H. Gordon (1920); D. C. Rife (1940, 1950); R. Howard and A. Brown (1970).

36. E. H. Lenneberg (1967).

37. For the opposite views, see B. T. Woods and H. L. Teuber (1973); H. L. Teuber (1975). For the subtler one, see H. Hecaen (1976).

38. M. J. Dennis and H. Whitaker (1976).

39. See also J. Mehler (1974).

40. P. Marler (1970).

41. P. D. Eimas (1975); K. Miyawaki et al. (1975).

42. S. Sasanuma (1975); M. Iwata (1984).

43. J. Elman et al. (1981).

44. For the initial findings, see R. Cameron et al. (1971). On the lack of confirmation, see A. R. Damásio et al. (1976).

45. A. Tzavaras et al. (1981).

46. G. S. Stent (1981).

47. J.-P. Changeux et al. (1973).

48. P. R. Huttenlocher et al. (1982).

8 Anthropogenesis

1. J. de Grouchy (1982).

2. W. Beermann and U. Clever (1964).

3. J. de Grouchy (1982); see also M. C. King and A. C. Wilson (1975).

4. M. C. King and A. C. Wilson (1975).

5. For references, see J. Ruffié (1976, 1982).

6. R. Holloway (1975); P. V. Tobias (1975, 1980); Y. Coppens (1981).

7. S. J. O'Brien and W. G. Nash (1982).

8. S. J. Gould (1977).

9. L. Bolk (1926).

10. Ibid.

11. W. Leutenegger (1972).

12. J. Catel (1953).

13. S. Packer and K. Gibson (1979).

14. B. Inhelder and J. Piaget (1964); J. Piaget (1977).
15. S. Saint-Anne Dargassies (1962).
16. F. Jacob (1979); U. Rutishauser et al. (1982).
17. See also R. Goldschmidt (1940); M. C. King and A. C. Wilson (1975).
18. G. D. Snell (1929); M. Wintzerith et al. (1974).
19. P. Evrard et al. (1982).
20. F. Gullotta et al. (1982).
21. G. Isaac (1978).
22. M. Godelier (1982).
23. J. Neel et al. (1964).
24. S. Mellen (1981).
25. See Y. Coppens (1976); see also J. Piveteau (1956).

9 The Brain—Representation of the World

1. See M. Piatelli-Palmarini (1979); M. Bunge (1980); S. P. R. Rose (1980); J. A. Fodor (1981b).
2. See J. A. Fodor (1975).
3. Ibid.
4. E. Mayr (1963); R. C. Lewontin (1974); T. Dobzhansky (1977); M. J. D. White (1978); S. J. Gould (1982).
5. B. André-Leicknam and C. Ziegler (1982).
6. N. R. Jerne (1967); J.-P. Changeux (1972); J. Z. Young (1973); G. M. Edelman and V. B. Mountcastle (1978).
7. M. Jeannerod and H. Hecaen (1979).
8. See P. Benoît and J.-P. Changeux (1978).
9. B. de Spinoza (1843).

Bibliography

Acher, R. (1981). Evolution of neuropeptides. *Trends Neurosci., 4,* 225–229.

Adrian, E. D. (1946). *The physical background of perception.* Oxford: Clarendon Press.

Afzelius, B. A. (1976). A human syndrome caused by immotile cilia. *Science, 193,* 317–319.

Altman, J. (1967). Postnatal growth and differentiation of the mammalian brain with implications for a morphological theory of memory. In *The neurosciences* (Quarton, G., et al., eds.). New York: Rockefeller University Press, pp. 723–743.

Alving, B. O. (1968). Spontaneous activity in isolated somata of *Aplysia* pacemaker neurons. *J. Gen. Physiol., 51,* 29–45.

André-Leicknam, B. & Ziegler, C. (1982). *Catalogue de l'exposition: Naissance de l'écriture—cunéiformes et hiéroglyphes.* Paris: Editions Réunion Musées Nationaux.

Angevine, J. B. & Sidman, R. L. (1961). Autoradiographic study of cell migrations during histogenesis of cerebral cortex in the mouse. *Nature, 192,* 766–768.

Annett, M. (1972). The distribution of manual asymmetry. *Brit. J. Psychol., 63,* 343–358.

Arai, Y. (1981). Synaptic correlates of sexual differentiation. *Trends Neurosci., 4,* 291–293.

Aron, C. (1974). Facteurs neurohormonaux du comportement sexuel chez la ratte. In *Problèmes actuels d'endocrinologie et de nutrition,* série *18: Le cerveau et les hormones,* 191–232.

Atlan, S. (1979). *Entre le cristal et la fumée.* Paris: Seuil.

Avery, O., MacLeod, C. & McCarty, M. (1944). Studies on the chemical nature of the substance inducing transformation of pneumococcal types: Induction of transformation by a deoxyribonucleic acid fraction isolated from *Pneumococcus* type III. *J. Exp. Med., 79,* 137–158.

Baer, K. von (1828–1837). *Entwicklungsgeschichte der Tiere: Beobachtung und Reflexion.* Königsberg: Bornträger.

Baillarger, J. (1840). Recherches sur la structure de la couche corticale des circonvolutions du cerveau. *Mém. Acad. Roy. Méd. Paris, 8,* 149–183.

Bain, A. (1855). *The senses and the intellect.* London.

Bauchot, R. & Stephan, H. (1969). Encéphalisation et niveau évolutif chez les simiens. *Mammalia, 33,* 228–275.

Beadle, G. & Tatum, E. (1941). Genetic control of biochemical reactions in *Neurospora. Proc. Nat. Acad. Sci.* (USA), *27,* 499–506.

Beerman, W. & Clever, U. (1964). The chromosomic puffs. *Sci. Amer., 210* (4), 50–65.

Bennett, D. (1975). The locus T of the mouse. *Cell, 6,* 441–454.

Bennett, M. R. & Pettigrew, A. G. (1974a). The formation of synapses in striated muscle during development. *J. Physiol.* (London), *241,* 515–545.

Bennet, M. R. & Pettigrew, A. G. (1974b). The formation of synapses in reinnervated and cross-reinnervated striated muscle during development. *J. Physiol.* (London), *241,* 547–573.

Benoît, P. & Changeux, J.-P. (1975). Consequences of tenotomy on the evolution of multiinnervation in developing rat soleus muscle. *Brain Res., 99,* 354–358.

Benoît, P. & Changeux, J.-P. (1978). Consequences of blocking the nerve with a local anaesthetic on the evolution of multiinnervation at the regenerating neuromuscular junction of the rat. *Brain Res., 149,* 89–96.

Bentley, D. (1971). Genetic control of an insect neuronal network. *Science, 174,* 1139–1141.

Bentley, D. & Hoy, R. (1974). The neurobiology of the cricket song. *Sci. Amer., 231* (2), 34–44.

Benzer, S. (1967). Behavioral mutants of *Drosophila* isolated by countercurrent distribution. *Proc. Nat. Acad. Sci.* (USA), *58,* 1112–1119.

Benzer, S. (1973). Genetic dissection of behavior. *Sci. Amer., 229* (6), 24–37.

Berger, H. (1929). Über das Elektrenkephalogramm des Menschen. *Arch. Psychiat. Nervenkr., 87,* 527–570.

Berger, H. (1969). Hans Berger on the electroencephalogram of man: The fourteen original reports on the human electroencephalogram. *EEG Clin. Neurophysiol.,* suppl. *28.*

Bergstrøm, R. (1969). Electrical parameters of the brain during ontogeny. In *Brain and early behavior* (Robinson, R. J., ed.). New York: Academic Press, pp. 15–42.

Bernard, C. (1857). *Leçons sur les effets des substances toxiques et médicamenteuses.* Paris: Baillière.

Bernstein, H. (1902). Untersuchungen zur Thermodynamik der bioelektrischen Ströme. *Pflügers Arch., 92,* 521–562.

Berridge, M. J. & Rapp, P. E. (1979). A comparative survey of the function, mechanism and control of cellular oscillators. *J. Exp. Biol., 81,* 217–280.

Bertalanffy, L. von (1973). *Théorie générale des systèmes.* Paris: Dunod.

Besson, J.-M., Guilbaud, G., Abdelmoumène, M. & Chaouch, A. (1982). Physiologie de la nociception. *J. Physiol.* (Paris), *78*, 7–107.

Bindman, L. J. & Lippold, O. C. J. (1981). *The neurophysiology of the cerebral cortex.* London: Arnold.

Binet, A. (1886). *La psychologie du raisonnement.* Paris: Alcan.

Blanc, M. (1982). Les théories de l'évolution aujourd'hui. *La Recherche, 13,* 26–40.

Bleuler, E. (1911). *Dementia praecox oder Gruppe der Schizophrenien.* Leipzig.

Bloom, F. E. (1981). Neuropeptides. *Sci. Amer., 245* (4), 114–124.

Bodian, D. (1952). Introductory survey of neurons. *Cold Spring Harbor Symp. Quant. Biol., 17,* 1–13.

Bodick, N. & Levinthal, C. (1980). Growing optic nerve fibers follow neighbors during embryogenesis. *Proc. Nat. Acad. Sci.* (USA), *77,* 4374–4378.

Bodmer, W. & Cavalli-Sforza, L. (1976). *Genetics, evolution and man.* San Francisco: Freeman.

Bolk, L. (1926). On the problem of anthropogenesis. *Proc. Section Sci. Kon. Akad. Wetens. Amsterdam, 29,* 465–475.

Bon, F., Lebrun, E., Gomel, J., Rapenbusch, R. van, Cartaud, J., Popot, J.-L. & Changeux, J.-P. (1982). Orientation relative de deux oligomères constituant la forme lourde du récepteur de l'acétylcholine chez la Torpille marbrée. *C. R. Acad. Sci. Paris, 295,* 199–205.

Bonin, G. von (1937). Brain weight and body weight in mammals. *J. Gen. Psychol., 16,* 379–389.

Boothe, R., Greenough, W., Lund, J. & Wrege, K. (1979). A quantitative investigation of spine and dendrite development of neurons in visual cortex (area 17) of *Macaca nemestrina* monkeys. *J. Comp. Neurol., 186,* 473–190.

Bouillaud, J. (1825). *Traité clinique et physiologique de l'encéphalite.* Paris: Ballière.

Bouillaud, J. (1848). *Recherches cliniques propres à démontrer que le sens du langage articulé et le principe coordinateur des mouvements de la parole résident dans les lobules antérieurs du cerveau.* Paris: Ballière.

Bourgeois, J.-P., Betz, H. & Changeux, J.-P. (1978). Effets de la paralysie chronique de l'embryon de poulet par le flaxédil sur le développement de la jonction neuromusculaire. *C.R. Acad. Sci. Paris, 286*D, 773–776.

Bourguignon, A. (1981a). Quelques problèmes épistémologiques posés dans le champ de la psychanalyse freudienne. *Psychanal. à l'Université, 6,* 381–414.

Bourguignon, A. (1981b). Fondements neurobiologiques pour une théorie de la psychopathologie: Un nouveau modèle. *Psychia. enfant, 24,* 445–540.

Bouveresse, J. (1979). Le tableau me dit soi-même . . . : La théorie de l'image dans la philosophie de Wittgenstein. *Macula, 5/6,* 150–164.

Bouyer, J. J., Montaron, M. F., Rougeul-Buser, A. & Buser, P. (1980). A thalamo-cortical rhythmic system accompanying high vigilance levels in the cat. In *Rhythmic EEG activities and cortical functioning* (Pfurtscheller, G., et al., eds.). Amsterdam: Elsevier, pp. 63–77.

Boyer, P. (1981). *Les troubles du langage en psychiatrie.* Paris: Presses Universitaires de France.

Brazier, M. A. B. (1977). La neurobiologie, du vitalisme au matérialisme. *La Recherche, 8,* 965–972.

Brazier, M. A. B. (1978). Architectonics of the cerebral cortex: Research in the 19th century. In *Architectonics of the cerebral cortex* (Brazier, M. A. B. & Petsche, H., eds.). New York: Raven Press, pp. 9–30.

Brazier, M. A. B. (1984). *A history of neurophysiology in the 17th and 18th centuries.* New York: Raven Press.

Breasted, J. H. (1930). *The Edwin Smith surgical papyrus.* Chicago: University of Chicago Press (2 vols.).

Breathnach, R. & Chambon, P. (1981). Organization and expression of eukaryotic split genes coding for proteins. *Ann. Rev. Biochem., 50,* 349–383.

Brecha, N., Karten, H. J. & Laverack, C. (1979). Enkephalin-containing amacrine cells in the avian retina: Immunohistochemical localization. *Proc. Nat. Acad. Sci.* (USA), *76,* 3010–3014.

Brecha, N., Karten, H. J. & Schenker, C. (1981). Neurotensin-like and somatostatin-like immunoreactivity within amacrine cells of the retina. *Neuroscience, 6,* 1329–1340.

Bremer, F. (1935). Cerveau isolé et physiologie du sommeil. *C.R. Séances Soc. Biol., 118,* 1235–1241.

Broca, P. (1861). Nouvelle observation d'aphémie produite par une lésion de la 3ème circonvolution frontale. *Bull. Soc. Anatomie, 6* (2ème Série), 398–407.

Brodmann, K. (1909). *Vergleichende Lokalisationslehre der Groshirnrinde.* Leipzig: Barth.

Broussais, F. (1836). *Cours de phrénologie.* Paris: Baillière.

Brown, M. C., Jansen, J. K. S. & Essen, D. van (1976). Polyneuronal innervation of skeletal muscle in new-born rats and its elimination during maturation. *J. Physiol.* (London), *261,* 387–422.

Buisseret, P. & Imbert, M. (1976). Visual cortical cells: Their developmental properties in normal and dark reared kittens. *J. Physiol.* (London), *255,* 511–525.

Bunge, M. (1980). *The mind-body problem.* Oxford: Pergamon Press.

Burden, S. (1977a). Development of neuromuscular junction in the chick embryo: The number, distribution and stability of acetylcholine receptors. *Dev. Biol.*, *57*, 317–329.

Burden, S. (1977b). Acetylcholine receptors at the neuromuscular junction: Developmental change in receptor turnover. *Dev. Biol.*, *61*, 79–85.

Burt, D., Creese, I. & Snyder, S. (1976). Binding interactions of lysergic acid diethylamide and related agents with dopamine receptors in the brain. *Mol. Pharmacol.*, *12*, 631–638.

Buser, P. (1980). Attention: A brief survey of some of its electrophysiological correlates. In *Functional states of the brain: Their determinants.* (Koukkou, M., et al., eds.). Amsterdam: Elsevier, pp. 175–188.

Byers, D., Davis, R. L. & Kiger, J. A. (1981). Defect in cyclic AMP phosphodiesterase due to the *dunce* mutation of learning in *Drosophila melanogaster*. *Nature*, *289*, 79–81.

Cabanis, P. (1824). *Rapports du physique et du moral de l'homme.* Paris: Béchet.

Cameron, R., Currier, R. & Haeper, A. (1971). Aphasia and literacy. *Brit. J. Dis. Comm.*, *6*, 161–163.

Campenot, R. B. (1977). Local control of neurite development by nerve growth factor. *Proc. Nat. Acad. Sci.* (USA), *74*, 4516–4519.

Catel, J. (1953). Ein Beitrag zur Frage von Hirnentwicklung und Menschwerdung. *Klin. Wschr.*, *31*, 473–475.

Caton, R. (1875). The electric currents of the brain. *Brit. Med. J.*, *ii*, 278.

Caviness, V. S. & Rakic, P. (1978). Mechanisms of cortical development: A view from mutations in mice. *Ann. Rev. Neurosci.*, *1*, 297–326.

Changeux, J.-P. (1972). Le cerveau et l'événement. *Communications*, *18*, 37–47.

Changeux, J.-P. (1980). Résumé du cours: Effets de l'interaction avec l'environnement sur le développement de l'organisation fonctionnelle du système nerveux. *Annuaire Collège de France*, 80th year, pp. 309–326.

Changeux, J.-P. (1981a). The acetylcholine receptor: An "allosteric" membrane protein. *Harvey Lectures 1981*, 85–254.

Changeux, J.-P. (1981b). Les progrès des sciences du système nerveux concernent-ils les philosophes? *Bull. Soc. Fr. Philosophie*, *75*, 73–105.

Changeux, J.-P. (1983a). Concluding remarks: On the "singularity" of nerve cells and its ontogenesis. *Prog. Brain Res.*, *58*, 465–478.

Changeux, J.-P. (1983b). Remarques sur la complexité du système nerveux et sur son ontogénèse. (Unpublished.)

Changeux, J.-P., Benedetti, L., Bourgeois, J.-P., Brisson, A., Cartaud, J., Devaux, P., Grünhagen, H., Moreau, M., Popot, J.-L., Sobel A. & Weber, M. (1976). Some structural properties of the cholinergic receptor protein in its membrane environment relevant to its function as a pharmacological receptor *Cold Spring Harbor Symp. Quant. Biol.*, *40*, 211–230.

Changeux, J.-P., Courrège, P. & Danchin, A. (1973). A theory of the epigenesis of neural networks by selective stabilization of synapses. *Proc. Nat. Acad. Sci.* (USA), *70*, 2974–2978.

Changeux, J.-P., Courrège, P., Danchin, A. & Lasry, J.-M. (1981). Un mécanisme biochimique pour l'épigénèse de la jonction neuromusculaire. *C.R. Acad. Sci. Paris, 292*, 449–453.

Changeux, J.-P. & Danchin, A. (1974). Apprendre par stabilisation sélective de synapses en cours de développement. In *L'unité de l'homme* (Morin, E. & Piattelli, M., eds.). Paris: Seuil, pp. 320–357.

Changeux, J.-P. & Danchin, A. (1976). Selective stabilisation of developing synapses as a mechanism for the specification of neuronal networks. *Nature, 264,* 705–712.

Changeux, J.-P., Devillers-Thiéry, A. & Chemouilli, P. (1984). The acetylcholine receptor: An allosteric protein. *Science, 225,* 1335–1345.

Changeux, J.-P., Heidman, T. & Patte, P. (1984). Learning by selection. *Dahlem Konferenzen* (in press).

Changeux, J.-P., Kasai, M. et Lee, C.Y. (1970). The use of a snake venom toxin to characterize the cholinergic receptor protein. *Proc. Nat. Acad. Sci.* (USA), *67,* 1241–1247.

Changeux, J.-P. & Mikoshiba, K. (1978). Genetic and "epigenetic" factors regulating synapse formation in vertebrate cerebellum and neuromuscular junction. *Prog. Brain Res., 48,* 43–64.

Chi, J. G., Dooling, E. C. & Giles, F. H. (1972). Left-right asymmetries of the temporal speech areas of the human fetus. *Arch. Neurol., 34,* 346–348.

Chomsky, N. (1980). Rules and representations. *Behav. Brain Sci., 3,* 1–61.

Chu-Wang, I. W. & Oppenheim, R. W. (1978). Cell death of motoneurons in the chick embryo spinal cord. *J. Comp. Neurol., 177,* 33–112.

Clarke, E. & Dewhurst, K. (1972). *An illustrated history of brain function.* Oxford: Sandford.

Clarke, E. & O'Malley, C. D. (1968). *The human brain and spinal cord: A historical study illustrated by writings from antiquity to the twentieth century.* Berkeley: University of California Press.

Claudio, T., Ballivet, M., Patrick, J. & Heinemann, S. (1983). Nucleotide and deduced amino acid sequences of *Torpedo californica* acetylcholine receptor delta subunit. *Proc. Nat. Acad. Sci.* (USA), *80,* 1111–1115.

Cohen, G. (1977). *The psychology of cognition.* London: Academic Press.

Collin, R. (1906). Recherches cytologiques sur le développement de la cellule nerveuse. *Névraxe, 8,* 181–308.

Colonnier, M. (1981). The electron-microscopic analysis of the neuronal organization of the cerebral cortex. In *The organization of the cerebral cortex*

(Schmitt, F. O., et al., eds.). Cambridge, Mass.: MIT Press, pp. 125–152.

Conel, J. L. (1939–1963). The postnatal development of the human cerebral cortex. Cambridge, Mass.: Harvard University Press (Vols. I–VI).

Coppens, Y. (1976). *Origines de l'homme: Catalogue de l'exposition.* Paris: Musée de l'Homme.

Coppens, Y. (1981). Exposé sur le cerveau: Le cerveau des hommes fossiles. *C.R. Acad. Sci., 292,* Vie académique, April suppl., pp. 3–24.

Corballis, M.C. & Morgan, M.J. (1978). On the biological basis of human laterality: I. Evidence for a maturational left-right gradient. *Behav. Brain Sci., 2,* 261–269.

Couteaux, R. (1981). Structure of the subsynaptic sarcoplasm in the interfolds of the frog neuromuscular junction. *J. Neurocytol., 10,* 947–962.

Cowan, W. M. (1979). Selection and control in neurogenesis. In *The neurosciences: Fourth study program* (Schmitt, F. O. & Worden, F. G., eds.). Cambridge, Mass.: MIT Press, pp. 59–79.

Cragg, B. G. (1975). The development of synapses in the visual system of the cat. *J. Comp. Neurol., 160,* 147–166.

Craik, K. (1943). *The nature of explanation.* Cambridge, Eng.: Cambridge University Press.

Crepel, F., Mariani, J. & Delhaye-Bouchaud, N. (1976). Evidence for a multiple innervation of Purkinje cells by climbing fibers in the immature rat cerebellum. *J. Neurobiol., 7,* 567–578.

Creutzfeldt, O. D. (1978). The neocortical link: Thoughts on the generality of structure and function of the neocortex. In *Architectonics of the cerebral cortex* (Brazier, M. A. B. & Petsche, H., eds.). New York: Raven Press, pp. 357–383.

Crum-Brown, A. & Frazer, T. R. (1868). On the connection between chemical constitution and physiological action: I. On the physiological action of the salts of the ammonium bases, derived from strychnia, brucia, the baia, codeia, morphia and nicotina. *Trans. Roy. Soc. Edinburgh, 25,* 151–203.

Crum-Brown, A. & Frazer, T. R. (1869). On the connection between chemical constitution and physiological action: II. On the physiological action of ammonium bases derived from atrophia and conia. *Trans. Roy. Soc. Edinburgh, 25,* 693–739.

Dahlström, A. & Fuxe, K. (1964). Evidence for the existence of monoamine-containing neurons in the central nervous system. *Acta Physiol. Scand., 62,* suppl. *232,* 1–55.

Dahlström, A., Fuxe, K., Olson, L. & Ungerstedt, U. (1964). Ascending systems of catecholamine neurons from the lower brain stem. *Acta Physiol. Scand., 62,* 485–486.

Dale, H. (1953). *Adventures in physiology.* Oxford: Pergamon Press.

Damásio, A. R., Castro-Caldas, A., Grosso, J. T. & Ferro, J. M. (1976). Brain specialization for language does not depend on literacy. *Arch. Neurol., 33,* 300–301.

Darwin, C. (1871). *The descent of man, and selection in relation to sex.* London: Murray.

Davidson, J. M. (1980). The psychobiology of sexual experience. In *The psychobiology of consciousness* (Davidson, J. M. & Davidson, R., eds.). New York: Plenum Press, pp. 271–332.

Deiters, O. (1865). *Untersuchungen über Gehirn and Rückenmark des Menschen und der Säugetiere.* Braunschweig: Vieweg & Sohn.

Dement, W. (1965). An essay on dreams: The role of physiology in understanding their nature. In *New directions in psychology,* vol. 2 New York: Holt, pp. 135–257.

Denis, M. (1979). *Les images mentales.* Paris: Presses Universitaires de France.

Dennis, M. A. & Whitaker, H. (1976). Language acquisition following hemidecortication: Linguistic superiority of the left over the right hemisphere. *Brain & Lang., 3,* 404–433.

Dennis, M. J. (1981). Development of the neuromuscular junction: Inductive interactions between cells. *Ann. Rev. Neurosci., 4,* 43–68.

Desmedt, J. E. (1977). *Attention, voluntary contraction and event-related cerebral potentials.* Basel: Karger.

Devillers-Thiery, A., Giradaut, J., Bentaboulet, M. & Changeux, J.-P. (1983). Complete mRNA coding sequence of the acetylcholine binding alphasubunit of *Torpedo marmorata* acetylcholine receptor: A model for the transmembrane organization of the polypeptide chain. *Proc. Nat. Acad. Sci.* (USA), *80,* 2067–2071.

Dickinson, A. (1980). *Contemporary animal learning theory.* Cambridge, Eng.: Cambridge University Press.

Diderot, D. (1769). *Le rêve de d'Alembert.* Paris: Garnier (1965).

Dobzhansky, T. (1977). *Génétique du processus évolutif.* Paris: Flammarion.

Dreyfus-Brisac, C. (1979). Ontogenesis of brain bioelectrical activity and sleep organization in neonates and infants. In *Human growth,* vol. 3 (Faulkner, F. & Tanner, J., eds.). New York: Plenum, pp. 157–182.

Du Bois-Reymond, E. (1848–1884). *Untersuchungen über tierische elektrizität.* Berlin: Reimer (2 vols.).

Dudai, Y. (1981). L'intelligence de la mouche. *La Recherche, 12,* 58–71.

Dutrillaux, B. (1979). Chromosomal evolution in primates: Tentative phylogeny from *Microcebus murinus* (prosimian) to man. *Hum. Genet., 48,* 251–314.

Dutrillaux, B. (1980). Chromosomal evolution of the great apes and man. In

The great apes of Africa (Short, R. V. & Weir, B., eds.). Colchester & London: Journals of Reproduction and Fertility.

Dutrochet, H. (1824). *Recherches anatomiques et physiologiques sur la structure intime des animaux et des végétaux, et sur leur mobilité.* Paris: Baillière.

Eaton, R. C., Farley, R. D., Kimmel, C. B. & Schabtach, E. (1977). Functional development in the Mauthner cell system of embryos and larvae of the zebra fish. *J. Neurobiol., 8,* 151–172.

Eccles, J. C. (1964). *The physiology of synapses.* Berlin: Springer.

Eccles, J. C., Ito, M. & Szentágothai, J. (1967). *The cerebellum as a neuronal machine.* Berlin: Springer.

Economo, C. von (1929). *The cytoarchitectonics of the human cerebral cortex.* London: Oxford University Press.

Edelman, G. M. (1981). Group selection as the basis for higher brain function. In *The organization of the cerebral cortex* (Schmitt, F. O., ed.). Cambridge, Mass.: MIT Press, pp. 535–563.

Edelman, G. M. & Mountcastle, V. B. (1978). *The mindful brain: Cortical organization and the group-selective theory of higher brain function.* Cambridge, Mass.: MIT Press.

Ehrlich, P. (1956). *The collected papers of Paul Ehrlich.* London.

Eimas, P. D. (1975). Auditory and phonetic coding of the cues for speech: Discrimination of the [r-l] distinction by young infants. *Perception & Psychophysics, 18,* 341–347.

Elliott, T. (1904). On the action of adrenalin. *J. Physiol.* (London), *31,* 20P.

Elman, J., Takahashi, K. & Tohsaku, Y.-H. (1981). Asymmetries for the categorization of Kanji nouns, adjectives and verbs presented to the left and right visual fields. *Brain & Lang., 13,* 290–300.

Elsberg, C. A. (1945). The anatomy and surgery of the Edwin Smith surgical papyrus. *J. Mt. Sinai Hosp., 12,* 141–151.

Euler, U. von & Gaddum, J. (1931). An unidentified depressor substance in certain tissue extracts. *J. Physiol.* (London), *72,* 74–87.

Evarts, E. V. (1975). Activity of cerebral neurons in relation to movement. In *The nervous system* (Tower, D. B., ed.), vol. I: *The basic neurosciences.* New York: Raven Press, pp. 221–234.

Evarts, E. V. (1981). Functional studies of the motor cortex. In *The organization of the cerebral cortex* (Schmitt, F. O., et al., eds.). Cambridge, Mass.: MIT Press, pp. 263–284.

Evrard, P., Gadisseux, J.-F. & Lyon, G. (1982). Les malformations du système nerveux central. In *Naissance du cerveau.* Monaco: Nestlé-Guigoz, pp. 49–74.

Ey, H., Lairy, G., Barros-Ferreira, M. de & Goldsteinas, L. (1975). *Psychophysiologie du sommeil et psychiatrie.* Paris: Masson.

Faber, D. S. & Korn, H. (1978). Electrophysiology of the Mauthner cell: Basic properties, synaptic mechanisms and associated networks. In *Neurobiology of the Mauthner cell* (Faber, D. S. & Korn, H., eds.). New York: Raven Press, pp. 47–131.

Faber, D. S. & Korn, H. (1982). Binary mode of transmitter release at central synapses. *Trends Neurosci.*, *5*, 157–159.

Falck, B., Hillarp, N. A., Thieme, G. & Thorp, A. (1962). Fluorescence of catecholamines and related compounds condensed with formaldehyde. *J. Histochem. Cytochem.*, *10*, 348–354.

Fambrough, D. M. (1979). Control of acetylcholine receptor in skeletal muscle. *Physiol. Rev.*, *59*, 165–227.

Feldberg, W. & Vogt, M. (1948). Acetylcholine synthesis in different regions of the central nervous system. *J. Physiol.* (London), *107*, 372–381.

Ferrier, D. (1880). *De la localisation des maladies cérébrales.* Paris: Baillière.

Finot, A. (1890). *Faune de la France: Insectes, orthoptères.* Paris: Deyrolle.

Fischbach, G. D., Berg, D. K., Cohen, S. A. & Frank, E. (1976). Enrichment of nerve-muscle synapses in spinal cord—muscle cultures and identification of relative peaks of ACh sensitivity at sites of transmitter release. In *The synapse. Cold Spring Harbor Symp. Quant. Biol.*, *40*, 347–357.

Fischer, E. (1894). Einfluss der Konfiguration auf die Wirkung der Enzyme. *Berichte der deutschen chemischen Gesellschaft*, *27*, 2985–2986.

Fischer, E. (1898). Bedeutung der Stereochemie für die Physiologie. *Hoppe-Seylers Zeitschrift für physiologische Chemie*, *26*, 62–63.

Fisken, R. A., Garey, L. J. & Powell, T. P. S. (1975). The intrinsic, association and commissural connections of area 17 of the visual cortex. *Phil. Trans. Roy. Soc.*, Series B, *272*, 487–536.

Flourens, P. (1824). *Recherches expérimentales sur les propriétés et les functions du système nerveux dans les animaux vertébrés.* Paris: Crouvost.

Fodor, J. A. (1975). *The language of thought.* Hassocks: Harvester.

Fodor, J. A. (1981a). *Representations.* Cambridge, Mass.: MIT Press.

Fodor, J. A. (1981b). The mind-body problem. *Sci. Amer.*, *244*(1), 124–132.

Forel, A. (1887). Einige Hirnanatomische Betrachtungen und Ergebnisse. *Arch. Psychiat. Nerv. Krankh.*, *18*, 162–198.

Fox, C. & Fox, B. (1971). A comparative study of coital physiology with special reference to the sexual climax. *J. Reprod. Fert.*, *24*, 319–336.

Fox, C. & Knaggs, G. (1969). Milk ejection activity (oxytocin) in peripheral veinous blood in man during lactation and in association with coitus. *J. Endocr.*, *45*, 145–146.

Fox, T. O. (1977). Estradiol and testosterone binding in normal and mutant mouse cerebellum: Biochemical and cellular specificity. *Brain Res.*, *128*, 263–273.

Frégnac, Y. & Imbert, M. (1984). Development of neuronal selectivity in primary visual cortex of cat. *Physiol. Rev., 64,* 325–434.

Freud, S. (1895). Project for a scientific psychology. In *The origins of psychoanalysis: Letters to Wilhelm Fliess, drafts and notes* (Bonaparte, M., et al., eds.). New York: Basic Books (1954).

Freud, S. (1914). Einführing des Narzissmus. In *Gesammelte Werke,* vol. 10. London: Imago, pp. 138–170.

Freud, S. (1920). Au-delà du principe du plaisir. In *Essais de psychanalyse.* Paris: Payot (1965), pp. 7–81.

Fritsch, G. & Hitzig, E. (1870). Ueber die elektrische Erregbarkeit des Grosshirns. *Arch. Anat., Physiol. & Wiss. Med., 37,* 300–332.

Fuster, J. M. (1980). *The prefrontal cortex.* New York: Raven Press.

Galambos, R. & Hillyard, S. A. (1981). Electrophysiological approaches to human cognitive processing. *Neurosci. Res. Prog. Bull., 20,* 141–265.

Gall, F. J. (1822–1825). *Sur les fonctions du cerveau et sur celles de chacune de ses parties.* Paris: Baillière (6 vols.).

Galvani, L. (1791). *De viribus electricitatis in motu musculari commentarius.* Bologna: Ex Typographia Instituti Scientarium.

Garcia-Bellido, A. (1981). From the gene to the pattern: Chaeta differentiation. In *Cellular controls of differentiation* (Lloyd, C. W. & Rees, D. A., eds.). New York: Academic Press, pp. 281–304.

Garey, L. J. (1984). Structural development of the visual system of man. *Human Neurobiol., 3,* 75–80.

Gazzaniga, M. S. (1970). *The bisected brain.* New York: Appleton.

Gerlach, J. von (1872). Ueber die Struktur der grauen Substanz des menschlichen Grosshirns. *Vorläufige Mitteilungen. Zbl. Med. Wiss., 10,* 273–275.

Geschwind, N. & Levitsky, W. (1968). Human brain: Left-right asymmetries in temporal speech region. *Science, 161,* 186–187.

Giacobini, G., Filogamo, G., Weber, M., Boquet, P. & Changeux, J.-P. (1973). Effects of a snake alpha-neurotoxin on the development of innervated motor muscles in chick embryo. *Proc. Nat. Acad. Sci.* (USA), *70,* 1708–1712.

Gilbert, C. D. & Wiesel, T. N. (1981). Laminar specialization and intracortical connections in cat primary visual cortex. In *The organization of the cerebral cortex* (Schmitt, F. O., et al., eds.). Cambridge, Mass.: MIT Press, pp. 163–191.

Glisson, F. (1654). *Anatomia hepatis.* London: Pullein.

Glisson, F. (1672). *Tractatus de natura substantiae energetica.* London: Brome & Hooke.

Glisson, F. (1677). *Tractatus de ventriculo et intestinis.* London: Brome.

Goldowitz, D. & Mullen, R. J. (1982). Granule cell as a site of gene action in the weaver mouse cerebellum: Evidence from heterozygous mutant chimeras. *J. Neurosci.*, *2*, 1474–1485.

Goldschmidt, R. (1940). *The material basis of evolution.* New Haven: Yale University Press.

Golgi, C. (1883–1884). Recherches sur l'histologie des centres nerveux. *Arch. Ital. Biol.*, *3*, 285–317; *4*, 92–123.

Golgi, C. (1906). The neuron doctrine—theory and facts. In *Nobel Lectures: Physiology and Medicine, 1901–1921* (1967), 189–217.

Goltz, F. (1960). On the functions of the hemispheres. In *The cerebral cortex.* (Bonin, G. von, ed.). Springfield, Ill.: Thomas.

Gordon, H. (1920). Left-handedness and mirror writing especially among defective children. *Brain*, *43*, 313–368.

Gorski, R. A. (1979). Long-term hormonal modulation of neuronal structure and function. In *The neurosciences: Fourth study program* (Schmitt, F. O. & Worden, F. G., eds.). Cambridge, Mass.: MIT Press, pp. 969–982.

Gould, S. J. (1977). *Ontogeny and phylogeny.* Cambridge, Mass.: Harvard University Press.

Gould, S. J. (1981). *The mismeasure of man.* New York: Norton.

Gould, S. J. (1982). Darwinism and the expansion of evolutionary theory. *Science*, *216*, 380–387.

Gouzé, J.-L., Lasry, J.-M. & Changeux, J.-P. (1983). Selective stabilization of muscle innervation during development: A mathematical model. *Biol. Cybern.*, *46*, 207–215.

Gray, E. G. (1959). Axo-somatic and axo-dendritic synapses of the cerebral cortex: An electron microscopic study. *J. Anat.*, *93*, 420–433.

Graybiel, A. & Berson, D. M. (1981). On the relation between transthalamic and transcortical pathways in the visual system. In *The organization of the cerebral cortex* (Schmitt, F. O., et al., eds.). Cambridge, Mass.: MIT Press, pp. 285–319.

Gros, F., Gilbert, W., Hiatt, H., Kurland, C., Risebrough, R. & Watson, J. (1961). Unstable ribonucleic acid revealed by pulse labelling of *Escherichia coli. Nature*, *90*, 581–585.

Grouchy, J. de (1982). Les facteurs génétiques de l'évolution. In *Colloques internationaux du CNRS, 599: Les processus d'hominisation.* Paris: Ed. CNRS, pp. 283–293.

Guillery, R. W. (1974). Visual pathways in albinos. *Sci. Amer.*, *230* (5), 44–54.

Guillery, R. W., Okoro, A. N. & Witkop, C. J. (1975). Abnormal visual pathways in the brain of a human albino. *Brain Res.*, *96*, 373–377.

Gullotta, F., Rehder, H. & Gropp, A. (1982). Descriptive neuropathology of chromosomal disorders in man. *Hum. Genet.*, *57*, 337–344.

Gurdon, J. (1974). *The control of gene expression in animal development.* Oxford: Clarendon Press.

Hadorn, E. (1966). Dynamics of determination. *Symp. Soc. Dev. Biol., 25,* 85–104.

Hadorn, E. (1968). Transdetermination in cells. *Sci. Amer., 219,* (5), 110–123.

Haeckel, E. (1874). *Histoire de la création des êtres organisés d'après les lois naturelles.* Paris: Reinwald.

Hahn, W., Ness, J. van & Maxwell, I. (1978). Complex population of mRNA sequences in large polyadenylated nuclear RNA molecules. *Proc. Nat. Acad. Sci.* (USA), *75,* 5544–5547.

Hall, J. (1978). Behavioral analysis in *Drosophila* mosaics. In *Genetic mosaics and cell differentiation* (Gehring, W., ed.). Berlin: Springer, pp. 259–306.

Hamburger, V. (1970). Embryonic motility in vertebrates. In *The neurosciences: Second study program* (Schmidt, F. O., ed.). New York: Rockefeller University Press, pp. 141–151.

Hamburger, V. (1975). Cell death in the development of the lateral motor column of the chick embryo. *J. Comp. Neurol., 160,* 535–546.

Hamer, D. & Leder, P. (1979). Splicing and the formation of stable RNA. *Cell, 18,* 1299–1302.

Harlow, H. F. & Mears, C. (1979). *The human model: Primate perspectives.* New York: Halsted Press.

Harlow, J. M. (1869). Recovery from the passage of an iron bar through the head. In *Proceedings of the Massachusetts Medical Society.* Boston: Clapp.

Harris, W. A. (1981). Neural activity and development. *Ann. Rev. Physiol., 43,* 689–710.

Harrison, R. (1907). Observations on the living developing nerve fiber. *Anat. Rec., 1,* 116–118.

Harrison, R. (1908). Embryonic transplantation and development of the nervous system. *Anat. Rec., 2,* 385–410.

Heath, R. G. (1972). Pleasure and brain activity in man. Deep and surface electroencephalograms during orgasm. *J. Nerv. Ment. Dis., 154,* 3–18.

Hebb, D. O. (1949). *The organization of behavior.* New York: Wiley.

Hebb, D. O. (1968). Concerning imagery. *Psychol. Rev., 75,* 466–477.

Hebb, D. O. (1980). *Essay on mind.* Hillsdale, N.J.: Erlbaum.

Hecaen, H. (1976). Acquired aphasia in children and the ontogenesis of hemispheric functional specialization. *Brain & Lang., 3,* 114–134.

Hecaen, H. (1978). *La dominance cérébrale.* Paris: Mouton.

Hecaen, H. & Albert, M. (1978). *Human neuropsychology.* New York: Wiley.

Hecaen, H & Dubois, J. (1969). *La naissance de la neuropsychologie du langage (1825–1865)*. Paris: Flammarion.

Hecaen, H. & Lanteri-Laura, G. (1977). *Évolution des connaissances et des doctrines sur les localisations cérébrales*. Paris: Desclée de Brouwer.

Heidmann, T. & Changeux, J.-P. (1980). Interaction of afluorescent agonist with the membrane-bound acetylcholine receptor from *Torpedo marmorata* in the millisecond time range. *Biochem. Biophys. Res. Comm.*, 97, 889–896.

Heidmann, T. & Changeux, J.-P. (1982). Un modèle moléculaire de régulation d'efficacité au niveau postsynaptique d'une synapse chimique. *C. R. Acad. Sci., Paris*, 295, 665–670.

Henderson, C. E. (1983). Role for retrograde factors in synapse formation at the nerve-muscle junction. *Prog. Brain Res.*, 58, 369–373.

Henderson, C. E., Huchet, M. & Changeux, J.-P. (1981). Neurite outgrowth from embryonic chicken spinal neurons is promoted by media conditioned by muscle cells. *Proc. Nat. Acad. Sci.* (USA), 78, 2625–2629.

Henry, J. L. (1980). Substance P and pain: An updating. *Trends Neurosci.*, 3, 95–97.

Henry, J. L. & Ely, D. (1976). Biological correlates of psychosomatic illness. In *Biological foundations of psychiatry* (Grenell, R. & Galay, S., eds.). New York: Raven Press, pp. 945–981.

Hess, W. (1964). *The biology of mind.* Chicago: University of Chicago Press.

Hickey, T. L. & Guillery, R. W. (1979). Variability of laminar patterns in the human lateral geniculate nucleus. *J. Comp. Neurol.*, 183, 221–246.

Hilgard, E. R. & Marquis, D. (1940). *Conditioning and learning.* New York: Appleton-Century.

Hillyard, S. A. (1981). In: Electrophysiological approaches to human cognitive processing. *Neurosci. Res. Prog. Bull.*, 20, 240–246.

Hillyard, S. A., Picton, T. W. & Regan, D. (1978). Sensation, perception and attention: Analysis using ERPs. In *Event-related brain potentials in man* (Callaway, E., et al., eds.). New York: Academic Press, pp. 223–321.

His, W. (1887). Zur Geschichte des menschlichen Rückenmarkes und der Nervenwurzeln. *Abh. K. Säch. Ges. Wiss., Math.-Phys. Klasse*, 13, 477–514.

Hodgkin, A. L. (1964). *The conduction of the nervous impulse.* Liverpool: Liverpool University Press.

Hodgkin, A. L. & Huxley, A. F. (1952). A quantitative description of membrane current and its application to conduction and excitation in nerve. *J. Physiol.* (London), 117, 500–544.

Hökfelt, T., Johansson, O., Ljungdahl, A., Lundberg, J. M. & Schultzberg, M. (1980). Peptidergic neurones. *Nature*, 284, 515–521.

Holloway, R. (1975). Early hominid endocasts: Volumes, morphology and significance for hominid evolution. In *Primates functional morphology and evolution* (Tuttle, R., ed.). Paris: Mouton, pp. 393–410.

Holloway, R. (1980). In *Am. J. Phys. Anthropol.*, *53*, 109.

Hood, L., Wilson, J. & Hood, W. (1975). *Molecular biology of eukaryotic cells.* Menlo Park, Cal.: Benjamin.

Hopfield, J. (1982). Neural networks and physical systems with emergent collective computational abilities. *Proc. Nat. Acad. Sci.* (USA), *79*, 2554–2558.

Howard, R. & Brown, A. (1970). Twinning: A marker for biological insults. *Child Dev.*, *41*, 519–530.

Hubel, D. H. & Wiesel, T. N. (1977). Functional architecture of macaque monkey visual cortex: Ferrier lecture. *Proc. Roy. Soc. Lond.*, Series B, *198*, 1–59.

Hubel, D. H., Wiesel, T. N. & Stryker, M. P. (1978). Anatomical demonstration of orientation columns in macaque monkey. *J. Comp. Neurol.*, *177*, 361–379.

Hudspeth, A. J. & Corey, D. (1977). Sensitivity, polarity and conductance change in the response of vertebrate brain cells to controlled mechanical stimuli. *Proc. Nat. Acad. Sci.* (USA), *74*, 2407–2411.

Hugues, J., Smith, T., Kosterlitz, H., Fothergill, L., Morgan, B. & Morris, H. (1975). Identification of two related pentapeptides from the brain with potent agonist activity. *Nature*, *258*, 577–579.

Hume, D. (1898). *A treatise of human nature.* New York: Oxford University Press, 1978.

Hummel, K. & Chapman, D. (1959). Visceral inversion and associated anomalies in the mouse. *J. Heredity*, *50*, 9–13.

Huttenlocher, P. R., Courten, C. de, Garey, L. J. & Van der Loos, H. (1982). Synaptogenesis in human visual cortex: Evidence for synapse elimination during normal development. *Neuroscience Letters*, *33*, 247–252.

Huxley, T. (1863). *Evidence as to man's place in nature.* London.

Imbert, M. & Buisseret, P. (1975). Receptive field characteristics and plastic properties of visual cortical cells in kittens reared with or without visual experience. *Exp. Brain. Res.*, *22*, 25–36.

Ingvar, D. H. (1977) L'idéogramme cérébral. *Encéphale*, *3*, 5–33.

Ingvar, D. H. (1982). Mental illness and regional brain metabolism. *Trends Neurosci.*, *5*, 199–203.

Inhelder, B. & Piaget, J. (1964). *The early growth of logic.* New York: Norton.

Innocenti, G. M. (1981a). The development of interhemispheric connection. *Trends Neurosci.*, *4*, 142–144.

Innocenti, G. M. (1981b). Growth and reshaping of axons in the establishment of visual callosal connections. *Science*, *212*, 824–827.

Innocenti, G. M. & Frost, D. O. (1979). Effects of visual experience on the maturaturation of the efferent system to the corpus callosum. *Nature*, *280*, 231–234.

Isaac, G. (1978a). Food sharing and human evolution: Archeological evidence from the plio-pleistocene of East Africa. *J. Anthropol. Res.*, *34*, 311–325.

Isaac, G. (1978b). The food-sharing behavior of protohuman hominids. *Sci. Amer.*, *238*, 90–109.

Ivy, G. O. & Killackey, H. P. (1982). Ontogenetic changes in the projection of neocortical neurons. *J. Neurosci.*, *2*, 735–743.

Jackson, J. H. (1868). In *Selected writings* (Taylor, J., ed.). London: Hodder & Stoughton, 1931.

Jacob, F. (1970). *La logique du vivant*. Paris: Gallimard.

Jacob, F. (1979). Cell surface and early stages of mouse embryogenesis. *Cur. Top. Dev. Biol.*, *13*, 117–135.

Jacob, F. & Monod, J. (1961). Genetic regulatory mechanisms in the synthesis of proteins. *J. Mol. Biol.*, *3*, 318–356.

Jacobsen, C. F. (1931). A study of cerebral function in learning: The frontal lobes. *J. Comp. Neurol.*, *52*, 271–340.

Jacobsen, C. F. & Nissen, H. (1937). Studies of cerebral function in primates: IV. The effects of frontal lobe lesions on the delayed alternation habit in monkeys. *J. Comp. Physiol. Psychol.*, *23*, 101–112.

Jakobson, R. (1968). *Child language, aphasia and phonological universals.* The Hague: Mouton.

Jan, Y. N. & Jan, L. Y. (1978). Two mutations of synaptic transmission in *Drosophila. Proc. Roy. Soc. Lond.*, Series B, *198*, 87–108.

Jeannerod, M. & Hecaen, H. (1979). *Adaptation et restauration des fonctions nerveuses.* Villeurbanne: Simep.

Jerne, N. K. (1967). Antibodies and learning: Selection versus instruction. In *The neurosciences: A study program* (Quarton, G., et al., eds.). New York: Rockefeller University Press, pp. 200–205.

Jessell, T. M. & Iversen, L. L. (1977). Opiate analgesics inhibit substance P release from rat trigeminal nucleus. *Nature*, *268*, 549–551.

Jones, E. G. (1975). Varieties and distribution of non-pyramidal cells in the somatic sensory cortex of the squirrel monkey. *J. Comp. Neurol.*, *160*, 205–268.

Jones, E. G. (1981). Anatomy of cerebral cortex: Columnar input-output organization. In *The organization of the cerebral cortex* (Schmitt, F., et al., eds.). Cambridge, Mass.: MIT Press, pp. 199–235.

Jones, E. G. & Powell, T. P. S. (1970). An anatomical study of converging sensory pathways within the cerebral cortex of the monkey. *Brain*, *93*, 793–820.

Jouvet, M. (1979). Le comportement onirique. *Pour la Science*, 136–153.

Jouvet-Mounier, D. (1968). *Ontogenèse des états de vigilance chez quelques mammifères*. Lyon: Imprimerie des Beaux-Arts.

Kaas, J. H., Nelson, R. J., Sur, M., Lin, C. S. & Merzenich, M. M. (1979). Multiple representations of the body within the primary somatosensory cortex of primates. *Science, 204*, 521–523.

Kaas, J. H., Nelson, R. J., Sur, M. & Merzenich M. M. (1981). Organization of somatosensory cortex in primates. In *Organization of the cerebral cortex* (Schmitt, F. O., et al., eds.). Cambridge, Mass.: MIT Press, pp. 237–261.

Karlin, A. (1983). Anatomy of a receptor. *Neurosci. Commentaries, 1*, 111–123.

Kandel, E. R. (1976). *Cellular basis of behavior: An introduction to behavioral neurobiology*. San Francisco: Freeman.

Kandel, E. R. (1979). Cellular insights into behavior and learning. *Harvey Lectures, 73*, 19–92.

Kandel, E. R. & Schwartz J. H. (1981). *Principles of neural science*. Amsterdam: Elsevier-North Holland.

Katz, B. (1966). *Nerve, muscle and synapse*. New York: McGraw-Hill.

Katz, B. & Miledi, R. (1972). The statistical nature of the acetylcholine potential and its molecular components. *J. Physiol.* (London), *224*, 665–699.

Katz, B. & Thesleff, S. (1957). A study of the desensitization produced by acetylcholine at the motor end plate. *J. Physiol.* (London, *138*, 63–80.

Kety, S. & Schmidt, C. (1945). The determination of cerebral blood flow in man by the use of nitrous oxide in low concentrations. *Ann. J. Physiol., 143*, 53–66.

King, M. C. & Wilson, A. C. (1975). Evolution at two levels in humans and chimpanzees. *Science, 188*, 107–116.

Klüver, H. & Bucy, P. (1939). Preliminary analysis of functions of the temporal lobes in monkeys. *Arch. Neurol. P. ych., 42*, 979–1000.

Koestler, A. (1967). *The ghost in the machine*. New York: Random House, 1982.

Kolb, B. & Whishaw I. Q. (1980). *Fundamentals of human neuropsychology*. San Francisco: Freeman.

Korn, H., Triller, A., Mallet, A. & Faber, D. S. (1981). Fluctuating responses at a central synapse: n of binomial fit predicts number of stained presynaptic boutons. *Science, 213*, 898–901.

Kosslyn, S. (1980). *Image and mind*. Cambridge, Mass.: Harvard University Press.

Kourilsky, P. & Chambon, P. (1978). The ovalbumin gene: An amazing gene in eight pieces. *Trends Biochem. Sci., 3*, 244–247.

Kraepelin, E. (1896–1915). *Psychiatrie*. Leipzig: Abel.

Kuffler, S. W. & Nicholls, J. G. (1976). *From neuron to brain: A cellular approach to the function of the nervous system.* Sunderland, Mass.: Sinauer Assn.

Kuffler, S. W. & Yoshikami, D. (1975a). The distribution of acetylcholine sensitivity at the post-synaptic membrane of vertebrate skeletal twitch muscle: Iontophoretic mapping in the micron range. *J. Physiol.* (London), *244*, 703–730.

Kuffler, S. W. & Yoshikami, D. (1975b). The number of transmitter molecules in a quantum: An estimate from iontophoretic application of acetylcholine at the neuromuscular synapse. *J. Physiol.* (London), *251*, 465–482.

Lacoste-Utamsing, C. de & Holloway, R. L. (1982). Sexual dimorphism in the human *corpus callosum. Science, 216,* 1431–1432.

Kühne, W. (1862). *Über der peripherischen endorgane der motorischen nerven.* Leipzig: Engelmann.

Laing, N. G. & Prestige, M. C. (1978). Prevention of spontaneous motoneuron death in chick embryos. *J. Physiol.* (London), *282,* 33–35P.

Lamarck, J.-B. de (1809). *Philosophie zoologique.* Paris (2 vols.).

La Mettrie, J. (1748). *L'homme machine.* Leyde: De Luzac.

Lamy, E. (1677). *Explication mécanique et physique de l'âme sensitive.* Paris: Roulland.

Langley, J. N. (1905). On the reaction of cells and of nerve-endings to certain poisons, chiefly as regards the reaction of striated muscle to nicotine and to curare. *J. Physiol.* (London), *33,* 374–413.

Langley, J. N. (1906). On nerve-endings and on special excitable substances in cells. *Proc. Roy. Soc. Lond.,* Series B, *78,* 170–194.

Langley, J. N. (1907). On the contraction of muscle, chiefly in relation to the presence of receptive substances: Part I. *J. Physiol.* (London), *36,* 347–384.

Lashley, K. S. (1929). *Brain mechanisms and intelligence: A quantitative study of injuries to the brain.* Chicago: University of Chicago Press.

Lassen, N. (1959). Cerebral blood flow and oxygen consumption in man. *Physiol. Rev., 39,* 183–238.

Lawrence, P. A. & Morata G. (1983). The elements of the bithorax complex. *Cell, 35,* 595–601.

Layton, W. M. (1976). Random determination of a developmental process. *J. Heredity, 67,* 336–338.

Lee, C. Y. & Chang, C. C. (1966). Modes of action of purified toxins from venoms on neuromuscular transmission. *Mem. Inst. Butantan Simp. Internac., 33,* 555–572.

Leeuwenhoek, A. van (1718). In *Epistolae physiologicae super compluribus naturae arcanis.* Delft: Beman.

Lejeune, J. (1977). On the mechanism of mental deficiency in chromosomal diseases. *Hereditas, 86*, 9–14.

Lejeune, J. Gautier, M. & Turpin, R. (1959). Étude des chromosomes somatiques de neuf enfants mongoliens. *C. R. Acad. Sci. Paris, 248*, 1721–1722.

LeMay, M. (1982). Morphological aspects of human brain asymmetry: An evolutionary perspective. *Trends Neurosci., 5*, 273–275.

Lenneberg, E. H. (1967). *Biological foundations of language.* New York: Wiley.

Leroy, Y. (1964). Transmission du paramètre fréquence dans le signal acoustique des hybrides F_1 et PxF_1 de deux grillons: *Teleogryllus commodus* Walker et *T. oceanicus* Le Guillou (Orthoptères, Ensifères). *C. R. Acad. Sci. Paris, 259*, 892–895.

Leuret, F. (1839) & Gratiolet, L. (1857). *Anatomie complète du système nerveux considérée dans ses rapports avec l'intelligence.* Paris: Baillière (2 vols.).

Leutenegger, W. (1972). Newborn size and pelvic dimensions of *Australopithecus. Nature, 240*, 568–569.

LeVay, S., Wiesel, T. N. & Hubel, D. H. (1980). The development of ocular dominance columns in normal and visually deprived monkeys. *J. Comp. Neurol., 191*, 1–51.

Levi-Montalcini, R. (1975). NGF: An uncharted route. In *The neurosciences: Paths of discovery* (Worden, F. G., et al., eds.). Cambridge, Mass.: MIT Press, pp. 245–265.

Levine, S. (1966). Sex differences in the brain. *Sci. Amer., 214* (4), 84–90.

Levinthal, F., Macagno, E. & Levinthal, C. (1976). Anatomy and development of identified cells in isogenic organisms. *Cold Spring Harbor Symp. Quant. Biol., 40*, 321–331.

Levitan, I., Harmar, A. & Adams, W. (1979). Synaptic and hormonal modulation of a neuronal oscillator: A search for molecular mechanisms. *J. Exp. Biol., 81*, 131–151.

Lewis, W. B. & Clarke, H. (1878). The cortical lamination of the motor area of the brain. *Proc. Roy. Soc. Lond.,* Series B, *27*, 38–49.

Lewontin, R. C. (1974). *The genetic basis of evolutionary change.* New York: Columbia University Press.

Lindvall, O. & Björklund, A. (1974). The organization of the ascending catecholamine neuron systems in the rat brain as revealed by the glyoxylic acid fluorescence method. *Acta Physiol. Scand.,* suppl. *412*, 1–48.

Linnaeus, C. (1770). *Philosophie botanique.* Vienna.

Little, W. & Shaw, G. (1975). A statistical theory of short and long term memory. *Behav. Biol., 14*, 115–133.

Little, W. & Shaw, G. (1978). Analytic study of the memory storage capacity of a neural network. *Math. Biosci.*, *39*, 281–290.

Livingstone, M. S. & Hubel, D. H. (1981). Effects of sleep and arousal on the processing of visual information in the cat. *Nature*, *291*, 554–561.

Lorente de Nó, R. (1938). Analysis of the activity of the chains of internuncial neurons. *J. Neurophysiol.*, *1*, 207–244.

Lorente de Nó, R. (1943). Cerebral cortex: Architecture, intracortical connections, motor projections. In *Physiology of the nervous system* (Fulton, J., ed.). London: Oxford University Press, pp. 274–301.

Lund, J. S., Boothe, R. G. & Lund, R. D. (1977). Development of neurons in the visual cortex (area 17) of the monkey *(Macaca nemestrina):* A Golgi study from fetal day 127 to postnatal maturity. *J. Comp. Neurol.*, *176*, 149–188.

Luria, A. R. (1980). *Higher cortical functions in man.* New York: Basic Books.

Macagno, E. R., Lopresti, U. & Levinthal, C. (1973). Structural development of neuronal connections in isogenic organisms: Variations and similarities in the optic system of *Daphnia magna. Proc. Nat. Acad. Sci.* (USA), *70*, 57–61.

McEwen, B. S. (1976). Interactions between hormones and nerve tissue. *Sci. Amer.*, *235* (1), 48–58.

McGaugh, J. M. (1973). *Learning and memory: An introduction.* San Francisco: Albion.

McGinnis, W., Garber, R., Wirz, J., Kuroiwa, A. & Gehring, W. (1984). A homologous protein-coding sequence in *Drosophilia* homoeotic genes and its conservation in other metazoans. *Cell*, *37*, 403–408.

McIntosh, F. (1941). The distribution of acetylcholine in the peripheral and the central nervous system. *J. Physiol.* (London), *99*, 436–442.

MacLean, P. D. (1952). Some psychiatric implications of physiological studies on frontotemporal portion of limbic system (visceral brain). *EEG Clin. Neurophysiol.*, *4*, 407–418.

MacLean, P. D. (1970). The triune brain, emotions and scientific bias. In *The neurosciences: Second study program* (Schmitt, F. O., ed.). New York: Rockefeller University Press, pp. 336–349.

Magoun, H. W. (1954). The ascending reticular system and wakefulness. In *Brain mechanisms and consciousness* (Delafresnaye, J. -F., ed.). Springfield, Ill.: Thomas, pp. 1–20.

Mariani, J. (1983). Elimination of synapses during the development of the central nervous system. *Prog. Brain Res.*, *58*, 383–392.

Mariani, J. & Changeux, J.-P. (1981). Ontogenesis of olivocerebellar relationships. *J. Neurosci.*, *1*, 696–709.

Marler, P. (1970). Bird song and speech development: Could there be parallels? *Amer. Sci.*, *58*, 669–673.

Marler, P. & Peters, S. (1982). Developmental overproduction and selective attrition: New process in the epigenesis of bird song. *Dev. Psychobiol.*, *15*, 369–378.

Martin, K. A. C. & Perry, V. H. (1983). The role of fiber ordering and axon collateralization in the formation of topographic projections. *Prog. Brain Res.*, *58*, 321–337.

Marty, R. & Scherrer, J. (1964). Critères de maturation des systèmes afférents corticaux. *Prog. Brain Res.*, *4*, 222–236.

Matteucci, C. (1838). Sur le courant électrique ou presque de la grenouille. *Bibl. Univ. Genève*, *7*, 156–168.

Matteucci, C. (1840). *Essai sur les phénomènes électriques des animaux.* Paris: Carilliau, Gœury & Dalmont.

Mayr, E. (1963). *Animal species and evolution.* Cambridge, Mass.: Harvard University Press.

Mazziotta, J. C., Phelps, M. E., Carson, R. E. & Kuhl, D. E. (1982). Tomographic mapping of human cerebral metabolism: Auditory stimulation. *Neurology*, *32*, 921–937.

Meech, R. (1979). Membrane potential oscillations in molluscan burster neurons. *J. Exp. Biol.*, *81*, 93–112.

Mehler, J. (1974). Connaître par désapprentissage. In *L'unité de l'homme* (Morin, E. & Piatelli-Palmarini, M., eds.). Paris: Seuil, pp. 187–319.

Mellen, S. (1981). *The evolution of love.* San Francisco: Freeman.

Mendlewicz, J. (1980). Les facteurs génétiques dans les syndromes dépressifs. *Riv. Psichiat.*, *15*, 62–73.

Mendlewicz, J., Linkowski, P., Guroff, J. & Praag, H. van (1979). Color blindness linkage to bipolar manic-depressive illness. *Arch. Gen. Psychiat.*, *36*, 1442–1447.

Mendlewicz, J., Linkowski, P. & Wilmotte, J. (1980). Linkage between glucose-6-phosphate dehydrogenase deficiency and manic depressive psychosis. *Brit. J. Psychiat.*, *137*, 337–342.

Meynert, T. (1867–1868). Der Bau der Grosshirnrinde und seine örtlichen Verschiedenheiten, nebst einem pathologisch-anatomischen Korollarium. *Vjschr. Psychiatr. Vienna*, *1*, 77–93, 198–217; *2*, 88–113.

Meynert, T. (1884). *Psychiatrie.* Vienna: Braumüller.

Mialet, J.-P. (1981). Les troubles de l'attention dans la schizophrénie. In *Actualités de la schizophrénie* (Pichot, P., ed.). Paris: Presses Universitaires de France, 195–226.

Michler, A. & Sakmann, B. (1980). Receptor stability and channel conversion in the subsynaptic membrane of the developing mammalian neuromuscular junction. *Dev. Biol.*, *80*, 1–17.

Mintz, B. (1974). Gene control of mammalian differentiation. *Ann. Rev. Genetics*, *8*, 411–470.

Miyawaki, K., Strange, W., Verbrugge, R., Liberman, A., Jenkins, J. & Fujimura, O. (1975). An effect of linguistic experience: The discrimination of (r) and (l) by native speakers of Japanese and English. *Perception & Psychophysics*, *18*, 331–340.

Monnier, M. & Hösli, L. (1964). Dialysis of sleep and waking factors in blood of the rabbit. *Science*, *146*, 796–798.

Monod, J. (1970). *Le hasard et la nécessité*. Paris: Seuil. (Translated as *Chance and necessity* (1976). Glasgow: Collins.)

Monod, J., Changeux, J. P. & Jacob, F. (1963). Allosteric proteins and cellular control systems. *J. Mol. Biol.*, *6*, 306–328.

Monod, J., Wyman, J. & Changeux, J.-P. (1965). On the nature of allosteric transitions: A plausible model. *J. Mol. Biol.*, *12*, 88–118.

Morata, G. & Lawrence, P. A. (1977). Homeotic genes, compartments and cell determination in *Drosophila*. *Nature*, *265*, 211–216.

Moreau de Tours, M. (1855). De l'identité de l'état de rêve et de la folie. *Ann. Méd. Psych.*, 361–468.

Morel. F., (1947). *Introduction à la psychiatrie neurologique*. Paris: Masson.

Morel, N., Israël, M., Manaranche, R. & Mastour-Frachon, P. (1977). Isolation of pure cholinergic nerve-endings from *Torpedo* electric organ. *J. Cell Biol.*, *75*, 43–55.

Morgan, M. & Corballis, M. (1978). On the biological basis of human laterality: II. The mechanisms of inheritance. *Behav. Brain Sci.*, *2*, 270–277.

Morgan, T., Sturtevant, A., Muller, H. & Bridges, C. (1923). *Le mécanisme de l'hérédité mendélienne*. Brussels: Lamertin.

Morin, E. & Piattelli-Palmarini, M., eds. (1974). *L'unité de l'homme*. Paris: Seuil.

Moruzzi, G. et Magoun, H. W. (1949). Brain stem reticular formation and activation of the EEG. *EEG Clin. Neurophysiol.*, *1*, 455–473.

Mountcastle, V. B. (1957). Modality and topographic properties of single neurons of cat's somatic sensory cortex. *J. Neurophysiol.*, *20*, 408–434.

Mountcastle, V. B. (1975). The world around us: Neural command functions for selective attention. *Neurosci. Res. Prog. Bull.*, *14*, suppl., 1–47.

Mountcastle, V. B. (1976). An organizing principle for cerebral function: The unit module and the distributed system. In *The mindful brain* (by Edelman, G. M. & Mountcastle, V. B.). Cambridge, Mass.: MIT Press (1978), pp. 7–50.

Mullen, R. (1977). Genetic dissection of the CNS with mutant-normal mouse and rat chimeras. In *Society for Neuroscience Symposia*, vol. II: *Approaches to the cell biology of neurons* (Cowan, W. M. & Ferrendelli, J., eds.). Bethesda: Soc. for Neuroscience, pp. 47–65.

Murphy, M. (1981). Evidence for the involvement of endogenous opiates in male sexual behavior. Proc. 5th World Congress on Sexology, Jerusalem.

Murphy, M. R. Bowie, D. L. & Pert, C. B. (1979). Copulation elevates plasma β-endorphin in the male hamster. *Soc. Neurosci. Abs.*, p. 470.

Nachmansohn, D. (1959). *Chemical and molecular basis of nerve activity.* New York: Academic Press.

Neel, J., Salzano, F., Junqueira, P., Keiter, F. & Maybury-Lewis, D. (1964). Studies on the Xavante Indians of the Brazilian Mato Grosso. *Hum. Genet.*, *16*, 52–140.

Nelson, P. G. & Brenneman, D. E. (1982). Electrical activity of neurons and development of the brain. *Trends Neurosci.*, *5*, 229–232.

Ness, J. van, Maxwell, I. & Hahn, W. (1979). Complex population of non-polyadenylated messenger RNA in mouse brain. *Cell*, *18*, 1341–1349.

Neubig, R. Cohen, J. (1980). Permeability control by cholinergic receptors in *Torpedo* postsynaptic membranes: Agonist dose-response curve relations measured at second and millisecond times. *Biochemistry*, *19*, 2770–2779.

Noda, M. et al. (1983). Structural homology of *Torpedo californica* acetylcholine receptor subunits. *Nature*, *302*, 528–532.

Oatley, K. (1978). *Perceptions and representations.* London: Methuen.

O'Brien, R. A. D., Östberg, A. J. C. & Vrbová, G. (1978). Observations on the elimination of polyneuronal innervation in developing mammalian skeletal muscle. *J. Physiol.* (London), *282*, 571–582.

O'Brien, R. A. D., Purves, R. D. & Vrbová, G. (1977). Effect of activity on the elimination of multiple innervation in soleus muscle of rats. *J. Physiol.* (London), *271*, 54–55P.

O'Brien, S. J. & Nash, W. G. (1982). Genetic mapping in mammals: Chromosome map of domestic cat. *Science*, *216*, 257–265.

Olds, J. & Milner, P. (1954). Positive reinforcement produced by electrical stimulation of septal area and other regions of rat brain. *J. Comp. Physiol. Psychol.*, *47*, 419–427.

O'Leary, D., Stanfield, B. B. & Cowan, W. M. (1981). Evidence that the early post-natal restriction of the cells of origin of the callosal projection is due to the elimination of axonal collaterals rather than to the death of neurons. *Dev. Brain Res.*, *1*, 607–617.

Oppenheim, R. W. & Nuñez, R. (1982). Electrical stimulation of hindlimb increases neuronal cell death in chick embryo. *Nature*, *295*, 57–59.

O'Rahilly, R. (1973). Developmental stages in human embryos: Part A. Embryos of the first three weeks (stages 1 to 9). Washington, D.C.: Carnegie Institution, Pub. 631.

Oster-Granite, M. L. & Gearhart, J. (1981). Cell lineage analysis of cerebellar Purkinje cells in mouse chimeras. *Dev. Biol.*, *85*, 199–208.

Overton, E. (1902). Beiträge zur allgemeinen Muskel- und Nervenphysiologie. *Pflüger's Arch.*, *92*, 115–280, 346–386.

Packer, S. & Gibson, K. (1979). A developmental model of the evolution of language and intelligence in early hominids. *Behav. Brain Sci.*, *2*, 367–408.

Palade, G. E. & Palay, S. L. (1954). Electron microscope observations of interneuronal and neuromuscular synapses. *Anat. Rec.*, *118*, 335–336.

Palay, S. L. (1978). The Meynert cell, an unusual cortical pyramidal cell. In *Architectonics of the cerebral cortex* (Brazier, M. A. B. & Petsche, H., eds.). New York: Raven Press, pp. 31–42.

Papez, J. W. (1937). A proposed mechanism of emotion. *Arch. Neurol. Psychiat.*, *38*, 725–744.

Pavlov, I. (1949). *Complete works.* Moscow.

Pellionisz, A. & Llinas, R. (1982). Tensor theory of brain function: The cerebellum as a space-time metric. In *Competition and cooperation in neural nets* (Amari, S. & Arbib, M., eds.). Berlin: Springer, pp. 294–417.

Penfield, W. & Rasmussen, T. (1950). *The cerebral cortex of man.* New York: Macmillan.

Perky, C. (1910). An experimental study of imagination. *Amer. J. Psychol.*, *21*, 422–452.

Peroutka, S. & Snyder, S. (1979). Multiple serotonin receptors: Differential binding of ^{3}H-spiroperidol. *Mol. Pharmacol.*, *16*, 687–699.

Pert, C. B. & Snyder, S. H. (1973). Properties of opiate receptor binding in rat brain. *Proc. Nat. Acad. Sci.* (USA), *70*, 2243–2247.

Pfaff, D. W. (1980). *Estrogens and brain function.* New York: Springer.

Phelps, M. E., Kuhl, D. E. & Mazziotta, J. C. (1981). Metabolic mapping of the brain's response to visual stimulation: Studies in humans. *Science*, *211*, 1445–1448.

Phelps, M. E., Mazziotta, J. & Huang, S. C. (1982). Study of cerebral function with positron-computed tomography. *J. Cereb. Blood Flow & Metabol.*, *2*, 113–162.

Piaget, J. (1977). *The development of thought: Equilibration of cognitive structures.* New York: Viking.

Piattelli-Palmarini, M. (1979). Structure distale et sensation proximale: Critère de co-traduisibilité. *Communications*, *31*, 171–188.

Piéron, H. (1913). *Problèmes physiologiques du sommeil.* Paris: Masson.

Pittman, R. & Oppenheim, R. W. (1979). Cell death of motoneurons in the chick embryo spinal cord. *J. Comp. Neurol.*, *187*, 425–446.

Piveteau, J. (1956). *Traité de paléontologie humaine.* Paris: Masson.

Popot, J.-L., Cartaud, J. & Changeux, J.-P. (1981). Reconstitution of a functional acetylcholine receptor: Incorporation into artificial lipid vesicles and pharmacology of the agonist controlled permeability changes. *Eur. J. Biochem.*, *118*, 203–214.

Postlethwaite, J. & Schneiderman, H. (1973). Developmental genetics of *Drosophila* imaginal discs. *Ann. Rev. Genetics, 7,* 381–433.

Powell, T. P. S. & Mountcastle, V. B. (1959). Some aspects of the functional organization of the cortex of the postcentral gyrus of the monkey: A correlation of findings obtained in a single unit analysis with cytoarchitecture. *Bull. Johns Hopkins Hosp., 105,* 133–162.

Preyer, W. (1885). *Spezielle Physiologie des Embryos.* Leipzig: Fernau, Grieben.

Prigogine, I. (1961). *Introduction to the thermodynamics of irreversible processes.* New York: Wiley-Interscience.

Prigogine, I. & Balescu, R. (1956). Phénomènes cycliques dans la thermodynamique des processus irréversibles. *Bull. Acad. Roy. Belg. Clin. Sci., 42,* 256–632.

Pull, C. & Pull, M.-C. (1981). Des critères cliniques pour le diagnostic de schizophrénie. In *Actualité de la schizophrénie* (Pichot, P., ed.). Paris: Presses Universitaires de France, pp. 23–55.

Quinn, W., Harris, W. & Benzer, S. (1974). Conditioned behavior in *Drosophila melanogaster. Proc. Nat. Acad. Sci.* (USA), *71,* 708–712.

Raichle, M. E. (1980). Cerebral blood flow and metabolism in man: Past, present and future. *Trends Neurosci., 3,* vi–x.

Rakic, P. (1974). Neurons in rhesus monkey visual cortex: Systematic relation between time of origin and eventual disposition. *Science, 183,* 425–427.

Rakic, P. (1976). Prenatal genesis of connections subserving ocular dominance in the rhesus monkey. *Nature, 261,* 467–471.

Rakic, P. (1977). Prenatal development of the visual system in the rhesus monkey. *Phil. Trans. Roy. Soc. Lond.,* Series B, *278,* 245–260.

Rakic, P. (1979). Genetic and epigenetic determinants of local neuronal circuits in the mammalian central nervous system. In *The neurosciences: Fourth study program* (Schmitt, F. O. & Worden, F. G., eds.). Cambridge, Mass.: MIT Press, pp. 109–127.

Rakic, P. & Goldman-Rakic, P. S. (1982). Development and modifiability of the cerebral cortex. *Neurosci. Res. Prog. Bull., 20* (4) 429–611.

Ramón y Cajal, S. (1909–1911). *Histologie du système nerveux de l'homme et des vertébrés.* Paris: Maloine (2 vols.).

Ramón y Cajal, S. (1933). Neuronismo o reticularismo? Las pruebas objectivas de la unidad anatómica de las células nerviosas. *Archos. Neurobiol., 13,* 217–291.

Ranvier, L. (1875). *Traité technique d'histologie.* Paris: Savy.

Redfern, P. A. (1970). Neuromuscular transmission in newborn rats. *J. Physiol.* (London), *209,* 701–709.

Reiness, C. G. & Weinberg, C. B. (1981). Metabolic stabilization of acetylcholine receptors at newly formed neuromuscular junctions in rat. *Dev. Biol.*, *84*, 247–254.

Rife, D. C. (1940). Handedness with special reference to twins. *Genetics*, *25*, 178–186.

Rife, D. C. (1950). Applications of gene frequency analysis to the interpretation of data from twins. *Hum. Biol.*, *22*, 136–145.

Ripley, K. L. & Provine, R. R. (1972). Neural correlates of embryonic motility in the chick. *Brain Res.*, *45*, 127–134.

Ritchie, A. D. (1936). *Histoire naturelle de l'esprit.*

Rizley, R. & Rescorla, R. (1972). Associations in second-order conditioning and sensory preconditioning. *J. Comp. Physiol. Psychol.*, *81*, 1–11.

Robertson, J. D. (1956). The ultrastructure of a reptilian myoneural junction. *J. Biophys. Biochem. Cytol.*, *2*, 381–394.

Roch-Lecours, A. (1983). Keeping your brain in mind. In *Neonate cognition: Beyond the buzzing, blooming confusion* (Mehler, J. & Fox, R., eds.). Hillsdale, N.J.: Erlbaum.

Rockel, A. J., Hiorns, R. W. & Powell, T. P. S. (1980). The basic uniformity in structure of the neocortex. *Brain*, *103*, 221–244.

Roland, P. E. (1981). Somatotopical tuning of postcentral gyrus during focal attention in man: A regional cerebral blood flow study. *J. Neurophysiol.*, *46*, 744–754.

Rolls, B. J. & Rolls, E. T. (1981). The control of drinking. *Brit. Med. Bull.*, *37*, 127–130.

Romer, A. S. (1955). *The vertebrate body.* Philadelphia: Saunders.

Roques, B. P., Garbay-Jaureguiberry, C., Oberlin, R., Anteunis, M. & Lala, A. K. (1976). Conformation of met-5-enkephalin determined by high field PMR spectroscopy. *Nature*, *262*, 778–779.

Rosch, E. (1975). Cognitive reference points. *Cognit. Psychol.*, *7*, 532–547.

Rose, S. P. R. (1980). Can the neurosciences explain the mind? *Trends Neurosci.*, *3*, 1–4.

Roux, W. (1895). *Entwicklungsmechanik der Organismen.* Leipzig.

Ruffié, J. (1976). *De la biologie à la culture.* Paris: Flammarion.

Ruffié, J. (1982). *Traité du vivant.* Paris: Fayard.

Rusconibus, G. de (1520). *Congestorium artificiosae memoriaer* Venice.

Russell, B. (1918). *The philosophy of logical atomism.*

Rutishauser, U., Hoffman, S. & Edelman, G. M. (1982). Binding properties of cell adhesion molecule from neural tissue. *Proc. Nat. Acad. Sci.* (USA), *79*, 685–689.

Saban, R. (1977). Les impressions vasculaires pariétales endocrâniennes dans la lignée des hominidés. *C. R. Acad. Sci. Paris*, *284* D, 803–806.

Saban, R. (1980a). Le système des veines méningées moyennes chez *Homo erectus* d'après le moulage endocrânien. *C. R. 105ᵉ Congrès national des Sociétés Savantes* (Caen), *3*, 61–73.

Saban, R. (1980b). Le tracé des veines méningées moyennes sur le moulage endocrânien d'*Homo habilis* (KNM-ER 1470). *C. R. Acad. Sci. Paris, 290*D, 405–408.

Saban, R. (1980c). Le système des veines méningées chez deux néanderthaliens: L'homme de la Chapelle-aux-Saints et l'homme de la Quina, d'après le moulage endocrânien. *C. R. Acad. Sci. Paris, 290*D, 1297–1300.

Saint-Anne Dargassies, S. (1961). Le premier sourire du nourrisson. *Dev. Med. & Child Neurol., 4*, 531–533.

Sallanon, M., Buda, C., Janin, M. & Jouvet, M. (1981). L'insomnie provoquée par la p-chlorophénylamine chez le chat: Sa réversibilité par l'injection intraventriculaire de liquide céphalorachidien prélevé chez des chats privés de sommeil paradoxal. *C. R. Acad. Sci. Paris, 291*, 1063–1066.

Salzarulo, P. (1975). Relationship between phasic events recorded in striate cortex and by surface techniques during sleep in humans. In *The experimental study of human sleep: Methodological problems* (Salzarulo, P., ed.). Amsterdam: Elsevier, pp. 37–49.

Sartre, J.-P. (1965). *Esquisse d'une théorie des émotions.* Paris: Hermann.

Sasanuma, S. (1975). Kana and Kanji processing in Japanese aphasics. *Brain & Lang., 2*, 369–383.

Saussure, F. de (1915). *Cours de linguistique générale.* Paris: Payot.

Savi, P. (1844). *Études anatomiques sur le système nerveux et sur l'organe électrique de la Torpille.* Paris: Fortin, Masson.

Scheller, R., Jackson, J., McAllister, L., Schwartz, J., Kandel, E. & Axel, R. (1982). A family of genes that codes for ELH, a neuropeptide eliciting a stereotyped pattern of behavior in *Aplysia. Cell, 28*, 707–719.

Scholes, J. H. (1979). Nerve fibre topography in the retinal projection to the tectum. *Nature, 278*, 620–624.

Schwartz, S. (1982), Is there a schizophrenic language? *Behav. Brain Sci., 5*, 579–626.

Segal, S. & Fusella, V. (1970). Influence of imaged pictures and sounds on detection of visual and auditory signals. *J. Exp. Psychol., 83*, 458–464.

Sharpless, S. & Jasper, H. (1956). Habituation of the arousal reaction. *Brain, 79*, 655–680.

Shatz, C. J. & Rakic, P. (1981). The genesis of efferent connections from the visual cortex of the fetal rhesus monkey. *J. Comp. Neurol., 196*, 287–307.

Shepard, R. N. (1978). The mental image. *Amer. Psychologist,* Feb. pp. 125–137.

Shepard, R. N. & Judd, S. (1976). Perceptual illusion of rotation of three-dimensional objects. *Science, 191*, 952–954.

Shepard, R. N. & Metzler, J. (1971). Mental rotation of three-dimensional objects. *Science, 171*, 701–703.

Sherrington, C. S. (1897). In *Forster's textbook of physiology*, 7th ed. New York: Macmillan.

Sherrington, C. S. (1906). *The integrative action of the nervous system*. New Haven: Yale University Press.

Shin, H., Stavnezer, J., Artz, K. & Bennett, D. (1982). Genetic structure and origin of t haplotypes of mice, analyzed with H-2 cDNA probes. *Cell, 29*, 969–976.

Sidman, R. L. (1970). Cell proliferation, migration, and interaction in the developing mammalian central nervous system. In *The neurosciences: Second study program* (Schmitt, F. O., ed.). New York: Rockefeller University Press, pp. 100–107.

Simon, E. J., Hiller, J. H. & Edelman, I. (1973). Stereospecific binding of the potent narcotic analgesic ^{3}H-etorphine to rat brain homogenates. *Proc. Nat. Acad. Sci. (USA), 70*, 1947–1949.

Simon, H. (1981). Neurones dopaminergiques A10 et système frontal. *J. Physiol. (Paris), 77*, 81–95.

Singer, W. (1979). Central-core control of visual-cortex functions. In The *neurosciences: Fourth study program* (Schmitt, F. O. & Worden, F. G., eds.). Cambridge, Mass.: MIT Press, pp. 1093–1110.

Slater, E. & Cowie, V. (1971). *The genetics of mental disorders*. London: Oxford University Press.

Sloper, J. J., Hiorns, R. W. & Powell, T. P. S. (1979). A qualitative and quantitative electron microscopic study of the neurons in the primate motor and somatic sensory cortices. *Phil. Trans. Roy. Soc. Lond.*, Series B, *285*, 141–171.

Snell, G. D. (1929). Dwarf, a new Mendelian recessive character of the house mouse. *Proc. Nat. Acad. Sci. (USA), 15*, 733–734.

Sokoloff, L., Reivich, M., Kennedy, C., Des Rosiers, M. H., Patlak, C. S., Pettigrew, K. D., Sakurada, O. & Shinohara, M. (1977). The ^{14}C-deoxy-glucose method for the measurement of local cerebral glucose utilization: Theory, procedure, and normal values in the conscious and anesthetized albino rat. *J. Neurochem., 28*, 897–916.

Sokolov, E. N. (1963). *Perception and the conditioned reflex*. New York: Macmillan.

Sotelo, C. & Privat, A. (1978). Synaptic remodeling of the cerebellar circuitry in mutant mice and experimental cerebellar malformations. *Acta Neuropath., 43*, 19–34.

Soury, J. (1899). *Le système nerveux central*. Paris: Carré & Naud.

Spann, W. & Dustmann, H. O. (1965). Das menschliche Hirngewicht und seine Abhängigkeit von Lebensalter, Körperlänge, Todesursache und Beruf. *Deutsche Zeitsch. Gerichtliche Med., 56,* 299–317.

Sperry, R. W. (1968). Hemisphere deconnection and unity of consciousness. *Amer. Psychologist, 23,* 723–733.

Spinoza, B. (1843). *Ethique.* Paris: Charpentier.

Springer, S. & Deutsch, G. (1981). *Left brain, right brain.* New York: Freeman.

Starck, D. & Kummer, B. (1962). Zur Ontogenese des Schimpanzenschädels. *Anthrop. Anz., 25,* 204–215.

Steinbach, J. (1981). Developmental changes in acetylcholine receptor aggregates at rat neuromuscular junction. *Dev. Biol., 84,* 267–276.

Stent, G. S. (1973). A physiological mechanism for Hebb's postulate of learning. *Proc. Nat. Acad. Sci.* (USA), *70,* 997–1001.

Stent, G. S. (1981). Strength and weakness of the genetic approach to the development of the nervous system. *Ann. Rev. Neurosci., 4,* 163–194.

Stent, G. S., Kristian, W. B., Friesen, W. D., Ort, C. A., Poon, M. & Calabrese, R. (1978). Neuronal generation of the leech swimming movement. *Science, 200,* 1348–1357.

Stephan, H. (1972). Evolution of primate brains: A comparative anatomical investigation. In *The functional and evolutionary biology of primates* (Tuttle, R., ed.). Chicago: Aldine, pp. 155–174.

Stern, C. (1954). Two or three bristles. *Amer. Scientist, 42,* 213–247.

Streeter, G. L. (1951). Developmental horizons in human embryos. Age groups XI to XXIII. Washington, D.C.: Carnegie Institution.

Stricker, E. M., Bradshaw, W. G. & McDonald, R. H. (1976). The renin-angiotensin system and thirst: A reevaluation. *Science, 194,* 1169–1171.

Strickland, S. & Mahdavi, V. (1978). The induction of differentiation in teratocarcinoma stem cells by retinoic acid. *Cell, 18,* 393–403.

Stroud, R. (1983). Acetylcholine receptor structure. *Neurosci. Commentaries, 1,* 124–138.

Strumwasser, F. (1965). The demonstration and manipulation of a circadian rythm in a single neuron. In *Circadian clocks* (Aschoff, J., ed.). Amsterdam: Elsevier, pp. 442–462.

Sullerot, E. (1978). *Le fait féminin (ouvr).* Paris: Fayard.

Sulloway, F. J. (1979). *Freud, biologist of the mind.* New York: Basic Books.

Taine, H. (1870). *De l'intelligence.* Paris: Hachette.

Terenius, L. (1973). Characteristics of the receptor for narcotic analgesics in synaptic plasma membrane fraction from rat brain. *Acta Pharmacol. Toxicol., 32,* 377–384.

Terenius, L. (1981). Médiateurs biochimiques de la douleur. *Triangle, 21,* 103–110.

Teszner, D., Tzavaras, A., Gruner, J. & Hecaen, H. (1972). L'asymétrie droite-gauche du *planum temporale:* A propos de l'étude anatomique de cent cerveaux. *Rev. Neurol., 126,* 444–448.

Teuber, H. (1975). Recovery of function after brain injury in man. In *Outcomes of severe damage to the nervous system.* Ciba Found. Symp., *34.* Amsterdam: Elsevier.

Thierry, A.-M., Blanc, G., Sobel, A., Stinus, L. & Glowinski, J. (1973). Dopamine terminals in the rat cortex. *Science, 182,* 499–501.

Thom, R. (1980). *Modèles mathématiques de la morphogénèse.* Paris: Bourgeois.

Thompson, W., Kuffler, D. P. & Jansen, J. K. S. (1979). The effect of prolonged, reversible block of nerve impulses on the elimination of polyneuronal innervation of new-born rat skeletal muscle fibers. *Neuroscience, 4,* 271–281.

Tobias, P. V. (1975). Brain evolution in the hominoidea. In *Primate functional morphology and evolution* (Tuttle, R., ed.). Paris: Mouton, pp. 353 –392.

Tobias, P. (1980). L'évolution du cerveau humain. *La Recherche, 11,* 282– 292.

Tolman, E. C. (1948). Cognitive maps in rats and men. *Psychol. Rev., 55,* 189–208.

Trevarthen, C. (1973). Behavioral embryology. In *Handbook of perception,* vol. III: *Biology of perceptual systems* (Carterette, E. C. & Friedman, M. P., eds.). New York: Academic Press, pp. 89–117.

Trevarthen, C. (1980). Neurological development and the growth of psychological functions. In *Developmental Psychology and Society* (Sauts, J., ed.). London: Macmillan, pp. 48–95.

Trevarthen, C. (1982). Social cognition. In *Studies of the development of understanding* (Butterworth, G. & Light, P., eds.). Brighton, Eng.: Harvester Press, pp. 77–109.

Trimble, M. R. (1981). Visual and auditory hallucinations. *Trends Neurosci., 4,* 1–3.

Tzavaras, A., Kaprinis, G. & Gatzoyas, A. (1981). Literacy and specialization for language: Digit dichotic listening in illiterates. *Neuropsychologia, 19,* 565–570.

Ungerstedt, U. (1971). Stereotaxic mapping of the monoamine pathways in the rat brain. *Acta Physiol. Scand. Suppl., 367,* 1–48.

Van der Loos, H. (1967). The history of the neuron. In *The neuron* (Hydén, H., ed.). Amsterdam: Elsevier, pp. 1–47.

Van der Loos, H. & Woosey, T. (1973). Somatosensory cortex: Structural alterations following early injury to sense organs. *Science, 179,* 395–398.

Vesalius, A. (1543). *De humani corporis fabrica libri septem.* Basel: Oporinus.

Vignolo, L. (1979). Utilita e limiti della tomographia computerizzata in neurologia. *Ital. J. Neurol. Sci.*, suppl. *1*, 64–72.

Vinci, L. da (1961). *Dessins anatomiques*. Selected & presented by P. Huard. Paris: Da Costa.

Vogt, M. (1954). The concentration of sympathin in different parts of the central nervous system under normal conditions and after the administration of drugs. *J. Physiol.* (London), *123*, 451–481.

von der Malsburg, C. (1981). The correlation theory of brain function. Internal report 81–2. Department of Neurobiology, Max Planck Institute for Biophysical Chemistry, Göttingen, July.

von der Malsburg, C. & Willshaw, D. (1981). Co-operativity and brain organization. *Trends Neurosci.*, *4*, 80–83.

Vries, H. de (1901). *Die Mutation Theorie*. Leipzig.

Vulpain, A. (1866). *Leçon sur la physiologie générale et comparée du système nerveux faile au Muséum d'Histoire naturelle*. Paris: Ballière.

Wada, J. A., Clark, R. & Hamm, A. (1975). Cerebral hemispheric asymmetry in humans: Cortical speech zones in 100 adult and 100 infant brains. *Arch. Neurol.*, *32*, 239–246.

Wada, J. A., Clark, R. & Rasmussen, T. (1960). Intracarotid injection of sodium amytal for the lateralization of cerebral speech dominance: Experimental and clinical observations. *J. Neurosurg.*, *17*, 266–282.

Waldeyer, W. (1891). Uber einige neuere Forschungen im Gebiete der Anatomie des Zentralnervensystems. *Dt. Med. Wschr*, 17, 1213–1356.

Wässle, H., Peichl, L. & Boycott, B. B. (1981). Dendritic territories of cat retinal ganglion cells. *Nature*, *292*, 344–345.

Watson, J. (1976). *Molecular biology of the gene*, 3rd ed. Menlo Park, Cal.: Benjamin.

Watson, J. B. (1913). Psychology as the behaviorist views it. *Psychol. Rev.*, *20*, 158–177.

Whitaker, P. & Seeman, P. (1978). In *Proc. Nat. Acad. Sci.* (USA), *75*, 5783–5787.

White, E. (1981). Thalamocortical synaptic relations. In *The organization of the cerebral cortex* (Schmitt, F. O., et al., eds.). Cambridge, Mass.: MIT Press, pp. 153–162.

White, M.J.D. (1978). *Modes of speciation*. San Francisco: Freeman.

Whittaker, V. P., Michaelson, I. A. & Kirkland, R. J. (1964). The separation of synaptic vesicles from nerve-ending particles ("synaptosomes").*Biochem. J.*, *90*, 293–303.

Willis, T. (1672). *De anima brutorum*. London: Davis.

Wimer, R. E., Wimer, C. C., Vaughn, J. E., Barber, R. P., Balvanz, B. A. & Chernow, C. C. (1976). The genetic organization of neuron number in Ammon's horns of house mice. *Brain Res.*, *118*, 219–243.

Wintzerith, M., Sarliève, L. & Mandel, P. (1974). Brain nucleic acids and protein in hereditary pituitary dwarf mice. *Brain Res., 80,* 538–542.

Wiesel, T. N. (1982). Postnatal development of the visual cortex and the influence of environment. *Nature, 299,* 583–592.

Wise, R. A. (1980). The dopamine synapse and the notion of pleasure centers in the brain. *Trends Neurosci. 3,* 91–95.

Wittgenstein, L. (1921). *Tractatus logico-philosophicus.* Paris: Gallimard.

Wolpert, L. & Lewis, J. (1975). Towards a theory of development. *Fed. Proc., 34,* 14–20.

Woods, B. T. & Teuber, H. L. (1973). Early onset of complementary specialization of cerebral hemispheres in man. *Trans. Amer. Neurol. Assn., 98,* 113–117.

Woolsey, C. N. (1958). Organization of somatic sensory and motor areas of the cerebral cortex. In *Biological and biochemical bases of behavior* (Harlow, H. & Woolsey, C. N., eds.). Madison: University of Wisconsin Press, pp. 63–82.

Wright, T. R. (1970). The genetics of embryogenesis in *Drosophila. Adv. Genet., 15,* 261–395.

Yasargil, G. & Diamond, J. (1968). Startle-response in teleost fish: An elementary circuit for neural discrimination. *Nature, 220,* 241–243.

Young, J. Z. (1964). *A model of the brain.* Oxford: Clarendon Press.

Young, J. Z. (1973). Memory as a selective process. *Austral. Acad. Sci. Report: Symp. Biol. Memory,* 25–45.

Young, R. (1970). *Mind, brain and adaptation in the 19th century.* Oxford: Clarendon Press.

Yunis, J. J. & Prakash, O. (1982). The origin of man: A chromosomal pictorial legacy. *Science, 215,* 1525–1530.

Zemb, J.-M. (1981). Discussion session, Feb. 28, *Bull. Soc. Fr. Philosophie, 75,* 105.

Zipser, B. (1982). Complete distribution patterns of neurons with characteristic antigens in the leech central nervous system. *J. Neurosci, 2,* 1453–1464.

Zipser, B. & McKay, R. (1981). Monoclonal antibodies distinguish identifiable neurons in the leech. *Nature, 289,* 549–554.

Index